soundworks
dworks

REFIGURING AMERICAN MUSIC *A series edited by Ronald Radano, Josh Kun,
and Nina Sun Eidsheim*   *Charles McGovern, contributing editor*

Anthony Reed

works

Race, Sound,
and Poetry
in Production

DUKE UNIVERSITY PRESS
Durham and London 2021

© 2021 Duke University Press. All rights reserved
Designed by Courtney Leigh Richardson and typeset in Portrait, Helvetica, and Canela by Westchester Publishing Services, Inc.

Library of Congress Cataloging-in-Publication Data
Names: Reed, Anthony, [date] author.
Title: Soundworks : race, sound, and poetry in production / Anthony Reed.
Other titles: Refiguring American music.
Description: Durham : Duke University Press, 2021. | Series: Refiguring American music | Includes bibliographical references and index.
Identifiers: LCCN 2020027632 (print) | LCCN 2020027633 (ebook)
ISBN 9781478010210 (hardcover)
ISBN 9781478011279 (paperback)
ISBN 9781478012795 (ebook)
Subjects: LCSH: Music and literature—United States— History—20th century. | American poetry—United States—African American authors—History—20th century. | African Americans—United States—Music—History—20th century. | Jazz—20th century—History and criticism.
Classification: LCC PN56.M87 R443 2020 (print) | LCC PN56.M87 (ebook) | DDC 811.009/896073—dc23
LC record available at https://lccn.loc.gov/2020027632
LC ebook record available at https://lccn.loc.gov/2020027633

Cover art: Singer, courtesy Digital Vision/Getty Images.

For Stokely and Nelson   For Emily

1
2
3
4

Contents

Acknowledgments / ix

INTRODUCTION / 1
Black: Sonic: Textuality

VOICE PRINTS / 23
Toward a Black Media Concept

COMMUNITIES IN TRANSITION / 61
A Poetics of Black Communism

TOMORROW IS THE QUESTION! / 103
Amiri Baraka's Poetics for a Post-Revolutionary Age

BODY/LANGUAGE / 143
The Semiotics and Poetics of Improvisation
and Black Embodiment

CODA / 181
No Simple Explanations

Notes / 195   Bibliography / 235   Index / 251

Acknowledgments

This book about recorded collaborations itself records many near- and long-term collaborations. The many years it has taken me to write it have been a period of intense personal and professional growth. These acknowledgments offer a partial account of all those who in one way or another have been pivotal to its fruition, with the usual caveat that it will necessarily be a partial list.

I would first like to acknowledge some of the women who taught me along the way, starting with three of my Harold Washington College colleagues—Raymonda Johnson, Della Burt-Bradley, and Rosie Banks—without whom my path would have a very different shape. Dr. Johnson hired me to join her department, and the experience of teaching there opened my eyes to the impact teaching and mentorship could have in the world. During what proved to be a pivotal moment in my life trajectory, Dr. Burt-Bradley offered profound advice. Dr. Banks gave me the nudge I needed to pursue a PhD. If you've paid attention to me, I hope all three of you feel validated by the steps I've taken and the work I've done thanks to your initial encouragement.

I've been fortunate to cross paths with many astounding peers and mentors. I would like to acknowledge Sharon P. Holland, from whom I've learned so much about intellectual and professional life. Likewise, Grant Farred has been a model of negotiating the demands of the job and the work, and not confusing the two. Joseph Roach, Hazel V. Carby, and Hortense J. Spillers, on the page and as colleagues, have been important models of intellectual generosity. There are many ways to inhabit this world and many ways to stay faithful to, or stray from, intellectual demands. Thank you for the gift of your work, your teaching, your example, and your friendship.

Many people have either invited me to present from this work as it developed or presented on panels with me and offered generous feedback. Thank you to my colleagues in Post45, who have been supportive throughout the process. I would especially like to acknowledge Tim Murray and the Society for the Humanities and Cornell University, where I was able to present to an audience including Tim, Lauren Berlant, Tsitsi Jaji, Suvir Kaul, and others. Your belief in the potential of this project sustained me through the inevitable twists, turns, and periods of doubt. Many years ago, Jacques Coursil answered my naïve questions about his collaborations with Frank Wright, and that conversation changed the course of my thinking. Colleagues at Duke University also were receptive to an initial version of these arguments, and I would single out Nancy Armstrong, Thomas DeFranz, Karla Holloway, Richard Powell, and Leonard Tennenhouse; your challenging questions and insights proved clarifying as I was beginning this project. Early on, I reached out to Steven Evans to compare notes when I discovered his project on the "phonotextual braid." Thank you for responding generously to a stranger. Thank you to Brent Hayes Edwards, Robert G. O'Meally, Farah Jasmine Griffin, George Edwards, Michael Veal, and others at the Jazz Study Group at Columbia University for your enthusiastic reception of these ideas. I'm grateful to have shared parts of this work with colleagues at Boston University (special thanks to Anita Patterson, Gene Andrew Jarrett, and Askia M. Touré), Concordia University (thanks to Nathan Brown and the Center for Expanded Poetics), Princeton University (thanks especially to Kimberly Bain and Jennifer Soong), New York University (especially Lytle Shaw and the Organism for Poetic Research), Northwestern University (special thanks to Harris Feinsod, John Alba Cutler, and the participants of our Radical Poetics Symposium—Chadwick Allen, Adrienne Brown, Kinohi Nishikawa, Urayoán Noel, Samantha Pinto, and Sonya Posmentier), the University of Michigan (special thanks to Hayley O'Malley and Kyle Fresina), and the University of Wisconsin (thanks to Adam Schuster, Timothy Yu, and others). Thanks to Sangeeta Ray, Mary Helen Washington, Hazel Carby, Caryl Phillips, and Eddie Chambers for engaging my work on dub poetry, which will ultimately belong to the next book. Thanks to Margo Crawford, Jeremy Matthew Glick, William J. Harris, Jean-Phillipe Marcoux, Carter Mathes, Fred Moten, Aldon Nielsen, and Tyrone Williams, who have been enthusiastic and challenging in their response to this work as it has evolved. Ron Radano invited me to participate in a Mellon Workshop at the American Academy in Berlin, where I was fortunate enough to be in the company of Nomi Dave, Eric Lott, Louise Meintjes, Phillip Miller, Rosalind Morris, Tejumola Olaniyan, Ciraaj Rasool, Michael P. Steinberg, Gavin Steingo, Jonathan Sterne, and Thuthuka Sibisi. At pivotal stages in the process, former Yale colleagues spoke to me about the manuscript, and I would single out Jacqueline Goldsby, Michael

Warner, and Ardis Butterfield for their care and attention. Nathaniel Mackey's invitation and provocation to dwell on the meaning of play proved decisive to the final shape of these arguments. Thank you all.

I could not have done this work without the generous and patient support of archivists, especially Kevin Young (then at Emory University), Julie Herrada, Curator of the Joseph A. Labadie Collection at the University of Michigan, and Nancy Kuhl and Melissa Barton at Yale's Beinecke Rare Book and Research Library. Special acknowledgement goes to Mark Bailey, Nick Forster, and Andrew Jones at Yale University's Historical Sound Recording archive. Thank you all for your patience and enthusiastic support.

As important has been the support of the musicians who have helped me develop the analytical method I use throughout the book. I was fortunate enough to have several conversations with Henry Threadgill about his poetry that proved formative when this project was nascent. Special thanks to Jason Moran, Tarus Mateen, and Nasheet Waits for their encouragement when this project was still germinal. Bob Stewart gave me a whole education on improvisation in one brief conversation. David Boykin invited me to participate in a celebration of Sun Ra and to be among such great scholars and musicians (including Marshall Allen, Dany Thompson, Greg Tate, Thomas Stanley, and Marvin X). That event helped me better conceive my audience and the stakes of this work. I was grateful to meet and learn from Gayle Wald, Nina Sun Eidsheim, Vijay Iyer, Jennifer Stoever, Alex Vasquez, and Wadada Leo Smith at an event Daphne Brooks and Brian Kane—themselves valuable interlocutors—co-organized. From the time we were in grade school bands together, Raphael Crawford has been a source of inspiration and knowledge about the music. His encouragement (and reassurance, when needed) has meant the world to me. Finally, to enter the music and write about it respectfully and knowledgeably I undertook to study saxophone with Frank Newton. From our first lessons I knew I was in the presence of a man whose involvement with the music is as profound as his gifts as a teacher. Being able to discuss music has proven a gift I will never be able to repay, but I want to acknowledge my debt and my appreciation for your instruction and your friendship, which sustained me and helped me stay grounded in the essential.

I cannot thank everyone who has helped or encouraged me along the way, but I want to acknowledge a few friends and colleagues who make this work sweeter. Thanks especially to Vanessa Agard-Jones, Elizabeth Alexander, Jafari Allen, Herman Beavers, Caetlin Benson-Allott, Rizvana Bradley, Nick Bromell, Joe Cleary, Soyica Diggs Colbert, David Coombs, Ian Cornelius, Aimee Meredith Cox, Ashon Crawley, Nijah Cunningham, Michael Denning, Laura

Doyle, John Drabinski, Erica Edwards, Daylanne English, Crystal Feimster, Rachel Galvin, Michael Gillespie, Glenda Gilmore, Ben Glaser, Langdon Hammer, Erica Hunt, Ulas Ince, Gerald Jaynes, Virginia Jackson, Meta DuEwa Jones, David Kastan, Vera Kutzinski, Wendy Anne Lee, Keguro Macharia, Lawrence Manley, Barry Maxwell, Kobena Mercer, Angela Naimou, Mark Anthony Neal, Steph Newell, Marisa Parham, Seth Perlow, John Durham Peters, Yopie Prins, Dixa Ramirez, Shana Redmond, Ed Rugemer, Evie Shockley, James Smethurst, Courtney Thorsson, and too many more to name. And special thanks to Dana Nelson.

Thanks to Ken Wissoker and everyone at Duke University Press, who have been models of professionalism and care through every step of the process. Thanks to Ron, Nina, and Josh for including the book in their series. And thanks to the anonymous readers whose encouragement and insights greatly improved this work.

My mother, Deborah, my brother Edward, my sister-in-law Tameka, and my nieces Nia and Soleil have been immensely supportive and inspiring throughout this journey. Please know that so much of what I do comes from the desire to make you all proud. My in-laws, Larry, Lorraine, Joe, Jeff, and Catherine, and my niece and nephews, Annalise, Sam, Alex, and Michael, have widened my sense of family, and I appreciate all of you more than these words will seem to say. Just know you're never far from my thoughts. While writing this book, we welcomed two sons, Stokely and Nelson. This book is dedicated to you, and to the worlds you will dream and build. May it contain something of the joy of word, music, and sound you have taught me. This book is also dedicated to Emily, my partner in all things. You inspire me, and I'm grateful to have you as my interlocutor, my friend, and so much more. This book is for the world we're making together.

Introduction

Black: Sonic: Textuality

I'm trying to find the concept according to which sound is renewed every time it's expressed.
—ORNETTE COLEMAN, "The Other's Language"

"We Are on the Edge." The first sounds: a trumpet (Hugh Ragin), a sound that recalls another you may have heard before. Roy Campbell? No, it sounds a little like Lester Bowie. Ragin plays an obbligato, answered by a unison line, played by an enlarged version of the Art Ensemble of Chicago, which his trumpet joins. Their union temporarily puts soloist/ensemble and improvisation/composition binaries in abeyance. After about three and a half minutes, the ensemble transitions to a vamp announcing some other event. Poet-performer Moor Mother (Camae Ayewa) soon provides and defers that event, announcing "we are on the edge / we are on the edge of victory." At first seeming to offer a familiar, gendered chastisement of "dope, and dancing, and drunkenness," she ends up underscoring the hollowness of victory that leaves many "dripping in blood from the rat race."[1] Stressing that the coming victory will be for "all of us," she reminds those who listen of prior victories' partiality. Refusing harmonic or conceptual resolution, audible within but not wholly enveloped by the traditions it invokes, I hear in "We Are on the Edge" a commitment to the dissolution and reconstitution of the "we" ("we are on the edge of existing"), which aligns it with the black experimental sound practice this book engages. Moor Mother's delivery, mode of address, and investment in the vernacular recalls Amiri Baraka, an influence on multi-reedist and co-founder of the Art Ensemble of Chicago Shaku Joseph Jarman, whose poetry is integral to the group's celebrated experiments with sound and theatricality. As on their former recordings, and in many other instances of the phonographic poetry studied here, "We Are on the Edge" joins poetry and music in a unity more complex and supple than a words/music dichotomy that prioritizes soundful words or meaningful sounds. Analyzing that greater complexity in conceptual, aesthetic, and historical terms is this book's abiding ambition. Its aim, in other words, is to learn to listen to phonographic poetry as a practice of black sound.

Knowing the fifty-year history of the Art Ensemble of Chicago does not fully prepare listeners for this recording, just as knowing Amiri Baraka's printed or recorded works does not substitute for listening to Moor Mother (or Joseph Jarman). One reason for this is that the prior works correspond to historical and social conjunctures whose conflicts, as the poem demonstrates, are at once extinct and still alive as urgent intellectual and political conflicts. Her refusal to convert historical sequence into unambiguous progress, her rejection of teleological certainty in favor of a reflexive disposition sounds a welcome reharmonization of the present's struggle with history. "We Are on the Edge" creates a musical and conceptual caesura, an aporetic pause between familiar paradigms, the history it sketches, and the particularity of its sound. In so doing, it invites and is *play*, a non-teleological commitment to what may happen in the course of an event's unpredictable unfolding. If, as we're accustomed to thinking, black sound offers itself as evidence of "some other kind of thought" or another way of knowing, we must remember that that thought does not exist independently of its material expression and that ways of knowing index conceptual apparatuses, that is, the sign complexes, theories, and texts through which we encounter and understand the world.[2] Sound is always (also) a re-sounding; it resounds in the presence of prior hearing and ways of hearing; it resonates within history's mutable chambers. It risks being, to borrow a term from Nathaniel Mackey, "hearded": "*Hear*'s past tense's past tense . . . multiply removed from the present, someone else's having heard presumed to be one's own."[3] What Mackey describes, I take it, is the process whereby music's putatively "internal" categories—pitch, timbre, intensity, duration, rhythm, melody, etc.—have to be in effect bracketed in order to define the experience as genre, as in the tradition. The part-whole relationship reverses itself, and the discursive map of the sonic overwrites its territory rather than describing the terrain.

Listening to black sound beyond the herding effects that discipline any experience of sound—starting with those epistemological and ideological mechanisms by which we separate music from random noise—requires reconceiving it as an evolving, open set of aesthetic practices that develop alongside the ideological and material forces that give those practices dimension and meaning. Black sound is the result of work, play, and contestation. This book listens to the insurgent sonic practices that have circulated between poetry and music and that have shaped a vital strand of black aesthetic production since the long Black Arts era (the late 1950s through the mid-1970s).[4] To listen requires reflexively engaging the time that frames the experience. Each present—each *now*—produces its own version of the past as part of its self-legitimation. Designating the present—post-Civil Rights, post-Ferguson—is political insofar as, drawing on Lauren Berlant, it requires a narrative accounting of those "forces [that] should be considered responsible and what crises urgent in our adjudication of survival strategies and conceptions of a better life."[5] The "historical present," what we collectively and individually live, is multiple rather than unitary; it often appears as what is intuitively true, what *feels* right; it is the starting point for knowledge projects, including the study of history. Every saying "now" is a tacit demand, assertion, and revisionary claim to collectivity and on the past (e.g., of the Civil Rights Era) that smooths out rough edges and contingencies according to narrative and generic conventions. Soundwork is a way of inhabiting and making claims to a collective present, both concrete and speculative. My analyses throughout attend to the rhythms of attachment, of community de- and re-formation, and the corresponding de- and re-formation of political aesthetics, dis- and re-enchantment with engaging the political.

To say that black sound in or across time resists social and political orders does not require listening to any note or analyzing any composition. Those narratives of resistance teach us about the nature of the crisis black life engenders within the deep economic, political, social, and epistemological structures of the West. They teach us that even as structures define themselves in opposition to blackness, blackness inhabits them as a destabilizing capacity. Ultimately, such resistance is tropological, a way of reading and thinking beyond the lived experience and positivistic accounts of black vulnerability. The first chapter tracks some of the figurative tendencies, which tend to be analogical (this aesthetic gesture is like a similar gesture in the physical world), metaphorical (the aesthetic gesture is symbolic action), allegorical (the ensemble models ideal sociality), metonymical (the aesthetic is juxtaposed with supposedly determining context), or some combination of these. Black sound, in these accounts, becomes an indicator of the radically emergent, a harbinger or emblem of utopian possibilities or at least the establishment of separate spaces for being and deliberating together. While I'm sympathetic to those ways of arguing (and inevitably argue that way myself at times), I practice listening as a historically grounded orientation toward the event with the understanding that no "pure" listening to music's "interior" aspects is possible because each—pitch, tonality, harmony, rhythm, duration, melody—already participates in a symbolic economy. Listening must contend with sound neither as pure presence nor as pure symbolic transcendence but as *text*, a structured weave of the phono- and typographic, the grammatical, and the semantic. As far as possible, I offer nonfigurative, theoretical descriptions of black sound's circulation and resonance in the world, with the assumption that reordered aesthetic experience intends new forms of community. I listen for what may have been possible to hear and desire in particular historical conjunctures without assuming the context to which the sound responds. Black soundwork does not simply express an evolving consciousness and orientation toward freedom; it does not reflect the world in which it resonates, but meaningfully changes it.

Soundworks' primary object of analysis is phonographic poetry, the recorded collaborations between poets and musicians, and the larger media history it refracts. Phonographic poetry allows me to track the changing practical and theoretical relationships among sound, text, and speech; among sound, song, and meaning; and among the sensuous, technical, and ideological forces that comprise the black sound object. It also foregrounds media—including paratexts such as interviews, liner notes, and titles—that coordinate artists' own (literal and figurative) voices, newly resonant vocal metaphors for instrumental sound (growl, scream, cry), and constitute and shape struggles within and against language.[6] Media are primary ideological and conceptual condensation points for the epistemological and ontological order that depends on maintaining a distinction between subjects and objects, between humans and things. These sound texts participate in contests over meaning and value and play out on a terrain structured by the culture industries and state cultural apparatuses. My interest is in the ways black sound, as sensual, sonic, and semantic, engenders the sense of ongoingness around which communities coalesce, fragment, and reconstitute themselves. Periods of political and aesthetic flux—for example, the late 1960s, the early 1990s following the Rodney King–inspired uprisings in Los Angeles, or the current era of protest against the nexus of policies, norms, and laws that reproduce black immiseration for which the extralegal murder of black people has been a focal point since 2014—tend to see an upsurge of phonographic poetry. Artists reach back to a prior generation's aesthetic and discursive modes. In the contemporary, this means returning to a Black Arts era aesthetic and political ethos, including its implicit assumption that communities must be built, and that black sound—poetry, music, and theatricality—is a means of building it. While recent recordings are not this book's primary object, I hope to contribute to an understanding of the politics and populism of the gesture.

Here, however, we hit a minor impasse. Aesthetic impulses tend to exceed even the most capaciously conceived historical schemas, even and perhaps especially in adversarial contexts. The relationship between black sound and history appears here as problem rather than solution. Especially since the 1950s, black poets and musicians have come to understand themselves, within their respective domains, to be experimental sound artists whose primary medium was verbal or nonverbal sound. If the poetry-jazz nexus was initially a site of interracial collaboration (usually organized around male homosocial bonds), the white avant-garde came to reject the so-called "tyranny of jazz" that informed abstract expressionism and the Beats.[7] Club owners, meanwhile, were wary of the new music even before critics associated it with black militancy because the kinds of listening it demanded were antithetical to a nightclub's economic mission. The alienation of black artists from putatively "white" spaces along with the development of a newly revalued blackness that included both the historical and then-decolonizing Africa accelerated the development of alternative spaces and institutions that inform the broader Black Arts era. As Aldon Nielsen observes, "black musicians, poets, and political activists all saw their work as part of a growing internationalist development" and, moreover, "recognized that there was little point in addressing themselves to the *New Yorker* and [instead] set about the construction of their own national and international networks of publications and readings."[8] To those institutions I would add the development of new performance venues, independent record labels, artist and composers' guilds, and outlets for criticism. In short, they set about creating an insurgent media infrastructure.

Starting from the presumption that aesthetic experience always has an aleatory, anarchic, and refigurative potential, I attend to the ways these poets and musicians play the changes of their moments within and against the contours of agency, understood in Gayatri Chakravorty Spivak's sense to refer to those forms of action institutionally and communally valid, even as they attempt to recreate institutions.[9] This framing encourages different perspectives on Charles Mingus's embrace of black vernacular forms, Langston Hughes's shifting sense of community, Matana Roberts's inheritance and transformation of an avant-garde legacy traceable to Archie Shepp, Amiri Baraka's poetics before and after his nationalist period, Cecil Taylor's embodied forms, and Jeanne Lee's aesthetic excess. Multi-genre, multimedia "live" performance plays a key role in the development of vernacular avant-gardes, and sound media play a similarly important practical and theoretical role, creating the conditions of spatial and temporal simultaneity in the service of reconfiguring the possibilities of tradition and community.

The material and ideological limits of calls for "black power" and its cognate demands for self-determination and local control of civic and economic institutions—including a missed opportunity to rethink politics on bases other than individual or collective rights and sovereignty—are well known. We might nonetheless see implicit qualm and qualification of institutions in the call itself. Rather than assume that everyone who rallied around "black power" naïvely sought black control or representation within liberal institutions and then-dissolving forms of direct domination, we might catch the outline of an anarchist- or communist-inflected imagination.[10] Driving this were new conceptions of the national and the nation-state, new faith in revolution and community, fascination with emergent forms of African and Caribbean socialism. If we take seriously the skepticism many black people had toward the ability of the state and capitalist social organization to answer their demands for freedom, we might better understand the suspicion many poets, musicians, intellectuals, and ordinary people felt *in the moment* about the relatively narrow interpretations of freedom available in the mainstream. For example, musician, poet, and activist Sun Ra said black people "were on the right road, but going in the wrong direction."[11] In this light, pragmatic forms of mutual aid and alternative institution-building resonate with black poets and musicians' evocations of both outer- and inner-space alternatives to then-extant cartographies of power and black life, alternative ways of being together. Although many of the figures I am concerned with here did identify as socialist, communist, or otherwise aligned with the radical left, I use the designation "communist-inflected" primarily to keep in focus the varieties of black political and social life that fall outside or exceed bourgeois norms of the acceptable or desirable.

I situate my analyses in what Richard Iton terms the "thickly dissonant space" between "the confidence of the teleological and the bittersweet . . . entanglements of the agonistic," between the certainties that attend some "liberationist narratives and the uncertainties and qualifications characteristic of an instinctively reflexive category of perspectives."[12] The liberationist impulse of cultural productions or the communist-inflected imagination is only one part of the story. Throughout this book, I focus on moments of ambivalence, where the "bittersweet entanglements of the agonistic" or quotidian struggle more perfectly overlap or undermine "confidence of the teleological." Any articulated telos—the good life, the liberated future—requires a calculation of what is possible, which is simultaneously an epistemological, historical, and political question: what do I know about the present, what can be hoped in the present, what can I convince others to want in the present?

When I started this project, I undertook intense study of music theory and performance (saxophone), intending to explain in technical detail how experimental music created fissures in the edifice of the so-called Western tradition. As my study advanced, however, I found it important to register the ways that black soundwork disturbs the intelligibility of the Western tradition, itself a mode of social reproduction whose models of the well-ordered function to exclude those non-European forms that cannot be appropriated or "refined." This is not to suggest that one cannot analyze the music according to the terms of Western musicology, but that doing so obscures more than it reveals. Black soundwork in all its varieties noisily calls into question the Western tradition's predicates and aesthetics from an outside that is always also at the very heart of that tradition's self-declared interiority. Rather than catalogue "call-and-response devices; additive rhythms and polyrhythms; heterophony, pendular thirds, blue notes, bent notes, and elisions; hums, moans, grunts, vocables, and other rhythmic-oral declamations, interjections, and punctuations; off-beat melodic phrasings and parallel intervals and chords; constant repetition of rhythmic and melodic figures and phrases . . . timbral distortions of various kinds; musical individuality within collectivity; game rivalry, hand clapping, foot patting, and approximations thereof; apart-playing; and the metronomic pulse that" Samuel Floyd argues "underlies all African American music" (in part because Floyd has already done that work), I have opted to underscore the unsuitability of certain musicological concepts for understanding—really listening to—the sounds of this music and its poetic symbiont.[13]

Foregrounding media enables sustained analytical attention to the interaction of the commodity form and class formations in a complexly postcolonial context that encompasses, as Stuart Hall argues, not only the end of direct European rule over the globe but the world-making projects that emerge from newly configured power/knowledge relations in which aesthetics had a role to play.[14] Drawing on Walter Benjamin's Marxian aesthetics, I understand sensory experience is historically situated rather than transcendent, and trace the ways technical apparatuses act in unevenly reciprocal relationships with that sensorium.[15] Accounts of voice that develop around and inform the idea of the

New Black Music and poetry, for example, reward the development of sound technologies that feature the voice in accord with those broader ideologies, which are in turn reinforced by those technologies. The voice becomes the central medium of the human soul or mind, technologies and material practices emphasize (or fetishize) the voice, voice and the metonymic chain it figures take on a phantom objectivity: it looks as though technology drives the centrality of the voice rather than collective desires, and it becomes difficult to see the ways ideas of voice drive the development of certain technologies and recording techniques, as well as the promotion of some performance styles over others. New aesthetics, metaphors, technologies, and material practices develop along those lines. Insofar as it is linked to aspirational collectivity (and aspirations to collectivity), black sound indexes a host of social changes and orientations toward alternative forms of social organization.

Soundwork in this sense also refers to the conceptual labor involved in producing black sound as a theoretical object that comprises practical, ideological, and epistemological structures.[16] Black sound gathers and encodes—sign-ifies—a set of rational, iterative practices that produce racial meanings (and race itself) through the circulation of sounds, texts, and attending discourses. Given the historical connection between black performance and compulsion—first by the dominant classes and then by the whims of the culture industries—we might say its mode is affirmation, a refusal to choose between containment and liberation, a noisy change of the question. I follow thinkers such as Alexander Weheliye in insisting that black soundwork, as aesthetic and political activity, is not merely reactive but constitutive of modernity and modern media. In Weheliye's account, which admirably maintains a reflexive stance toward the history it charts, black sound is not "merely a byproduct of an already existing modernity, ancillary to and/or belated in its workings, but a chain of singular formations integrally linked to this sphere, particularly as it collides with information technologies."[17] Conceiving black sound as a "series of relational singularities that refuse to signify any ontological consistency before and beyond" and of tradition as "activating difference" outside an original/copy binary allows more highly attuned listening to specific sonic events.[18] However, in order for them to signify as "afro-modernity" they have to relinquish some of their singularity in order to become exemplary, in the manner of synecdoche, of a larger formation that still needs to be historicized. For that, I remix Weheliye with Stuart Hall, understanding black sound as the ground of constitutive differences upon and through which cultural meanings are inscribed, contested, worked out, and reactivated. There is no "as such" or ontological ground upon which to rest; the question of black sound only has meaning in relation to the specificity of specific moments.[19] Soundwork, then, is necessarily theoretical work, requiring an account of sound's effects that corresponds to particular historical conditions. Such framing avoids the sense of black sound (or culture) existing as either timeless or as the autonomous unfolding of a unitary tradition or consciousness, while having the benefit of allowing a further question of the relationship between historically specific articulations of blackness and its texts.

A Vernacular Avant-Garde

Sound recording and reproduction technologies further aided in the transforming relationship between sound and source, making available, plausible, and desirable new cultural spheres and aesthetic forms. New forms of social organization made it possible to value and promote sound recording and reproduction technologies in concert with transformed relations to time, space, community, and aesthetics. The new and transformed often appears first in the guise of the old, and the process of transformation reveals an often explosive potentiality latent within the familiar—the unorganizable within social and aesthetic organization. Structurally unorganizable particularity is also a futurity beyond the conceptual limits into which sound is he(a)rded. To substantiate my claims that the sounds change contexts rather than metonymically, metaphorically, or otherwise reflecting them, I propose the term *vernacular avant-garde*. This framing allows us to acknowledge participation in the culture industry as important but not determinant, to acknowledge cynical marketing of black rebellion as an attempt to short-circuit the real thing, and to acknowledge the ways new performance styles required shifts in the ways engineers recorded.[20] The term *vernacular avant-garde* also captures relays between popular forms and their aesthetic elaboration and imagines them as simultaneous, rather than reinscribing modernism/mass culture binaries. I use it to hold space open for listening for the ecstatic and riotous within black aesthetics. "Riotous" refers to those apparently spontaneous acts that reveal the fictive and arbitrary nature of existing social relations and in so doing introduce the possibility of different desires and arrangements. These range from avant-garde performance, which targets the line between art and non-art, to the spontaneous urban uprisings that revealed the degree to which black leadership neither directed nor straightforwardly reflected people's quotidian "upworking" of new political desires, or revolutionary ideals.[21] The rhetoric of spontaneity tends to discredit those ideals and political means, while tacitly reinforcing and legitimating the hegemonic order. The structurally unorganizable, the structurally uncountable, is riotous potentiality.

Even when the riot does not manifest as punctual event or conflagration, the riotous imprints itself in the fabric of everyday life. What happens to aesthetic forms that seem linked to moments whose questions and solutions seem misfit in subsequent moments? What becomes of yesterday's riots? Learning to listen means resisting the urge to hastily declare failure or supersession (soul or R&B or rap music supersede jazz as "people's music") where there is instead rearticulation of common elements. Thus, if the persistence of free jazz, certain modes of political poetry, and other vernacular avant-garde practices appears atavistic or revenant, the fault lies in our conceptual and critical frameworks.[22] No matter how often we are told that vernacular avant-garde modes have been superseded, they persist, and continuing investment in those modes is perhaps symptomatic of a too narrowly conceived concept of the beautiful and "the popular," themselves tethered to forms of social organization that are ultimately too narrow.

Drawing on Miriam Bratu Hansen, Ralph Ellison, and Christopher Small, my understanding of vernacular "combines the dimension of everyday usage and cultural practices with its connotations of discourse, idiom, and dialect, with circulation, promiscuity, and translatability,"[23] outlines a historically particular "process" embedded in the (re)production of racial logics rather than a preexisting set of practices and styles,[24] and tracks the "anarchistic resistance to classification" that informs suspicion toward and rejection of genre distinctions (e.g., jazz) for the artists in this study.[25] Hansen's account, in particular, helps to keep the recording apparatus visible as a constitutive component of vernacular art rather than imagining a black sound essentially prior to recording. "Vernacular" specifies one way of considering in aggregate processes of reappropriating and redirecting of the riotous, insurrectionary capacities of outmoded forms, of inventing in the style of the past with an eye toward new historical conjunctures and horizons not previously imagined beyond the dissolution of black communities into their constitutive, antagonistic class fragments, and more broadly the domestic and international class-shuffle that characterizes the sixties. I also draw on James Smethurst's notion of a "popular avant-garde": "a paradoxical . . . avant-garde that had roots in actually existing and close-to-home popular culture and that was itself in some senses genuinely popular while retaining a countercultural alternative stance."[26] "Popular" here is a rough synonym for "mass" rather than "high" culture (forms of culture enabled by emergent culture industries) and counts a large number of people ("genuinely popular"). It also signals attachment to the "synthesi[s] and revis[ion of] a cultural inheritance derived significantly from the Popular Front, using the 'new thing' jazz or 'free jazz' of the late 1950s and the 1960s as a model."[27] The semantic drift and malleability makes "popular" a tricky word to describe the phenomenon I describe, which tends to involve recontextualizing—re-signifying—the sources of "the people." I prefer the term *vernacular* because of its insistence on the shifting ground of relation in contrast to *popular*'s ambiguous position between the descriptive and the valorized, its insistence on forms of social mobility not guaranteed to the musicians and writers that I analyze. Smethurst's insistence on the continuities between the black left in the Popular Front era and the period that follows is salutary, and his notion of an avant-garde reframes the emphasis on direct emotional expressivity and the New Black Music's embrace of "uglier modes."[28] *Avant-garde* as I use it here signals the effort to continually recreate the ground of aesthetic practice, to create practical and conceptual openings for new systems of value or thought; it is a way of occupying the interludes between emergence and appropriation. *Vernacular avant-garde* is ultimately my way of conceiving both the reappropriation (in all senses of the term) of mass cultural elements and the modes of address and resonance within and across shifting national and communal boundaries where the status of "the people" is uncertain. The term refers to a mode of collective politics and poetics in deep conversation with the apparatuses of the culture industry in a period defined by hostility to collective imaginings of freedom (and collectivity itself).

Though not always acknowledged, racial logics have important media components, and vice-versa: media emerge in and contribute to specific racialized contexts whether engaged practically or theoretically. Early ethnographic recording helped legitimate phonography's medium. Ideas of black sound, circulating under the sign of Negro or "world" music, helped to popularize it.[29] Recent scholarship reveals the centrality of African American vaudeville performers and public figures, early ethnographic records, and vernacular music to the legitimization and popularization of phonography.[30] One way of narrating the history of the medium is the gradual becoming-autonomous of the phonographic sound object, its evolution from storage medium or index of prior performance to an aesthetic medium in its own right. The rise of commodity culture and concomitant transition from the Victorian parlor to the modern living room (hence the invention of the private domestic space) is one precondition for sound reproduction technology finding recorded music as a primary function. It overlaps population shifts from rural to urban centers and from agricultural to industrial labor, and expansions of imperialism and domestic rights, among other shifts. There was, as Jonathan Sterne argues, "a new level of plasticity in the social organization, formation and movement of sound," which informed the emergence of new media, or the designation of new functions for existing technology.[31]

One of sound recording's first functions was to communicate the dominant values of bourgeois society through important speeches, poems, and symphonies. As Michael Denning and others have shown, the communication and dissemination of alternative, anticolonial, or counter-hegemonic values coexists with its other functions, such as producing and aestheticizing the exotic in the interest of normalizing imperial relations.[32] The latter function became a dominant way of hearing by reducing aesthetic excess to appropriable surplus, making "world music" the sign of either an exotic or a recently departed elsewhere. Records helped create and disseminate a sense of shared social experience across geographically and temporally diverse terrains, contributing to shifting racial attitudes and geographies, and ultimately helping shape the racialization of sounds themselves. The modern, including black sound, depends on hidden or obscured colonial relations, and the transition from racial abjection to liberal freedom, historically paired with the waning of sovereignty as political virtue, has continually meant the spatial and conceptual displacement of dispossession of unfreedom along lines of gender, race, and geographic difference. To conceive of black soundwork as liberatory requires thinking beyond the boundaries and histories of individual nation-states, and reconceiving the alternative maps and geographies implied and traced by the circulation of black sound. If early sound recording's traffic in vaudeville suggests an effort to create shared social experience for the white bourgeoisie, the traffic of "race records" and other vernacular music remade modernity's collective ear, enabling new collectivities organized around and through the sonic.[33]

Phonographic poetry is one element in that development. Its emergence provides insights into the evolving techniques of poetic, sonic, and racial production. It emerges in the context of a general social reorganization of the ways we listen, what we listen for, what we hear, and who counts as "we." One well-developed axis of analysis emphasizes white hipster engagements with African American and global black culture, which follows the trajectory of love and theft Eric Lott analyzes through his study of blackface minstrelsy. Having been, however ambivalently, the soundtrack of youthful rebellion and antibourgeois self-fashioning for white hipsters, jazz's meanings have become increasingly diffuse and contested, especially along the color line, which I would argue made it vulnerable to the emergence of rock and roll (which also had roots in the black "folk") to become the soundtrack of white youth culture. Simultaneous with that, one sees the rise of poetry as a counterculture, with recordings of Dylan Thomas, Allen Ginsberg, and the Beats playing a key role.[34] Less emphasized, however, is the new self-assertion of black poets and musicians who, through "soul jazz," capaciously conceived avant-garde and other forms that used sound to hail new black publics and counter-publics into being in the context of the culture industries' consolidation. Musicians and poets positioned audiences to receive new sounds and definitions of blackness—corresponding with new notions of "the people" and the community.

Such transmission is never straightforward, and the positions of sender and receiver are dynamic and reversible. Although the outcome Theodor W. Adorno seems to have at once predicted and feared—that music would "become" writing—has not happened, listening to sound as text, as material always already worked on, requires attention to what is and remains troubling. Medium, and with it the possibility of animating re-hearing, plays a central role. Rather than "relinquish[ing] its being as mere signs," phonographic sound emerged from and participated in overlapping ethnographic and commercial processes that enabled new grammars of listening, and new modes of signification in excess of those grammars.[35] Each citation of a sonic "truth" of race also plays in the interstitial zone between reinscription and potential resignification or transformation. Phonographic poetry is among the new forms electric sound recording made available, transforming and extending music's productive force rather than extinguishing it. Nonetheless, its producers mobilized it in the interest of transformation of "the most recent sound of old feelings" into simultaneously archaic and avant-garde texts that bear without being reducible to knowledge to come.[36] Phonography, even with the most carefully planned recording session or reading, unavoidably creates the conditions for hearding—hearing that more or less willfully confuses text and subtext. Phonography never entails the simple transmission of a message, the translation of sound from one medium (air, built environments) to another (durable storage media): textuality's inevitable surplus always also bears along what is not yet communicable.

New Words, New Worlds

Through mixed-media, vernacular avant-garde textual practice, black poets and musicians sought to reconceive community and the common that subtends it. Keeping attention on the sound-specific practices and texts through which people shape and contest meaning, I avoid reference to "blackness" in the abstract. While I've learned from Moten's understanding of blackness as "an ongoing irruption that anarranges every line," my question involves the ways black *texts* produce, contest, and disseminate the meanings of blackness, a social relation, which then obtains a "phantom objectivity" as "para-ontological" (ante-/anti-) presence.[37] *Text* does not refer to recording or writing but to something closer to medium and the surplus generated by what grammar and intertextuality produce in the interstitial play between different kinds of utterances. Attention to text allows simultaneous attention to the constitution of black sound as a set of relations among economic, political, professional, and affective interests (rather than a narrower understanding of the music industry). From this vantage point, I attend to the aesthetic possibilities afforded by new performance, recording, transmission, and playback techniques and technologies to take on dimension. *Text* thus refers to open-ended material practices/processes and objects as well as the interaction among temporal, grammatical, material, and figural processes of signification that allows blackness to appear as both an open set of incongruous and contested meanings and a transcendental signified or objective thing rather than the social relation it is. My framing allows a richer picture of the theoretical, physical, and political investments black sound practice encodes. Moreover, this framing requires attention to the media concepts or historically contingent desires that make black sound work.

Black soundwork, rather than assuming a stable audience as recipient, often does the work of calling to a prospective audience, of drawing together a "we." Drawing on the work of Jacques Rancière, Saidiya Hartman, Fred Moten, and others, I'm interested in the ways aesthetic projects imagine collectivity and ongoingness, and in the ways they participate, modifying Rancière, not in the production but in the *improvisation of the common*, the improvisation of communism.[38] Rather than institutional forms (e.g., the Party) or debates (e.g., reform or revolution), *communism* refers primarily to conceptions of social organization that are not organized around property relations or capital. "Improvisation of the common" holds space open within which to conceive and take seriously alternative social structures where production is not necessarily the production of value. Black community, never a defensive exclusivity or formation grounded in origin or originary rupture, might best name the socio-spatial forms produced by—and that condition the production of—marginal social life, where "margin" indicates the continued production of an outside to a putative mainstream. At its most radical, black soundwork is a practice of black collective thinking that opens onto new configurations of the social. Analysis of phonographic poetry through medium requires a different line of thinking about the ways sound practice draws on the past (itself mediated by previous texts), not simply to affirm belonging to a group or historical formation but to attempt to imagine and call into being new ways of being collective.

In Rancière's account, "the political (*la politique*) arises from a count of community 'parts,' which is always a false count, a double count, or a miscount."[39] Relatedly, the "distribution of the sensible," referring to "the system of self-evident facts of sense perception that simultaneously discloses the existence of something in common [*le commun*] and the delimitations that define the respective parts and positions within it," serves as the point of articulation between politics and aesthetics.[40] At bottom, for Rancière, is a question of *logos*, and those identified with it via a familiar logocentricism that equates intelligible speech with being human and unintelligibility with the condition of the subhuman. Nonetheless, the notion of the common usefully recalls other shapes of the social than those corresponding with logocentric cartographies. As Michael Hardt puts it, the common "is the scene of encounter of social and political differences, at times characterized by agreement and at others antagonism, at times composing political bodies and at others decomposing them."[41] The boundary separating sensible/insensible and *demos*/non-*demos* is the police order (*le politique*). The count of democracy's *demos* always produces a surplus—the part that has no part. Politics, for Rancière, exists when domination is interrupted or resisted by the dominated, and that resistance constitutes the dominated as a political entity. Freedom is a "pure invention," an act of claiming equality carried out by the "part that has no part," the dominated who are structurally excluded from the *demos* and therefore visible only within the police order as an element to suppress. A long history of black sound reveals that crossing the line into intelligibility does not eliminate the operation of the police order. As often as not, emerging intelligibility—legitimacy—can intensify policing, allowing cover for the continued murderous segregation that produces the "part that has no part," reframed as the spectacularly or sacrificially excluded upon whom the security of the *demos* depends.

This is not to answer a theoretical question empirically. Rancière's arguments for the ways societies respond to il/legitimate claims to freedom from those whose systematic and strategic exclusion shapes the political give me pause. Rancière cites Herodotus writing about a Scythian slave revolt (it is easy to imagine more contemporary slave revolts) where the enslaved "decided that, until proved wrong, they were the equal of the warriors" and engaged in armed revolt.[42] The enslavers eventually put aside their spears—signifying their intention to engage the rebels on their terms—and took up whips: "struck by the spectacle, the slaves took to their heels without a fight." His point is to strategically position such uprising as the "disorder of revolt" beyond the sphere of the legitimately political—beyond the realm of the intelligible—and thus discredit it. The enslaved spoke themselves into the social order, and the police order reasserted itself and, moreover, revealed the degree to which it had imprinted itself in the self-understanding of the enslaved. Putting to one side disagreement over the potential of popular uprising, it remains unclear how or whether the police order might be not simply disrupted but dismantled, or whether there are ways of resolving the theoretical and structural problem posed by the "part that has no part" that fundamentally alter the terrain of the political. That, I take it, has tended to be the aim of "slave rebellions" and similar uprisings.

But what if we read those revolts through Saidiya Hartman's analysis of the "longstanding and intimate affiliation of liberty and bondage," and her injunction to consider "freedom independent of constraint or personhood and autonomy separate from the sanctity of property and proprietorial notions of the self"?[43] If the most radical claims for the new music and new poetry stem from their respective reimagining of experience itself, grasping the full impact of black soundwork and the forms of community it discloses requires reconsidering the claims to subjectivity and subjective experience that tend to inform the discourses and cultures surrounding the music and poetry, each understood as the other's spur and limit. Producing the common ought to be a name for the pre- and re-figurative work of overturning the very ground of the political in light of the structural miscount. For this reason, and because the outcomes are not guaranteed, I prefer to think in terms of what Spivak might call the concept-metaphor of improvisation. The uncounted are structurally excluded; the part that has no part is neither inside nor outside; as riotous supplement, it might turn this mother out.

In its ideal forms, improvisation requires both play and reciprocal attunement—commitment to sympathetic vibration, social disposition, and embodied practice. This does not simply mean commitment to rule breaking or violating norms but a collective commitment to yet unrealized alternatives, to revolutions that yet have no name. In its commitment to that "yet" it opens onto the unthought, to experiments with freedom reflexively aware of their complicity and insufficiency but nonetheless oriented toward something else to be completed by and through the future engagement phonography provides. Reciprocal attunement requires play, a commitment to what may happen in the course of the event's unfolding, as well as an openness to conceptual revisioning to make room for the forms of transformation of self and others that may come. Play, in ensemble, likewise requires reciprocal attunement. Improvising the common, then, is the search, through play, for a freedom that does not necessarily recapitulate the structure. I'm interested in black soundwork's speculative capacities, its capacity to invoke aspects of lived experience of renewal in Ornette Coleman's sense in the epigraph above. The sanctity of property and the norms of propriety and autonomy that issue therefrom have as their avatars bourgeois white men, and are defined in opposition to the slave and the feminine. What we need is not the universalization of patriarchal, capitalist freedom but its abolition, along with its conceptual dependencies—personhood, autonomy, individual sovereignty—understood to mark the boundaries of legible and desirable selfhood. Abolition in this sense is at stake in the black soundwork this book studies. What we need is a set of collective capacities for which we do not have names, and which black soundwork gives one way of conceiving.

In his discussion of Amiri Baraka, Fred Moten refers to "a massive intervention in and contribution to the prophetic description—a kind of anticipatory rewriting or phonography—of communism that is, as Cedric Robinson has written, the essence of black radicalism."[44] In light of his subsequent work, we can understand that remark in terms of his ongoing engagement with a long phenomenological tradition that separates subjects and objects, which subtends his powerful critique of the proper and property. If, following Moten and Robinson, we understand blackness as the historically specific and enduring form of a more general racialization and production of the social's excess or "outside," we might understand the long, discontinuous history of black struggle as a series of contests staged in the name of a freedom more profound than those oriented around self-possession. Taken together, Hartman, Moten, and Robinson offer exemplary critiques of the social forms predicated upon freedom to enter into contracts, formal equality, property, and the "invisible hand"—in a word, critiques of the forms of life thinkable from within capitalism—that substantively engage slavery and its afterlives. Substantive freedom requires social forms and transformation beyond what we usually mean by diversity, inclusion, and similar terms. But it will also mean that the "we" that becomes free will differ from the "we" that fights for freedom. The fight for freedom is a fully transfigurative fight to reshape the discursive and political terrain upon which people struggle, a fight for new ways of imagining collective action and collectivity itself without guarantees of their future shape. Here we might again recall that the name musicians and critics give to musical activity is *play*, and consider the full range of things played on and with. We might, as I attempt, consider the relationship between improvisation and surprise as a way of registering the unexpected, the riotous, what was immanent but unrecognized, what was still possible in what was thought outmoded.

To ask about black sound's media is to ask about the history of the past, the relationship of culture to the present, and ultimately the improvisation of the common whose range of effective circulation we term community, but whose most radically conceived form is communism. Focus on collaboration, meanwhile, creates conceptual space through which to consider the mutual constitution of poetry and music. Rather than understand these collaborations in terms of the available histories of poetry and music, this book listens for artists' negotiation of aesthetic fields that shaped and were shaped by their institutionally legible and illegible actions. Using experimental modes, they engaged textual practices that expanded the possibilities of art, and those texts refract—recode and engage through field-specific logic—broader social conflicts and contradictions while retaining a relative autonomy and a specific discursive, economic, and political field. This orientation encourages consideration of the aesthetic field's relative autonomy, seeing aesthetic conflicts as having an actuality beyond simply reflecting or expressing broader social and historical processes.[45]

What *Is* This Thing Called *Jazz*?

Insofar as I am invested in the potentialities and latencies as born by black sound, especially music, I grapple with what is regressive or inadequate in the music's history and historiography, which discourses surrounding the music can tend to replicate. Throughout, I grapple with the predominant maleness of the archives of free jazz and phonographic poetry. The persistent conceptual and practical exclusion of women from jazz should remind us that no aesthetic form or practice is inherently liberatory or progressive.[46] The word *jazz* names multiple vectors of desire, power (including the power to define what is and is not jazz), relations to music, and sites of conflict, and that multiplicity defines its being. Perhaps above all, it designates a discursive field, that is, an evolving set of questions and answers, claims and explanations, within which evolve narrative and tropological tendencies and ideal ways of linking aesthetics and historical context. It sets the conditions for hear(d)ing the music, for converting non-meaning sound into predetermined symbolic relations (e.g., syncopation as indicative of a basic savagery in one moment, recoded as a freedom drive in another). The line between meaning and non-meaning is a historical question regarding the specific contexts in which black sound comes to be read as an independent phenomenon. Rather than recite familiar lists of performers, composers, debates, tendencies, legacies, and landmark recording sessions, it seems more productive to consider the processes by which critics, musicians, and listeners alike have produced ideas of jazz as the name for a singular impulse. What are the semantemes (base units of meaning) and how do they control its morphology, the torque of its tropes? Sherrie Tucker argues that what we study is "the desires mapped onto representations of and narratives about jazz and the connections and disconnections between them and jazz practice."[47] Those representations and narratives are constitutive of jazz, and those representations, which encode and fuel collective desires, suffuse the experience of jazz practice, even as that practice necessarily exceeds them. Tucker calls for critics to consider those practices, players, and audiences jazz studies excludes in order to define its object—"to narrate with an awareness" of narrative's limits and produce more adequate representations. The more radical implication of the deconstruction she calls for (riffing on Scott Deveaux's influential essay "Constructing the Jazz Tradition") would be to track the ways those bodies, desires, and practices strategically excluded from the jazz tradition as discourse turn out to be conditions of possibility for thinking or narrating jazz. Insofar as the anarchic, unorganizable, or unruly name jazz's ideal promise, our analysis should probe the serial exclusions upon which its symbolic unity relies. I am ultimately interested in the kinds of listening and analysis that become possible, and necessary, when we treat "jazz" as a process rather than an entity, and examine the vectors of power that shape its being. As with poetry and other genres, the whole to which jazz belongs is an effect of the discursive operations that make singular performances or styles effective. Poetry is no more stable as referent or archive than jazz is, and while I do not study spoken word directly, its performative mode bears a family resemblance to those I do study. One could trace the emergence of phonographic poetry through the archives of poets reciting and performing their own poetry in the nineteenth and earlier twentieth centuries, whose function gradually shifted from demonstrations of elocution, to instill virtue and discipline speech and to encourage self-expression, to a means toward an additional plane of analysis where the author's own inflections became most vitally important.[48] The public reading, parallel with the use of early sound recording to transmit great oratory, eventually gave way to broader practices of literary entrepreneurialism, where charismatic lectors developed rhetorical and performance practices to promote their work and supplement their income. In that relay between print and performance modern poetry constitutes itself. The spaces, practices, and functions of poetry proliferate through the twentieth century, with poets adapting new technology as it emerges. Along the way they effect crossings among (invoking in Don Ihde's terms of "the word as soundful" or "songful") "sounds as meaningful" and "the [technical] transformation of [sound] experience itself."[49] Poetry mediates soundful words and meaningful sound; phonographic poetry remediates poetry, music, and the community theater projects specifically for intended black audiences. Media analysis is key to reconstructing this cartography of desires, narratives, and competing claims to legitimacy within and beyond the bourgeois sphere of culture. Framed by economic and cultural relations and antagonism, medium is a name for a "recurring set of contingent social relations and social practices."[50] One name for that contingency, of course, is history, analyzed in terms of the shifting economic and political terrains, the processes of emergence and incorporation, and the vectors of power and social positionality that shape and animate mutually informing class, race, and gender relations. This project investigates the media of poetry and the work of poetry as mediation in a specific context where black sound takes on new political meanings.

Collection: Time

A project concerned with sound recordings is also concerned with collection—re-constellating commodity objects in into new networks of desire and value. Obsession, which marks a perversion or diversion of libidinal energies toward potentially perverse, even liberatory (mis)use, is its intellectual mode. And, as will be clear from its analysis of the shifting meanings and functions of black sound, the analysis of phonographic poetry probes the boundaries between art and non-art as (related to) the boundary between socio-ethical and economic value, understanding that with each binary one pole contaminates the other. A simple opposition of "idealist" (black sound reflects or expresses an underlying black consciousness) and "materialist" (black aesthetic practice responds to concrete historical antagonisms) theories of black soundwork is unhelpful, even symptomatic, if it simply proposes sound as materiality or pure use-value. Use-value, as Gayatri Chakravorty Spivak has argued, is "both outside and inside the system of value-determination," neither simply host to parasitic exchange-value (inside) nor calculable within the definition of value.[51] Spivak's reminder, via Marx, that "a thing can be a use-value without being a value" reminds us of the theoretical difficulties entailed in framing black sound as wholly resistant and extrinsic to capital or capitalist modernity. (It also tells us something about those whose lives and labor are at once central to and external to bourgeois conceptions of the good life.) One way, then, of conceiving black soundwork is by thinking about those similarly inside and outside capitalist modernity, those whose desires to "consume the (affect of the) work itself" always point to a strategically excluded possibility of, and riotous supplement to, that modernity. In its claims to and mobilization of common content, this aesthetic and theoretical practice I study here is most generally concerned with the improvisation of alternative forms of value. As obsessive pursuit (thinking here of the sheer duration of the labor entailed in being able adequately to develop one's own sound concept), it allows collaborators to imbue with value the objects, questions, concerns, and positions drawn from within stratified social structures, and outline at least a fantasy of autonomous, auto-telic production. Yet, though durable, obsessions are also mutable, ultimately deferring and differing the compulsion to circulation and value.

If, as Jacques Attali argues, records store "use-time" (on the model of use-value), the record collection is also an archive of intimacies and desires, uses beyond utility and surplus.⁵² Yet, "use-time," like use-value, is heterogeneous, only ambiguously related to larger determinations of value. While workers disposing of their time as they will registers as theft from the perspective of the capitalist, it is also clear that the record collection potentially represents something more subversive than people "stockpil[ing] what they want to find the time to hear."⁵³ Attali's unfortunate analogy of "exchange-time" to money ("a supposedly stable sign of equivalence") is beyond the scope of my present argument. Suffice it to say that as with traditional Marxist accounts of use-/exchange-value, the two change sides, and eventually use-value has to be strategically excluded in order for his temporal schema to work. What I want to suggest is that we might be able to read his terms differently in order to rethink the record collection in light of the concerns with which I began this introduction.

One might agree that sound recording reifies labor (use-time) into a commodity. One could also note that legitimating early sound recording required understanding it to belong to a broader social hygiene project, ensuring the transmission of bourgeois cultural values to the proletariat. Neither of these "materialist" accounts, however, account for the perversity of collection as a site of conflicting desires and uses, not all of which correspond with market values in any straightforward way. Collection indexes affects at once intrinsic and extrinsic to social reproduction; it points to affectively necessary surpluses that have no correlate within the production of commodity value. But, returning to Nathaniel Mackey and the Art Ensemble of Chicago, I wonder about other forms of "exchange-time," which is to say I wonder about the normative situation Attali and others imagine of the solitary listener with his (usually a man) records, waiting for the time to listen. Could we conceive of such time as the imagined time of an encounter, the prospective, future-perfect time of listening in a world that differs from the world of the initial sounding? Exchange-time becomes a way of describing a moment when things fall into place—the right moment, the right sound, the right company, the right occasion to share listening. Mackey's character N. decries "someone else's having heard presumed to be one's own." But Mackey's work—in prose, in verse, and as a longtime host of a radio show called *Tanganyika Strut*—reminds us of the pleasure and possibility of making one's listening available to others. Listening is reflexive, but its autonomy heightens the desire for another to listen to my listening and through that imagine a community of listeners "that each wants to make itself heard hearing."⁵⁴ This doubled scene of listening—being affected by sound and imagining others hearing my hearing—marks the resonant body of the community of listeners.

One's personal collection of sound objects—I can no longer say "record collection"—is advance preparation for an encounter with someone who shares in the project of counter-knowledge at the heart of black (sound) studies. Collection touches on alternative temporalities and intimacies, alternative relations to the objects one concerns oneself with that are not about consumption, absorption, integration but instead about reoriented relations to the world. This attention is necessary as this book considers the circulation of texts, the different meanings sound takes on or is refused at different moments across time and space, in the interstices of communal formation between the here/now and the potential. As much as a sound recording, like any document or archive produced under capitalism, is also a document of dispossession, alienation, and exploitation, it also indexes "some other kind of thought," points that will have been locatable on a map of counter-formation. This is a formation written on the B-side of the archival records of black negation, the fetishistic ac/counting of black vulnerability, the mathematics and ledgers of black undoing. Listening is a proto-political, critical practice aimed at what in the past is not yet exhausted, at forms of life still on the horizon. Those riotous forms of life are immanent; they beckon still—if we make time to listen.

In the beginning there were no words. In the beginning was the sound and they all knew what that sound sounded like. —TONI MORRISON, *Beloved*

The voice becomes more and more relevant to contemporary jazz. From the vocal quality of the most impressive horns, to "A Love Supreme," or Archie Shepp's spoken "Malcolm" . . .
—AMIRI BARAKA, *Black Music*

Voice Prints
Toward a Black Media Concept

Fugitive Voicing

Black sound emerges as what refuses, interrupts, or redirects the energies of extant discourses and their subtending epistemologies. Considered historically and theoretically, it is also a fundamentally textualized discursive field. To track its oscillation between these poles, and the political visions and desires to which each refers, is to rewrite the history of the black sonic avant-garde as a continual reinvention of its conceptual ground, negotiation of its relation to other discursive fields, and coordination of technical, sensuous, and ideological elements. While black sound tends to appear as extra-discursive plenitude, as medium for preserving and disclosing practices of resistance and structurally inarticulable postulates of freedom—and collective black sound *practice* has indeed worked that way—black sound as concept yokes together fields of signification continually contested within and reinvented across generations. Without denying its extra-linguistic or extra-semantic meanings, I would argue that it is *primarily* textual. By "text," I do not mean writing in the narrow sense, but an open-ended will to systematicity, structured by relations of power and capital, that draws and redraws the horizon within which sound techniques, gestures, dispositions, and so on take on meaning. The multi-phonic, altissimo saxophone note becomes legible as "scream" only insofar as it can serve as a metonym for black rage and aspiration, which in turn requires a cultivated habit of hearing in the grain of every sound the inchoate "voice" of *some* subaltern people making ambiguous transition to the popular, those whose desires and actions become legible and generalizable within a hegemonic order—that is, as the hegemonic order transforms in response to mass mobilization. (This is one way of describing the heterogeneous but overlapping, mutually inflecting struggles for liberation that characterize the 1960s beyond relatively narrow frames such as "Civil Rights," a term that names the response to black freedom struggles but not their demands.) Attending to sound's textual remit and transmission, as shaped by the rapidly transforming institutions within and around state cultural apparatuses, has the advantage of conceiving of artists as agents navigating a terrain shaped by the traditions they claim (and that claim them) alongside the institutions that frame agency. Insofar as that context makes every aesthetic gesture at least potentially symbolic, it becomes tempting to read every stylistic choice in terms of symbolic action—for example, resistance to a norm whose supposed externality helps delimit the thingness of black sound. To focus primarily on pain and privation puts the music in a primarily reactive stance, which can obscure the complexities of its emergence in the field of the social, its multiple significances, the theoretical challenges that play as oblique or eccentric engagement with a situation, form, or discourse. To infer connections between black sound practice and concrete social antagonisms requires deeper engagement with what Adorno terms the "total social process," more attention to processes of mediation, of condensation and displacement, if we are to listen rather than fetishize sound as inherently oppositional.[1] Here, that attention registers in tracked relays between text, voice, and other sound practices as they shape and modify black sound understood as theoretical object.

Engaging disparate sound experimentalists Archie Shepp and Matana Roberts, the former exemplary of Black Arts–era political engagement and the latter of more elusive contemporary politics, I seek to historicize the tendency to read sonic aesthetic agency in symbolic terms, and by foregrounding considerations of medium to counteract that tendency. My aim is not to posit Roberts's indebtedness to Shepp, or Shepp's priority for reading Roberts, or to claim them both as cartographic points in a map of a singular tradition. Instead, drawing on their implicit and explicit accounts of and approaches to history, genre, and medium, I read their practices intertextually. Shepp's generation provides a set of coordinates of interpretation that Roberts, despite the divergent regimes of black sound as discourse and possibility that link and separate them, must navigate. While Shepp understood himself to be making art for "revolutionary times," taking advantage of then-ongoing class reorganization in the transition between imperial regimes, Roberts emerged in a period where black public life is broadly characterized by exhaustion with both politics and the political, yet still in pursuit of alternatives not yet named. Behind this is a set of questions regarding the discrepancies between Shepp's music, his claims for the music, the divergent ways Impulse! and critics framed him as an "angry black tenor man," between the objective historical conditions to which his sound practice refer and its re-signification in the present, tarrying with the durability of medium, the way sound and sound techniques persist across time and attach themselves to new conditions of legibility and audibility and thus new possibilities of meaning. It can also help us contend with the fact that "angry African American tenor player" sounds a false note insofar as we can take the individualizing term "African American" as a marker of historico-political shift rather than identity. African Americans may be angry, and may play saxophone, but the social world has shifted beneath their feet, and there are few contexts in which their anger will read as legitimate, much less answerable.

I am inspired by what Alexander Weheliye terms the "oral performative dimensions of written language," and want here to account for the obverse: the textual dimensions of sound—not the recovery of a positive "origin" of sound or phonic materiality but the ultimate unavailability of an origin for sound other than the destabilizing conduct of intertextuality.[2] Part of my investment here is to insist upon, and analyze, contradictions between texts, their continuities as well as their discontinuities, the discursive backdrop against which they take shape and the theoretical contexts within which they take on meaning. The scream and other gestures that counter standards (which change from generation to generation) of "good" musicianship or "beautiful" sound could stand as catachrestic invocations of the people for whom current representational schema are inadequate. Proceeding this way, I change the question of tradition from a *what* (canons and key figures) to a *how* (the means by which knowledge, virtues, practices, worldviews, and so on, are handed down), which requires attention to media. A related aim, fundamentally at stake in free jazz and its poetics, is a desire to conceive music beyond representation, which, as Sylvia Wynter argues, participates in the larger project of creating a repertoire of visceral responses in support of the ascriptive hierarchies upon which capitalist relations of production depend. Music and poetry, with their respective emphasis on the physicality of sounding, and of sounding for its own sake, both eschew representation in favor of expressive modes and accounts of the visceral that stray from or otherwise resist recuperation into a symbolic order. The supposed return to "craft" in poetry and jazz following the putatively undisciplined art of the Black Arts era (for instance, the "Young Lions" in jazz and other neo-formalists) tells us something about the shift in politics between the 1960s (when the unruly element was the politics themselves) and the depoliticizing tendencies of following periods during which the management of social antagonism through procedural fixes and voting emerge as the only legitimate political strategies. Yet, factoring in platform shift (e.g., the ascension of the compact disc), and the overlapping historical media work of CD reissues and prominent anthologizing, those preferences surely felt organic to the moment, since the "return" was simultaneous with the reappearance of sounds framed as "traditional." Considering them in tandem reveals something about the communities between and among which artists and intellectuals imagined texts circulate, and what they imagine texts do. It tells us, in other words, about the changing *idea* of black culture, and of culture itself, and relatedly about the changing relationships among aesthetics, technology, communication, transmission, and society.

Attending to the textuality of black sound can help us better see how culture interacts with broader political shifts without seeing the former as mere reflection of the latter. One way this chapter coordinates its analysis across spatiotemporal disjuncture is by attending not only to mediation (the intellectual procedure of linking fundamentally unlike ideas or phenomena in one conceptual frame) but to media as well. Although some scholars have attended to the critical role black people have played in the development and popularization of media technologies, and others have attuned us to the effects changes in the nature of print or recording media have had on black cultural production, interrogations of the complex of assumptions and understandings of the relationship between technology, communication, transmission, and society are rare. Yet some analysis of the ways different artists have understood the dynamic relationships between aesthetic practice, communication, and the intended publics or communities—here referred to as "media concept"—can help us better understand the continuities, permutations, discontinuities, and intertextual play that shape any claim to or refusal of tradition.[3] *Medium* here functions partially as a proxy term for the processes whereby changes in social relations encourage or make visible new uses of existing technological or expressive forms, that is, for changes in the underlying discourses of and epistemologies that form the horizon, limits, and enabling propositions that shape sound practice in relation to other domains of meaning and action. In every moment that sound appears to be the dominant mode of black "consciousness" and its cognates, we should consider the underlying social relationships, genres, languages, and material practices that make it so.

In Alexander Weheliye's influential account, the interplay of music's ephemerality and the materiality of sound technologies and practices "provides the central, non-sublatable tension at the core of sonic Afro-modernity."[4] We must conceive this tension, I argue, in terms of the black sound object's relation to the circuit of capitalist production, aided by the advent of sound recording technologies that engender new ways of configuring sound and writing. Sound technologies—which by turn encourage, challenge, and reify the idea of sound's pre-technical plenitude—necessitate both a deconstruction of the orature/literature binary and a different historical frame through which to understand the emergence of sound reproduction technology. Weheliye claims those technologies' emergence "did not cause the same sorts of anxieties about the legibility of music as it did in mainstream [Euro-]American culture"; but black people, for whom the public/private binary has always been fraught, did experience the reorganization of space and the recalibration of the sensorium in which sound reproduction technologies participated. That reorganization, and the corresponding transformation, invoking Elizabeth Alexander, of the black *and* bourgeois interior, allows new understandings of sound and new functions for existing music technologies. Hence, for example, we can understand the centrality of the phonograph (and black women's voices) to Langston Hughes, Ralph Ellison, or James Baldwin's self-narration. The separation of sound and source and the concomitant transformation of the theoretical and material object of black sound create new points of contact between performers and listeners, the semantic and the somatic, the phonic and the graphic. Within poetry, the interplay between the in-time and the over-time, between the ephemeral and the durable, creates new paradigmatic and syntagmatic possibilities for black soundwork, that is, new sources of aesthetic pleasure, new ways of apprehending the sensualities of the sonic that might carry us beyond the constellation of self-possession and the proper. In this and following chapters, investments in and refusals of certain models of subjective interiority, investments in and refusals of models of aesthetic ecstasy for those pleasures that yet have no name, are key topoi.

The renewed emphasis on voice Amiri Baraka declares in this chapter's epigraph is in fact a question awaiting theoretical clarification. For black and other minoritized artists, voice splits its function. On the one hand, it operates conventionally to connote the carrier and sign of an inalienable and singular inner self, soul, mind, and so on. On the other hand, voice hovers in that uncertain zone between synecdoche (the individual self that stands in for the collective) and metonymy. "All calls to collectivity," Gayatri Chakravorty Spivak argues, "are metonymic because attached to a situation. And they work by synecdoche."[5] At stake in the newly significant voice Amiri Baraka describes and calls for are forms of collectivity that might lie beyond metonym/synecdoche political performativity, and in excess of the figurative. In order to hear the radicalness of the New Black Music and avoid re-situating it in the musical and political configurations it rejected, in the paradigms of voice as unmediated bearer of inner truth of the self or the community (although some did discuss their work in those terms), it's important to trace the ways the re-signified voice is adequate to the emergent forms of consciousness and political aspiration among those who in a moment of crisis, in the caesura of the everyday, understand the need for new forms of political being.

Drawing on Joy James's analysis of Frantz Fanon and Nathaniel Mackey's discussions of music (which themselves re-ground faith in alternative or dissonant aesthetics following the anti-collective politics of the 1970s and '80s), I propose the term "fugitive voice" for this new, speculative relationship between "voice" as intertextual performance of collectivity—a double inscription that makes "the people" legible and makes an individual representative of a collective whose presumed presence authorizes speech—and a call to those who would, in the *henceforward* that designates the revolutionary moment's uncertain aftermath, understand themselves as a collectivity despite there being no necessary a priori unity to join them. James conceives of the rebel as an unexampled confluence of mechanical, biological, and divine temporalities and modes of action without necessity, and without the assumption that revolution will be progressive. In the wake of rebellion's defeat, the energies of the *henceforward* do not simply dissipate but reorganize in forms waiting to reactivate in later moments. Mackey offers the term "metavoice" as a name for a supplemental voicing for a constitutively irreparable collectivity, a fictional collectivity whose realization will have followed the utterance, if utter is what this voice does. Fugitive voice similarly names a confluence of the technical (including the mechanical), the biological, and a speculative or experimental practice conceived as message emanating from the other side of the henceforth, a hailing of subjects yet to emerge. Both, in my reading, at least gesture toward the speculative temporality of the *henceforward*, oriented toward solidarities unforeseeable in reified accounting of present possibilities. Both metavoice and fugitive voice play in the interval between disposition and dispossession, and I would emphasize voicing as othering, as gift, as what comes from the "outside" of being. In this, Mackey's account of music as phantom limb, "phantom reach with/after something you have but don't have," something you might hold (or that might hold you) but never possess, is illuminating. "Voice" may operate on one register as the index of subjective interiority, but its self-excessive tendency, its tendency to stray or "slide away from the proposed" (Amiri Baraka's description of saxophonist John Tchicai), marks it as always also a sign of alterity, of differing and transformation. It is the voice as a sign of that dispossession, voice as a gift from the outside of being, from the outside of the subject, a marker of the space between being (or history, or experience) in general and the subject as focal point for intelligible narrative. Recentering this discussion in terms of discourse and text, I'm sympathetic to Fred Moten's arguments for tradition as a text cutting and augmenting itself (indeed, particular ways texts cut and augment themselves as an index of history itself), with the difference being that where Moten sees "a cry from the outside," "figure[d] subjunctively" as a central component of this "internal disruption,"[6] I emphasize what is internal to but not governed by the internal arrangement of materials of texts themselves, what I referred to above as a "gift" from the outside, what we might name (following a range of thinkers from John Coltrane and Cecil Taylor to Moten himself) surprise or wonder, understood as that which, in the gap between all of the things one is and the narrative framing of the subject, can be cognized but not fully incorporated. We might more simply term it invention, the potentially revolutionary reworking of the given world, the precondition of any emancipatory politics.[7]

Listening for the fugitive voice, for speculative collectivities beyond the national, alongside the media that bear, distribute, and transform it, helps us hear emergent forms of sonic practice that still lack adequate names. I am trying to name the intrusion of those forms of experience that might lie beyond or be misunderstood by an economy of expression. In this sense, "fugitive voice" is a term for what is excessive or dissonant in a performance vis-à-vis the tradition or conventions it is supposed to exemplify, and the ways that excess makes retrospectively visible the social contradictions out of which formal innovations, as indices of the struggle over the sensible, emerge. At stake is not just messages but also their means of conveyance, not just codes but also the social actors that activate their meanings—a media concept. We might read, say, saxophonist Steve Coleman's claim that "sonic structures (forms, rhythms, and tones plus intent, emotion, and intuition) that masquerade as compositions" allow for "a more direct transmission of information than ordinary language" in light of both his millennial context and the fact that those sonic structures, mediations of "Kemetic astrological, astronomical and metaphysical sources," required re-mediation through liner notes.[8] How does sound as source, spur, and horizon or knowledge provide a basis for invention, including, in Sylvia Wynter's terms, the "invention of the concrete self" to be the "subject" of the new communities, the new communism?[9] How have people, thinking beyond the limited framing of reaction, response, or representation, conceived blackness in positive terms, as social poetics, as invention and reinvention? How have they conceived the possibilities of communication beyond "expression"?

Black sound, understood as a set of heterogeneous practices and discourses, indexes both a drive toward freedom and, as Simone White terms it, the negotiation of "the feeling of unwanted feeling" and the realities of the many forms of unfreedom and unliving that continue to shape black sociality (and creativity).[10] However, my larger concern is not the degree to which, say, Matana Roberts's experimental sound practice "sounds somewhat ineffectively into rap's vortical socio-symbolic domination of the black music space" but the degree to which her music necessarily engages the seeming "intractability of black misery," whose "unwanted feeling" indexes the pervasive anti-collective ideology that individualizes social antagonisms. "Unwanted feeling," the feeling of something missing or unexplainable, becomes the basis of new political solidarities. At least it gives us new points of departure, new maps and territories of invention. If one tracks the development of the New Black Music alongside the emergence and dominance of rhythm and blues, and Archie Shepp's example encourages thinking of the two dialectically, White's framing correctly identifies a shift, but misnames it: in Shepp's period, prominent proponents of the new music had access to non-specialist audiences thanks to a media ecology that included both mainstream and small independent publications, "big" and "little" magazines, including *Negro Digest*, *Soulbook: A Quarterly Journal of Revolutionary Afroamerica*, *Down Beat*, the *Cricket*, the *Grackle*, and many in between. At present, rap music's apparent "vortical socio-symbolic domination of the black music space" looks (or perhaps "feels") different because one usually encounters dissenting voices, especially those keen to maintain relative prestige (e.g., Wynton Marsalis's occasional comparisons of rap music to blackface minstrelsy)[11] through the presumptive lens of generational change. White's critique of the orthodoxy surrounding the music (which, ironically, tends to stand as an example of disrupted or refused orthodoxies) that imputes to the music an anarchic freedom drive serves as check and spur to recontextualize the accounts of community and collectivity I offer here.

A Genealogy of Black Sound

Black sound refers at once to material sounding in space and time, including the recording's reconstituted space-time, as well as a set of intertextual discursive acts that shape a field of enunciation—a process of negotiating what and how practices are discussed (or become legible as discrete practices), a delineation of what does and does not belong to it, a group of concepts and permissible/illicit choices and desires between a Foucauldian technology and a metaphorical assertion of the meaningfulness—that must be thought in concert with the plurality and complexity of black life in excess of its predicates. At key moments, thinkers such as Fred Moten have conceived it as akin to "the tenor's irruptive habitation of the vehicle," a flight from meaning that becomes the pathway to other meanings and ways of meaning.[12] Those discussions re-sign-ify the confluence of sensuous materiality, techniques, and ideologies that make sound meaningful, and in the process change ideas about its transmission, circulation, and possible audiences. Although the word *media* is seldom used, successive theoretical accounts of black sound as occult knowledge make legible the development and evolution of a media concept—a way of discussing a text as a transmission of effects not fully covered by the notion of mimesis or communication. One might think here of Amiri Baraka's early account of music, discussed below, which emphasizes collective activity and participation in musical acts (process) over commodifiable records (product) as the source of meaning, which allows him to separate the legitimate from the illegitimate. Insofar as technical media are usually what we mean by "media," and "medium" refers to material with and upon which aesthetics work, we might say that media (social relations that promote novel uses of existing technologies) mediate (provide a conceptual framework for thinking together apparently contradictory ideas) mediums (the material forms within which aesthetic effects are realized and conveyed). Mediums in turn participate in a broader process of mediating symbolic forms and practices. The tendency of these terms to blur together is part of my point.

Though there are other paths and nodes, I trace a movement from Frederick Douglass through W. E. B. Du Bois and Zora Neale Hurston, ending with longer analyses of Shepp and Roberts.[13] My aim is not exactly to chart a developmental model of black sound—each of these figures produced a conception of black sound that persists. As black sound has no singular origin, so is there no "as such" to black sound; yet, to interrogate its apparent material existence is to presuppose the priority of an onto-phenomenological question, or at least to venture into a discursive field shaped by such questions. If, as I argue, each generation must reinvent a notion of black sound, then what I offer here is a set of successive origins, with *origin* understood in Walter Benjamin's sense not as the singular moment black sound emerges but as a way of naming succeeding conceptions that remediate black sound as practice, usually through understandings of communication or mimesis. Disarticulating black sound as real and theoretical object, I track the serial formation and re-formation of black sound as theoretical object (a structured complex of sensuous, technical, and ideological forces). Doing so, I'm interested in the repertory of strategies, epistemological assumptions, and political gestures that bind black sound and endow it with the appearance of solid objecthood.

In his 1845 *Narrative*, Frederick Douglass famously writes that when he was "within the circle," he could not "understand the deep meaning of those rude and apparently incoherent songs."[14] Separation from—or at least imagining an inhabitable position outside—"the circle" is a condition of knowing the circle. Douglass, in other words, *appropriates* the "apparently incoherent songs" as abolitionist testimony, makes them into an object of knowledge. His text mediates "unmeaning jargon" and meaningful song—writing an allegory of his own experience in order to make the songs legible within narrative and generic codes whose partial fulfillment makes experiences legible and shareable, and whose partial violation points to the more profound processes and meanings genre obscures. Mediating the songs of the enslaved for audiences who are also "outside the circle" (who mistook them either for a sign of savagery or contentment) allows him to understand and transmit the knowledge that "every tone was a testament against slavery." Jon Cruz traces back to Douglass the process of appropriating black sound as meaningful.[15] Doing so, Cruz shows the ways phonography's legitimation as an instrument of scientific preservation is linked to techniques of culture and "race" as filiation and class belonging. The very logic of racialization, allowing white, bourgeois subjects to imagine themselves to be the representative, ideal subjects of experience, permeates the early uses of sound recording and transmission technologies from the telephone to the preservation of voices (and languages) of those threatened with either extinction or absorption as imperial capital extended its borders and incorporated ever more of the world.

The production of meaning around black sound is irrevocably linked with the production of value. Noting the ways sound recording changed the social, cultural, and legal status of the voice, creating new forms of value around a property regime that promoted the idea of inalienable aspects of a person as property, we could conclude that questions of value and subsumption (the transformation of labor processes in response to the dictates of capital) are ultimately at stake in the genealogy I offer here.[16] Signs of humanity easily become an appropriable surplus, and play easily becomes another modality of labor. Insofar as the appropriation of black sound as a discrete object (e.g., a sign of humanity) imbues it with specific pseudo-use value (i.e., not the value sound practice has within communities on their own, non-universalizing terms), black soundwork exists in ambivalent relation with capitalist production rather than outside of it.

Writing and print are only analogous to sound recording. They help engender the broader shifts in cultural understanding that will allow sound reproduction technologies to become media, which later form the metaphorical backdrop for conceiving sound as always already reproduction, a point on a textual chain of tradition. In Fred Moten's influential reading of this passage, he urges readers to "be attuned to the transmission of the very materiality that is being described while noting the relay between material phonography and material substitution," which helps us conceive together broken familial and hermeneutic circles in order better to apprehend the stakes of this episode in Douglass's narrative.[17] Writing and print are part of a larger textual mediation in which sound, voice, and meaning appear as metaphors for each other under the sign of a circle whose inside and outside continuously change places. The formation of a "circle" (which inevitably recalls circulation—especially the circulation of [ideas about] the unruly noise of the slave songs as indicative of mental inferiority, contentment, or both) is another. The conversion of sound into song creates a frame for relating and conceiving of a totality of individual and collective experience transmitting that experience to others. It gives form to the material facts of life while allowing persons linked by slave status to think of themselves in positive term as a slave *community*. Douglass's project involves aesthetics in the broadest sense—determining the line between sensation and the sensible, between meaningful sound (song) and "incoherent" noise. Claiming the slave songs to be proto-abolitionist texts, Douglass authorizes his own text as part of that tradition, implicitly claiming for himself the essential power and opacity ("They would sometimes sing the most pathetic sentiment in the most rapturous tone, and the most rapturous sentiment in the most pathetic tone"). He implicitly links learning to listen with learning to read. His claim that "the mere recurrence to those songs, even now, afflicts me" so that he is moved to tears while writing, puts writing into the same textual weave that connects sound, voice, and meaning. Yet, it's also clear that the meaning he assigns serves to limit the play—and possibility—of sound's signification, its aspiration to expressive modes for which codes have not coalesced. Outside the circle, black singing appeared to be unintelligible or unmeaning (unmediated) sensuality, an instance of the voice failing, or indeed exceeding its function as index of the human. Aligning the songs of the enslaved with abolitionism, Douglass at once makes them legible and reduces the power of the fugitive voice: the sound of a community in formation.

Even prior to music's centrality to sound recording, sounds meaningfully derived from minstrel versions of black and other racially marked sounds helped determine the popularity of sound reproduction industries from sheet music to phonographs, which in turn helped shape changes in the ways audiences listen to and value sonic detail. Coinciding with the Great Migration of African Americans from rural to urban spaces and from South to North, black sounds appeared in living rooms outfitted with record players as listening transitioned from a public to a private activity.[18] This commercial backdrop, along with the development of the modern living room (likely equipped with a piano), adds one layer of significance to *The Souls of Black Folk*'s sheet music epigraphs. They reappropriate and remediate the already mediated forms of black music then circulating with the Fisk Jubilee Singers and other groups, even as "The Sorrow Songs," a late addition, further remediates the music in terms similar to Douglass, whose "wild notes" reverberate in Du Bois's characterization of the "wild" or "weird" music of black "folk."[19] Du Bois adds what would prove to be a decisive dimension, nationalism ("the only American music which welled up from black souls in the dark past"), which naturalizes citizenship, the institution of culture, and "true manhood" as unassailable political goods. Nationalism for Du Bois always sat in uneasy relationship to Pan-Africanism, and here it's also important to mark his argument for the invaginative force of blackness as that which is at once excluded from civil and cultural life and as that which defines it. The "circle" from Douglass to Du Bois apparently expands. If before Douglass rhetorically excluded some of the slave song's singularity so that it could become synecdoche, Du Bois similarly subordinates its surplus—its noisy excess to signification—in order to metonymize a particular collective. By rhetorical sleight of hand, it becomes metonymy of "the singular spiritual heritage of the nation," and thus evidence of the centrality of African American culture to US culture more broadly.[20]

Troubled maternity subtends Du Bois's account of the music. His grandfather's Senegambian grandmother's song—rendered "Do bana coba gene me, gene me!"—comes to figure what precedes the slave past, and the continuity of traditions among people of African descent. As Farah Jasmine Griffin notes, in context readers "know little of what the words mean, but that doesn't matter because the meaning is in the sound and only the initiated can hear."[21] Here is an early instance of the conflation of African ancestrality as conduit to apparently unmediated communication. The semantic meaning is lost; the sound, phonetically preserved, becomes the medium through which "things to come from those now gone" (borrowing a phrase from Muhal Richard Abrams) resonate as if from the future. African ancestrality in this sense informs a good deal of literature during the New Negro period, ranging from Claude McKay's *Banjo* to Gwendolyn Bennett's "Song" or Zora Neale Hurston's "How It Feels to Be Colored Me," where the tom-tom and ideas of African rhythm stand in for the repaired temporality whose rupture is the Middle Passage.

The development of mass culture informs another shift. Increasingly, rather than learning in face-to-face situations, people learned the tradition through phonograph records. As Michael Denning shows, those records engendered a complex anticolonial phonopoetics enabled and mediated by a relative plasticity in regimes of domination. But this situation would prove problematic for those versions that understood it to be emblematic of "folk" culture, not least because of the ways reconfigurations of political space disrupted the temporal scheme that made those remote from colonial/metropolitan centers also temporally or developmentally regressive. The solution for many was figuring sound itself as bearer not of slave culture or "Africa" but black consciousness left intact by regimes of segregation.

Zora Neale Hurston is one thinker in that line. In important ways breaking with Du Bois, her essay "Spirituals and Neo-Spirituals," included in Nancy Cunard's 1934 *Negro: An Anthology*, marks an important node in the genealogy I'm tracing. It offers among the first accounts of black expression and black sound, as "unceasing variations around a theme," a changing same.[22] Hurston carefully disarticulates black sound from its media by insisting on the in-person transformation of songs, whether printed or otherwise transmitted, by new collectives for their own ends. "The nearest thing to a description one can reach," she writes, "is that they are Negro religious songs, sung by a group, and a group bent on expression of feelings and not on sound effects."[23] Nonetheless, she isolates and delineates the formal features that aid group expression, famously including "jagged harmony," "dissonances," "shifting keys and broken time," and spontaneous arrangements that make "each singing of the piece . . . a new creation."[24] Her primary aim is to claim the unruly spirituals against the neo-spirituals, codified and commodified versions of African American "folk" music she understood to be something other than "the songs of the people, as sung by them."[25] As with Douglass, Hurston insists on a (hermeneutic) circle and alternative or counter-circulation where the real "songs of the people," extended into preaching and other liturgical practices such as corporate prayer, have their proper resonance. The need for such a circle indicates the impossibility of such a circle, an appeal to a radical exteriority to capital and national(ist) projects increasingly difficult to imagine because of the coincident de-composition of traditional black communities in the midst of the Great Migration and burgeoning "race record" markets. The existence of "neo-spirituals," the presence of the inauthentic alongside the authentic, requires appeal, borrowing a phrase from Fred Moten, to a "radically exterior aurality" that, inevitably, threatens to undo even the stability of blackness as identity, since, as for Douglass, blackness simultaneously circulates as sign and commodity.[26] Black folk themselves become final arbiter of what could count as "songs of the people," and because they could not represent themselves, members of the intelligentsia would have to represent them. The unteachably "jagged harmonies" of the spirituals, like the requirement of group singing in the context of remote churches, sits uncomfortably with the awareness that, by 1934, a massive effort was underway to record these spirituals to ensure an archival trace, an effort Hurston's own descriptions and discussions of the spirituals, the sermon, and the prayer participated in. Hurston effectively rewrote these signs of radical exclusion into a decision for outsideness, breaking with older traditions that linked black aesthetic achievement to arguments for integration. Doing so, she made the fraught and "wounded kinship," the fraught and wounded claims to belonging, the fraught and wounded critique of propriety the music sounded into a virtue through which to conceive the music. Techniques become a way not only of separating the authentic from the inauthentic, the "performative essence," as it were, of black aural aesthetics as a stance vis-à-vis industrial capitalism, but a sign or reflection of an underlying group consciousness.[27]

Where Hurston does not make gender a theme in her analysis, Du Bois in subsequent retellings would stress the centrality of women in the transmission of the kernel of black expressive culture. Amiri Baraka, more than half a century later, re-genders transmission male in part through invocation of a more familiar medium: records. He offers a memorable account of the education he and A. B. Spellman received in poet and Howard University professor Sterling Brown's living room in the early 1950s: "There in a center room was a wall, which wrapped completely around our unknowing, of all the music from the spasm bands and arwhoolies and hollers, through Bessie and Jelly Roll and Louis and Duke, you know? And we watched ourselves from that vantage point of the albums staring haughtily at us, with that 'tcch tcch' sound such revelations are often armed with."[28] The phenomenological implications of subjects watching themselves listening from the place where the records watch them merit future attention. He attributes to Brown the claim, "This is the history. This is your history, my history, the history of the Negro people." Baraka's own relationship to records is more ambivalent. In a later essay on Albert Ayler he writes, "There are no records of Albert [Ayler] (no precise replications), only *Rumors*, but more faithful, more moving.... As outstanding as they are, the recordings only get the tops or edges of the sound, but not the unnerving deepness of the sound's force!"[29] This is at once a comment on the limitations of the medium and on what sound communicates.

In a typical gesture, he describes the music as "touching," "but its touch was 'past' aesthetic/psychological; it was bluntly physical, not just being heard, but being felt... the whole body became a field of sonic ideational penetration."[30] He had previously argued that "Music... is the result of thought. It is the result of thought perfected at its most empirical, *i.e.*, as *attitude*, or *stance*."[31] Shortly thereafter, he wrote of "the sound itself [becoming] a basis for thought."[32] Sound is the catalyst and music is the result; records both bear and distort history, but the *idea* of the history that black sound bears catalyzes thought. The point is the transfigurative possibility, the reminder that things can be otherwise. As he wrote of then-emergent avant-garde music: "If you can hear, this music will make you think a lot of weird and wonderful things. You might even become one of them."[33] The music's apposition (if not opposition) to the modes of social reproduction that create the "West" creates fissures or tears in the texture of quotidian experience and allows us to imagine, however briefly and imperfectly, life otherwise.

Without citing Hurston, Amiri Baraka would elaborate one line of her analysis in his epochal *Blues People*, which similarly worries about black sound in the context of the ongoing transformation of the conceptual and concrete realities of the "black community." Hurston and Baraka agree that black music is fundamentally improvisatory and collective, but where Hurston insists on the adequacy of technique to separate the inside from the outside of the circle, the three decades between her writing and Baraka's witness the proliferation of records through which any musician could access and master black sounds. The counterfeit can circulate freely and with the same value as the real. Baraka's response to this, and to the general anthropological vogue in things Negro, is to argue for black sound as a unified whole greater than the sum of its parts or features:

> Just as some of the African customs survived in America in their totality, although usually given just a thin veneer of Euro-American camouflage, so pure African songs, dances, and instruments showed up on this side of the water. But I consider this less significant because it seems to me much more important, if we speak of music, that features such as basic rhythmic,

harmonic, and melodic devices were transplanted almost intact rather than isolated songs, dances, or instruments.... But the survival of the *system* of African music is much more significant than the existence of a few isolated and finally superfluous features. The notable fact is that the only so-called popular music in this country of any real value is of African derivation.[34]

He goes on to cite historian Brooks Adams in order to argue that the Western prioritization of economic reasoning over the imagination disrupted a traditional African conception of the essential unity of life and art, and, importantly, introduced a distinction between "high" and "low" forms of music. As much as his concern is to argue for the essential unity of black musical expression rooted in the particularities of U.S. chattel slavery and its aftermath—especially the ambivalent incorporation of newly minted African Americans into the social order as nominally "free"—his concern is also to establish black sound outside of the logic of the thing, of commodification, in order to understand music as what's given in and as not time but *history*.

In the course of these arguments, black sound has become at once a way of mediating history and itself a medium of transformative energy—what Larry Neal would term "the modern equivalent of the ancient ritual energy"—defined by its opposition to existing conditions of capitalist modernity.[35] Rather than being the vanguard expression or reflection of the inner strivings of "the community" or "the people," its value lies in its impulse toward the freedom it intends, an impulse I discuss in the third chapter under the rubric of invention. To say the music is revolutionary is perhaps to mischaracterize it, as Amy Obugo Ongiri shows in her analysis of the ways in which black intellectuals like Archie Shepp and Larry Neal sought to fuse the dissonant impulses of the music they embraced with the more popular rhythm and blues or soul music. Neal stresses the "internal spiritual aspects of art" that placed it beyond the reach of Marxist analysis of the aesthetic labor process and "Western analytical methods."[36] The music had to bear the spirit of the people, and received understandings of form, balance, purposelessness, and so on were inadequate tools for evaluating work that stood on different aesthetic bases. Here would ordinarily follow a critique of the fundamentally intuitive accounts of blackness Neal and others in his generation advanced (and ultimately abandoned).

The predication of sound as medium responds to the antagonisms and exploitation inherent in the labor processes of music production by insisting on a more fundamental use-value that escapes the logic of capitalist circulation. We also come full circle to the ambivalent ways Douglass used sound-as-medium to strategically subordinate some of its noisy surplus in order to self-authorize and make the music metonymize a collective. "My music is functional . . . My music is for the people," Archie Shepp would declare;[37] black art should "reflect and support the Black Revolution," Ron Karenga pronounced.[38] These confident pronouncements make the most sense in the face of anxieties over the flux not only within the music industry and the jazz world—vanishing venues and hostility among entrenched cultural gatekeepers among the primary concerns—but also in popular understandings of aesthetic value. We can retrospectively read investment in the reciprocal production of race and sound techniques as a canny anxiety regarding the shifting nature of blackness amid postwar class reorganization. As we have seen, ideas about black sound tend to be proxies for thinking about black community, enabling the idea of a coherent, singular slave culture; a notion of centrality to the nation built on the exclusion and enslavement of blackness; and a set of practices indexed to alternative social structures whose relationship to nation is uncertain. Critiques of questions or answers that now seem outmoded miss the importance of the circulation, adaptation, and transformation of forms, and the simultaneous development, which worried thinkers in the Black Arts era, of apparently contradictory, but ostensibly black, forms that appealed to different segments of the working classes. The desire to imagine a transhistorical blackness that unfolds as a singular contradiction in the Western world is historically conditioned.

Rather than critique Shepp's account, which appropriated moments of divergence from Western aesthetic norms as signs of difference in which revolutionary blackness inhered, I would emphasize his deep listening and insight into both the new music and the rhythm and blues that emerged alongside it. For both, past forms were not to be repeated but listened to again with the aim of capturing and amplifying those unrequited desires and impulses to collectivity that I have termed fugitive voice, and in that the two practices are two sides of a single coin, pun intended. The New Black Music's free manipulation of existing musical forms and genres, its re-sign-ification of the wild or unruly elements of black traditions was valorized precisely for its refusal of the prevailing logic of entertainment. Black sound no longer needs the mediation of print, transcription, or even hermeneutics: the music itself, understood as the bearer of meanings, becomes medium of transformative energy. It becomes a name for the de-structuring or de-orchestrating effects of such alternative understandings of communal and political organization. With music—or black sound more generally—itself as medium, we can better understand calls such as Larry Neal's for the "destruction of the text" not exclusively in terms of a desire for greater immediacy, but as an emphasis on the mediality of sound as such.

I have been tracking a transition from text as a way of appropriating sound to sound itself *as* text, which is in turn figured as counter-inscription or counter-code. "Text" is also a term for an essentially contentless *process* of dissemination, bearers of "legends, stories, history, and above all historicity" that, for Fanon, make the body legible by reducing its ungeneralizable and libidinal excess.[39] Texts are sites of encounter between discourses and discursive levels; they are intertextual and productive, oriented toward the production and dissemination of the common. For Neal, destruction aims at the latter sense in the interest of creating conditions of possibility for new meanings and forms of community. For all the accounts of black sound I've touched on here, something like poetic language remains a key medium for at once containing and disseminating the raw semiotic force of the black (male) signifier whose model is James Brown's scream and Malcolm X's vernacular speech cadences (both most widely available through records). For poets to answer Larry Neal's call to "learn to sing, dance, and chant their works [and] be a kind of priest" returns to poetry its pre-capitalist, ritual function, thereby re-enchanting it. However, as Tony Bolden observes, James Brown's falsetto screams, the product of countless hours of rehearsal, are only available because they have been recorded, that is, made into texts.[40] The same is true of Malcolm X's speeches, published in print and on record. Neal's argument that black poets should write poetry that aspires to the condition and power of a primal aurality that roots itself in "ancient ritual energy" implicitly acknowledges that signs both permeate and mediate racial experience, creating the effect of "authentic" or originary racial being. But it also situates black soundwork as a practice predicated on acts of critical listening, not raw experience but the textual mediation of experience. This is also to stress black cultural production as necessarily *intertextual*, which establishes commensurability between poetry, James Brown's scream, and Malcolm X's diction. Therefore, rather than assume a unitary object, we might think of text as a complex weave of social and historical processes legible in objects that link grammatical, experiential, and historical time, and whose textuality requires consideration of both the personal/collective utterance and the processes that make utterances meaningful. Such a reading allows us to connect arguments about the text with the broader critique of Western aesthetics (what Neal termed the "white thing") at stake in the same era. What's "destroyed," in this way of reading, is the myth of the text as neutral, self-contained, or spontaneous self-expression in favor of more open-ended accounts of black performance.

The problem of the text, which a study of recorded collaborations must confront, links considerations of access (who can record and under what conditions), use, and tradition.[41] "To what extent," Margo Natalie Crawford asks, "are literary and cultural movements inevitably reconstructed and remembered as textual objects as opposed to process-oriented, anti-object collaborations?"[42] The text, reified as a work to be studied from a posture of contemplation, becomes a fetish object that obscures more fundamental relations between aesthetic agents. Crawford resolves the problem of the text dialectically by arguing that Black Arts poetry emphasizes processes *within* texts that disclose the means by which they produce meaning, which in open-form jazz and other experimental sound practices (including poetry) re-map the critical terrain and invite analysis beyond rehearsals of cultural nationalist politics and their limitations. However, if one takes seriously the idea of aesthetic *production* (as Crawford does), and considers the possibility of production beyond exchange-value, it's possible to take seriously the connections many black creative intellectuals drew between their art and community, even as we might be critical of the versions of "the community" they advanced. One can see the relationship between aesthetic production and the improvisation of the common. To the degree that no text—poem, recording, painting, or other art object—exists exclusively as a "pure" use-value, to the degree that "sound for sounding" ineluctably implies an appropriable surplus beyond utility, it is theoretically impossible to distinguish the production of use-value ("function") from the production of exchange-value.[43] Each text belongs to an economy of production and reproduction governed by the intertextual play of grammar and reference, but each text in its navigation of the norms governing legibility and pleasure in a specific aesthetic context produces something unanticipated that could develop into a meaningful, even liberatory practice.

Revolutionary Times; or, Archie Shepp's Voice

Archie Shepp, saxophonist, poet, and playwright, is an exemplary producer of phonographic poetry. Reading his early work, I want to make clear the interactions of race, gender, sound, and medium I have been discussing. This discussion will also allow me to say a few words about the notion of voice, whose importance to recited poetry is unavoidable. Like other performers of the word, Shepp draws attention to the voice not as an index of some "intimate kernel of subjectivity"[44] (although intimacy is important to the overall effect of the performance) but as an index of mediation. Just as "jazz" does not refer to sounds alone, so does voice abide in that conflictual zone between the singular and the general, between the Barthesian "grain" and the signature, with all the legal and economic resonances of that term.[45] But one should underscore the degree to which Shepp attempted to develop a materialist analysis of politics and of art, even within a context shaped by idealist understandings of black sound as group expression, and "the people" constituted out there and shaped by externally defined "interests" and supposed "consciousness." Shepp threads the needle between understandings of revolutionary art in the heroic-voluntarist sense of cultural nationalists ("My music is functional . . .") and the expansive sense figured by the fugitive voice, which entails the free manipulation of culturally specific genres and style markers in and through which the historical text, as precondition of the future, can be rewritten.

Medium—especially the speed with which recorded material could circulate—played an important role in Shepp's explicit politics on record, as well as serving as the means by which he was able to sustain himself as a professional artist. A onetime John Coltrane protégé, Shepp rose to prominence thanks in part to Coltrane's mentorship and his association with pianist Cecil Taylor and trumpeter Bill Dixon, whose Jazz Composer's Guild he departed in order to sign with Impulse! Records.[46] His first album for Impulse!, *Four for Trane*, features Coltrane on its cover, making public the older artist's behind-the-scenes endorsement of Shepp (Coltrane had lobbied producer Bob Thiele to record Shepp and other younger, experimental musicians). His second, the 1965 *Fire Music*, which features his phonopoem "Malcolm, Malcolm—Semper Malcolm," would solidify his aesthetic and political ambitions. Shepp recorded the bulk of the album on a session with a sextet on February 16, 1965, but returned to the studio March 9, just over two weeks after Malcolm X's assassination, with bassist David Izenon and drummer J. C. Moses to record the phonopoem. According to journalist Nat Hentoff's liner notes, "Malcolm" was initially part of a longer piece called "The Funeral," dedicated to Medgar Evers, a Civil Rights activist assassinated in 1963. (In August 1963, shortly after Evers's June 12 assassination in Mississippi, Shepp had recorded a piece called "Funeral" with a cooperative quartet whose other members were alto saxophonist John Tchicai, bassist Don Moore, and percussionist J. C. Moses for the album *Rufus*.) Shepp reconceived the earlier piece and composed the poem he would read as the lead track on *Fire Music*'s second side.

"Malcolm, Malcolm—Semper Malcolm" functions as a curiously and appropriately *open* work of mourning, a generous structure that accommodates the dead still to come, among whose number Shepp obliquely includes himself. He offers his own story of migration as metonymy, but the result is ambiguous. Interpolating his own story with Malcolm X's, the scale is intimate, the loss personal. Shepp reads the poem softly and slowly alongside Izenon's bowed and then plucked bass, gradually building intensity; the whisper, rather than the stereotyped scream, is crucial to the phonopoem's blend of the intimate and distant, the quotidian and the occult.[47] Aldon Nielsen suggests that the opening line, "A song is not what it seems," "seems a description of both jazz and the lives of black Americans," and concludes that Shepp's poem marks "a nearly final loss of trust in liberal promises of national amelioration."[48] Hentoff quotes Shepp saying Malcolm X was "the first cat to give actual expression—though he didn't act it out—to much of the hostility that most American Negroes feel"; Hentoff concludes, "The music . . . is meant to symbolize the various elements in Malcolm's life and spirit, and in the life and spirit of this country's black people. Including Charlie Parker."[49] The poem lends itself to synecdochic reading, where Malcolm's assassination becomes the suffering of all black people ("we're murdered," Shepp recites, "in amphitheaters / On the podia of the Audubon"). The whisper's intimacy, however, refuses the suppression of singular subjectivity that would allow Shepp to metonymize Malcolm and claim to speak for collectivity at any scale. The poem's paratactic last lines ("Philadelphia / 1945 / Malcolm / My people / Dear God / Malcolm") raise the ante on that anti-representational strategy. They create the effect of montage, while Shepp's slow, breathy reading has the gravity of testimony or prayer. When Shepp's saxophone takes over from his voice, it continues in the same exploratory or contemplative vein, building tension without directly resolving it. He starts softly, achieving flute-like sonority in his tenor saxophone's upper register, offering a parallel line of articulation that approaches the sudden absence created by Malcolm's death. His improvisation engages Izenon and Moses in something more akin to dialogue than a conventional soloist-accompanist relationship. After initial soft, contemplative passages on voice and saxophone, Shepp plays with his full tone—warm, gruff, redolent of swing-era players like Chu Berry and Don Byas, but thoroughly modern (i.e., post-Coltrane). Abruptly (and satisfyingly), the ensemble lands on an R&B-inspired syncopated line (accenting the initial downbeat and second upbeat, pause, then a stuttering sixteenth-note figure connecting the first upbeat and second downbeat, completed with a glissando starting on the third upbeat, alternating between concert B♭ and C♮)—a performative stagger, a theatrical stutter. "Malcolm, Malcolm—Semper Malcolm" seeks formal unity between speaking and instrumental voice that finally lands on an unexpected moment of convergence through recourse to a surprising moment of closure. Read symbolically, the conventional harmonic and rhythmic resolution seems to mark the fated end of an era and uncertainty of what will come. Within the mini-drama of the phonopoem, Shepp finally finds his "voice" (political and aesthetic sensibility) in a communal form that remains adjacent to a marketable or commercial form (i.e., R&B), but that finds a line of flight away from the culture industry's gravitational pull. It touches on and tampers with the reciprocal limits of voice, of poem, of song to produce meanings not necessarily available in one medium alone.

Jonathan Sterne observes that "the cultural status of the voice transformed sound recording."[50] The relationship is reciprocal: sound recording helped reinforce, distribute, and generalize understandings of the voice and its function. The emphasis on the human voice as a sign of consciousness and interiority helped shape the institutions, practices, and meanings of sound recording as medium, an iterable set of social relations that naturalize mediation. Shifts in sound culture enhance and underscore the ways a certain notion of voice sutures phenomenal subjectivity and political subjecthood. It is not enough simply to critique or deconstruct "voice" and the privileging of speech over writing throughout a certain history of Western metaphysics, which is by now a familiar gesture. The point is to listen for all those ways voice fails to fulfill that function, how it can become sign of madness or insufficient individuation, index of a sociality in conflict with dominant social forms. Yet the whisper, suggestive of conspiracy and difficult beginnings, intimacy and withdrawal, of coming to voice and losing it, suggests an entwinement of self and other that may proffer deeper communion. A whisper is a sounding that threatens to lose itself in surrounding sounds, at once a separation and a joining of self and other. For who can bear the secrets, the new sound concepts this phonopoem brings?

Above, I alluded to the practical issues jazz musicians faced, including vanishing venues and wariness among cultural gatekeepers who resisted the new forms of play and playing. The "plasticity in the social organization, formation, and movement of sound" I invoked earlier extends to "jazz" itself, no longer definable through any one element.[51] Swing had enjoyed the status of quasi-universal structuring element: it was no longer the "nodal point" or master signifier around which other elements in jazz's discursive field could be unreflexively coordinated in hierarchical structures. The freedom artists enjoyed to redefine rhythmic, melodic, harmonic, and timbral possibilities coincided with what for many was a worsening economic situation for performers, especially those inclined to experimentation with "uglier modes."[52] Many innovators of the new music articulated their frustrations in forthrightly political and historical terms. Ornette Coleman said bluntly, "It seems that production and publicity are so closely related that they turn into the same thing . . . [I]n jazz the Negro is the product."[53] Shepp's pronouncements were even starker. Referring to white-dominated record production, dissemination, and criticism, he argued: "[Y]ou own the music, we make it. By definition, then, you own the people who make the music. You own in us whole chunks of flesh."[54] The "freedom" of free jazz does not exclusively refer to musical concepts, but to the whole discursive and economic apparatus within which aesthetic effects take on meaning.

Let us reconsider "Malcolm, Malcolm—Semper Malcolm" in this fuller context. Baraka's assertion, cited in this chapter's epigraph, that "the voice [was] becom[ing] more and more relevant to contemporary jazz," has multiple valences, one of which is its ambivalent "liberation" from its representative function, even as many figures sought that role. Empirically, Baraka refers to a host of albums, including John Coltrane's overdubbed chanting on *A Love Supreme* (1965) and *Om* (recorded in 1965 but posthumously released in 1968); Abbey Lincoln's ecstatic vocalizations on *We Insist!* (1961) and those of saxophonist Frank Wright, especially on *Your Prayer* (1967); and of course recorded collaborations between poets and musicians, aided by new recording technologies. In a wider frame, the claim also encompasses the vocal experiments of such diverse musicians as Donald Byrd (*A New Perspective*, 1964), Eddie Gale (*Ghetto Music*, 1968; *Black Rhythm Happening*, 1969), and Andrew Hill (*Lift Every Voice*, 1970), all of which to different degrees attempted, as Shepp did during his Impulse! years, to harness the energies of rhythm and blues or gospel. (One should also consider Nikki Giovanni's 1971 *The Truth Is on Its Way* and Sarah Webster Fabio's 1976 *Jujus/Alchemy of the Blues* along these lines.) The "relevance of the voice" encompasses "the persistent, insatiable drive toward articulacy at the core of the music" that Brent Hayes Edwards observes, even as extended vocal techniques such as whispers, rasps, cries, and moans remake articulacy, foregrounding the transmission of sound over the transmission of message.[55]

It has become customary for cultural critics and historians to narrate the history of black aesthetics through institutions—independent press, coteries, artist collectives, bands, independent record labels, and so on—which are important to my analyses. But I also want to place these within a broader political and aesthetic field. "Institutions" also refers to poetry and music themselves as epistemological, aesthetic, and discursive fields in meaningful contact with capitalist modes and relations of production. Indeed, the "drive toward articulacy" resonates with the anxieties generated by nonverbal or extra-semantic sound conceived as medium, making voice a kind of supplement or balm against the radical claims made regarding "sound for sounding" or Larry Neal's self-effacing text.[56] Finally, acknowledging that Baraka's "contemporary" radiates from the New Black Music, his claim about voice's importance metaphorically encompasses a shift in the ways some artists related to jazz as a field of cultural production. What if we consider the increased autonomy of the voice in experimental black music and poetry—its liberation from the obligation to express or represent—as the condition under which one can start to talk about black sound as a discrete object? As trombonist-composer-scholar George E. Lewis argues, "By the mid-1960s, many musicians were reconceptualizing the discursive, physical, and economic infrastructures within which their music took place," with artists to varying degrees abandoning the nightclubs, major labels, and established festivals.[57] Here one can consider the proliferation of independent labels and artist collectives alongside the increasingly outspoken nature of many of the musicians through the 1960s who articulated political visions for their work in interviews, articles, liner notes, song titles, and other discursive forms that blurred the line between sonic text and paratext, but also transformations of the sound-text itself.

Shepp belongs to that generation of thinkers eager to find or create a space for aesthetic, social, and political being beyond the reach of culture industries, even as his vernacular avant-garde practice requires the use of state cultural apparatuses. A major part of that effort—and a sticking point for critics—is his professed aim to make "popular art." "Popular," in Hentoff's gloss, names "social responsibility," a desire to make "music that has relevance to the actual lives of a broad spectrum of people, not just the insular elitists."[58] Striking is the degree to which Hentoff, who editorializes about the problem of "words that have been worn smooth" and "the brittle evasions of the non-livers—those who just exist," understands himself to be in league with Shepp, despite (or because of) the latter's explicit racial politics. If we take seriously Hentoff's situation of Shepp within a broader postwar context defined by individualism, homogenization, fragmentation, and the production of a nonpolitical (or depoliticizing) social formation, we can see the extent to which his invocations of Medgar Evers and Malcolm X entail not just the politics of those figures but also their media circulation. The whisper, with its implied intimacy, brings Malcolm X away from "brittle evasions" and rearticulates him as part of a broader story of black life that includes Shepp's (whose family moved from Florida to Philadelphia in 1945). Shepp's is a canny use of sound media but also the mass media, played against the grain.

Contemporary critics have underscored the resulting ambiguities. Ongiri, in a longer argument about the class politics of ways black creative intellectuals fetishized "the black community," notes Shepp's difficulty "articulat[ing] the relationship between the jazz avant-garde and the African American working-class community that appeared to be rejecting it."[59] If we recall that musicians like Shepp were proletariat in Marx's sense—the class that, compelled to "freely" sell its labor, "produces both the accumulation of capital and the means by which it is itself made relatively superfluous"—we can better situate those musicians' incisive critiques of the jazz industry and produce a clearer account of their class politics.[60] Moreover, many other proletarian innovators of the New Black Music were acutely aware of their relatively precarious position but nonetheless invested in the reproduction of the bourgeois nation-state. This certainly includes Shepp himself, who, channeling Du Bois, argued that members of his cohort should "take advantage of a certain overview that we [black artists] have that others don't have" in order to translate an "intuitive working class instinct" into something ordered and meaningful.[61] Shepp's analysis here is inadequate, not least because it requires reifying the black working classes as a stable, externally defined, and internally coherent "community." Moreover, black life possibilities, especially in the US context, alter belonging to the middle class as a matter of relative wealth, access to cultural and material capital, and the specific mechanisms of domination. All of this calls for new frameworks that tease apart class and taste. In the introduction I suggest the term "vernacular avant-garde" as one way to work through this set of concerns; I will elaborate below.

Ambiguities around class inform many contemporary analyses of the era. In his discussion of Shepp, Eric Porter notes the artist's "desire to create a music that could conform to the tastes of a larger audience without being too 'commercial.'"[62] He goes on to cite Shepp in the liner notes to *Fire Music*: "We have to get into their [the people's] lives which is one way of saying we have to get more and more into our own lives and know who we are so that we can say all that's on our minds." Such sentiments get to the heart of the doubleness of the artist's position in this period and reveal the importance of attachments and identifications that allow black creative intellectuals to conflate political and affective solidarities. That conflation is evident in Larry Neal's famous declaration that black art (especially an ascending hierarchy of poetry, theater, and music) was "the aesthetic and spiritual sister to the Black Power concept."[63]

As Shepp would tell Neal, those were "*intense* political times," even "revolutionary times," characterized by the sense of political possibility awakened by the transition from one imperial regime to another, effected largely through semi-coordinated, global, popular struggles.[64] From this distance, some view skeptically those "revolutionary times" and revolutionaries, holding the latter up for special scorn insofar as they either became elected officials, or helped, directly or indirectly, to elect leaders who were inadequate to their political moment. Such a perspective tends to shift blame to the defeated (labeled the "professional managerial class," the "elites," and so on) and away from the victors, the newly multiracial dominant classes, for which mandated integration created a new form of ideological cover. The black boss or mogul is both sign of the "success" of the revolution, if its goal is understood as expanding access, and sign of its defeat. Invoking Raymond Williams's taxonomy, one must consider the interplay of the emergent and the residual (remembering that "emergence" is an ambivalent category without guarantees), and thinking across periods requires, I argue, reckoning with what never fully emerged in the past. Stalled emergences of all scales comprise the historical text. Moreover, Archie Shepp's view was more or less the ruling consensus. As black thinkers had long been critical of the New Deal's racial politics, people in the moment saw the beginning of the end of the liberal New Deal order as an opportunity for more radical transformations. These often self-consciously articulated race and class even as changes in the racial formation, especially in the United States, augured more attention to the constitutive place of gender and sexuality within the concrete and symbolic administration of race. This is to read against conventional understandings of Black Power as a northern (i.e., urban and working class—although "proletariat" better describes and unifies actors across regions and fields of employment) counterpart to the "minimalist program of interracialism and integration," and thus to reorient critics to the figurative and literal terrain of black organizing.[65] There was nothing "minimalist" about "interracialism" in practice. The subversion of the demand, to cite one famous example, for "Jobs and Freedom" into "equal opportunity" requires political analyses that go beyond critiques of the black "elites" or members of the "managerial class" most likely to benefit from that subversion. Members of a globally emergent managerial class strata most adept at negotiating then-available structures of race leadership certainly were in the best position to benefit from the Civil Rights Movement's "gains," but exclusive focus on who most gains short-circuits analysis of the political terrain itself.[66] The bourgeoisie and petit-bourgeoisie by definition are most likely to gain from "equal access" and the formal equality that follows from freedoms predicated on the free disposition of property, including labor. The bigger question is how to recover alternative articulations of freedom. The aesthetic is one path.

Along similar lines, one should resist the argument that so-called avant-garde or free jazz helped usher the music into the academy and away from "the people." *Some* experimental jazz, claiming a root in the vernacular cultures of the black and interracial inner cities, was commercially quite successful, but where Herbie Hancock or Miles Davis managed to emerge from the era critically intact, other politically outspoken and aesthetically daring figures, such as Archie Shepp, receive more skeptical treatment. For example, Ongiri argues,

Shepp and many of the jazz avant-garde attempted to negotiate the complications of the period immediately following desegregation by organizing in collectives such as the Jazz Composer's Guild, Charles Mingus' Jazz Composer's Workshop, and the Association for the Advancement of Creative Musicians, out of which they hoped not only to control musical production resources but also to create a broader, community-based popular reception for the avant-garde stylings.[67]

Underlying calls for Black Power and the promotion of the "new black music" and "new black poetry" are desires for economic and political control. The latter two negotiated a view that art must express vital aspects of "the people," understood to be relatively homogeneous. Such understanding allows rhetorical alignment of "the people" and their "authentic" nature as incipient revolutionary bloc in a move familiar at least since Frederick Douglass. Shepp speculated, as did many others, that he was witnessing the emergence of new collective identities, new subjects of history, and political possibilities. The defeat of this formation has a number of causes, among them the rise of a global petit bourgeoisie in the wake of the global erosion of direct domination as a means of what David Harvey terms "accumulation by dispossession" (colonialism, Jim Crow) in key geopolitical sectors. Neocolonialism, alongside the erosion of public institutions that follow Jim Crow, enabled the re-entrenchment of bourgeois ideology now supporting neoliberal governmentalities. Without treating freedom dreams as homogeneous, fugitive voice names an attempt to take seriously the ruins of futures past as they shape the objects and collaborations we read now, and the desire to rethink present possibilities. What seemed possible or desirable? How did people define their present and shape practices to those presents?

Shepp's generation of artists and thinkers sought to find or create a space for aesthetic, social, and political being beyond the reach of culture industries through vernacular avant-garde practice that required engagement with the culture industry apparatuses. The one who uses the culture industry will surely be used in turn. Even as Shepp tried to marshal the energies of marginal spaces not fully absorbed where "authentic" cultural production seemed possible, the response was a near-simultaneous spectacularizing of his refusal of certain bourgeois norms via the "Angry Black Tenor Man" trope that shaped his early commercial career. That era's unfinished business marks our intellectual (and physical, in some cases) landscape as so many ruins to negotiate and shapes our reception of Shepp's utopian claims for his art. We know, for example, that "the people" and "the community" are gendered concepts; we know, invoking Hortense Spillers, that "the old 'community' is neither *what* nor *where* it used to be."[68] The incorporation of *some* black people into the American national project marks the emergence of a new anti-collective, anti-political cultural logic that exploits group (especially racial group) membership selectively, often disciplinarily, buoyed by the theoretical and practical avoidance of black (or any other) unity. If popular culture refers to what Michael Denning calls "that contested terrain structured by the culture industries, the state cultural apparatuses, and the symbolic forms and practices of the subaltern classes,"[69] then the absorption of the signs and symbols of black protest into capitalist spectacle, as Ongiri and Angela Davis respectively note, partially defines the current situation.[70] We encounter the raised fist, solidaristic slogan, and other objects locked in association with a no-longer-available politics of the sixties as commodities for individual consumption or nostalgia.

Settling for critique of the terms artists and intellectuals set themselves, critics risk reifying cultural distinction into either elitism or an elite-pluralist model of leadership that takes for granted a homogeneity of black culture and externally determined or "objective" interests. As one example, Eric Porter concludes his excellent analysis by declaring that "[t]here was certainly no danger of Shepp's [experimental arrangement, on *Fire Music*, of Antonio Carlos Jobim's international 1965 hit song] 'The Girl from Ipanema' becoming a best-selling single [as Jobim's had the previous year]. Thus, like many of the works composed by the poets and playwrights of the Black Arts movement, Shepp's version of African American expressive culture was probably 'relevant' only to a small audience."[71] Among other things, this reading has to discount the fact that many people would have been at least passingly familiar with a recent hit song. Even if one assumes, with Pierre Bourdieu, "the hostility of the working class and of the middle class fractions least rich in cultural capital towards every kind of formal experimentation," the choice of a commercially successful song as the basis to introduce new techniques would give listeners a familiar ground from which to follow flights into the unfamiliar.[72] Something similar happened with spirituals and the blues, and one can't dismiss the possibility that these experiments *could* have succeeded. There *was* danger of Shepp's song catching on if one accepts his and others' claims for what that aesthetic shift would mean. That possibility, it seems to me, was the whole point. The reasons it did not succeed are not exclusively aesthetic. Shepp's revision and restaging of the familiar, it seems to me, should be the starting point of an analysis of the "success" of his work, and that analysis should also consider the ways bossa nova itself remediates working class samba for international, female-identified middle-class audiences. It is difficult to see otherwise how one avoids a class essentialism that reinforces the critic's cultural capital—as she who can apprehend and appreciate "avant-garde" art—at the expense of "the people."

Yet if, as James C. Hall argues, artists like Shepp sought to transform black "consciousness into an art that often anticipates the difficulties inherent in its reception," we would do well to take seriously the relationship between formal innovation and "the development of a new order of interpreters."[73] To some degree, their failure to achieve greater success speaks to the ambitiousness of their project to reimagine the social basis of their art, by reimagining and remapping the social, and to the real resistance they met. Although their attempts to present avant-garde aesthetics as expression of group consciousness could not have the success of Douglass or Du Bois, records were crucial to this project. But what the artists often rejected, and what the more established institutions of industrial culture could provide, is a fantasy bribe—something to persuade people to maintain faith in the existing order, rather than insisting on a radical break into unknown worlds. This is to take the *aesthetic* component of black aesthetics as seriously as we do its blackness. At the same time, the politics of aesthetics exceeds an artist's claims or explicit intentions, and even exceeds the situation Phillip Brian Harper identifies (discussing poetry, but I think it equally applies for the music that grows in tandem with the poetry) that black art tended (tends?) to be "*heard* directly by whites and *over*heard by blacks."[74] "[T]he project of Black Arts poetry," he continues, "can be understood as the establishment of black nationalist subjectivity—the forcible fixing of the identity of the speaking I—by delineating it against the 'non-I person.'"[75] That speaking *I*, conventionally conflated with the authorial *I*, effectively retraces social distinction between the black creative intellectual and the ordinary black people apparently addressed insofar as, for Harper, that address is mediated through a white audience whose listening is primary. Yet in the terms of the present discussion, Harper describes a more general process of navigating synecdoche and metonymy as an artist in a society "structured in dominance." But what if one listened for those fugitive aspects of the aesthetic project that exceed such explicit modernist opposition to society as its means of sociality? Although Shepp would claim, in conversation with Amiri Baraka, that "the Negro people through the force of their struggles are the only hope of saving America, the political or the cultural America," his music reveals that international freedom struggles influenced his sense of politics and "the people" well beyond the inner cities.[76] His work therefore expresses an ambivalence toward the US as the ultimate *telos* of aesthetic and political activity and a sense that "integration" would require the transformation of existing institutions into ones compatible with the fullness of black life, which is to say life as such. Albums such as *The Magic of Ju-ju* (Impulse!, 1967) and *Live at the Pan-African Festival* (BYG Actuel, 1969) (recorded in Algiers and featuring Ted Joans and Haki R. Madhubuti proclaiming jazz "an African music," a prodigal son that had "returned" to the continent) figured a Third World or diasporic public sphere united by listening. At stake is not just an alternative map of the world and new understandings of the past but new possibilities for organizing life starting with the idea of repairing the rupture of those timelines deemed "pre-modern." On other Shepp albums, such albums as *For Losers* (1970), *Attica Blues* (1972), or *The Cry of My People* (featuring legendary R&B drummer Bernard "Pretty" Purdie and bassist Cornell Dupree), the results of his adaptation of African American vernacular into "trans-African" music give a good sense of what a successful alchemy might sound like. When Shepp declares his willingness to "get into rock and roll, somehow . . . , to slide into that, and refer to the people so that they'll know what I mean," he apparently speaks of "the people" as a homogeneous, implicitly male group awaiting leadership and political symbols.[77] Considered as aesthetic practice we might hear something else: an effort to constitute a people, largely hailed as consumers rather than citizens, by rearticulating familiar vernacular gestures. This is a historically specific goal; if few poets, musicians, or critics working today would proclaim such a quixotic agenda (just as few poets would insist on being labeled "jazz poet"), what has changed are contemporary assumptions about what poems and songs do, particularly in an era hostile to the idea of collective freedoms, and collectivity in general. The questions that worried Shepp as poet and musician no longer directly resonate in the present, but the critic's response should not be simply to critique him but also to consider the shifting possibilities, real and imagined, that his work reflects in order to sharpen our analysis of his work and better hear what, in Cecil Taylor's words, "continues begging."[78]

Connecting these concerns are the discursively and textually mediated black sounds themselves. Engaging those unavoidably requires engaging the ways those sounds were supposed to communicate alongside what they communicate. Media in this sense significantly inform the rise of sound recording and its industries, which in turn informed moments and texts key to the self-definition of modernity, and the multi-generic practices of modernism. The advent of sound recording and its widespread commercial availability allowed for two paradoxical tendencies: the privatization of the listening experience and the possibility of a mass, geographically dispersed, and temporally nonsynchronous audience. The presumed and imagined forms of intimacy sound recording techniques engender create the effect not of "speaking for" but "speaking to" or with its various audiences. In the place of the second-person and first-person plural as a means to resolve class and other social divisions, phonographic poetry's implicit injunction to listen to and with the poet invites intersubjective relationships between performers and listeners. Here, then, one can hear Shepp's "Girl from Ipanema" as a more complicated putting-to-work of the shifting nature of class, racial, and sexual desire (recall the song's theme of unrequited love), missed international encounters and possibilities for other futures. If one further recalls the role gender plays in the development and definition of middle-class culture, the sign under which bossa nova circulated in the United States, the interpretive possibilities for Shepp's cover—I am tempted to call it an inter-vernacular avant-garde but that obscures the complex, overlapping vernaculars of Jobim's composition and its bilingual performance—expand.

Celebrate (Black) Life

How does one recognize (or analyze) the end of revolutionary times? What follows in their wake? Michael Denning suggests that an adequate analysis must think on multiple time scales: "the conjunctural, the generational, and the epochal."[79] Insofar as the black media concept I've been tracing encompasses the remediation of older forms—first through performance and then by direct appropriation in DJ practice, sampling, and other techniques—it keeps in sight coexisting structural contradictions (e.g., between tradition and innovation within the field of jazz) and articulating those in a widening context. Such an account helps us situate artists who follow and transform Shepp's aesthetic, including Steve Coleman, Ambrose Akinmusire, Nicole Mitchell, and others. Rather than emphasize priority, succession, influence, or other flattening temporal schemes, I listen for the ways contemporary artists and critics contend with and participate in a thickening textual weave, whose pattern a certain version of the New Black Music generates. I turn now to saxophonist, vocalist, composer, and experimental sound artist Matana Roberts's ambitious, projected twelve-"chapter" *Coin Coin* series, a multimedia work with an evolving cast of musicians and media configurations. What emerges is a layered account of media, family, and site-specific histories, with an emphasis on what remains unsettled and on the unsettling nature of the past as source and resource. Offering as much a theory of history as of medium, Walter Benjamin argues that "[t]he medium through which works of art continue to influence later ages is always different from the one in which they affect their own age."[80] "Medium" includes not just recorded sound or written signs but the mediations that make them sensible. *Mediation* is a term both for those conceptual frames that claim a necessary relation between contradictory elements, and what object-ifies those frames and makes them available to thought. Benjamin points to the necessity of remediation as a way of making past works resonate in the present, with the understanding that they will harmonize without being identical. Fredric Jameson helps work out relation as a product of intellectual labor (under historically specific conditions) rather than an innate or objective ordering of things to be intuited or otherwise discovered. Tradition itself, from this perspective, is another word for mediation facilitated by media forms (print, sound recording); it names the ways communities apprehend—chart and fight over—the fugitive voice of past historical practices, impulses, values, languages, and so on, making the present appear to have a continuous, evolutionary relationship with the past.

Matana Roberts and her ensemble recorded *Coin Coin*'s first chapter, *Gens de couleur libres*, "live" in a studio before a small audience and then edited it for release. The resulting sound text mediates history through "very, very particular stories passed down to me orally via ancestral elders living and dead in my family line."[81] In an artist's statement, Roberts describes her interest in "human trace; the whispers, the secrets, left behind, sometimes by those never given a chance to really claim them. I wish for my work to sit firmly as a historical document of these universal, sometimes forgotten, moments."[82] At an initial read, Roberts seems very far from Shepp's easily caricatured investments in "the people," which I argue above reveals the line between synecdoche and metonymy, between the subaltern and the popular, as a central contradiction of black cultural production. However, considering the media concept I've been tracing, I want to show the lines of commonality, regarding their stance toward tradition as mediated by texts.

In the period of his greatest fame, Shepp forthrightly avowed a certain blackness, and sought to appropriate elements of an "African" past as the basis for imagining liberated futures. Roberts, by contrast, identifies class-based anxiety, the "dichotomy of going back and forth of am I black enough, can I be accepted in these white institutions," as a central conflict of her aesthetic and personal development.[83] Where Shepp spoke of living in "revolutionary times," Roberts understands herself to represent "a generation of African American women who ha[ve] more choices about ways of being than any other generation preceding it: this [i]s exciting, but also at times incredibly confusing, and in some ways it ma[kes] my creative path quite harrowing."[84] A onetime member of the Association for the Advancement of Creative Musicians (AACM), she counts Fred Anderson, George Lewis, and Muhal Richard Abrams as important mentors, and in interviews insists on the importance of artistic community. But where Shepp's outspokenness and "blunt speech" has been a source for celebration, Roberts expresses greater caution, an almost resigned sense of obligation to make committed art: the likelihood of state surveillance is "an intense reminder that you might as well do exactly what it is you want to do with your work, as what freedom do you really have to lose at this point?"[85] Ultimately, then, shifts in the relationship between artists and the state cultural apparatuses, including the myriad ways the state responded to artists and activists like Shepp, require "a different way of cracking the idea of culture, class," and the persistence of unfreedom as the ground of black life.[86] Roberts tracks the transition from revolutionary to post-revolutionary time, but like those of the prior generation holds black traditions as a "beautiful oeuvre of work around dealing with a political system that refused to include them in the process."[87] But where artists of Shepp's generation claimed to draw inspiration from past traditions as an authenticating mark of their own practice, Roberts approaches traditions more explicitly as text, citing her "deep interest in American history and old oral traditions developed, deconstructed, merged together often times through profoundly contradictory means."[88]

Although in 2013 Roberts presents herself as relatively sanguine about the prospects of US political institutions and the place of black people within them, her work opens onto a more complex, open-ended, and reflexive engagement with what looks less like triumph than exhaustion, less like victory than détente. Her series initially seems to be a reckoning with slavery's afterlives, a commemoration of survival and accounting for black life and live-ness beyond what Katherine McKittrick has termed "the documents and ledgers and logs that narrate the brutalities of this history [and] give birth to new world blackness as they evacuate life from blackness."[89] In that regard, it seems to be a literary project of recovery concerned with the singularity of a life held between the competing, abstracting logics of synecdoche and metonymy, and an interrogation of the limits of a freedom forged in and defined by slavery. On a more fundamental level, though, Roberts's series is also a mediation on the texts and other media that make slavery knowable in the first place, with the understanding that such knowledge, necessarily incomplete, partially occludes its object. Slavery is an obvious theme, especially of the first chapter, but it is just one element in Roberts's "panoramic sound quilting" approach, a figure for the processes of history rather than primary theme.

"Coin Coin" refers both to a historical woman—distant relative Marie Thérèse Coincoin—and to Roberts (her grandfather nicknamed her Coin Coin) engaging the historical text to re-sign-ify events and patterns of the past. *Gens de couleur libres*, the first "chapter," draws on the narrative of the historical Coincoin, a manumitted enslaved woman who in the eighteenth century founded a community of free and enslaved people, some of them family members of whom she assumed legal possession. Roberts narrates songfully (but usually not tunefully) Coincoin's experience of slavery and freedom in the first person. Her parents die of yellow fever; she attempts to save an unborn sibling. She enters into a marriage neither recognized nor sanctioned by the state with her enslaver, Claude Thomas Pierre Metoyer. In a devastating moment of poetic compression, she understates the line between sharing a bed and having a spouse, between bearing children and mothering: "I bore him fifteen children, ten of them his" (i.e., all of the children became his legal possessions, and he was biological father of ten).[90] Facing social pressure, Metoyer marries a white woman; he subsequently manumits Coincoin. She sets upon purchasing her children, who've been sold into slavery, and with them she builds a large settlement of free people of color. Roberts casts her as a "hustler" who wanted her children to have a better life than she did.

Throughout, Roberts's reading is rhythmic, propulsive, tonally varied, and conversational, possessed of a semi-spoken, semi-sung eloquence; all words are clearly enunciated, yet the musicality and songfulness at times run contrary to the story's emotional resonance. The discrepancy between musical and literary tone seems to underscore sonic resistance to the enclosures of familiar narrative movement. That reading, however, may be too valedictory, or at least too quick a conclusion, especially given the project's investment in the transmission and circulation of stories. Roberts overlays independent texts—a tone poem and a discursive one—and synchronizes those discrepant writings into something new: a phonographic poem. The story Roberts adapts, meanwhile, illuminates the lines of continuity between slavery and freedom from the perspective of black life.

Gens de couleur libres meditates profoundly on the complexities of reproduction and kinship, registering a certain ambivalence toward the domestic institutions of home as those are intimately tied to the reproduction of slavery and freedom alike. In several instances, the poem insists on the realities of Coincoin assuming possession of children, grandchildren, "cousins, mothers, brothers, uncles, aunts, daddies, mothers," from white enslavers. Their labor enabled the expansion of her property and family. The seductions and selective inductions that make the liberal order celebrate the black entrepreneur who "makes it" without making thinkable in the same frame the ways the production of freedom on those terms (i.e., the freedom to occupy the office of the exploiter or enslaver) simultaneously reproduces unfreedom as the norm of black life.

The *Coin Coin* series not only participates in prior traditions, including Shepp's, but cites them. "Rise," the overture to *Gens de couleur libres*, opens with a buzzed saxophone note that recalls John Coltrane's famous altissimo register "screams," while the visceral scream at the start of "Pov Piti," the next movement, sung in a gruff chest voice that occasionally cracks into falsetto, recalls Abbey Lincoln's famous performance with Max Roach on the 1960 *Freedom Now* suite. Considering tradition as a form of affiliation, the differences between Roberts and the antecedent texts she recalls are not only significant but are made to signify. Whereas Coltrane's "screams" extend the range of the saxophone by "overblowing" so an overtone sounds as the primary note (a technique that recalls the bar-walking saxophonists Coltrane heard while coming of age), Roberts's buzzed note (concert A♯) falls within the common range of the alto saxophone. In the context of a piece titled "Rise," both assent and ascent are resonant but (technically) limited. Similarly, where Lincoln's scream, building from moan to hum to shriek, sounds what Fred Moten calls the "locus of an ongoingly other recording of event, object, music," Roberts's relative restraint on "Pov Piti" and "I Am," in both instances building from semi-articulate vocables to fuller cry, strike my ear as anti-cathartic, coiling rather than releasing, as if outlining the promise of a counterfeit freedom as one more hump to get over.[91] Rather than emerging from intensifying blues moan, as Lincoln's does, Roberts's cry punctuates a series of "low hoarse key" vocalizations that sound like either a beginning or refusal of speech: "sounding out the words as the noose is 'round my neck."[92] All of this suggests an alternative pathway between song and speech that, like her inflected, singsong recitation, denies any essential difference between the two. The voice, meanwhile, becomes a blunt instrument whose materiality—its phonemic and rhythmic aspects—appears in non-hierarchized relationship with its semantic function, putting what the voice does on nearly the same plane as what it says or symbolizes, without making the sound of the voice another unit of meaning. As is true with sound recording broadly speaking, to listen is to rescale units of attention, units of expression, recalibrating a sense of the whole and its effects.

Running throughout the series, the phonopoems (her term is "wordspeak") play thematically in the spaces between institutionalized social bonds—especially those of maternity, paternity, and marriage—and social reproduction. The sheer variety of familial forms—mixing blood-based filiation with broader forms of affiliation for which "kinship" is too inflexible a term—are one feature of black life Roberts invites us to celebrate. Some version of "community" often, in a double movement, opens and sutures the space between filiation and affiliation, bolstered by vernacularizing mass media and producing aesthetic and critical aims opposed to existing forms of social reproduction. Rather than imagining itself to address a pre-constituted public, the series' ultimate theme relies on shifts in the locations and meanings of community—the real and fictional overlay of filiation and affiliation—imagined as the space within which dispersed (mediated) black sounds could circulate and resonate. If throughout the long Black Arts era and beyond poets and musicians claimed the source of their exclusion as the foundation for new improvised forms of community, then one hears in their collaborations an echo of the impossible: the epistemico-critical event of black freedom in the fullest sense. Something, that is, free of the circle and what it encloses.

All four chapters of Roberts's *Coin Coin* series to date foreground storytelling as a thematic and formal concern. Roberts highlights those refusals to tell that mark broader refusals, gaps within the subjection of blackness within which black freedom has flourished. Recalling and advancing a standing tradition of phonographic poetry, the series outlines a broader tradition of sounding and sound collaboration, which is thematically what articulates—joins and separates—generations. "Honey, there's some things I just can't tell you about," words Roberts attributes to her grandmother, forms the second chapter's refrain. The series makes the theoretical point a theme, insisting on the dimly remembered, misremembered, or untold pasts that shape black lives and kinship. It also makes the point formally through its deep engagement with a long media history, which indexes the means through which the knowledge and practice of slavery and freedom are preserved and transmitted, and the ways preservation, transmission, and circulation alter knowledge and experience.

In addition to the performance traditions referenced above, the series's four chapters weave together an impressive range of folk song, spirituals, performed interview and speech transcripts (including excerpts from Fannie Lou Hamer's 1964 testimony before the Credentials Committee at the Democratic National Convention), field recordings (from Roberts's time in Mississippi), and recorded speeches by Malcolm X. This is perhaps the most explicit example of remediation in the sense I've been discussing. Lingering in this concentrated media history, which refracts concern with the intersection of modern technical media and the older sense of art making, might encourage different questions about the media and mediation of black soundwork. The media of sound reproduction—encompassing sheet music, electric recording, and literature—have shaped both the theoretical and empirical object black sound, and the *Coin Coin* series retraces some of that history. Returning to the first chapter, "Pov Piti," whose motifs recur, modified, throughout the first volume, revises "Pov Piti Mamzelle Zizi," a Creole song popular in the nineteenth century. That music provides the basis for the "wordspeak" spoken in a singsong cadence doubled throughout the first volume by co-vocalist Gitanjali Jain's lag-behind French. The effect is at once amplification and refusal of more familiar narratives of US slavery taking place within a monolingual South, where slavery figures primarily have overcome a shameful past.

Prior to relating the story of Coincoin's manumission and reconstitution of her family and extension of kinship through property, Roberts and Jain co-present a version of Oscar Brown Jr.'s "Bid 'em In," from his 1960 album *Sin and Soul*. Where Brown gives singsong voice to an auctioneer who in rhythmically free time tries to sell a woman who will "make a fine lady's maid when she's properly whipped," Roberts makes the auction rhythmic, lyrical, seductive—even joyous and celebratory. Once they finish with Brown's text, Roberts sings solo, with a menacing sweetness, from the perspective of the woman to be enslaved, selling "you" on the benefits of winning this auction: "You can rape my mother, you can beat my daddy. . . ." She invites the other musicians—"Mr. Bass" and "Mr. Keys"—to join in, and the result is an infectious, bluesy jam that becomes increasingly free harmonically, marking one of the few (ambivalently) cathartic moments of the suite.

Gens de couleur libres culminates with a poem that in one gesture celebrates the preciousness of each moment and (black) life itself. The call to "celebrate life" alternates with the question "how much would you cost?" Celebrating (free) life is a method for managing ambivalence—noticing and reveling in what is, while continuing to feel the pressure of something missing, unnamed, or inadequately named. To celebrate on those terms is to refuse the choice between seeing Coincoin as black or human, where the definition of the human, as free, exists in necessary opposition to the black, as enslaved. The undecideability of this opposition, black and free, even in the face of the necessity of decision, limns the ideological contours that structure available choices. The best option is to decide for both, to *affirm* blackness, and in the space of that affirmation point to a space of improvised freedom and social organization pursued by black soundwork. Such affirmation amounts to reframing the situation to better specify what is at stake, and what remains unthinkable, in this case about a host of matters from slavery and the human to life itself. Taken in its most expansive and capacious sense, such reframing is the task of black soundwork, for which critics must listen: an affirmation—indeed, celebration—of black life and its possibilities as they overflow available frames of thought, without conflating the distinct, overlapping irrationalities and discontinuities of sound, music, text, and blackness. "Celebration" might be a name for desiring and pursuing blackness beyond the conditions of alienation that shape its emergence, a way of attaching oneself to a world, or something in the world that may not yet have a name. It might be a name for love, at once risk, promise, and "subversive gift."[93]

While Roberts and her predecessors all pursue uses of the voice that liberate it from vehicle of personal expression alone, the conditions under which they work change, as do the meaning and value imputed to black sounds. If Black Arts–era theorists assumed a relatively easy relationship between black aesthetic radicalism and the creation of radical black consciousness, the intervening years have sharply attenuated both the possibility and desirability of the radical. The end of the sixties is marked by a series of painful reminders of the limitations of blackness as parapolitical formation. The succession of electoralist politics that demobilize and discredit black (self-)organization, urban policies that demonize and marginalize the poor majority, and punitive state policies have undermined even the idea of a black community so central to Shepp and his cohort. Yet the promise of the medium as transmitter of values, practices, unarchived dreams, and political yearnings persists in Roberts's practice, which stunningly turns to records themselves—of leaders and landscape—and starts to chart a more capacious and complicated sense of collective history, and of collectivity, which is urgently needed. Engaging media and transmission have played a significant role in writing that history and helping to conceive the collective, to improvise the common—processes the following chapters analyze.

To me jazz is a montage of a dream deferred. A great big dream—yet to come —and always *yet*—to become ultimately and finally true. —LANGSTON HUGHES, "Jazz as Communication"

Communities in Transition
A Poetics of Black Communism

The title poem to Langston Hughes's 1926 collection *The Weary Blues* establishes themes that recur throughout his work, including the production of music art as mediator of labor and leisure, alongside the blues as an aesthetic resource for managing and expressing difficult feelings. This poem establishes a relationship between word and music, musician and listener, around which I frame this chapter's investment in Langston Hughes's 1958 collaboration with bassist, composer, and bandleader Charles Mingus. Hughes does not imply a relationship of influence between poetry and music, but rather suggests a deeper entwinement. Grammar, registered as temporal ordering, is key to the poem's apposition of word and music, which never exactly resolves. The first sentence, spread across three lines, begins with a dangling modifier. It reads: "Droning a drowsy syncopated tune, / Rocking back and forth to a mellow croon, / I heard a Negro play." The poem's organizing consciousness, its "I," is the grammatical agent of *droning, rocking,* and *hearing.* Yet, most readers will assume that the musician produces the music. From the beginning, then, both speaker and musician are involved in making music—the speaker's interrupted by hearing "a Negro play," the Negro's continuing with no apparent regard for the speaker. This also initially establishes a relationship for the speaker that falls between spectator and witness, an impasse only resolved in the poem's conclusion.

While the poem's location is concrete and specific (Lenox Avenue, Harlem), its time ("the other night") remains vague: Harlem becomes a space formally in transition, a vantage point from which to engage broader changes. The musician, illuminated by "the pallor of an old gas light," appears on the verge of modernity defined by electric lights, and the "pallor" foreshadows the poem's ending. Rather than present blues-like stanzas, lyrical interjection here stands in for the ecstatic apostrophe that might characterize ad libs, or the broad flexibility singers and players have for interpreting lyrics. The interjections "O Blues!" and "Sweet Blues!" mark both a response to the music and a translation into poetry that eschews direct representation. This is not, in other words, a form of ekphrasis whose object is sound, but an instance of what Brent Hayes Edwards might term "pseudomorphisis," the translation or reinvention of a parallel text in another medium.[1] At least at first glance. At stake is a profound question of the relationship between poetry and music as a relationship of labor and figuration that informs much of Hughes's subsequent writing.

The stanza break between the first and second verses also marks the poem's shift of perspective from witness to a more profound relationship: "The singer stopped playing and went to bed." If we understand the speaker to be witness watching the singer sleep, there seems to be a deeper, potentially sexual intimacy between the two. Not content with that, the poem adds a clause: "While the Weary Blues echoed through his head." The union of observer and observed halts or at least complicates a reading that would make the musician or his life an allegory of the music. The weariness of the blues and the weariness of the man are not the same. By the end of the poem, the musician is objectified to the point of figurative or literal lifelessness: "He slept like a rock or a man that's dead." If up to that point the poet-speaker encountered the freely expressive musician as ego-ideal, by the end a reversal has happened, and figuration (*like a rock . . .*) has to supplement the music that had seemed the animating vitality of the poem. I read this as a caution about the limits of the legitimate relationship between poem and music, with the former having the obligation to maintain distance from the latter lest the music be drained of its animating vitality.

Because of his decision to focus on "low-down folks, the so-called common element [who] are the majority—may the Lord be praised," Langston Hughes's most celebrated poetry oscillates between making black vernacular culture into a sign of the people and an interrogation of the contradictory impulses surrounding the music that simultaneously invoke a reified version of "the people" and make the actual lives and aspirations of those people unthinkable.[2] The transformation of the blues singer into inert matter at the of the "The Weary Blues" speaks to a contradiction at the heart of the culture industry that also concerned Archie Shepp and others in subsequent tendencies. The tendency to champion the culture but not the "low-down folks" who produce or consume it sits in tense relationship with Hughes's investment in the possibilities of represented performance, on the one hand, and the figures around which thought coalesces or loses itself, on the other. Hughes's poetics mediate this contradiction through attention to the figural and sequential processes by which people create their own sense of a present against the backdrop of dominant narratives of global/national progress and the rhythms of dispossession. We might nickname those dominant narratives "Time," capital "T." Hughes's project is not a simple or sentimental representation of the microtemporalities of black life; instead it captures the rhythmic *feeling* for life within which official or dominant notions of Time appear in distorted ways.

I use the musico-tactile metaphor "feeling" here not only because this chapter is concerned with Hughes's collaborations with Charles Mingus, but to underscore the degree to which Hughes's work tends to eschew a hegemonic sense of order—whether national or counter-national—in favor of a composite of interlocking and conflicting desires and aspirations for which one term is community. The reconstructed vernaculars—the heterogeneous social poetics of unidealized black life—for which both Hughes and Mingus are justly celebrated becomes at one level a graph of collective or communal sensibilities and social formation, and a property that no one can possess. The vernacular for both becomes a spatio-temporal graph of that community-in-progress, which unfolds via "crablike meander and drift"[3] rather than developing according to familiar narrative expectations or teleologies. Because this unfolding is often ad hoc and contingent, one might refer to it as the improvisation—or, more precisely, amending one of Charles Mingus's terms, the "spontaneous group composition" of the common as culture. Collaboratively and respectively, Hughes and Mingus invite consideration of what it means to make something out of nothing, something out of what "nobody would want or care about."[4] Though both emphasize the underclasses, that category remains capacious and open to all those who, like these artists, cannot define their projects on their own terms. This chapter refers to such rooted practice, not just a citation of the vernacular but using it as a template for invention, a poetics of black communism.

Charles Mingus's conception of composition emphasized the input of each member of the ensemble, each person's idiosyncratic understanding of those parts of the past to which he is responsible. His poetic and musical temporal innovations, which typically stress the importance of writing and iterability ("I question whether most musicians can even repeat their solos after they've played them once on record," he quipped), similarly enflesh community as interlocking, common time, rooted in a feel for the moment as well as for tradition.[5] Mingus's tongue-in-cheek observation that most musicians would not be able to reproduce their own solos is part of his deeply ambivalent relationship to the avant-garde tradition of which he was both progenitor and antagonist, and a reference to early practice where audiences expected musicians to reproduce their recorded solos note-for-note. He shares with Hughes a sense of displacement, what Vera Kutzinski, discussing Hughes, describes as "perpetual exile, of being misrecognized wherever he went . . . of being at home nowhere."[6]

Bearing in mind the limits of community as a discursive and theoretical formation in whose name many reactionary stances self-legitimate, this chapter conceives community with Langston Hughes's Harlem in mind. *Community* names a contingent formation through which to conceive and practice individual and collective subjectivities and agency. Communities are at once material sites within which strategies for collective survival emerge—adaptation, refusal, and other forms of negotiating the contradictions of the present—and a name for desires beyond the narratives, soundscapes, and semiotic economies of the present. They are material and conceptual spaces wherein people conceive of their past and future, struggle to claim or reorient values of the past and conceive a future, and form the institutions within which their actions take on meaning. I conceive community in the etymological sense of "conspiracy" that poet-musician Jeanne Lee outlines: a space of breathing together, not of harmony or accord but common struggle.[7] Rather than consensus or ideal unity, irritation, dissensus, and disagreement may reign. What binds people is a desire for things to work out, and a fundamentally shared sense of what things are important, which things will matter for the future, which elements of the past are important to note, which tendencies to nurture and promote. We might think of community on this view as a way of deorchestrating Time to create not a home but a resting place from which to imagine home.

Hughes and Mingus collaborated throughout the 1950s in Greenwich Village clubs. On record, they indirectly collaborate on "Scenes and the City" (the opening selection on Mingus's 1957 *A Modern Jazz Symposium of Music and Poetry*) and directly on one side of the 1958 album *Weary Blues*. These rich texts encourage us to attend not only to the musical aspects of Hughes's work, a familiar critical task, but also to the *literary* aspects of Mingus's work, from his provocative song titles, self-composed liner notes, memoir, and recited poems to his conception of spontaneous composition and "rotary perception," his alternative to swing. What's more, his collaboration with Hughes provides an opportunity to think together two artists who might not otherwise be considered together politically or aesthetically, despite the common formal resonances, aesthetic concerns, and similar politics of community that have further implications for the ways we think this era. As I will show, sound media are central to their respective ways of conceiving and writing time—both the present and the imminence of social change—as a central problematic of post–World War II–era black life.

Mingus, like many musicians of his and the following generation, chafed under the label "jazz," yet that term haunts him and sets the terms of his historical (mis)recognition. If by the late 1950s critics accused Langston Hughes of having forgone aesthetic and intellectual development in pursuit of money and prestige, the younger Mingus's reputation was on the rise.[8] Mingus had come to prominence in the bebop era, where he collaborated with such luminaries as Charlie Parker and Bud Powell. He rose to notoriety owing to his independent spirit; along with drummer Max Roach and then-wife Celia Mingus Zaentz he cofounded Debut Records in 1952, partially to protest the ways the record companies mistreated black artists. That spirit, along with his other political stances, volatility, and tendency to self-mythologize, got him stereotyped as the "Angry Man of Jazz," a reputation that tends to make the lurid details of his many verbal and physical fights—with band members, club owners, and unappreciative audience members—central to his story in ways that eclipse his genius.[9] His biographers and other critics have tended that ground well, so I will have little to say on it.

Likewise, despite his strenuous attempts to reconceive America on principles other than capitalist exploitation, Hughes's continued (mis)recognition depends on ambiguities surrounding the overlapping but apparently incommensurate versions of radicalism he pursued across his career. Many discussions of Langston Hughes's literary politics follow two broad tendencies. The first marks a break between his radical period in the 1930s and the modernist periods that surround it, whose engagement with black vernacular sources tends to be the emphasis.[10] Scholars such as James Smethurst problematize the idea of such a supposed break with Popular Front organizations, contextualizing Hughes's public "evasiveness and denials" in a larger African American response to the Cold War.[11] The second tendency, typified by scholars such as Steve Tracy or Maryemma Graham, emphasizes Hughes's vernacular sources and argues for an "essential harmony" between Hughes's politics and aesthetics rooted in his knowledge of and commitment to "the interests and aspirations of the masses of working-class people and an understanding of social and economic history."[12] Graham argues that Hughes "worked out a revolutionary method that takes cognizance of the historical experience of black people, the experience of racial oppression and resistance to that oppression as represented through cultural forms."[13] These two approaches need the other. "[T]he historical experience of black people" is an abstraction Graham's own attention to the operation of class processes (i.e., exploitation) at work *among* black people calls into question. The history in "the historical experience of black people" threatens to become a cypher that enables attention to intergroup conflict while obscuring in-group antagonisms. The relationship between "popular," its cognates ("the people," "the masses"), and "folk" is not synonymic but metonymic. "Popular" tends to mask internal class processes, while "folk" recodes class distinctions in regional and temporal terms (the "folk" are less developed). If we consider Hughes to be interested in the subaltern, those who are, in Gayatri Chakravorty Spivak's terms, "removed from all lines of social mobility" and denied a "recognizable basis of action," we find in his work an examination of the vernacular as process that at once renders the (sonic) color line permeable and reinscribes it.[14] The citations of black vernacular (or subaltern) culture *as* popular culture is indeed a "revolutionary method" that affirms a people-in-formation despite the historical forces that tend toward group deformation. Undeniably, Hughes's poetics emphasize and draw on the energies of mass culture and the class processes Graham points to. It is similarly clear that, following Smethurst, we need to read these formal strategies alongside his continued commitment to some versions of formal left politics. Framed this way, we might try to account for the aesthetic theory irony, discrepant juxtaposition, and citations of black vernacular culture imply. Although most black people continued to be excluded from lines of social mobility, as daily black culture continued to be stigmatized as disordered and illegitimate, the cultural forms black people produced within the culture industries enjoyed a good deal of cultural mobility and legitimacy.

The phrase "communities in transition" comes from Hughes's description of his 1951 *Montage of a Dream Deferred*, the work that forms the basis of many of his and Mingus's phonopoems. I use the phrase to index the enhanced plasticity and possibility around social organization, especially as indexed by the meanings, formation, and circulation of sound that Mingus and Hughes's collaborations register thematically and formally. Their collaborations took shape amid anti-colonial movements abroad, as well as a domestic social order in which the prospect of mass utopia took both capitalist and socialist forms. Their respective and collaborative aesthetics index disorganized as well as non- and occasionally anti-institutional practices of the quotidian, emergent groups and forms of consciousness for which names did not exist, which I will discuss in this chapter through the capacious term *black communism*. Transition, of course, does not intrinsically carry positive or negative valences, but in this context points to inchoate forms of life not yet classified or policed by ruling power. Hughes and Mingus's phonopoems, which tend to be present-oriented, focused on the development of the "present" as if to catch the possibilities and limitations of transformation, thematizing transition in ways that pose profound questions about social life and the long 1960s and, indeed, about the 1950s. This is a period defined by the overlapping emergence and intensification of struggles for economic, political, and sexual self-determination. "Jazz" had an unusual degree of flexibility, as it was being pressed into service in the name of both liberal individualism and black liberation. Those visions of jazz, as they might reshape liberal individualism, are at stake in what I am characterizing as a poetics of black communism. One way to read Hughes's and Mingus's vernacular avant-garde practice, especially its emphasis on the impoverishment of those whom the music would otherwise "represent" in the zero-sum game of incorporation into the normative bourgeois order, is as a critique not of the human, which is in current vogue in black studies, but of property and the property relations the human subtends.

Black Communism and the Undercommons

Here I should say a word about the relationship of the argument I'm developing to the notion of the undercommons as articulated by Fred Moten and Stefano Harney, one definition of which is "the practice of space and time that does not conform to the space and time of the sovereign, self-possessed individuals or the states they plot."[15] It is an immanent disruption of the "outside" that reveals the ultimate fictionality of the social order and the narratives of Time that enable it. As with Moten's definitions of blackness elsewhere, the excluded or external element—intimate with what refuses it—tends to destabilize or de-structure what's built on exclusion. This is not an analysis of subject position but of the non-sites (the modalities of refused relation) from which one lives her exclusion—the place at once "outside" and intimate to the "common" from which one might imagine its fundamental reordering.

Above, I stress the vernacular as poetics rather than representation, a way of marshaling the energies of a common culture that escape or run alongside commodity culture and the culture industries. By the 1950s, Hughes could argue that "Negro syncopation [had become] the popular music of America."[16] It's a familiar problem: black culture was popular (in the fullest sense of that term, meaning it figured the putative inner longings of "the people" or the nation), but black people were not. Indeed, the continual exclusion of black people—the positioning of black aesthetics as a kind of inert thingliness Hughes diagnoses in "The Weary Blues"—may be a precondition of black cultural forms' availability as "universal." In any event, representation should be the beginning rather than the end of the conversation. For that reason, I underscore Hughes's (re)construction of the communal sensibility that drives the development of vernacular forms, which link quotidian practices of timing and official Time. The vernacular allows Hughes to present black culture as itself historical, as embedded in larger social processes, yet holding (not possessing) an integrity of its own. Hughes's poetics use the vernacular to orient readers toward social and collective commitments rather than sentimentality, pity, or subjective feelings. He does not just draw on "folk" traditions but positions vernacular forms, as distillations of communal sensibility, in order to insist on their historical resonance as action rather than their idealist expression of an unfolding "spirit." For Hughes, all society is class society and hence predicated on exploitation. Race belongs to a discursive project that delimits in advance the range of intelligible black utterance. His poetics thus engage not just black culture as resource but that culture's role in the subalternization of black folk. Unlike a nationalist project where the point is to gain authority through avowal of racial signifiers, Hughes tends to dialectically arrange those signifiers in the service of improvising the common. This is similar to what Robert Young terms "disalienation," a "poetics of recognition and estrangement," but I stress Hughes's seeming awareness of black sound's ambiguous position owing to class processes and alienation: it is not "the reader" that needs disalienation but African American culture itself.[17] At stake is not jazz or the blues per se but their dialectical repositioning and transformation, imagining what the blues and black culture might become following the annulment of the conditions that produced them. This is what I term *communist poetics*.

More than another investigation of Hughes's formal relation to Left institutions, I use the term *communism* to name a refusal of the proper, of propriety, of property. In positive terms, the term names the desire for communities committed to the imagination and practice of freedom beyond the value form and its governmentalities and subordinativities (borrowing a term from Richard Iton).[18] I highlight not just acts of refusal, but counternarratives and desires, trial runs and experiments in freedom that I hear in both Hughes's and Mingus's work. Framed this way, I intend to open questions regarding the genres of experience and politics habitually excluded by conventional historiographical schemas that center the nation-state, and those stigmatized as deviant to the moral ordering of hetero-patriarchal capitalism. Insofar as aesthetic forms index specific historical, political, and epistemic regimes, their political content always works against art institutions, whose mechanisms of appropriation neutralize that political content. Vernacular avant-garde practice makes neutralized aesthetic content common again, reappropriating and redirecting the energies of inherited traditions that have been, in a sense, liberated from the concrete conditions to which they correspond.

"Negro syncopation" becoming the pulse of the United States is politically ambiguous insofar as it means that an aesthetic mode supposed to be the site of alternative deliberation has become part of a regime of segregation in Fred Moten's terms: "the modality in which the alternative is subjected to genocidal regulation and reproduction."[19] Hughes, of course, deploys an older model of aesthetic politics, but the implications for mainstreaming the culture but not the people are clear. I use "communism" primarily as a speculative frame within which to hear the collaborations between Langston Hughes and Charles Mingus sound alternative socialities eclipsed by the terms of their respective institutionalization.[20] Hughes and Mingus conceive and work through a notion of community as more than the voluntary association of "free" individuals; instead, community—a conceptual, sociospatial, and sonic space within which we can hear alternative social, political, and aesthetic forms, immanent to this one that never came to be—is the ground of individuality. Communism thus alternates between theme and theoretical notion that, in this mid-century context, shaped as much by the Cold War as by the Civil Rights Movement, we might hear as a call for the abolition of segregation rather than a call for integration. Reading Hughes and Mingus through the double inscription of the aligned social hygiene projects of the Cold War and Civil Rights Movement, I trace their respective refusal of the inducements of bourgeois normativity that grounded the ultimately successful versions of integrated citizenship.

Listening/reading for a poetics of black communism requires attention to text as transmission between places and times, through historical and cultural contexts. It requires, that is, attention to Hughes's and Mingus's respective relationship to media. Both engaged mass cultural forms and techniques figuratively (e.g., montage, portraiture, and other media forms invoked metaphorically) and practically (poetry readings, sound recordings, television appearances, and so on). To make an implicit point explicit, neither Hughes nor Mingus ever formally joined the Communist Party of the United States of America (CPUSA), and neither's personal commitments were uncomplicatedly leftist. Among other transformations and reversals during the Cold War, Vera Kutzinski notes that, following his appearance before Joseph McCarthy's Permanent

Subcommittee on Investigations of the Committee on Government Operations, Hughes severed ties with radical poets and fellow travelers in Haiti and Cuba.[21] Around that time, he began to forge new ties and collaborate with African and African American musicians, including Mingus and Randy Weston. I relate these collaborations to his expanded activities in other mediums, such as his celebrated Jesse B. Semple columns, which debuted in the *Chicago Defender* in 1943. Part of my argument here is that the best way to outline Hughes's aesthetic theory is to attend to his engagement with different media, from which we can further glean a sense of his shifting conception of the relationship between media and community. This in turn reveals something about his desire to develop, in Elizabeth Davey's terms, "a black public . . . for black writing," which entailed "introduc[ing] black audiences to the possibilities of literature representing their own creativity, aspirations, and experiences."[22] Describing Hughes's reading practices for those audiences, Davey provides a helpful insight into his early activity, especially his early annotations of his poetry with detailed notes scoring "musical accompaniment that drew from popular war songs, blues, jazz, and spirituals, 'played,' Hughes fancifully dictated, 'by a piano or an orchestra.'"[23] Articulating such sources as part of a common vernacular is a way of improvising a common culture, a new configuration of familiar elements. Here, I think, is where he overlaps, in the late 1950s, with Charles Mingus, who through the collaborative development of independent record labels and other means sought maximal freedom to shape his music and its public.

Attending to the ways Mingus and Hughes play the changes of their moment, not just responding to what was happening but also trying to intervene in their moment, we might unsettle familiar narratives that, for example, situate Charles Mingus's turn to "soul jazz" in the late 1950s in ways that overemphasize his reaction to claims that his music was inauthentic and didn't swing. One celebrated touchstone is his 1960 album *Blues and Roots*.[24] Atlantic Records producer Nesuhi Ertegun wanted *Blues and Roots* to be "a barrage of soul music: churchy, blues, swinging, earthy" that for Mingus recalled his youth in Watts. "The blues was in the Holiness [Church of God in Christ] churches—moaning and riffs and that sort of thing between the audience and the preacher" that Mingus remediated into that album and other performances from the period.[25] Considering the different motivations Mingus and Ertegun may have had—for Mingus, collaboration with Hughes may be one, as might a challenge from Miles Davis that his music was like "tired modern paintings"—we might include among them a desire to engage a black public as the source and intended audience of the emotional immediacy he championed.[26]

A poetics of black communism is also related to what Fred Moten terms "a poetics of the undercommons": "a constant process where people make things and make one another or, to be more precise, where inseparable differences are continually made. They make the sociality in which they live and often that sociality within which they live is conceived of, in relative terms, as nothing, as something nobody would want or care about."[27] This "something" is, I would amend, not of no value, but its value contingently stands athwart a commodity logic, a logic of circulation, accumulation, surplus, and appropriation. Moten, in this articulation and in his collaborative work with Stefano Harney, helpfully keeps attention on the growing pool of the dispossessed, and on the intensification of dispossession as a process that defines capitalist modernity. In a wider frame, he's primarily concerned with the transmission of virtues, values, and practices forged in the encounter between black people, blackness as a culturally necessary sign complex unassimilable to Western modernity, and the forms of culture forged in the wake of the Middle Passage and chattel slavery. The improvisation of the common—the attempt to think something in common beyond available frames of understanding—tends also to produce its outside, its strategically excluded and structurally unaccountable. The historically contingent forms of that exclusion presume capitalist relations of labor exploitation, resource extraction, and policing as ideological and material support for racial and gendered dispossession. "Undercommons" bears a hard-to-miss echo of common(s) and communism. It speaks to a concern that haunts what I insist on referring to as black communism: the practical and theoretical difficulties translating the terms and affects of solidarity, for example, the inter-vernacular (impossibility of) translating, say, "The Interationale" or the terms of proletarian revolution for a subalternized workforce. Yet the unsanctioned and institutionally illegible imagining of material forms of freedom, acknowledging the real risks such illegibility bears, remains my focus. The poetics of black communism analyzes one vector along which people have imagined, pursued, fought over, and lived their pursuit of substantive freedom for themselves and each other. I insist on "communism" in order to keep the history of struggles, dreams, and aspirations for forms of social organization other than capitalism in clear view. Communism, the communist-inflected imaginary, brings into view the world imagined from within the positionality of the logically excluded. Such imagining, registered in acts, attitudes, and dispositions toward illicit forms of freedom, and both practiced and represented by Hughes and Mingus's collaboration, affirms modes of production that are not always already fated to subsumption by capitalist modes of production. Communism is a world-making project that starts from the question of the social forms imaginable absent the commodity form and property as such.

The phrase "black communism" signals the implicit modalities of desire and attachment, of being and doing rooted in the non- and anti-institutional forms of living that one might find beneath—or alongside, or wandering away from—the figure Mingus termed "underdog." How do we understand forms of play and production that do not produce alienable surplus because, existing on the margins of political economy, they develop their own incommensurate logics? This does not mean, of course, that people in such economies—including Langston Hughes and Charles Mingus—did not pursue money or have a rent-seeking relationship to their own work, or that they somehow acted outside capitalist relations. The underdog participates in the game as an unfavored opponent whose success directly benefits others, while also justifying the game as such with the idea that anyone can win. To be *beneath* the underdog is to have a position of adjacency, a way of playing beyond the rules of the set game, a game that may have improvised rules and relative freedom, depending on whether or how the main game absorbs it. This is a tenuous space, but it reflects those for whom willful adjacency marks a primary relation to the game. Hughes's and Mingus's respective and collaborative vernacular avant-garde practices draw attention to and intervene in the unequal distribution of time and of history, allowing community to appear as a set of forms through which people struggle against the commodification of time and history.

The Poetics of Black Communism

Hughes and Mingus's collaborations first came about after Hughes published a glowing review in the *Chicago Defender* of a 1956 performance by Mingus's Jazz Workshop at the Newport Jazz Festival. Mingus, biographer Gene Santoro writes, had been experimenting with multimedia, hoping to forge new connections between "[p]oetry and music, theater and music and dance."[28] At the time of Mingus and Hughes's collaborations, poets such as Kenneth Patchen (who also collaborated with Mingus), Lawrence Ferlinghetti, Kenneth Rexroth, and later Jack Kerouac and David Amram were rising to prominence and collaborating with jazz musicians, with mixed results.[29] Following one such performance, in New York City, Mingus reportedly complained to Amram, "They're stealing our music anyway and not doing it right. The cats that create this music should be part of the whole picture."[30] Hughes, on the other hand, had been an innovator of jazz-poetry collaborations, and according to biographer Arnold Rampersad had "first included blues and instrumental jazz on his reading program in 1926," decades prior to the association of the practice with the Beat writers.[31] However, his bebop-influenced *Montage of a Dream Deferred*

(1951) was widely disparaged for what seemed to be mere gimmickry. Mingus, at the time of their collaboration, was routinely criticized for having abandoned "swing," a broad metonym for jazz conventions and, especially, black cultural specificity. The pairing, in that regard, makes sense: two under-acknowledged innovators found common ground around their shared investments in the developments of music, literature, and (though I have not emphasized it to this point) sound recording. Yet I want to suggest a deeper connection between these artists' separate musical and literary projects by conceptualizing their joint black communist poetics. At the cusp of the postwar Civil Rights Movement, focusing attention on those whom integration would structurally exclude draws attention to the limits of an integration that does not—or is prevented from—interrogating the very grounds of American social life.[32] Simultaneously, the transformation of jazz from a set of counter-symbols and -formations into a "popular," race-transcending "American music"—a project that was led by white hipsterism and that culminated in the transformation of jazz into "America's classical music"—changed the nature of this black-identified music.[33] Critics staged contests in jazz (as they did in poetry and other black arts) over the very nature of the form, and what it meant to consider the form black.

Thematically, their collaborative works stage a contest between Harlem's subaltern and hegemonic times. If "Harlem" names a community whose "unity" is not given but worked on and worked out, then their shared act of composition makes an otherwise heterogeneous temporal fabric legible as something greater than the sum of its parts. Considering Mingus's fascination with psychoanalysis—a key component of his "self-composition" (as he termed it in his memoir, *Beneath the Underdog*)—I stress that the superimposition of structure and play is central to his notion of spontaneous composition. The spontaneity, after all, comes from the obligation of each member of the ensemble to improvise their way through an arrangement. "Jazz Workshop," like "Harlem," is only the name for a space of interaction and inscription. Recalling Jacques Derrida's engagement with Freud, writing is "the interruption and restoration of contact between the various depths of psychical levels"; it supplements "lived time."[34] Lived time is not perceived directly, but as an effect of retrospection, and in that way phonography is a primary component, thematically and materially. Phonography—sound production and enregistration—is a key to grasping the philosophical and political levels of Hughes and Mingus's respective and collaborative work, from Hughes's early experiments in *The Weary Blues* through Mingus's famous vocalizations and "rotary perception."

A complex aesthetic immediacy informing their project makes thinkable an abstract black situation as emergence and emergency. I do not mean to paper over their points of aesthetic and political divergence, only to make the point that they stage similar problems of community that have further implications for the ways we think their era. Both Hughes and Mingus were active during a cultural moment characterized by worry over American standardization, a trend best figured by metronomic time and predictable, fateful cadences. We can think of them both in line with Hughes and his Harlem Renaissance cohort for whom, as Keith Leonard argues, "the complex negotiation of individuality and poetic achievement" was "the means to construct a communal cultural identity," rooted in "common consciousness and a life in common."[35] The concern Langston Hughes had voiced in 1926 over "pouring racial individuality into the mold of American standardization" had only become more acute; Mingus's emphasis on emotionalism and individuality, through which he extended the traditions of Thelonious Monk and his idol Duke Ellington, was one response.[36] As Mingus strongly implies in his criticism of David Amram cited above, racial individuality had been generalized and neutralized, alienating the racially marked innovators from their own inventions, even as the societal benefit of what Hughes called the "vogue in things Negro" was at best ambiguous for the majority.

In this context, attention to their textured interaction (which, as Meta DuEwa Jones notes, requires notions beyond mere "accompaniment")[37] reveals black musicking—Christopher Small's term for "what people do as the take part in a musical act"—like poetry, to be an activity that abuts social stratification.[38] In this case, it mediates the dreams of transcendence captured in contemporary reference to "black excellence" and the despairing sense of black social abjection. Riffing on Ralph Ellison's "antagonistic cooperation," Scott Saul refers to the dynamic among members of the Jazz Workshop—whom Mingus once described as "people set to free themselves in music"—as "antagonistic liberation."[39] This notion captures an aggressive approach to managing, thwarting, and reshaping audience expectation, but understates the degree to which the Workshop endeavored to continually (re)make its own ground. We might more simply conceive of their dynamic, characteristic of the avant-garde more generally, as a form of play—open-ended, non-teleological, reflexive engagement with others in time. Such agonistic play deorchestrates the grammatical and tropological operations that constitute it as such, as self-identical iteration of a tradition. As subversive gift, play's successful transmission requires retuning the sensory apparatus, opening it to "the interruption and restoration of contact between the various depths of psychical levels" that constitute "lived time" and experience. Reinvented ground destructures the semantic stability of existing discourses—such as freedom or community—making space for what tends to be strategically or logically excluded from those concepts.

In Hughes and Mingus's practice, composition and improvisation mutually constitute and transform one another, under the sign of play, as practices of freedom. That proposed freedom is one place where we can start to conceive of gender's undoing. The specificity of Harlem, as a site of both adjacency to death and alternative practices of freedom, allows them to sketch the limits of any form of "inclusion" that leaves intact the power to exclude, as well as the limits of the refusal to play the game. Long an ideal site through which to imagine black community within and beyond the United States, Harlem sits at the crossroads of nation and world, past and anticipated future. Their phonopoems, in other words, inscribe Harlem as a disruptive and disrupted locale that does not so much reflect the global as it marks what is excessive to geo-spatial order that may yet institute a different culture. That culture is at once "out" in the colloquial sense and eccentric, a space of enclosure and opening—"dream within a dream."

The poetics of black communism are anticipatory—an orientation captured by Mingus's conception of composition as a framework for interpretive action, as well as Hughes's conversational discursive mode and rhetorical questions ("ain't you heard?"). One finds this sense of anticipation in Hughes's description of jazz as anticipation ("always yet") or Mingus's notion of "rotary perception," a theory and practice of ensemble timing that "gives [each member of the ensemble] a feeling he has more space" by making them intimately aware of another's "feel" for the pulse.[40] In more negative terms, one can think of Mingus's phonopoem "Freedom," which, after a list of all those for whom freedom was imminent concludes, with a descending blues scale line, "no freedom for me." Yet my thinking emerges out of the problem of anticipation as a way of attaching oneself to a particular moment. I take the open-endedness of the anticipatory, alongside the use of the vernacular as a way of thinking from the future, as a cue to consider Mingus and Hughes's affective and intellectual openness to fulfillment *or* catastrophe. The phrase "communities in transition" implicitly anticipates at once the destructive and reconstructive tendencies of modernity, the dissolution and reconstitution of all social groups and thus the pending crisis of all aesthetic production rooted in group life.

I read Mingus and Hughes through this frame: anticipating the promise of community alongside the reality of communal dissolution and reconstitution. If one still insists on reading them in terms of the Civil Rights Movement, let us recall that that movement is best understood through its many contingent coalitions. Those sectors of the movement that encouraged self-fashioning in the mode of the bourgeoisie—mocked by both Hughes and Mingus across their respective oeuvres—are not the only important elements of the moment to which they might respond. On the contrary, their collaborations remind us of those aspects of black life—and those activist calls for freedom and self-determination—that intended something more profound than equal access or freedom to compete in class society. The erasure of the Civil Rights Movement's radical elements from public commemoration is one way neoconservative (and neoliberal) reframing of the era, aided by the fusion of red- and race-baiting, which "spawn[ed] a dense network of 'little HUACs' and 'little FBIs,'" artificially untangles what Jacqueline Dowd Hall calls the "Gordian knot that ties race to class and civil rights to workers' rights."[41] Hughes and Mingus, in their flirtation with and movement away from more recognizably leftist positions, reflect the foment of overlapping radical and mainstream positions, as both seek to anticipate changes that neither could predict.

The Literary Mingus

Central to Mingus's emergence in the mid-1950s with his Jazz Workshop is writing—encompassing written marks, the medium of writing, and the aural transmission of ideas. In the liner notes to *Pithecanthropus Erectus*, which Mingus authored for his 1956 debut with Atlantic Records, he makes an astonishing claim:

> My whole conception with my present Jazz Workshop group deals with nothing written. I "write" compositions—but only on mental score paper—then I lay out the composition part by part to the musicians. I play them the "framework" on a piano so that they are all familiar with my interpretation and feeling and with the scale and chord progression to be used. Each man's own particular style is taken into consideration, both in ensemble and in solos. For instance, they are given different rows of notes to use against each chord but they choose their own notes and play them in their own style, from scales as well as chords, except where a particular mood is indicated. In this way, I find it possible to keep my own compositional flavor in the pieces and yet to allow the musicians more individual freedom in the creation of their group lines and solos.[42]

Brian Priestley argues that with his aural approach Mingus "had become the first 'jazz composer' (as opposed to a tune-writer such as [Thelonious] Monk) whose pieces were not written down, and the first since [Duke] Ellington whose definitive works were to any extent 'co-composed' by his sidemen."[43] Priestley's gratuitous dismissal of Monk underscores several unresolved tensions in the reception of jazz and the New Black Music, especially the tension between "serious" music (implicitly long and intricately structured) and "tune writing" (implicitly referring to short themes accompanied by chord structures that serve as vehicles for improvisation). Those tensions underpin Mingus's own claims for his art, especially the question of what counts as writing ("I 'write' compositions—but only on mental score paper"). His approach blurs the line between improvisation and composition, creating structure for the former ("they are given different rows of notes to use against each chord") and maximum freedom for the interpretation of the latter, so that playing a written part within the ensemble becomes a creative act. Seeking to destabilize distinctions between composition and improvisation, his music is neither wholly spontaneous in the style of automatic writing, nor wholly composed if that means conventionally notated. His music holds open a place for complexity—of the (historical and punctual) moment, of interaction, of the intellectual labor involved in making "Mingus music" rather than jazz[44]—against the ideological forms of black spontaneity against which, say, "cool jazz" positioned itself.[45]

The Workshop extended Duke Ellington's tradition of drawing on the individual strengths and talents of its members. Like Thelonious Monk or, later, Cecil Taylor, Mingus insisted that bandmates learn songs by ear and improvise arrangements within fixed parameters. (If one considers the graphic scores favored by musicians ranging from Wadada Leo Smith to Matana Roberts, a whole history of jazz and other experimental black sound practice waits to be told that would specifically foreground ambivalence toward the forms of textual transmission the music depends on as tradition and repertoire.) Composition—Mingus would later call himself a "spontaneous composer"—thus became an interpersonal, embodied activity that incorporated and moved beyond the harmonic theory bebop (especially Charlie Parker) had introduced. Combined with other influences—the black church and Duke Ellington most prominently—his approach to composition produced a music of often astonishing stylistic and emotional range. To listen to Mingus's music is to listen in a sense to an inventory of past listening and collaboration. Where Hughes is among the innovators of reading poetry with jazz and of the use of urban vernacular speech patterns as theme and compositional element, Mingus is a progenitor of "avant-garde" jazz—music that broke rules of functional harmony, song structure, rhythm, and tonality and proceeded through new conceptions of the collective responsibilities of music making, including collective composition.

If one is inclined to hear jazz, in Brent Hayes Edwards's apt phrase, as "a performative archive of historical experience," an Ellingtonian "tone parallel" rather than expression of history, the possibilities afforded by sound recording, and a long history of interaction between record and stage, is central to Mingus's work.[46] Poetry was central to his compositional approach from his earliest compositions, such as "The Chill of Death," which he wouldn't record until near the end of his career, on his 1971 *Let My Children Hear Music*. The recording studio—and the apparatus of records including the "micro-poetics" of song titles, liner notes, and promotional genres such as interviews—would prove similarly central both to his compositional process and his framing of jazz as an intellectual tradition.[47] While recording engineers and record producers had used overdubbing to correct mistakes, or to splice together composite "master takes" from multiple sessions, Mingus pioneered the use of overdubbing and editing to shape a composition on his 1963 album-length composition *The Black Saint and the Sinner Lady*.[48] In order to situate Mingus's direct collaboration with Hughes, I want to develop a sense of the literary Mingus, a brief account of some of the ways he used text and other forms of writing that were central to his art.

Mingus frequently sought to square improvisation's inventiveness and the record's invitation to recursive listening. Rather than alienating people from their initial experience, he seems to imagine Coleman Hawkins or Jean-Baptiste "Illinois" Jacquet "memoriz[ing] their solos and play[ing] them back for the audience" to be affirming, perhaps because the practice could minimize the myths of spontaneity that otherwise haunt black performance. This allows him to proclaim Charlie Parker or Bud Powell "spontaneous composers," the tradition in which he locates himself, rather than the "pencil composers" of the Western art music tradition. He refers to one of his solos as a "composition" that was "on the whole as structured as a written piece of music," able to convey "one feeling, or rather, several feelings expressed as one."[49] Implicitly, he is targeting other musicians' technical ability, musicianship, and conscious plan. But it is also worth underscoring the deeper media historical point. Composition played an important role in canonizing the solo in jazz history. Louis Armstrong composed his famous solo on King Oliver's "West End Blues," as was common practice in the 1920s, and other trumpeters transcribed and attempted to play his solo in concerts. We might pair Mingus's criticism of those who could not reproduce their own performances with his charge against the avant-garde that they were not "playing feeling" but instead "playing anything they want to play: noise, squeaks, hollers, yells, banging bells, with no continuity to it, no recapitulation, no form."[50] Phonography—sounds *and* their circulation, comprising interviews, profiles, and albums—is central to his conception of "spontaneous composition." The emphasis belongs on *composition* as the production of iterable structures belonging to a tradition rather than *spontaneity*. What separates the spontaneity Mingus valorizes from that which he abjures is institutionally valid practice. We might best appreciate Mingus as a transitional figure, and wonder what more he might have had he been able to hear the intense planning or appreciate the forms of study that comprised the avant-garde developing around him.

The destabilization of the border between "pencil" composition and improvisation provided an important means by which Mingus negotiated the racial presuppositions surrounding jazz, even as the ecstatic shouts for which his 1950s work is famous reinforce racist typologies of the jazz musician. We should also consider the importance of his song titles, which helped frame his relationship to his moment. Mingus is far from alone among artists in the long Black Arts era in his use of song title to signal political awareness, but his titles stand out as especially and consistently provocative. Bristling with wit and insight, the song titles help index the compositions to particular historical moments and specify the historical situation that occasions them. Titles such as "Fables of Faubus" (responding to Arkansas governor Orval Faubus's refusal to allow integration in Little Rock schools) or "Remember Rockefeller at Attica" (commemorating the 1971 Attica Prison uprising) recall specific moments, while titles such as "Don't Let It Happen Here" (an anti-fascist poem featuring a revision of Martin Niemöller's famous "First They Came . . ." poem), "Suite Freedom (A Lonely Day in Selma, Alabama)," "Once There Was a Holding Corporation Called Old America," "Meditation for Integration (Or for a Pair of Wire Cutters)," or "Haitian Fight Song" point to broader, if understated, politics engaging the fundaments of the historical present. The song titles are malleable: "Once There Was a Holding Company Called America" becomes "The Shoes of the Fisherman's Wife Are Some Jive Ass Slippers," similarly witty but even less clear as critique.[51] Some of these songs feature spoken texts, while others rely on the liner notes, the "paratexts"[52] of the record or live performance, to convey their political content. Phonography gives a sense of the possible forms of interactivity—one wants to say shared responsibility—between musicians and audience in the anticipated moment of listening. It provides, quite literally, a medium for Mingus's improvisatory practice and inchoate or under-articulated politics.

One of his earliest recorded instances of playing on the border separating music from other texts is "The Clown" (1958), an allegory in the form of a radio play that features radio personality Jean Shepherd performing a semi-improvised text (based on a story Mingus outlined). The story concerns a struggling artist whose corniest routines are the biggest crowd favorites, and whose fatal accident on stage in Dubuque, Iowa, is his greatest success. That performance, Mingus's first to combine both instrumental and verbal improvisation, builds on his earlier experiment with *musique concrète*—a compositional practice based on environmental or "found" sounds and montage techniques repurposed from cinema—on his 1956 recording of George Gershwin's "A Foggy Day," which appears on his Atlantic debut, *Pithecanthropus Erectus*.[53] But his liner notes suggest a different lineage: "You might be tempted to laugh on first hearing—and a good, healthy laugh never hurt anyone—but on second hearing, try to imagine the tenor playing the melody as John Doe walking down Market Street to the Ferry Building, hearing the sounds of a big city on a foggy day . . ."[54] While one might be inclined to hear the simulated sounds of sirens, police whistles, fog horns, and car horns during J. R. Monterose's tenor sax solo in line with musical concretism, Mingus's reference to vaudeville-derived "hokum" techniques recalls Jelly Roll Morton's earlier experiments, such as his 1927 "Sidewalk Blues," which begins and ends with dialogue and street sounds.[55] The reference to vaudeville reminds us that black artists had to negotiate the postwar landscape shaped by a historical modernism partially fueled by racial anxieties. Those anxieties, which shaped racial ventriloquism and racist caricature alike, remained deeply ingrained. The technical ability to reshape traditional aesthetic practices, however, made modernism itself available for critical revision even as broader historical shifts eroded even the notional line separating modernism from mass culture. This sets the stage for the vernacular avant-garde practice Mingus would develop with Langston Hughes.

Scenes in the City

Except for his use of "canned" laughter on "The Clown," the RCA recording of "Scenes in the City," to which I now turn, is the only other instance in this period of Mingus experimenting at this border of hokum, concretism, and spontaneous composition (unless one considers his vocal simulation of the Sanctified church during this period along those lines). In Mingus's discography, "Scenes in the City" follows both "A Foggy Day" and "The Clown," and we might read "Scenes" as the latter's companion piece, focusing on the travails of the audience rather than the artist. Together, they offer a powerful perspective on the different locally grounded ways one participates in a musical act, and the ways sound both establishes and disrupts the local and the subjective. For the text of the phonopoem, a dramatic monologue originally entitled "I Live on Music,"[56] Hughes collaborated with playwright Lonne Elder III,[57] himself active in the Harlem Writers Group founded by Rosa Guy, John Oliver Killens, and John Henrik Clark. Hughes sent corrected copies of the script sent to Mingus and Mel Stewart, but it's difficult to discern how much Hughes contributed to the finished product. It is clear is that the music cues (e.g., when the trumpet would play, whether the speaker would hum with the trumpet, when the band would pick up the tempo) are scripted. Elder, Mingus, and Hughes imagined text and music as part of an integral composition rather than as discrete entities. Mingus recorded a version of the phonopoem with Elder reading the text during the sessions that produced *Tijuana Moods* under the title "A Colloquial Dream" in July 1957. Because of legal wrangling, RCA would not release that album until 1962, and Elder's reading would remain unavailable until a 1999 CD box set included it. In October 1957, Mingus rerecorded the phonopoem with the title "Scenes in the City." On this recording, the lone phonopoem on Mingus's 1958 *A Modern Jazz Symposium of Music and Poetry*, actor Mel Stewart—a frequent collaborator of both Hughes and Mingus—read the text.[58] That Mingus decided to rerecord the work, perhaps because he saw that RCA was delaying *Tijuana Moods*' release, speaks to its relative importance in that moment as part of his continued multimedia experiments.

This complex, episodic text resists narrative summary. Mingus referred to it as one of his "sketches of New York City."[59] While Hughes's biographers ignore this collaboration, Mingus's biographers both unimaginatively say that it speaks of "black sensitivities in a hostile environment"[60] or "black feelings in a hostile environment."[61] A poem about a person on the edge of starvation is not a poem about a "hostile environment" but one about a social order that tolerates dispossession whose rationalization is the result of an underlying racecraft.[62] Sonically, "Scenes" offers a space alive with sociality that opposes or critically navigates dominant forms of social organization. In "Scenes," to live with music, to be surrounded by it, is a simultaneously ambivalent and pleasurable fantasy of the oceanic in psychoanalytic terms, a "return" to a pre-subjective, oceanic state of unity between body and its sonorous environment (i.e., the mother's body).[63] Given that the "environment" apparently refers to attempts to inscribe a fantastic origin in the "lived experience" of the present, I would stress the degree to which listening is a creative act, another supplementation of "lived time." The phonopoem moves through connected spaces. It begins on a barstool in a café bar across from a theater where the speaker, a frustrated actor, cannot afford to purchase even the cheapest seat, much less perform. It then moves to the dynamic sonic space of a Harlem tenement building. The music, presented as agent, initially seems unbounded. By the end, it is subject to the contours of lived space, falling up the stairs and then staying with the speaker. Being "always with the blues," as the speaker describes himself, allows an unsustainable fantasy of listening without a body, or with the external world reduced to a field of impulses, sounds, and receptive bodies without the need for mundane material support. The speaker's most abstract ruminations end with the sudden irreducible problem of the (implicitly) raced body. With its sonic construction of spaces and archives, "oceanic space" merges with the uncomfortable experience of space permeated by others' sounds and soundings.

"Scenes in the City" shuttles between monologue and poem, between downtown and Harlem, the text falling between commentary on the music ("that's jazz music you're hearing") and element of composition with its own rhythmic contours and melodic propulsion in excess of narrative progression. Mel Stewart's reading is dramatic and lively, not rhythmic but in step with the underlying beat. His baritone conveys the lively rhythms and inflections of a professional actor's everyman. Like much of Mingus's music of this period, the composition unfolds through multiple sections, with corresponding shifts of mood and tempo. It opens with an up-tempo, blues-based unison triplet line played by Jimmy Knepper (trombone), Shafi Hadi (alto saxophone), and Clarence "Gene" Shaw (trumpet), propelled by Dannie Richmond's ride cymbal and Mingus's walking bass line. The piece abruptly transitions to an adagio duet between Stewart and Mingus's arco bass. "Well," Stewart intones resignedly, "here I am. Right where I was yesterday, and the day before and the day before that: sitting on a high bar stool holding my dreams up to the sound of jazz music." Richmond joins with finger cymbals as the speaker sketches his situation: living uptown but preferring to be downtown where the music is, and "always with the blues," prone to talking to himself and humming jazz tunes. He has given up his dream of being an actor, is desperately poor ("I've got fifteen cents between me and starvation"), and figures his love of jazz as an addiction ("I'm on that music again").

The mood shifts when he discusses jazz, largely thanks to a shift in instrumentation—rather than a trio with Mingus accented by Dannie Richmond's finger cymbals, he reads and sings along with Shaw's muted trumpet rendition of the main theme. This accompaniment inspires the speaker to break the fourth wall: "That's jazz music you're listening to." He describes it as "pretty," then self-corrects to "beautiful," and likens the music to a hypothetical sexual encounter: "like a woman you might have been with last night. Or, say, an hour ago. Sad, huh?" If the music threatens to be the fantasy thing, the "reminder" of an imagined encounter, his next chain of thought—the room he lives in, the landlady to whom he owes three weeks' rent and whose sensitivity to sound interrupts his enjoyment of the music and homosocial bonding with a friend who visits with a "mouth full of jive"—defers that fantasy. This theme—and attempt to elide the music with "a woman"—recurs at the end of the piece in a context I will discuss below.

On first listening, the interjection "that's jazz music you're listening to" is odd, even corny. What listener who purchased or otherwise encountered the album (and looked at its title) would need that clarification? Considered in a broader context of Mingus's career and concerns, this is a mildly confrontational moment. It speaks to critics who claimed Mingus's music did not "swing" and therefore was moving away from jazz. The very moment when the phonopoem enunciates "jazz" in order to figure subjective immersion in the music is also the moment where the work reveals the heterogeneity of "jazz." If, say, Dave Brubeck (himself the target of a charge, from Mingus, that his music did not swing) topped *Down Beat* or other polls, Mingus here claims the authority to define jazz. The direct address invites shared listening—shared immersion in what Langston Hughes called a "sea of jazz." More than speaking from the margins, the direct address makes marginality audible. The second person serves as an invitation to consider the activity of listening and, potentially, to consider what one does *not* hear in the music. His story is one of surviving day by day, barely staving off starvation, "always with the blues"—both the music and the sense, articulated in the blues idiom, that bad luck is the only luck he can have. Importantly for a text with the narrative-adjacent title "scenes," he does not belong to any obvious narrative of personal or political progress. He wonders why things are so bad for him without hazarding an explanation. His activity of making time—what one might call his improvisatory or even spontaneously composed life—calls progress into question.

Until he directly refers to the music around him, a written script would achieve comparable effects. When the speaker says, "That's jazz music you're listening to," a reader might well conjure her own representative tune or sound, or be content to understand what jazz signifies. "Now catch this," he says, animatedly marking a transition to the second movement; Jimmy Knepper improvises on the opening triplet figure, inviting alternating solo and unison lines with the other horn players against Mingus, Richmond, and Horace Parlan's rhythm section. This allows for both a musical and spatial transition, relocating the opening "here" from the Village back to Harlem and from Shaw's dirge-like descending melody line to Mingus and Richmond's propulsive swing: "Now, here I am standing at my window in my old building." The world of the old building, in contrast with the Village's cafés, is a world of sonic overlap. A male voice, presumably a bus driver, offers to take people to work. Some voices call for quiet, some cry or holler, another directly comments on the text (when the speaker worries about disturbing his landlady lest she remember his past-due rent, a male voice asks, as scripted, "What kind of landlady you got, man?"). The speaker responds only to the implied voice of a friend he begs to be quiet, lamenting to him that because he has pawned his record player they cannot listen to the music together. The real and implied voices both set and *are* the scene, and Harlem becomes a site of mixed sonic impressions. Released from the conventions of linear narrative, these sounds create an impressionistic sense of the speaker's lived aural world.

From a different perspective, these sounds create an aural sign of Harlem as an oceanic space of listening, where one is always connected to others in ways that disallow the kinds of "threshold crossing" that might lend the music the therapeutic quality the speaker apparently desires. In this regard, the phonopoem offers a vision of participating in the music that remains stubbornly tethered to historical and personal contexts. In "Scenes in the City," there is no music separate from imagined subjective experience, the listening of the other. Simultaneously, and somewhat paradoxically, music seems formative of subjective experience. A sign of witness and voyeurism, listening remains autonomous from the demands of narrative. The phonopoem underscores what is unruly—formative and disfiguring—in listening, calling into question even Mingus's ideal of the artwork as a monad of musicians listening to each other, an ensemble in which audience response "wouldn't matter."[64] It displaces the stable site of listening, reinscribes it as a fiction—the place from which the other listens. The speaker's "here I am" serves as the aural sign of stasis, indicating what resists full immersion into a phantasmatic union with the music and the always already present and receding black undercommons. To listen to such a person is to begin to sense the mythic work of jazz as a sign of spontaneous creativity content, to ignore the historical limits of such creativity, and to disregard or minimize broader questions of social poetics. Importantly, attention to social poetics is not a form of protest—claiming black humanity, for example—but rather encourages consideration of alternative modalities of the human. Rather than prefiguring calls for interracial listening or "dialogue," the phonopoem asks us what kind of activity listening *is*.

The work anticipates diverse listeners and ways of listening. The pedagogy of "that's jazz music" later becomes a thematic element in a comic sequence near the middle of the piece.[65] During this sequence, the speaker describes teaching his mother to love jazz by playing her the music of several iconic musicians. Listeners are expected to recognize (or infer) Shafi Hadi's imitation of Charlie Parker, Bob Hammer's imitation of Bud Powell, Clarence Shaw's imitation of Miles Davis (using the Harmon mute that characterized Davis's sound in this period), Jimmy Knepper's imitation of J. J. Johnson, Mingus's imitation of Jimmy Blanton, and Dannie Richmond's imitation of Max Roach. Later, listeners are expected to recognize Jimmy Knepper softly playing Thelonious Monk's "'Round Midnight," the song that finally converts the speaker's mother by convincing her to spend her "nights in Tunisia" (a reference to Dizzy Gillespie's "A Night in Tunisia"); to catch the transition to a minor blues when the speaker says, "Somewhere along the line the blues walked in"; and to appreciate Shaw's quote of "Someday My Prince Will Come" (popularized by Miles Davis) when he repeats "the blues walked in." There is an uneven implication of listeners, some excluded from the world of those who "wake up with jazz in the morning" (an allusion to a characteristic blues lyric) and those who presumably need to have jazz (correctly) identified for them. Part of the pleasure is catching the playful musical references and puns. Simultaneously, the scene of pedagogy implies at least a reach beyond the jazz that signals engagement with the black situation, and a desire to bring women into the reimagined world the phonopoem figures.

Semi-improvised modes of living adjacent to—but not fully defined by—the dominant normativities that structure the modern characterize the poetics of black communism I'm developing. Black vernacular traditions here serve as an instance of the common and offer immediate and urgent itineraries for living otherwise, using an aesthetics of immediacy ("that's jazz music you're listening to") to point the way to a different present. These itineraries ineluctably issue from a gendered undercommon, insofar as the vernacular materials reworked as common tend to originate in social and aesthetic forms—like jazz—that rely on gendered hierarchies. The common easily devolves into a discursive reframing of male homosociality—in Eve Kosofsky Sedgewick's terms, "men promoting men's interests"—functionally indistinguishable from a scheme of male unification and mutual support whose ultimate aim is the continued domination and exclusion of women.[66] Such a drama plays out here, and it is worth underscoring the extent to which what is ultimately at stake in Hughes and Mingus's collaboration can easily become black *male* communism. The last thing anyone needs is another masculinist utopia. I don't think that's a necessary outcome, but it is an important internal limit on this and perhaps all arguments about black vernacular culture's utopian potential.

The poem's last section starts to undo the ironic in-group nature of the address, reminding that, diegetically, the speaker has had to hock his record player so that although the music surrounds us all, his listening is either indirect or occurs only in memory. He wonders why it is so "tough" for him: "Tough like when I can't make that morning meal. When I'm ducking the landlady. When everything I have is in hock. Like when I think." It is an arresting moment, one that his semi-optimistic citation of Richard M. Jones's "Trouble in Mind" ("the sun's gonna shine in my backdoor someday") fails to resolve. The band returns to the slower, secondary theme and again he sings along and again calls it "Beautiful. Like a woman. A real woman." With this, he again makes the music a fantasy object—or, better, makes the fictional "real woman" a fetish for what the music lacks.

Musically, there is a similar play between resolution and irresolution. To speak technically for a moment, the piece begins with one of the most common chord sequences in jazz, a ii-V7-I: a ii chord (the minor chord based on the second scale degree of a major scale) followed by a V7 (a major "dominant" chord based on the fifth scale degree), which usually resolves to the I (major tonic). The "function" of the dominant or flatted seventh in this chord is to create tension that pulls the harmony back to the tonic. The closing theme is less conventional. It begins with the sequence Am7-D7 (ii-V7), implying G major, but then substitutes B♭-m7 (the ii-chord of A♭ major), which does not resolve but rather begins a second cycle based on a chord a semitone away from the expected tonic. It continues this way, finally ending on a IV chord (based on the fourth scale degree) that does not technically resolve, although it is "stable" (and conventional). Like the text, the music provides an ending but not a resolution—a choice that is likely deliberate, especially in light of Mingus's ongoing multimedia experiments with music and text. The clichéd analogy of music to a woman marks what David Schwarz in another context terms "an emergence of conventionality" that allows for closure without tarrying with the lack, the catastrophe it refuses to name.[67] We might simply call this History in its varied senses: personal regarding subject formation; social regarding the origins of dispossession; local regarding Harlem and the music itself; and so on.

The phonopoem cannot quite escape a metaphysical impulse to understand the music outside of history. Considering the many musical references and jokes, one way to participate in the musical act is through accepting the invitation to think historically its verbal and musical references. There, the phonopoem most belongs to history. In its apparent desire for an unmotivated out, into the ether of unclaimed or lapsed attachment, it floats free of the very community it works for and into a stereotyped world between the pretty and the beautiful, the archetypal and the "real." Between its image of Harlem as a zone of picturesque poverty and Harlem as an unthinkable (not to say "unimaginable") site that was never in vogue, it points to a certain void, what Suzan-Lori Parks might term the Great Hole of History, a generative "nonplace" neither inside nor outside but marked by the structured exclusions of historical experience.[68]

Mingus's multi-part composition, slightly at odds with the text, shuttles between humor and pathos, between traditional structure and collective improvisation: it suggests another relationship to history. It helps create the montage effects that characterize his music, and the sense of an unsettled, in-transition moment *felt* rhythmically and intuitively rather than charted "empirically." Above, I referred to a rhythmic feeling for life that generates its own hierarchies of value and attachment, and which informs cultural inscriptions within which official notions of Time appear in distorted ways. I want to take a moment to situate Mingus's musical project historically as well as thematically, through a brief consideration of his revisions of swing and collaborative composition. Mingus's music generally—but especially here and in his subsequent collaborations with Hughes—emerges at a moment of uncertainty within the field of jazz. New improvisational possibilities suggested by modal playing (organized around principles of sound other than those of the "functional" harmony a ii-V7-I progression implies), alongside increased interest in black vernacular forms (e.g., the blues, gospel, and polyrhythms associated with the decolonizing African world), challenged settled critical narratives of progression from swing to bebop's radical transformations of received song structures. In his perspicuous account of the era, composer and critic Ekkerhard Jost argues, "Mingus accepts the old formal patterns, but alters them by filling them with new content."[69] Jost's metaphor, surely meant to give Mingus his due as an innovator, understates the radical nature of his intervention within the field of jazz precisely insofar as it re-inscribes the thingness of what Mingus attempts to reanimate. Jost would have it seem that although Mingus draws on the lives, experiences, and emotions of the black people who played the music, the underlying form remains primary. Stable form amounts to the dialectical sublation (or cancelation) of content: the familiar modernist understanding of form as the "refinement" of folk materials. In short, new content reanimates old forms, which amount to the "transcendental signified" that ultimately subverts the grammars constitutive of Mingus's music. Modernist framing is a way of not listening to the challenge his music poses to so-called jazz precisely by reanimating what "refinement" reifies.

Like the music that surrounds the speaker of "Scenes in the City," Mingus's collaborative approach to composition and arrangement becomes a matter of embodied practice and memory, of intimate transmission and collaborative creation. One of the most distinctive features of his music in this period was the shifting moods, tempos, and rhythmic feel that he termed "rotary perception." As he put it in his semi-autobiographical *Beneath the Underdog* (1971):

> There was once a word used—swing. Swing went in one direction, it was linear, and everything had to be played with an obvious pulse and that's very restrictive. But I use the term "rotary perception." If you get a mental picture of the beat existing within a circle you're more free to improvise.

People used to think the notes had to fall on the center of the beats in the bar at intervals like a metronome, with three or four men accenting the same pulse. That's like parade music or dance music. But imagine a circle surrounding each beat—each guy can play his notes anywhere in that circle and it gives him a feeling he has more space. The notes fall anywhere inside the circle but the original feeling for the beat isn't changed. If one of the group loses confidence, somebody hits the beat again. The pulse is inside you. When you're playing with musicians who think this way you can do anything.[70]

Fred Moten draws out the implications of Mingus's recourse to metaphors of the circular and centripetal, with particular reference to Mingus's critiques and ambivalent praise of Ornette Coleman, whom Mingus, in 1964, referred to as a "calypso player" who lacked the feel for African American rhythmic conceptions.[71] Moten powerfully unpacks the intra-racial dynamics that shape the formation of an African American identity distinct from a broader black identity. However, in 1959 Mingus had told Leonard Feather: "Now, aside from the fact that I doubt he can even play a C scale . . . in tune, the fact remains that his notes and lines are so fresh. So when [disc jockey] Symphony Sid played his record, it made everything else that he played, even my own record that he played, sound terrible. I'm not saying everybody's going to have to play like Coleman. But they're going to have to stop playing like Bird."[72]

Intra-racial—and imperial—dynamics enfold and are refracted by aesthetic and professional concerns. Like Charlie Parker before him, Coleman introduced not just a new style but, in the cant of musicians, a new *language* or *idiom*—a new approach to harmony and melody, a new way of interpreting and negotiating preexisting "content," including ideas of the past, to generate (invoking Duke Ellington) a new "feeling of jazz." The "feeling of jazz," and what it does or does not improve, is fundamentally at stake in scenes of pedagogy, where we consent to hear another's hearing and to be transformed by it. To change the language and feeling of the music is to change the structure of desire and intersubjective relation, to reorganize music as a "fantasy space." Innovations—from bebop's rewriting of the rhythmic and melodic rulebook to Mingus's rotary perception and a commitment to greater emotionalism—suggested new modalities of lived (musical) time. These musical innovations shift the parameters of the acceptable disruptions, suspensions, and accentuations of metronomic, regular time, whose colloquial term is "feel."

In response to the new feeling of jazz, Mingus initially assembled a freewheeling pianoless quartet in the Coleman vein, featuring Eric Dolphy, Ted

Curson, and Dannie Richmond. Following Dolphy's decision to leave Mingus's band (and his premature death), Mingus expressed his alienation from the new modes (and the accolades afforded the new players) in familiar reactionary terms, implying his own approach to be "authentically" black. Having already accepted Nesuhi Ertegun's challenge to make a "churchy, blues, swinging, earthy" album, Mingus claimed his music's synecdochic relation to black aesthetic practices and hence claimed belonging to a collective that validated his music. Belonging to the collective as the expressive part of a larger whole emerged as the figurative/discursive frame through which critics could hear innovation as purposeful agency rather than disordered noise. "Authenticity" became a kind of commodity object, and those things without use-value held an ambiguous position, similar to those practices that could not claim collective validation. There could only be one, hence Mingus's discursive othering of Coleman as synecdoche for a different (scorned) tradition. But what of those actions, like those of "Scenes'" speaker, that do not rise to the status of synecdoche? The dynamic clarifies the personal, historical, and potentially political stakes of "Scenes'" production of ambivalent musical space.

The work's overall concern with the sociality of feeling raises the larger question of what it might mean to "live on jazz." Extending Thomas Carmichael's influential reading of Mingus's autobiography, we see here "jazz life" as neither "subversive mimicry [presumably of bourgeois norms] nor the experience of the blues as a counter-hegemonic strategy, but the expression of a profound ambivalence with respect to the affiliations of culture and identity" that structure black subjectivity.[73] Here, then, we can account for the two material realities—race and poverty—that block the speaker's ability to "lose himself" or dissolve the threshold separating his self from the music. While race remains implicit, poverty in "Scenes in the City" is a social problem that only ambiguously hails a collective solution. Neither is the speaker's hunger the basis for a romantic vision of the artist or the noble poor. On the contrary, the narrator's desperate situation is a problem because it affects him and many like him, similarly nameless, anonymous despite the ubiquity of the music that represents them. The speaker must improvise a relation to a social world in which improvisation is recontextualized in the contested conceptual and material terrain from which it (improvisation) emerges. This phonopoem syncopates calls to synecdochic collectivity—the speaker cannot claim to represent anything bigger than himself, yet does not rise to the level of individual. It defers the figurative ground from which recognizable agency might emerge. In this way, claiming a collectivity but refusing to be counted either on the demographer's or race leader's ledger, he gives voice to—demands an audience for—those who never speak as the nation or "the people," those around whom more adequate versions of community might coalesce. Such ambiguous giving voice is a hallmark of Hughes's work, including his collaborative *Weary Blues*, to which we turn now.

Consider Me

Langston Hughes's ambition, his desire to support himself through his writing alone, seems to have encouraged him to take on ever more projects to ensure his legacy and day-to-day survival. For both Hughes and Mingus, actualizing any politics of improvisation required negotiating the complex interplay between the demands of commerce and the demands of art. In his prefatory note to *Montage of a Dream Deferred*, Hughes conflates bebop's "conflicting changes, sudden nuances, sharp and impudent interjections, broken rhythms" and the nature of Harlem itself, drawing on "the jam session, sometimes the popular song, punctuated by the riffs, runs, breaks, and disc-tortions of the music of a community in transition."[74] Remembering Mingus's praise for Bud Powell and Charlie Parker's "new and good melodic structures—on such simple chord changes," we might ask how bebop's innovations, many rooted in blues harmonic and melodic concepts, alter Hughes's sense of or feel for the blues.[75] We might consider, from this perspective, other forms of freedom (expressive or otherwise) his late poetry represents. The vernacular—understood as simultaneous ground of semantic intelligibility and unintelligibility, a marker of what resists universalizing abstraction—becomes a heuristic for perceiving the subterranean practices of making and valuing time that accompany official timekeeping. Read in light of "Scenes in the City" and his earlier work's attention to those not considered in dreams of integration, *Weary Blues*'s poetics plays on the immediacies of lyric address and "spontaneous composition."

Across his career, Hughes regarded jazz, the blues, and other black commercial fields as sites of simultaneous achievement and restraint. Yet, he also seemed to see in them the possibility of a broad-based mode of belonging that could include all black people, allowing for intimacy with them without relying on their (or his own) "authenticity." He sought, in other words, ways of speaking not *for* the "so-called common element" but *with* them, to and alongside them. This vision of mass culture contrasts with the folkloric or romantic approaches to the "folk" that develop alongside the emergence of phonographic folklore studies, where encroaching commerce and modernization required arguments for a distinct, uncontaminated folk culture, which ultimately needs the "folk" as an alter-native to modernity's mechanization.[76] This vision also contrasts with the idea of vernacular culture as a legitimating sign or referent through which to perform one's own distinctness. Finally, this vision marks out a similar ambivalent musical space as that Mingus achieves in "Scenes," with particular interest in highlighting (those who) work from eccentric margins. Nathaniel Mackey's provocative claim for black art is especially resonant in Hughes's work: "Black art, like any other, is innovative, demanding, and/or outside to the extent that it addresses the wings and resistances indigenous to its medium qua medium.... To don such wings and engage such resistances as though they were the stuff of identity and community is to have taken a step toward making them so."[77] Mackey's formulation identifies outfulness as aspiration, "always yet" as Hughes might say. From early poems such as "The Cat and the Saxophone," whose graphic presentation recalls and distances itself from T. S. Eliot's "The Waste Land," jazz becomes one more element in a montage of black life—a dialectical juxtaposition of elements that forges new connections and allows for new questions and answers. Jazz belongs to a set of discursive and aesthetic operations marshaled toward the attempt to find adequate form for the complexities of the common and common practices.

Setting out on these terms, I hope to rethink the interplay of the general and the particular in Hughes's poetry as a way to reconsider his consistent uses of vernacular linguistic structures and poetic devices rooted in "low-down" black subaltern populations across his career. Writing in 1951, Hughes argued, "Poetry is rhythm—and, through rhythm, has its roots deep in the nature of the universe.... The rhythms of poetry give continuity and pattern to words, to thoughts, strengthening them, adding the qualities of permanence, and relating the written word to the vast rhythms of life."[78] That comment takes on a slightly different character when read alongside his claims for "Negro syncopation" discussed above. The rhythms of living vary, and at different moments will be legible in different ways to different audiences, so "writing about things they live and know" will help poets "bridge the often imagined gulf between literature and life."[79] Taken together, and with the earlier concerns about the rhythms of life with and against the dominant graph of Time, we can perhaps analogize Hughes's stated approach to rhythm to Mingus's theory of rotary perception. Both offer a way of unfixing time in order to give form to black life as social poetics, a way of conceiving individuals separate from (but imbricated in) the larger social world, and of capturing and building from the eccentric and exorbitant to make and remake culture.

In *Weary Blues*, one of jazz's functions is to measure quotidian routines and temporary freedoms against a larger, elusive freedom. But the difficulty of Hughes's version of jazz is that it also includes and ambivalently retraces a history of people-as-property as well as the "valuational grids and grammars of feeling" that result from that freedom.[80] If by the late 1950s, through displacement and condensation, the music in the popular imaginary (i.e., "America's classical music") evinces no sense of the lives and lifeworlds actively involved in its creation, one of Hughes's projects is to disrupt the abstracting logics that allow it to stand as an ideal of human freedom. If this can constitute the "oceanic" in the sense discussed above, one must always ask exactly which thresholds and which selves are in play. Jazz poetry in this sense is concerned with the contest between the black popular, those black people deemed suitable for inclusion within the larger *demos*, and the black subaltern structurally excluded from the integration that "whispered promises" foretold: the pimps and sex workers that fascinated Mingus, the drug addicts and autodidacts of jazz lore, the riotous, the strivers whose desires beyond bare survival pose unintelligible demands.[81]

The first side of the MGM release *Weary Blues* features Hughes with a band (Henry "Red" Allen, trumpet and leader; Vic Dickenson, trombone; Sam "The Man" Taylor, tenor saxophone and clarinet; Al Williams, piano; Milt Hinton, bass; Osie Johnson, drums) playing a suite of compositions by jazz critic and historian Leonard Feather, who produced the album. The second side features Hughes with Mingus's Jazz Workshop: Horace Parlan, piano; Jimmy Knepper, trombone; Shafi Hadi, tenor saxophone; Charles Mingus, bass; Kenny Dennis, drums.[82] Hughes reads twenty poems with the Leonard Feather group across seventeen musical compositions; thirteen poems with the Jazz Workshop across eight compositions. Meta DuEwa Jones, in one of the few sustained analyses of the recording (she primarily focuses on the first side), notes that Tom "Curly" Ruff's digital remaster and transfer puts both sides of the original LP on one track, making it difficult to align the fifteen tracks listed on the back of the CD with the twenty-six audible breaks between recorded segments.[83] Perhaps the engineers and others working on the CD transfer wanted listeners to hear the album as one continuous mix, one that would highlight the dialectical interplay between poem and song within and across compositions, approximating the experience of hearing Hughes performing with these bands at a nightclub. In order that this analysis can be useful to listeners who encounter the poem through that CD, I refer to it rather than the LP and delineate discrete poems by time.

Mingus and the Workshop primarily perform music written specifically for this collaboration. For reference purposes, the composition listed as "Consider Me" aligns with Langston Hughes's poem "Consider Me"; "The Stranger" groups "Warning: Augmented," "Motto," and "Dead in There"; "Midnight Stroll" groups "Final Curve" and "Boogie 1 A.M."; "Backstage" groups two poems from "Seven Moments of Love"; "Dream Montage" groups "Tell Me," "Good Morning," and "Harlem"; "Weird Nightmare" collects "Same in Blues" and "Comment on Curb"; "Double G Train" pairs "Freedom" and "Island" with a composition later recorded as "Wednesday Night Prayer Meeting"; and "Jump Monk" pairs the song of that title with Hughes again reading a shortened version of "Warning: Augmented" that emphasizes the poem's humorous admonition to "curb your doggie / Like You ought to do, / But don't let your dog curb you!" Most of the poems Hughes performs with Mingus come from *Montage of a Dream Deferred* ("Warning: Augmented," "Motto," "Dead in There," "Boogie 1 A.M.," "Tell Me," "Good Morning," "Harlem," "Same in Blues," "Comment on Curb," and "Island," with additional poems published in *Jim Crow's Last Stand* ("Freedom"), *Shakespeare in Harlem* (two poems from the cycle "Seven Moments of Love"), and the journal *American Scholar* ("Consider Me").

"Consider Me" (beginning at 23:35) opens with Shafi Hadi playing a plangent theme on tenor saxophone accompanied by Mingus's arco bass, creating a mood similar to the second motif of "Scenes in the City." Hughes reads with a lively tone, drawing out the poem's drama and deliberately fitting the cadences of his reading to the music. As with all the other poems Hughes reads for this recording, the speaker is apparently male. "Consider Me," which Hughes would revise for inclusion in his 1959 *Selected Poems*, deploys a deceptively simple diction that in this case masks a larger existential question. The poem, from the perspective of a poor "colored boy," offers a first-person description of the black communist poetics at the center of this chapter's concerns. He describes his daily routine ("Downtown at eight, / Sometimes working late"), and the respite the weekend offers ("On Friday / The eagle flies. / Saturday / Laughter, a bar, a bed."). The phrase "consider me" serves as a refrain that, through repetition, transforms from plea to question.

Hadi's theme provides the musical backbone for the composition, which lasts about three minutes twenty seconds, and consists of three sections: the adagio introduction, a two-feel ballad section (24:35), and a double-time swing section that accompanies the weekend section (23:53). The speaker is a "boy," older than sixteen, "once nobody, / Now me," who traces his lineage back to "Original Pa— / spelled G-o-d," God "meaning mystery."[84] Horace Parlan punctuates the moment with a left-hand discord, marking the transition to the ballad section. Hughes reads with a clear, unhurried baritone, not quite keeping time with the music except when he pauses for musical interludes, particularly at the beginning of the double-time section, where he pauses longer as if to showcase the complexity of the unison horn lines and the suppleness of the Workshop. The effect links Hughes and the Workshop in a deliberate interaction.

He becomes akin to a soloist, not to say "improviser," who merges his self with the group concept. That Hughes was not primarily a performer is evident—his pauses sound deliberate, but not smooth—and this makes his apparent commitment to the group concept even more striking.

The one significant variation between the recorded and printed poem occurs when Hughes seemingly improvises a refrain: the speaker refers to being "caught in a crack" that splits the world from China to Harlem's Lenox Avenue. Hughes repeats the phrase "To Lenox Avenue," which marks a transition, a break for instrumental response. (His reading of those lines, "Black / Caught in a crack," is rhythmically syncopated, irregular on the page and in performance.) The speaker of this and most of the poems Hughes remakes with Mingus into phonopoems participates in the music as neither artist nor entertainer. He is subject, not citizen, and the mundanity of his poverty positions him proximate to the trope and specter of "the nigger"—the archetype of the noncitizen who evidences both the need for reform and predicts the failure of reform efforts. It is to this figure that the common refers.

The maleness of the speaker is a key element of the poem's attempts to make him legible, and a limit on its politics. That his "Sugar" has to work signals the speaker's economic and epistemological poverty, his cruel attachment to a suffocating social form. His inability to occupy normative bourgeois masculinity describes the historical situation of unmarried African American migrants, where women could often find domestic work but men had a harder time. His exclusive attention to his own limited participation in the system obscures both her oppression and their alternative freedoms. Yet, although his ability to imagine transformative possibilities remains tethered to the mutually constituting structures of sexual and racial difference that, as with "Scenes in the City," transforms the music into a woman and the ideal listener—the one asked to "consider"—into a male, the phonopoem underscores the ambiguities. When the speaker asks reader-listeners to "consider" his "Sugar," Jimmy Knepper and Dannie Richmond engage in a short, syncopated musical conversation, audible as a destabilization of the musical context, a sonic aporia. The musical dialogue between men underscores the predicament of the speaker, his detachment from legitimate lines of social reproduction and his subaltern status even within black communities. But it also invites consideration of the woman in the same predicament, who cannot speak at all. (One wonders whether the Knepper/Richmond moment is mimetic, symbolizing an argument between the speaker and his lover.)

Hughes's pauses, though not occurring in rhythmically or prosodically unusual places, accentuate the line "Sunday prayers syncopate glory," which occurs during a broad rewriting of the lyrics to T-Bone Walker's "Call It Stormy Monday." Walker's song laments the end of the weekend, and the drudgery, uncertainty, and unfulfilling nature of the work from which the weekend provides brief respite. Hearing that song in light of the gender role disruption I've been discussing, one might wonder whether women who work as a domestics or take in laundry experience Sunday. In regular meters, syncopation underscores and reinforces the main pulse in much the way that the weekend parties interrupt and propel the patterns of the workweek, serving as an alternative end where other avenues of freedom appear blocked. In some accounts, including Hughes's, syncopation is synonymous with black music, which encourages one to recall that in musical terms syncopation uses brief interruptions to propel and to produce variation within a larger rhythmic context. With "prayers syncopate glory," however, Hughes invents a new vernacular phrase. The most straightforward reading is that Sunday prayers mark the end of the weekend's revelry ("glory"), and thus mark the boundary to the fantasy of revelry as an alternative, rather than dialectical flipside, of quotidian drudgery. But if Sunday prayers "syncopate glory," then glory is ongoing, despite the start of the workweek, and the prayers are an irregular rhythmic variation of the main time. The non-idiomatic phrase produces its own "syncopation" of the lines that precede it, arresting and propelling meaning in a manner similar to "Black / Caught in a crack" with regard to the rhythm of Hughes's reading.

Syncopation suggests something more than commodifiable style, a discrepant time practice that occasionally intrudes into and reframes Time. Referring to similar working-class black activities in the Jim Crow South, Robin Kelley argues, "Most people attended these events to escape from the world of assembly lines, relief lines, and color lines, and to leave momentarily the individual and collective battles against racism, sexism, and material deprivation."[85] Yet, escapism tells only part of the story: "seeking the sonic, visceral pleasures of music and fellowship, the sensual pleasures of food, drink and dancing" amounted to disorganized and non- if not anti-institutional practices of the quotidian. In this case, these practices inscribe a social poetics geared toward creating space for black people to forge "a common vernacular filled with a grammar and vocabulary that struggled to articulate the beauty and burden of their racial, class, and gender experiences."[86] Such social poetics create a swerve or hiccup in the implicit graph of Time, and if they are not revolutionary they at least pose different demands to different people, and outline possibilities that otherwise remain unthinkable.

As Hazel V. Carby notes of Hughes's use of the blues to structure his poetry in general, "Consider Me" attempts to provide "access to a social consciousness through the reconstruction and representation of nonliterary, contemporary, cultural forms that embodied the conditions of social transformation."[87] Beyond its explicit reference to the recent demographic shifts from rural to urban living, the poem locates its speaker in world history. He declares himself "Descended also / From the / Mystery," and that declaration, inscribing blackness in the unknowable origins of the universe itself, works on at least two levels. On the one hand, "Mystery" functions as a nickname for ongoing processes of mystification—the public amnesia that Aimé Césaire referred to as modernity's "forgetting machine"—whereby one sees and stigmatizes the beggar or the criminal for lacking work ethic, rather than interrogating the production of social abjection.[88] On the other, we might see Hughes evoking a countermystification whose function is fundamentally therapeutic, locating the black *man* at the beginning of time rather than incidental to it, and thus insisting on black people as integral to any holistic account of the universe (or, in the context of this poem, the global). In both instances, what is at stake is an alternative timeline, an alternative past to recover.

Hughes's poetry tends to be paradigmatically "lyric" insofar as it presents a fictive situation of address into which anyone can imagine herself as the addressee, but not just anyone can imagine herself to be the speaker. It preserves fragments of history, but—as with the Mystery—without the solace of an originary wholeness to be reconstituted. Instead, Hughes's poems present elements of a montage without the benefit of a definite narrative or cinematic framework, which demands and frees the reader to reconstruct what was not previously whole, to create in the absence of a model, investing familiar signs and objects with new subjective meanings. Although the mode of address recalls similar monologues meant to invite public sympathy, this speaker retains a fundamental opacity. The more he asks listeners to "consider me," the more of a challenge it seems to put together the fragments of his life, what he is now who was "once nobody," descended from "the / Mystery" and still a mystery to listeners, who presumably is not a Harlem resident. Then again, one might imagine that Hughes's poem addresses people like the poem's speaker, who do not need references like "On Friday the eagle flies" (i.e., people "sport away" their pay) to be translated, and who likewise see in their own lives something to consider, despite—or because of—their social isolation.

Here, as across Hughes's work, his poems invest worn-out forms like popular blues lyrics and even the form of alienated life and its object world with new subjective meanings, producing what Walter Benjamin termed "dialectical images."[89] Thus, my version of Hughes departs somewhat from, say, Anita Haya Patterson's modernist Hughes, for whom the "risk of incomprehensibility" indicates "his right to creative freedom of expression."[90] Reading incomprehensibility in temporal terms, it becomes a sign of figuring futures that are not repetitions of the social divisions and antagonisms that shape the present, without being reducible to programmatic statements. Hughes's invocation of the communal sensibility that cultural forms carry—keeping the sense of "carry" as activated both in metaphor (to carry over) and in alienation ("taken my blues and gone")—more than signifying affiliation attempts to create new sensibilities by rearticulating cultural forms as common. Attention to smaller scale practices of social formation as well as the broader conditions in which that formation takes place—the mutual blindness and dependency of local and structural forces—is at the heart of his work on *Weary Blues* and elsewhere.

The investments of Hughes's speaker remain opaque because they are not available as a prescription beyond the redundant, even mocking demand "consider me." From a different perspective, that opacity points to the limitations and meanness of available configurations of common life, and the imaginaries that subtend them. Like Mingus's "Meditations (On a Pair of Wire Cutters)" or some of Hughes's explicitly political texts, the implied question is what constitutes an adequate thought or action. The difference is that we hear in Mingus an interventionist impulse, a desire to sound the demand for action Ralph Ellison's narrator in *Invisible Man* hears in Louis Armstrong's music, but equally to acknowledge some unspecified accountability to a community—a graph of interlocking and conflicting desires and strivings undergirded by a common feel for the moment and for tradition. Hughes, with his greater investment in formal devices and the distancing effects made possible by the page, tends to be after something more ambiguously implicative, but no less urgent. One feels at times that his keen ear for the rhythms of language—and of the lives of those who use it—allows him write at the vanishing point between a communal spirit and the community's transformation.

With these reflections in mind, I turn to "The Stranger" (26:57), where Hughes reads the whole of "Warning: Augmented," "Motto," and "Dead in There" from *Montage of a Dream Deferred*. As with "Consider Me," the phonopoem moves through different moods, beginning with an out-of-time figure that builds to an abrupt, staccato note that introduces the first poem. Shafi Hadi humorously interacts with Hughes's list of dogs, then takes a one-chorus solo on a blues-like theme, which sets up "Motto," read mostly in duet with Mingus. A slower blues theme akin to "Goodbye Porkpie Hat" accompanies Hughes's apparently improvised narrative segue, transforming his reading into an act of "spontaneous composition" rather than poetry with a jazz background. As "Motto" reaches its climax, the band plays a decelerando to transition to a new interlude, which begins, "Well, that's the motto of a hepcat" ("dig and be dug in return"), a "cool bop daddy" who died young, ironically because of "too much good time-ing," a diagnosis that is aurally indistinguishable from "too much good timing." Describing the man's nighttime funeral procession down Lenox Avenue, Hughes states (and repeats) the title "Dead in There," along the way explaining that sometimes in Harlem "we have night funerals." The band hits one more accented note a beat after Hughes reads, *"Wake up and live!"* The improvised narrative achieves the effect of the offset, italicized or capitalized lines in the other poems in *Montage* and throughout Hughes's oeuvre, syncopating the imagined singular voice of the lyric mode with a communal or objective narratorial comment.

The staccato horn notes that frame the composition introduce an unexpected element of humor, especially to the ironic, makeshift epitaph "wake up and live," which in turn sets up the ironic turn of the end where those who didn't "dig" the hepcat in life now dig his grave and "plant" him. But that continuity is illusory: while Hughes's new narration links "Motto" to "Dead in There," one is left to infer from their placement alongside "Warning: Augmented" that the dead "bop daddy" had less sense than the dogs Hughes describes in "Warning." Hughes's ad hoc narration stands as an objective statement that asks listeners to consider but not identify with the motto of the dead bop daddy, or with the man himself. The next poem in the sequence, "The Stranger," finds in the dead man both dream image (insofar as he represents the fulfillment of an ultimately ungeneralizable model of social transformation) and ruin of "a community in transition." The stranger of the title becomes a floating signifier referring at different points to the poem's narrative persona (who at once identifies with and floats free of Harlem); to listeners (positioned as non-residents eager for insider information); and to the dead man (estranged from the community of workers who will ultimately bury him). The dead man is, on one level, the ultimate telos of the speaker of "Scenes in the City," and thus an end of the fantasy of immersion in the music. The narrative persona and (non-resident) listeners are strangers insofar as they represent the hepcat's constitutive "otherness"; his "good time-ing" ultimately estranges him from his own body. The Workshop's abrupt, staccato notes finally serve as alienation effects that, like Hughes's humor, discourage sentimental identification. Their respective and collaborative alienation effects show the ways sentimental identification produces everyday estrangement.

"Double G Train" extends that figuration to the community of Harlem itself. About a year after recording *Weary Blues*, Mingus would rearrange and record this composition, without poetry, as "Wednesday Night Prayer Meeting" for the album *Blues and Roots*, released in March 1960, where it appeared alongside such famous works as "E's Flat, Ah's Flat Too" and "My Jelly Roll Soul."[91] The title change signals that these are qualitatively different compositions, in contrast with "Jump Monk," which features Hughes reading "Warning: Augmented" as an introduction. "Double G Train" begins with Hughes reading "Freedom," from the 1943 volume *Jim Crow's Last Stand*, without accompaniment. Beginning "Democracy will not come / Today,"[92] this poem has learned the lesson that, as Arthur P. Davis would declare, "a global victory for democracy [i.e., the Allied victories in World War II] does not necessarily have too much pertinence at home."[93] Nor, as Hughes's increasingly outward-looking politics would attest, had there been a truly *global* victory for democracy, just détente among competing imperial nations. Davis tracks the ways that Harlem shifts across Hughes's poetry from *The Weary Blues* to *Montage of a Dream Deferred*, from a space of interracial fantasy to a "class-conscious Harlem" that offers refuge from the white world—an ebullient, mournful space that is no longer a symbol of the "all-inclusiveness of American democracy."[94] Yet Harlem continues to oscillate between symbol and reality, the "dark tenth of a nation" serving as a location for the transformation of people from Puerto Rico, Cuba, Haiti, Jamaica, the South, and elsewhere, "dark / wondering / wide-eyed / dreaming" to carry out the hard work of constituting themselves as a people, if not the popular.[95]

The Double-G train in New York was a crosstown Brooklyn-Queens train (now the G train), and the poem plays on two senses of local. One is the outer boroughs, not accessible to black Harlemites via that train, which suggests the difficulty of even cross-*city* alliances even as the city's black populations were diverse, and diversifying. Simultaneously, the phonopoem invokes the local rhythms and sounds of a Sanctified church (albeit without Mingus's famously ecstatic hollers). "Wednesday Night Prayer Meeting," with its explicit sonic invocation of the space of the church referenced in "Consider Me," accompanies "Freedom" and "Island," which in effect brings the suite of phonopoems full circle. The black church, metonymic of the prayers that "syncopate glory," at times figures a quasi-counter-institutional space that, like the spaces of revelry, offers a compensatory or figurative democracy. One can read it, then, as related to Mingus's own poem "Freedom," built around a riff that recalls the spirituals. In both cases, I would stress the forms of expert, active, embodied listening on the part of the performers that in turn implicates listeners. Of course, by 1958 both Hughes and Mingus were aware of the southern Civil Rights Movement for which the church proved vital. Rather than symbol, though, the church (and the relatively disorganized spiritual practices the spirituals symbolize) represents here the alienated form of African American life subjectively reinvested with the dream image of a world that could yet emerge. The phonopoem is not a representation of the church or an attempt to ground its aesthetic authority in a "people's culture," but creates a vanishing point between the cultural act and the spirit it supposedly expresses. Indeed, Hughes's line "I do not need my freedom when I'm dead / I cannot live on tomorrow's bread" rhymes with the familiar critiques of Christianity for encouraging African Americans to look to heavenly rather than terrestrial salvation. That Mingus plays a short motif to introduce "Wednesday Night" as Hughes is reading "I want freedom / Just as you" suggests that the music symbolizes both a freedom (substituted for the titular "democracy") still to come and an alienation from the larger "you" the poem addresses. Hughes reads the second poem, "Island," after a full statement of the melody and ends, "Ain't you heard?" as Hadi continues a short blues-based solo whose beginning overlaps with Hughes's conclusion. Mingus begins his solo by modifying the motif with which Hadi ends. In succession, the effect is to draw attentive listeners to the active listening between Hughes and the members of the Workshop. "Ain't you heard?" marks an invitation to imagine listening to someone else listen. During Mingus's solo, members of the Workshop clap on the off-beats (following his audible exhortation), evoking the sound of the storefront church that might well connect black Harlem to the outer boroughs, to the South, to Watts, or, as people increasingly started to think, to the African diaspora insofar as the basic beat seemed to be the same. Since "Island" makes Harlem emblematic of migration, the storefront becomes a metonym for the African diaspora, and "Democracy" comes to figure not "America" but a new configuration of black politics.

Insofar as the closing line "ain't you heard?" doubles as a challenge—did you listen?—it requires response without prefiguring the form response might take. The second poem of "Double G Train" shifts address from the presumably white "you" of "Freedom" to the "daddy" addressed throughout *Montage* and *Weary Blues*, and with that from an appeal to the white world to a black one with whom the music and speaker both seem to be aligned. Above all, it doubles, again, as an appeal to listen and to respond, ideally, in some new way. Harlem's "dream within a dream" (Hughes revises the next line from "*our* dream deferred" to "*Harlem's* dream deferred") figures the larger struggles of the black community to gain consciousness of itself as historical. Hughes and Mingus's collaboration figures Harlem as what John Lowney terms a "geography of desire, a geography of disappointment, a geography of militant rage, a geography of 'dark' meditation"—a bound and unbounded space in which new expressive forms, now utopian and now testaments to failure, emerge.[96]

If, for poets such as William Carlos Williams or writers like Norman Mailer, black music powerfully testifies to alternative masculinity, these poems are also powerfully concerned with moving black masculinity from the domain of mythic power into the quotidian world of pleasure and vulnerability where women and men suffer alike—even as male suffering, especially in "Consider Me," is thinkable primarily as "feminization." "Weird Nightmare," where Hughes reads "Same in Blues," coordinates three scenes of frustrated sexual relationships undone by money or sexual dysfunction. Hughes's reference to "a certain amount of impotence in a dream deferred," in a putatively objective voice—offset and italicized in print and marked by a change in timbre in performance—undermines the supposed hyper-virility of the African American male and of the bluesman. The sexual relation remains a key component of the experience and naming of racial oppression, but the point seems to be that racial oppression undoes the sexual relation.[97] There is no "freedom *from* a confinement associated with women" and no "freedom *to* escape to a world defined by the creativity of men": the two remain connected, here, via nondialectical mediation: each is the other's metaphor.[98] Differences of race, class, gender, sexuality, and different ways of relating to that extraterritorial locality termed "the community" appear liberated from an underlying historical situation—it is a period of flux. Such liberation is ambivalent, but it also defines a moment we retrospectively think of as "the sixties," with its new subjects of history and new internationalisms. Aligning the subjunctive punctualities of improvisation and lyric utterance—the moment, liberated from chronology, from which lyric subjects speak and from which creation begins—Hughes and Mingus continually wrest that moment back to ordinary, historical time. They create a series of moments whose significance comes from the events they constellate, the overlapping nows of different speakers and their implied communities and assumed listeners, and the recursive time—"disc-tortions"—of the phonograph.

As important as the disciplined practice of improvisation is to Mingus and Hughes's collaboration, I hear, or want to hear, in their collaborative work an invitation to reconceive their insistence on the punctual, the now. In different terms, I hear, or want to hear, an inchoate version of Audre Lorde's call to develop new ways to relate across differences.[99] I do not mean to suggest that they are feminist—proto- or otherwise—only that in bringing us to a point of considering the limits of current patterns and imitations of progress new possibilities become not only imaginable but desirable. New possibilities seem immanent in the forms of relation and social poetics whose inadequacy may point to a different set of possibilities. Hughes and Mingus find a different future in and for the present, and we can understand the jazz they embrace as avant-garde practice to be black communist poetics rather than mere style.[100] The *immediacy* of the experience of any improvisation has as its ground an implied inscription, through which a *then* emerges in the *now* of lived time, without the two times being reducible to each other, or to a simple narrative sequence. There is no "as such" to improvisation. The task is to think its implied "we" beyond simple aggregation of present-to-one-another subjects. Thus, improvisation may be thought of as a disavowal of *the* self, insofar as the self is assumed to be singular, present to itself, and persistent through time. This, then, aligns it with the common revolutionary hope for a total reinvention—or at least recasting—of social relations so that existing differences will have to change in the world still to be imagined.

But of "Modern" we must begin to ask,
"What does Modern Mean?" and "What is the
Future?" or "Where Does One Want to Go?"
or "What Does One *Want* to Happen?"
—AMIRI BARAKA, "The Changing Same"

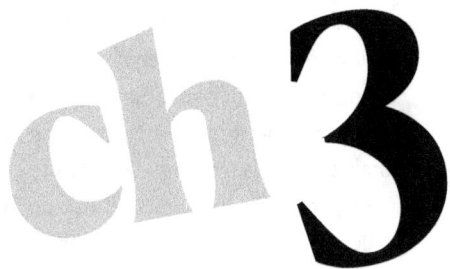

Tomorrow Is the Question!
Amiri Baraka's Poetics for a Post-Revolutionary Age

I take this chapter's epigraph from Baraka's appraisal of Archie Shepp, with whom Baraka would collaborate on a 2001 album, *Live in New York*. Trombonist and co-leader Roswell Rudd (who had collaborated with both Baraka and Shepp during the 1960s), bassist Reggie Workman, and percussionist Andrew Cyrille round out the group. Baraka reads his poem "Funk Lore" as part of a phonopoem entitled "We Are the Blues," which describes a "we" "half here / half gone." Baraka's reading conforms to a twelve-bar blues pattern, elongating and modulating his tone to fit the rhythmic pattern, performing at the threshold of song. Deploying a remarkable array of techniques—including repetition, changes of tempo, and remarkable vocal dexterity—his reading of 208 words takes almost six minutes and maintains a high level of focused intensity the whole time. The temporal dilation creates a sonic space in which one might imaginatively locate oneself in a post-expectant history that includes "12 / bars / like the stripes / of slavery / on / our flag / of skin" and includes "us" as "the 1st / Caucasians."[1] This thematic and performative play registers the crisis of temporality that characterizes much of Baraka's published and recorded work across his career and reflects an uncertainty, to invoke a question he himself popularized, about what time it is. The temptation to understand Baraka as primarily declamatory or hortatory, or to read him in light of nostalgia (or disdain) for an earlier period avoids reading him as an important thinker of the resistance to transformation and the resistance transformation occasions, of the demands and promise of history beyond the narratives of progress with which we contain it.

I draw the term "post-expectant" from Nathaniel Mackey, who uses it to analyze the discrepancy between the dream and its fulfillment or disappointment, the wake of what did not come to be, or the discrepant fulfillment of a desire. This notion frames this chapter's understanding of what Baraka termed the "letdown of a post-revolutionary age."[2] It also helps us glimpse the underlying temporal concerns and anxieties that would increasingly inform his work. "The Revolutionary Theatre," for example, "must take dreams and give them a reality."[3] To give dreams reality—through dramaturgy, representation, or "language ... tightened by the poet's backbone"—is not the same thing as fulfilling them. The discrepancy between revolutionary dreams, hints, impulses, and intuitions and the forms of their fulfillment, defeat, or abandonment is one of this chapter's primary concerns. How do people, including revolutionary artists, navigate pasts and aftermaths, the sense of looming unfinished business and obsolescence that shapes the post-expectant politics and aesthetics that characterize the era that follows "revolutionary times." If the seemingly imminent transformation of black social organization spurred theories and practices of aesthetic production—and aesthetic production *as* social production—how can critics account for a seeming continuity of revolutionary aesthetic techniques even as the questions to which they served as answers are no longer pertinent?[4] One of Baraka's solutions is to engage the past as history and personal/collective inventory mediated by (ambivalent figures of) mass culture. Artifacts of popular culture matter precisely because they are sticking points for broader histories individuals cannot immediately recognize or name. History becomes a set of given texts, distorted by the ideologies that uphold racial capitalism, which serve as a basis for invention.

This chapter cannot do full justice to the complexities of Baraka's politics, which would require, as a beginning, taking seriously Baraka's shift to Third World Marxism and embrace of "Marxism, Leninism, Mao Tse-Tung Thought," best reflected in the transformation of the nationalist Congress of African People (CAP) into the Maoist Revolutionary Communist League, which was related to the New Communist Movement.[5] For the most part, critics have followed Baraka and William J. Harris to designate periods of his aesthetic production—the "Beat" period, the cultural nationalist period, and his final Third World Marxist stage, by far the longest and most productive period of his career and the least studied.[6] Most of these accounts, like accounts of his politics, downplay the Marxism of his post-1974, Third World Marxist period. This chapter primarily addresses his collaborations in that period, especially those on *In the Tradition*, his 1982 collaboration with David Murray and Steve McCall, and his 1999 collaboration with the New York Art Quartet (NYAQ). These periods—"Beat," cultural nationalist, Third World Marxist—roughly mark his evolving ways of theorizing relationships between class, race, the state, capital, imperialism, and ideology. But that development is neither linear nor continuous; it does not follow expected trajectories. Moreover, his poetics do not neatly correspond with his political self-description. Contrary to some powerful critical accounts, his aesthetics and politics appear to be mutually informing. Ideas he formulates in his notes on "The Revolutionary Theater," for example, are present in his earlier poetry. Some of the techniques and concerns of the so-called "Beat" period, which I address through analysis of his 1964 collaboration with the NYAQ and his contemporaneous writing on music, resonate across his career. His phonographic poems across four decades confront readers and listeners with the challenge of understanding and fighting for the present—this despite the eventual marginalization of both his experimental aesthetics, and the more radical forms of black politics supposed to correspond with those aesthetics.

As I observed in the first chapter, Baraka credits sound media with helping to shape his consciousness. Sound media are also central to his mature conception. In a 1980 interview with Harris, he makes a case for the importance of *recorded* sound: "The page doesn't interest me that much—not as much as the actual spoken word. The contradiction with that is that I should be *recording* all the time, which I'm not for obvious reasons. I'm much more interested in the spoken word, and I think that the whole wave of the future is definitely not literary in a sense of books and is tending toward the spoken and the visual."[7] Harris had suggested that Baraka's Marxist poetry pursued an immediacy that made it more score-like, "less, and less about the text" or written word. Pausing to note that scores are themselves written, one might expect Baraka to proclaim the importance of live performance, which comrades such as Larry Neal had associated with "ancient ritual energy."[8] Recordings, however, enable broader circulation and repeated play allows for the kinds of inventive listening that might animate historical latencies. They open onto national and international vernacular avant-garde networks. Having a durable copy that can circulate beyond the immediate bounds of a spatially delimited community is as important to Baraka's aesthetic and political projects as the "content" of the recordings. Critics hoping to develop a full understanding of Baraka's aesthetic and political projects, including his emphasis on "orally conceived" poetry and even "the music," would do well to reconsider the importance of media, both sound and print.[9]

Across several time periods and ideological orientations, Baraka bore witness to the variegated emergence of the present and the ways capitalist novelty and neutralization of past forms mirror erasure. Remembering poorly or partially is tantamount to forgetting. Behind this claim is a sense of what "it" Baraka passed through, and of the key changes not only in his poetics and ideology but in the world around him: the transition from "the sixties" to a post-revolutionary age. Baraka's iconic question "What time is it?" (the answer was "Nation Time!") remains pertinent because the political project of producing a present wherein one might be able to declare readiness at last for revolution is a key to his late poetics. Particularly in his Marxist period, Baraka's strident—even militant—investment in black culture and black particularity, his insistence on blackness as a name (or site—"In America, 'black' is a country") for autonomous production could seem atavistic, "anti-poetic" in the ways John Coltrane was termed "anti-jazz."[10] It is fair, of course, to question what Marxism does for Baraka's poetics, and better to ask whether one can discern a materialist aesthetic theory informed by class antagonism or historical contradiction. However, such questioning should oblige one to engage the work in detail rather that dismissively sneer that Baraka "does not urge an alternative black cosmology" when in fact alternatives accumulate exorbitantly throughout his work, even during his cultural nationalist period (roughly 1965–74).[11] "Black Art," which I discuss in the next section, and "Ka 'Ba," which ends asking "What will be // the sacred words?,"[12] both appear in *Black Magic: Poetry 1961–1967* (1969). Tracking the troubled temporality of his poetry, of which interest in media is one component, I argue that we can in fact observe a surprisingly stable set of aesthetic concerns that persist across quickly changing times and corresponding configurations of the political. I draw out the implicit understanding of capitalist modernity as a crisis of temporality, a crisis of the now, particularly for black people. Citation of the past as *inventory* and (source for/product of) *invention* becomes a strategy bound up with the practice of emphasizing and nurturing alternative black cosmologies that unites Baraka's different periods. By pairing these terms, which share a common etymological root meaning "to come upon," I want to reconcile Baraka's abiding interest in models of selfhood other than bourgeois individualism with the avant-garde techniques he insisted were "contained in the residue of history or in the now-swell of living."[13]

Baraka's work gathers elements of the past and present, articulating them in new forms so that each becomes to an extent deformed by the process. But if we are to understand his contribution to a black radical aesthetic practice and theory, we need to understand how race functions alongside his overall social analysis, which is primarily concerned with processes that divorce art from quotidian practice, or obscure the nature of the quotidian. Insofar as it claims universality, canonical Marxist aesthetic theory assumes the uniformity of society and/or the working classes, which sharply limits its explanatory power and foregrounds the bourgeoisie.[14] (This category overlaps with, but is not the same as the heterogeneous "middle class" of US political argot, which is less a relationship to the means of production than an affective relation to the current order of things.) Here we might see a different theoretical function of *voice* in his thinking, not just as a sign or reflection of racialized presence but the continual *production* of racial difference as inchoate political consciousness, mobilized against the standardizing impulses of mode of life built around the alienation of labor power from the laborer. Conceiving the mediated voice as in the passage cited above or his understanding of poetry as "speech *musicked*" as part of what interrupts that process of separation, we can open new interpretive horizons.[15] But in light of the sense of temporal dislocation discussed above, "speech musicked" is a more radical notion than it might appear. It belongs to a cluster of concepts and affects that borrowing from Walter Benjamin's account of Charles Baudelaire, placing modernity's "shock experience at the very center of his art."[16] It makes perceivable the crisis of experience that, for Baraka as well as for Benjamin, capitalist modernity engenders. The question of time is not just rhetorical. If, for Benjamin, "experience is indeed a matter of tradition, in collective existence as well as private life," capitalist modernity and the racial dispossession whose continual forgetting/misremembering is a condition of its functioning generalize and thus neutralize traditions and the groups to which they belong.[17] The loss and reconstitution of tradition—as a name for coordinating collective and individual lives in history—is a central concern of Baraka's work.[18]

As class divides among black people intensify following the partial incorporation of the black middle class into "mainstream" institutions, "black" stops being able to contain or coordinate the heterogeneous histories, experiences, and practices the characterize people of African descent, especially after nationalism loses its political and epistemological salience amidst the post–World War II global class shuffle. From this perspective, it is easier to contextualize, in Richard Iton's terms, the "anarchist-inflected imagination" that informs the counter-aesthetics and counter-institutions—artist guilds, workshops, and independent record labels—through which black creative intellectuals have improvised alternatives—and alternative modes of attachment—to the national and the nation-state.[19] The modern, including black sound, depends on hidden or obscured colonial relations, and the transition from racial abjection to liberal freedom, historically paired with the waning value of sovereignty as political virtue, has continually meant the spatial and conceptual displacement of dispossession of unfreedom along lines of gender, race, and geographic difference. Slogans such as "black unity" became increasingly contentless (and increasingly commodified) as neocolonialism followed colonialism, bloody proxy wars revealed the limits of allowable freedom in the Cold War context, and many would-be radicals confronted the difficulties of Pan-African organization. Simultaneously, familiar concerns over a growing black bourgeoisie—and black "middle class" as discussed above—resurfaced and informed Baraka's occasionally voluntarist class politics. This underlines the importance of what Baraka often called the artist's "stance," a mode of positioning oneself with respect to old and new conflicts in a changing political landscape. The overall situation, where yesterday's freedom dreams echo unanswerable in today's, registers as a post-expectant tear in the texture of lived time. For Baraka, solutions involve a non-melancholy lingering over the fragments of the past, continually rearranging elements in ways that displace official narratives and their dependencies. This is one way the past functions in Baraka's work: it stands as an abstract individual-collective will to narrative that gathers and orders half-remembered fragments into a graph of collective memory.

Rather than devise plans aimed at the given self's wholeness, Baraka's work moves in the opposite direction, best summarized by his description of the New Black Music: "find the self, then kill it." I take this slogan as a call to give up the versions of (black) selfhood that engender alienation (because they unreflexively reproduce the versions of alienated selfhood inherent to capital) and get down to the "invention of Black Lives."[20] Aldon Nielsen argues that Baraka's poetry works in two simultaneous modes: "One mode gathered up the loose ends and unfinished projects of the modern; the other returned to the modern and located within it new beginnings. The result is a set of aesthetic motions that are at once in the tradition and counter to its direction."[21] To this I would add that the temporal displacement I've characterized prevailed across each of his self-defined periods, so part of that work was also to (re-)invent the tradition. Invoking another of Baraka's great descriptions of the music that influenced him (and that he influenced), he had a playful, "anarchic regard" of tradition. Without mistaking his work as a vanguard to follow—the centrality of agonistic forms of ensemble interaction to his practice may be a necessary check on that tendency—his conceptions and practice of black sound as unruly play in the margins and archives of Western modernity remains generative in its unruliness, in its continual invention of alternatives from within what appear as settled matters.

A Poetics of Liberation

Among his many activities,[22] Baraka tirelessly worked to build the kinds of institutions—artist collectives, workshops, "concert spaces, theaters, clubs, recording companies, publishing companies, and periodicals"—that have helped sustain and nurture radical black art and sensibilities and foster a separate black counter-public sphere.[23] In the field of jazz alone, a number of journals emerged (e.g., the *Cricket* and the *Grackle*)[24] that helped black artists advance, debate, and refine ideas and practices of creative autonomy, often implicitly or explicitly linking aesthetic autonomy and political autonomy. Practically speaking, these alternative institutions constitute the infrastructure through which Baraka and like-minded black creative intellectuals advanced a *poetics of liberation*. "Liberation" here encodes both the promise and threat of a substantive black freedom (about which more below) in the context of the long Black Arts Movement. I'm using the term in its fully ambivalent sense to name the freedom fought for and the "liberation" or disarticulation of race from class struggles. Thus depoliticized, those struggles find themselves, invoking Fredric Jameson, released "to find new modes of social and political expression."[25] Simultaneously, the flux surrounding the authenticating institutions—imagined to be drawn from and to reflect the "collective experience of marginal pockets of the social life of the world system"—was partially rooted in a growing skepticism toward the idea of collective experience, and therefore rendered the idea of a large-scale aesthetic project problematic.[26] The alternate institutions Baraka championed and facilitated, in and beyond the 1960s, operated in uneasy conjunction with other institutions, including the mainstream press and universities that hosted aesthetically and politically radical black artists. Yet Baraka's institutions were necessary for black artists whose work sought and stimulated what Baraka termed "some other kind of thought."[27] Baraka's collaborative sound recordings enable the dissemination and potential re-experiencing of "the emotions ... some of them completely new" as the aesthetic basis for new concepts and avenues of thought.[28]

The term *freedom* and its cognates surround the New Black Music and "New Black Poetry" of the long Black Arts era. Some orienting references include Sonny Rollins's 1958 *Freedom Suite*, Max Roach's explicitly political *Freedom Now* suite (1960), and of course Ornette Coleman's 1961 *Free Jazz*. One touchstone is the unfolding postwar Civil Rights Movement, occasionally termed the Freedom Movement. What if we understand the discursive, intellectual, and aesthetic commitment to freedom among people who'd never experienced it as transcending the bounds of the existing social order, including the centrality of the transformed nation-state as the *telos* of imaginable political transformation? What if, in a different register, we aligned such commitment with the unthinkable itself: forms of individuality and social organization that transcend the "intimate affiliation of liberty and bondage," that articulate "freedom independent of constraint or personhood and autonomy separate from the sanctity of property and proprietorial notions of the self"?[29] Such a reading would return to the Black Arts era its anarchic, refigurative force, allowing us to hear the continued reverberation of what may yet prove necessary.

To imagine a robust black freedom requires methodological attention to the contingent practices of freedom (and attending ways of imagining selfhood, touched on in the next chapter), and conceiving of "the present" as something other than the past's future or fulfillment. If the Black Arts critique of the West largely remained somewhat diffuse, its most robust version of human freedom nonetheless illuminates the new and influential forms of ensemble interplay that shift the basis of improvisation from the virtuosic "solo flight" that defines an ensemble as an aggregate of individuals to the thicker forms of communion that characterize the New Black Music.[30] More broadly, the "revolutionary moment" of the Black Power era provides a brief opening out beyond the horizons of what Saidiya Hartman has called the "burdened individuality" that defines emancipation for black subjects, who are "self-possessed and indebted, equal and inferior, liberated and encumbered, sovereign and dominated, citizen and subject."[31]

Here, then, I will offer a sense of the relationship between invention and inventory as they move toward the unburdened individuality at stake in Baraka's vernacular avant-garde practice. I'll offer two citations, one already invoked. In his liner notes for John Coltrane's *Live at Birdland*, Baraka writes, "If you can hear, this music will make you think a lot of weird and wonderful things. You might even become one of them."[32] In *Blues People* he writes, "Music, as paradoxical as it might seem, is the result of thought. It is the result of thought perfected at its most empirical, *i.e.*, as *attitude*, or *stance*. Thought is largely conditioned by reference; it is the result of consideration or speculation against reference, which is largely arbitrary."[33] Synthesizing these statements, the music does not give listeners symbols or directives, but gives them objective confirmation of their own thinking. Music, in other words, is the result not only of musicians' thinking but also of listeners'. The musical act has two components. First, there is the materiality of the sound itself (pitch, duration, intensity, rhythm, and so on) within a context where the sounds seem to refer to one another in one musical text. Either memory or sound media—what he calls "artifacts" or, elsewhere, "rumors"—serve as more or less durable and stable references confirming that some sound happened.[34] Next, listeners and musicians must connect their own experiences and memories to a broader set of references that they consider or speculate against, creating the sense of where the music has come from (an inventory of tradition[s]) and where it might be going. Musician and critic need not agree: Baraka's account, in fact, strongly suggests their separation, making tradition itself a matter of emergence rather immanence, something produced or happened upon rather than an empirical property of things. The music, thus, does not directly affect the attitude or stance (although the experience, even imperfectly recalled via phonographic or other recording, "can place you somewhere a long way off from anything ugly").[35] Here again the phrasing matters: it can "place" a listener away from ugliness, but it does not displace ugliness. As Theodor Adorno puts it, "the social alienation of music . . . cannot be corrected within music, but only within society: through the change of society."[36] Listening is a creative act, and it inspires creation, which in turn implicitly requires removing whatever blocks beauty. Adorno's worries that jazz and other aesthetic forms whose modern emergence coincides with the culture industry would necessarily corrupt themselves parallel Baraka's own concerns across the body of his jazz criticism. What could not be co-opted was the music's "valid separation and anarchic disregard of"[37] Western aesthetic ideals, popular and otherwise, its "attitude or stance," its participation in what Julian Mayfield has termed "the business of making revolution" that transcends or motivates technical advances.[38] A revolutionary change of society would bring about the conditions of a truly revolutionary music, rather than vice versa. The avant-garde was a kind of rough draft for the music—and society—to come.

Returning to *Blues People* can help us develop an account of the music that was so often model or analogue for Baraka's poetics of liberation. Through analogy, historical analysis, and sociological argument, Baraka wanted to make critics of jazz and blues—"Negro music"—responsible for a larger history of black life without simply melting jazz as commercial form into a general US or Western culture. As he would argue in his essay "Jazz and the White Critic," to study black music adequately would require different paradigms from those developed to evaluate European art music.[39] Baraka rejects a reading of jazz as a projection of or resource for US democracy (although, ambiguously, he would later refer to it as "American classical music").[40] Instead, he claims it as an authentically particular cultural production rooted in the historical and persistent exclusion of black people from public life. The importance of black music lies in its resistance to the push toward homogeneity (e.g., the "melting" of older ethnic identities into a singular American identity) that drove in both positive and negative terms the domestic ideologies through which the United States normalized its emergence as a global superpower.[41] Although Baraka's arguments in *Blues People* rhyme with other midcentury critiques of mass culture of the 1950s, I think something more is at stake than what John Gennari calls a "racialized version of existential hip."[42] His earliest collections repeatedly interrogate the difference that race and processes of racialization make, and the intersection of race and affect in the individual psyche. On the cusp of desegregation, one of the questions *Blues People* asks is what role black people and culture could play in ongoing debates; it asks readers to consider the implications of social homogenization for those historically excluded from full political and social participation. From that perspective, Baraka's critique of what he saw as the vapidity of contemporary society doubled as a call to other black cultural producers.

Blackness—which in *Blues People* is at once historically specific and transhistorical, predicated in materialist and idealist terms—represents a particularity not yet absorbed into "mainline" American culture or capitalism's homogenizing project. Remembering Baraka as a preeminent poet and thinker of alienation (I'm thinking of early poems such as "An Agony. As Now" with its Du Boisian overtones), blackness also offers here and would continue to offer a paradoxical transcendental rootedness as a balm or salve against the objective conditions of deprivation and deracination he analyzes throughout *Blues People* and elsewhere. Transcendental rootedness is a theoretical (and therapeutic) response to the conditions of possibility that create and require black culture as, for him, untethered to any nation-state. Paul Gilroy's account of the music of the African diaspora here is apt: "What was initially felt to be a curse—the curse of homelessness or the curse of forced exile—gets repossessed. It becomes affirmed and is reconstructed as the basis of a privileged standpoint from which certain useful and critical perceptions about the modern world become more likely."[43] It also, Gilroy continues, "represents a response to the successive displacements, migrations and journeys (forced and otherwise) which have come to constitute these black cultures' special conditions of existence."

Yet in contrast with black modernists of the previous generation (e.g., James Reese Europe, Will Marion Cook, and Black Swan Records founder Harry Pace), Baraka was skeptical of attempts to "refine" black "folk" traditions into high art on the European model. Simultaneously, he broke both with the New

Negro generation's desire to make art that would win white society's esteem, and ultimately rejected that generation's investments in individuality as a solution to racial antagonisms. He considered black culture protection *against* an increasingly dehumanized, mechanized and alienated society, which is to say he theorized black culture as opposition to that society and took affirmation of that opposition to be both politically and aesthetically necessary. His class critique is indistinguishable from his concern over the degree to which black people have acclimated to "the sinister vapidity of mainline American culture." In such a situation, "separation from, and anarchic disregard of, Western popular forms" become not only "valid" but a political obligation *if the art is to be of use*.[44] Indeed, Baraka defines black art as a permanent avant-garde, an insurgent practice of self-authorized outfulness.

In his famously caustic review of *Blues People*, Ralph Ellison rejected what he saw as that book's unduly "sociological" framing. Although he had his own normative sense of what constitutes legitimate black culture, Ellison most strenuously objected to Baraka's claim for black separateness from the "mainstream" of US society.[45] In their divergent appraisals of a particular ensemble, the Modern Jazz Quartet (MJQ), which featured John Lewis on piano, Milt Jackson on vibraphone, Percy Heath on bass, and Connie Kay on percussion, the terms of their disagreement become clearer. The MJQ rose to fame primarily through its affiliation with the so-called "Third Stream," a movement that self-consciously appropriated elements from "classical" music. Baraka critiqued such aesthetic developments perhaps most clearly in his assessment of fusion, where his description of "the funk bottom or rhythm . . . harnessed gently to the cooled-off top or melodic and harmonic lines" served as an image of integration-as-incorporation. Such thinking also informed his criticisms of the MJQ: he recognized Lewis as a fine player of the blues and declared the MJQ "has been responsible for some of the most exciting jazz of the last few years." Baraka tempered this praise with criticism of "Lewis's attempts to 'combine' classical music and jazz" as aesthetic rather than categorical failures.[46] For Baraka, to make jazz appeal to popular tastes in this way would signal the "*final* dilution of Afro-American musical tradition[s]"[47] that Baraka's anti-incorporation arguments sought to avoid. Ellison's criticism was less conciliatory: "There is even a morbid entertainment value in watching the funereal posturing of the Modern Jazz Quartet"; part of the fascination was "the anticipation that during some unguarded moment, the grinning visage of the traditional delight-maker . . . will emerge from behind those bearded masks."[48] Both Ellison and Baraka emphasize the necessity of thinking black performance in the context of both capitalist exchange and racial domination, assigning the maintenance of racial specificity both ethical and aesthetic value. The question is not whether black artists engage "European" sources—both see the "liberation" and rearticulation of European aesthetics as a precondition of modern art. The question is whether they do so imaginatively, whether it guards against (Ellison) or facilitates (Baraka) the transformation of black traditions. The past and traditions exist as resources, but the ends to which they are to be used remains an open question.

Their deeper and related disagreement is the status of the nation-state, for there they most sharply diverge over the meanings and obligations of black aesthetics. Considering the larger context—which includes the Freedom Movement (Ellison's preferred term for the Civil Rights Movement), mid-century pressure toward homogenization and against cultural or racial particularity, *and* the Cold War's mapping of legitimate politics—the discussion of black music allowed intellectual cover for a more thoroughgoing critique of the thin grammars of US freedom and citizenship. In *Blues People*'s opening pages, Baraka proclaims the book a "strictly theoretical endeavor" that proceeds "by means of analogy and some attention to historical example, to establish certain general conclusions about a particular segment of American society." The status of the enslaved individual is a key point of contention: the enslaved and their descendants, as a class, Baraka argues, can never be incorporated, whereas Ellison, emphasizing individual aspiration and self-understanding, argues that the culture of the enslaved imprints every aspect of public life, so much so that it is a fundamentally American culture.[49] Recalling Saidiya Hartman's argument that "the advent of freedom marked the transition from the pained and minimally sensate existence of the slave to the burdened individuality of the responsible and encumbered freedperson," Ellison emphasizes the individuality, while Baraka stresses the burden.[50] Yet that burden, that outsider status, in a familiar move, grants the music "most closely associated with [black people]: blues and a later, but parallel development, jazz" authentic autonomy from "the sinister vapidity of mainline American culture." In this, Baraka resolves the tension between aesthetic production rooted in "the people" and a rigorously autonomous art by declaring the permanent autonomy of the people. If their autonomy seems lost to capitalist projects, the fact that it ever existed means one can return to it; it can appear in the present as a flash from the past that illuminates new pathways for the future. The music thus becomes an allegory, or a constellation of allegories that are all in some way metonymic for freedom: "what is soulful expresses not a metaphysical freedom as the *surfaces* of the old spirituals did, but speaks to the liberation of a living people (just as many of the old spirituals did, laying on more symbol as well)."[51] Liberated from the assurances and promises of an earlier era, and from an era's fealty to a post-expectant future, these practices continue to hold a capacity to indicate a new point of departure for something yet to emerge.

Here in the World

I turn now to a brief analysis of Baraka's much discussed and enigmatic poem "Black Art," which is often taken to be an *ars poetica*. Its enigmatic nature derives from its being at once programmatic and evasively unprogrammatic; it arguably sees social transformation as the spur to aesthetic revolution rather than vice versa. Yet, as we see in the unfolding of his debate with Ralph Ellison, the more uncertain the status of blackness as theoretically distinct becomes, the more insistent are Baraka's claims to it—both as historical specificity and as unrealized capacity. In this light, we can read "Black Art" as primarily a prefigurative attempt to *make* black art, something wholly invented, that will "Let Black People understand that they . . . Are poems & poets & / all the loveliness here in the world."[52] The poem exemplifies the processes of invention and inventory as I have been discussing them, offering an inventory of possibilities for what a poem can be and do in order to "clean out the world for virtue and love" and invent new possibilities for black life. Its 1965 publication as a sonic text prior to its initial print publication in *Liberator* (1966) reveals, as Howard Rambsy II argues, "Baraka's cutting-edge commitment to utilizing audio production as a means of transmitting verse."[53] Transmission, allowing this poem and "Black Dada Nihilismus" to "change the drawing rooms into places where real things can be said about a real world, or into smoky rooms where the destruction of Washington can be plotted," is part of both the aesthetics and politics of these works.[54]

"Black Art" is one of the four tracks on percussionist Sunny Murray's album *Sonny's Time Now* (featuring Don Cherry on trumpet, Albert Ayler on tenor saxophone, Henry Grimes and Lewis Worrell on bass, and Murray), which was distributed by Baraka's own Jihad Records. (The other titles on the album are similarly abstract: "Virtue," "Justice," and "The Lie.") The phonopoem opens with an out-of-time, three-note mock-heraldic motif, played twice. Wit, rarely acknowledged, characterizes the music and Murray's physical approach to "Rhythm as occurrence. As natural emphasis."[55] Carter Mathes describes the opening as "rushed, as if the listener has been thrust into a scene's frantic climax," and the piece retains that intensity while remaining relatively spare, ludic in its conception.[56] The playfulness marks its attempt to decenter, from within, the norms governing the music. One must listen beyond the aesthetic norms that, say, Charles Mingus championed (continuity, recapitulation, recursive form),[57] to hear continuity with Mingus's project. However, Grimes and Worrell apparently lay out during Baraka's reading. Without the bottom, the music attains a spaciousness, an emphasis on breath that for some listeners might recall the open field poetics so influential to Baraka. This is "free jazz," but it has little in common with the churning, roiling, raucous spirituality of John Coltrane's late groups with Pharoah Sanders and Alice Coltrane, which have little do with early Ornette Coleman's advanced bebop. For that matter, the playing on *Sonny's Time Now* does not resemble the independent work of either Ayler (whose 1965 *Spiritual Unity* would feature Murray and bassist Gary Peacock) or Don Cherry, who would record and release his first album as leader, *Complete Communion*, the following year. Under Murray's leadership, the music emphasizes unusual timbres, subtle group interaction, and an exploration of free space and time presented as a continual break that treats even the discography of Ornette Coleman and Cecil Taylor—with whom Cherry and Murray, respectively, first emerged—as a historical text to be unwritten and rewritten. When Baraka begins reading, his voice startles not just because of the surprise of hearing a human voice calmly intone against the faux heraldry, but also because the pitch and timbre of his voice is so distinct from Cherry's trumpet and Ayler's extended-technique whine. Murray's cymbals create a sense of space rather than rhythmic propulsion. The microphone sounds too close. Plosives pop; voice doubles as irregular percussion. To the degree that "Black Art" is an instance of black art in process, rather than a blueprint for creating black art, the phonopoem is an ideal realization of a work moving beyond the solace of the figurative or lyrical.

Discussing the poem in the context of Baraka's ideological shift following his trip to Cuba, William J. Harris argues, "In the late 1950s Baraka was drawn to the white avant-garde in art because its celebration of the imagination reflected his own valorization of fantasy. As he became more and more involved in the world of black politics and the economic and social reality, however, he had to reconsider the importance of the creative imagination."[58] I am unpersuaded, however, that "Baraka wanted to place real objects in his poems to create a black world that would *reflect* the lives of black people."[59] On the page and in performance, the poem has recourse to onomatopoeia—Baraka's imitative airplane complemented by Don Cherry's imitation air siren—which seems to acknowledge the poem's limitations as agent, while also acknowledging the material limits on the creative imagination "here in the world." If we understand "reflection" in the idealist sense—to embody and participate in the "essence" or spirit of black life, which accords with his apparent understanding of black music in *Blues People* and *Black Music*—the sheer diversity of things, not to mention forms and aspects of life in the poem, suggests Baraka may have been on his way to considering the ways the world forms consciousness rather than vice versa. This is just to say that the transition Harris identifies may have been more profound than he states. Baraka, in his proto-nationalist phase, would likely have found the notion of reflection—the theoretical position that aesthetic objects and practices "express" underlying social phenomena or realities as their truth in a more or less mechanistic and causal manner—unobjectionable. But to the degree that reflection involves the movement of the contemplative subject's mind, it's difficult to square with the blunt physicality "Black Art" ascribes to poetry ("teeth or trees or lemons piled / on a step"), a physicality the phonopoem achieves through layered literary and musical reference. Neither the phonopoem nor the printed poem express blackness as a collective ethos. Both proclaim need for invention adequate to blackness as it will extend into the future.

Most profoundly, the poem is worried about forms of sociality that might be structured around the invaluable, around the displacement of value: the acts of violence it describes, after all, may be retributive response to local strife in segregated cities, but it is also nonproductive. Note the pun, the reference to "black magic," with its claims to conjure, to transmute material properties, to generate alternative values. The proximity of blackness to (market) value, to thingliness, is at once the historical problem that informed much of Baraka's thinking, and one way of parsing the "we" as re-marking and refusing imposed forms of individuation and denied capacity to individuate. Capitalist societies are organized around the production of value, so imagining new forms of value and society, if not revolutionary, occupies a position difficult to grasp and as such effects a syncope in the rhythms of the ordinary. The specific objects and activities "Black Art" names belong to a fantasy construction so idiosyncratic and repellent—shocking—that it is difficult to hear its first part as anything other than an affirmation of the black rebellion many whites (and "middle class" black people) desired and feared.

Read in the context of the new inventory of "African" polyrhythms alongside the sounds, sentiments, and symbols of the African American church that characterize the New Black Music, people may well have heard emergence in Raymond Williams's sense, an example of "those alternative acts and alternative intentions which are not yet articulated as a social institution or even project."[60] Emergence might double as a new inventory that becomes the basis for those alternative acts and intentions, a resolution of the crisis of experience that shapes the black experience of modernity. This is the perspective from which, in Werner Sollors's terms, "poetry must die so that the poem can kill," provided that we understand "poetry," like Larry Neal's "text," to be one of the things the poem attempts to kill.[61] The world the poem announces and pursues waits in such not-yet-organized spaces of civil society, and represents the effort to overcome racial reification, a problem of social reproduction informed by the relative autonomy of racial antagonisms from broader class struggles.

The poem concludes, "We want a black poem. And a / Black World. / Let the world be a Black Poem." The conflict between the expressive and the inventive in the poem shapes its social poetics: aesthetic practices and objects oriented toward the black world to come. The question is not just how to know but how to *use* the past, and what to do, after the kairological event of Black Art (a metonym for a revolutionary revaluing of black life) with those who will be incompatible with the new "black world." Care for, attention to, and construction around such revenants—an obligation to what slips determination in graphs of communal spirit or progress—structures Baraka's poetics of liberation.

Taking Hazel Carby's argument that "music embodies *but also produces* the social values of its time," we might contribute to a more general understanding of the major rhythmic shifts initiated by funk, on the one hand, and by free jazz, on the other. Taken together, these provide a way to hear the temporal disjunction the ensemble produces under Murray's leadership.[62] I argue above that this moment—when declarations of new black music and poetry coincided with the calls for "liberation," organized protests, and spontaneous mass uprisings across US cities—revealed and emerged from an unprecedented shift in the structures of racial thought and feeling (and of the administration of racial differences). It is tempting to read Sunny Murray's (and other percussionists', such as Milford Graves's) exploration of rhythmic concepts that evade regular patterns and meters as allegorical expression of the unease of the uncertain moment. The time is free because skepticism toward teleologies of progress make people question metronomic propulsion as a way of relating to one another. However, I think Baraka's sense that these musical experiments with time and timing represented a (re)turn to something more vital (in line with, for example, Mingus's rotary perception) provides a needed check on allegorical readings. The ensemble's tone is often mocking, their interplay loose. Cherry, for example, seems not to anticipate that Ayler will repeat the opening gesture and ends up slightly out of sync. The phonopoem is evocative, even antic in its deformation of military music (which is characteristic of Ayler's approach, and also legible through Sunny Murray's innovations as a drummer) and in Cherry's occasional echoes of bebop melodic patterns. The text is similarly ludic. Alongside Baraka's mockery of the "middle class"—affectively oriented toward the nation-state's and capitalism's perpetuation—cloaked in justly criticized misogyny, the poem also ridicules the class strata responsible for social management: "the Liberal / Spokesman for jews," and three "negro-leaders." Rather than a model of democracy, this ensemble effectively refuses hierarchy, approaching even the recently emergent traditions of black music with anarchic regard.

In utopian accounts, the social ensemble selects moments from the past and present to revisit, revise, reimagine, or let pass, and through that critical activity reconceives the possibilities of being together. The phonopoem "Black Art" stops short of this last step. It names a future poem that will make black people conscious of their "loveliness"—their lovability, the validity of their attachments to this world and each other. However, its excoriation of black leaders, "mulatto bitches," and "slick halfwhite politicians"—indeed, its indecision between the concepts that poems *are* black people (and vice versa) and that poems *do* (black?) things—destabilizes the meanings of blackness and poetry. Its model of ambivalent attachment represents continuity with, rather than a break from, Baraka's concerns in "Black Dada Nihilismus," which he had recorded the previous year with the New York Art Quartet (NYAQ).

Dimensions of Invention

Against the grain of scholarly narratives that suggest that Baraka's radicalization represents a sharp break, I will show that "Black Dada Nihilismus" contains a revolutionary energy continuous with "Black Art" and with his concerns in his music writing about reification. Reification, in Adorno and Horkheimer's analysis of the culture industry, casts already alienated social relations in aesthetic terms, the better to create libidinal investments in consumer goods, and in consumption itself. Adorno valorized bourgeois art while Baraka stressed vernacular aesthetic practices that engaged the culture industries without being wholly determined by them. But they each stress a separate, critical, subversive aesthetic domain contingently removed from capital's homogenizing processes. Concern over specifically racialized forms of reification resurface in the later poems this chapter examines: "Class Struggle in Music" and his reunion with members of the NYAQ. I will focus especially on "Black Dada Nihilismus's" use of lists and its famous concluding inventory of famous and infamous black people. That inventory allows him to confront readers and listeners, particularly black readers and listeners, with the shock of unresolved problems from the past, which it shows to be fully implicated in the modern. If the threat of reification—particularly of signs and symbols of black protest—

implicitly underwrites the proliferation of non-commodifiable stances and acts listed in "Black Art," it plays no less decisive a role in "Black Dada Nihilismus."

Given that even the most radical black expressions were subject to commodification, as Baraka well knew, we might understand the threat of commodification, along with his desire to fit into established norms of poetry reading (to which his friend Allen Ginsberg presented one powerful alternative), as one reason for his preferred reading style at this point.[63] What he says of alto saxophonist John Tchicai, a member of the New York Art Quartet, applies to his own reading: "His tone is dry, acrid, incisive; his line spare and lean, like himself; and his phrasing at times reminds one of Mondrian's geometrical decisions, or lyrical syllogisms."[64] As Aldon Nielsen observes, the "terrifying tensions" of "Black Dada Nihilismus" depend on "the dissonance between the apocalyptic words of the poem and the almost overly calm fashion in which Baraka reads it."[65] (One might also consider in these terms Malcolm X's speeches, which began appearing on record around this period. His calm incisiveness could seem counter to his incendiary content, and certainly distinct from the preacherly tradition against which people would hear him.) Moreover, relatively quiet intensity built from incrementally added elements in a harmonically and rhythmically open context typifies the ensemble's style. The phonopoem is a group effort. Rather than creating an atmosphere of freedom shaped by intensity and duration, the NYAQ makes dynamic use of ensemble interplay through which it generates an almost conversational sense of tension and release, sound and silence.

The printed version of "Black Dada Nihilismus" appeared in Baraka's *The Dead Lecturer* in 1964, the same year he recorded the poem with the NYAQ (Congolese-Danish saxophonist John Tchicai, white trombonist Roswell Rudd, African American Lewis Worrell and Jamaican-born Milford Graves on bass and percussion, respectively) on their self-titled debut album, released on Bernard Stollman's ESP-Disk. The NYAQ's playing is abstract, defined by open space and supple interaction rather than the lengthy harmonic explorations of Coltrane's late period, the advanced bebop of Ornette Coleman's early quartet, or Cecil Taylor's lyrical physicality. Their aesthetic has more in common with the spacious approach rooted in advanced harmony and a relatively free approach to time that characterized, say, the Art Ensemble of Chicago. Such an approach, rather than privileging soloists, tends to create improvisational eddies where musicians operating with maximum independence within the group concept occasionally intersect to produce spontaneous counterpoint and countermelodies. According to Baraka, there was no fixed plan for the reading: "It was just look at this poem; this is what I want to do."[66] Reading into Baraka's statement, it is likely that he shared the poem and approached them with a sonic concept. Their performance, which uses Roswell Rudd's composition "Sweet V" as its basis, shows a profound engagement between Baraka and the NYAQ. The piece has two sections. In the first, Baraka reads alongside Worrell and Graves, who create a sonic landscape that does not so much illustrate as it complicates the text. In the second, Tchicai and Rudd play and improvise around a boppish theme whose triplets, paired with their just-off unison, creates the effect of stumbling, of being borne along toward a place to conclude but not to end or rest (i.e., harmonically resolve).

Fred Moten frames his reading of the printed poem through a question: "What does it mean to suffer from political despair when your identity is bound up with utopian political aspirations and desires?" Despair, for Moten, refers to the tragic dimension of Baraka's work, or more precisely to his way of laboring in the wake of the "unsayable claims of black utopian political desire, an unrequited love after the fact."[67] From this perspective, Moten reads "Black Dada Nihilismus" in terms of "the absence, the irrecoverability of an originary and constitutive event; the impossibility of a return to an African, the impossibility of an arrival at an American, home."[68] From there he moves into a meditation on the relations between tragedy, elegy, and improvisation; that is, elegy mourns for the lost or longed-for home that conditions tragedy, while improvisation allows for an experience of what exceeds the oppositions—for example, of Africa and America, impossible abstractions—that engender such longing. Moten's reflections are at once a heterodox and, perversely, commonsensical way of outlining a genealogy of Africa American "(re)visions of Enlightenment formulations of universality and freedom."[69] Yet, I think the poem reverses Moten's implied temporality, presenting despair as anticipatory, unrequited love *before* the fact—thus engendering a crisis of temporality. "Black Dada Nihilismus" enacts a drama of seeking, and failing to find, new vocabularies and ways of relating across difference. It adds new ambivalence over the mass forms that create virtual or "imagined" community among those whose only connection is their shared investment in texts mediated by the culture industries. After all, the poem begins with misplaced punctuation—a period that apparently links the final, unpunctuated sentence to the beginning (this is an effect Rudd's melody line nearly duplicates: its final note is a semitone away from the first).[70] The poem expresses an anticipatory loss, a shaken faith, even as it strains after versions of community and solidarity that exceed thinkable forms of sociality.

Both Baraka's poem and Rudd's composition have two sections and use vernacular gestures (Rudd's bluesy descending triplet figure, Baraka's interjection "got it, *Baby!*") to announce a conclusion.[71] The poem's first section outlines a set of questions that either upends the notion of the poem as expression of subjective experience, or suspends the link between sensual experience, cultural experience, and knowledge. It traces a fragmentary process of observation and position taking, interrelating racially particular sensory experience and utterance in a landscape whose symbols have been stripped of their habitual associations. Signifiers appear in a jumble, either unmoored from or too close to their referents: the church ("protestant love") with its stained glass windows recalls Piet Mondrian, but also (presumably) the Stations of the Cross. Jesus's crucifixion in turn evokes the Holocaust ("ugly silent deaths of jews")—and a profane image of "sacrifice" for the sake of a certain vision of the human—which in turn resolves into the more mundane figure of surgery-enabled assimilation, a kind of racial self-sacrifice, which in turn conjures images of assimilated black people. This signifying chain finally rests on Hermes Trismegistus, the Greek god of magic and writing whom the poem credits with creating "the blacker art." Hermes is the very figure of the hermeneutics, and as such is invoked as if to comment on both the desire for a new signifying logic and the alienating enclosure of the speaker's consciousness from others in what is a radically de-peopled landscape.

Reification—the transformation of subjects into objects knowable and legible only through exchange that here has an ambiguous racial element—drives the poem's implied fragmentation. The poem reduces sense experience to a congeries of encounters, associations, and positions without a master code, a set of hyper-material signifiers disconnected from a stable signifying structure. Yet the suspension of the signifying structure in the first part of the poem is also the revolutionary desire of the poem to understand things otherwise. Here, the importance of the music, reflective of an important tendency of the free music in general, merits comment. The ensemble's move away from traditional song and musical structures enables new relationships between players (including Baraka's voice, featured as if he were a soloist). From moment to moment, the musicians imply tonality, tempos, and rhythmic feel, but they shape their performance, as Nielsen demonstrates, around the thematic and rhythmic content of Baraka's reading. "[T]he musicians on the *New York Art Quartet* recording," he argues, "sound as if they have not only listened to Baraka's poem but have taken positions inside its stanzas from which to elaborate their contribution to the new ensemble structure built upon the poem."[72] In other words, Baraka, Worrell, and Graves create a space within which collective consciousness emerges through constructive, anticipatory listening.

Both music and the primarily visual world evoked in the poem's first section are audible as a set of deliberative thoughts and negotiations of sound and silence. An additional sense of "free time," of overlapping co-temporal black performance traditions, governs the concluding dedication-as-litany:

> For tambo, willie best, dubois, patrice, mantan, the
> bronze buckaroos.
>   For Jack Johnson, asbestos, tonto, buckwheat,
>   billie holiday.
>   For tom russ, l'overture, vesey, beau jack,
> (may a lost god damballah, rest or save us
> against the murders we intend
> against his lost white children
> black dada nihilismus

The list blends familial (Tom Russ, Baraka's grandfather), public, and legendary figures. It mixes archetypes of black inferiority (Buckwheat, Asbestos) with those of black self-esteem and revolution (W. E. B. Du Bois, Patrice Lumumba, Toussaint Louverture, Denmark Vesey); figures of art (Billie Holiday—the only woman, and the only musician) with those of entertainment (*Bronze Buckaroo* star Herb Jeffries, comedians Willie Best and Mantan Moreland, boxers Beau Jack and Jack Johnson).[73] To list in this way is to appropriate a past that includes the fallen, understood as neither pure victims nor pure heroes, as if to overcome temporal unease in favor of the open space-time of imagination. But that creative space is never empty; invention, in contrast with *ex nihilo* creation, always draws on the given world. Rather than read the inventory as a recuperation of the black entertainer from the overdeterminations of the minstrel stage (and thus to read Black Dada Nihilismus as a kind of avenging angel figure), we might better understand it through the lens of ambivalence and (the fear of) complicity. Rather than engaging a fantasy of the subject's auto-intelligibility, the poem decomposes intelligibility into the fragments of ambivalent attachments to a past and a people. Returning to an earlier argument, we might further understand the poem to seek alternative forms of subjectivity and freedom. Such a reading would make it clearer how this work rhymes with Baraka's contemporaneous poems' interest in suicide, and even his anti-programmatic call to "find the self, then kill it." Temporal unease, here manifest through a gathering of living and dead ancestors from the distant and recent past, articulates the disruptions inherent in modernity. Likewise, Worrell and Graves's interaction with Baraka creates a space at once resonant and lacking familiar markers of stable rhythm or tonality. Imagining "freedom independent of constraint or personhood and autonomy separate from the sanctity of property and proprietorial notions of the self" leaves us, at the end of the poem, uncertain where we stand or what comes next.[74]

Part of the point, then, is the inability to imagine what kind of art, society, or subjectivity would follow the pseudo-cathartic or proto-revolutionary violence. Baraka's performative reticence, like the restraint of other ensemble members, creates its own unreleased tension, and in that way refuses the lure of marketable rebellion. Worrell and Graves's interaction with Baraka creates an uncanny resonance, at once familiar and lacking familiar markers of stable rhythm or tonality. The phonopoem is a tapestry of concentrated, anticipatory listening whose overall effect is a graph of inventive interiority that transforms uncertain waiting into strategic inaction. The poem creates a space of invention, a site where one might produce the present by lifting past fragments from the narratives that usually link them. If part of Baraka's concern is the "co-optation and commodification of aesthetic modernity represented by the transformation of the conflictual elements of modernism into the official culture"—particularly, in a context where the divide between high and low culture was becoming at once less meaningful and more strenuously policed—his response is to create a "blacker art" from the ruins of the culture and its unburied dead.[75]

While Baraka's earliest work may present an alienated, "transgressive" interiority,[76] the poems of *The Dead Lecturer*, "Black Dada Nihilismus" in particular, mark a transition to new formal strategies and political concerns that predate Malcolm X's assassination—strategies and concerns, in other words, that scholars tend to point to as spur to Baraka's embrace of black nationalism. If instead of Malcolm X's assassination our periodization instead foregrounds his trip to revolutionary Cuba, as Cynthia Young urges, we can better situate the Beat period in the context of global and domestic liberation struggles that mark the rise of a global middle class, the sudden availability of new frontiers of capitalist expansion.[77] Amid the continued appropriation of racial markers to be disseminated by the culture industry and analyzed by a primarily white commentary class, by 1964 Baraka faced both racial reification and racial dislocation among white liberal friends who were committed to ignoring politics.[78] Readings of "Black Dada Nihilismus" tend to emphasize the speaker's call to "black dada nihilismus" to "come down" in order, as Kimberly Benston argues, "to regenerate a sanctified collectivity from the conditions of defilement";[79] or they see the poem as an early attempt to generate a cathartic free jazz "scream" in poetry. Yet on the record, the relative restraint of both Baraka and ensemble suggests that regeneration may turn out to be a sonorous event. One reaches the end of the printed poem to find the final punctuation withheld, which makes the end a point of departure for the phonopoem's next wordless movement. An apparent mode of continual ascesis—"find the self, then kill it"—simultaneously traces a process of materialization that reduces identities to objects that relate to one another and impersonal processes of reproduction. Overall, the phonopoem makes a tentative claim to modes of sociality not yet subsumed by capitalist spectacle.

While the poem primarily moves through a distressed subjectivity unable to make sense of the visual world, a vernacular call—"got it, *Baby!*"—sets up its inventory of unaccountable, illegible, undercommon forms of blackness now revalued as spiritually or politically salvific. If invention—the act of rearticulating the past in the present as disruption rather than continuity—is at stake, perhaps it is subjectivity itself being invented: as ear- rather than eye-based, and as flowing from intersubjective rather than individual experience. Sound's circulation within and beyond existing economies of circulation and value, from this perspective, is crucial to this poem's staging of the new black music as a blacker, unappropriable art.

Though Baraka wavered between seeing music as community-based art and commodity, depending on which performers or tendencies he analyzed, its abstract value lay in his view that aurality falls outside a more general logic of alienation and reification. Listening thus becomes a site of production, an act capable of producing particular affective-intellectual responses such as a feeling of being home in the world. Like "Black Dada Nihilismus," "A Poem for Willie Best" uses the vernacular to pose "the whole question of how does one relate realistically to one's environment if one feels estranged from one's environment and especially a black person in a white situation."[80] That makes the function of the inventory in "Black Dada Nihilismus," its blend of the heroic and the abject, even more ambiguous. In context, we might read the figures in that list as ambivalent household gods whose seeming omnipresence demands some offering, a beginning, the revolutionary end of the world. Like Billie Holiday (the only woman, and perhaps the least co-opted) they are all figures one imagines a young Baraka encountering at home or at the homes of friends and relatives—in that utopian sense in which the culture industry does not just enforce uniformity but enables forms of tradition, ways of relating to the present shared across geographic domains. Such optimism, which ultimately suggests a pliability of aesthetic and libidinal investments, runs through much of Baraka's thinking from the mid-sixties on, though it is not necessarily articulated as such or systematically developed as a theory. That optimism allows us to read and hear his later work—the bulk of his career—without the tragic sense that he gave up too much in his various ideological and geographical shifts.

A Post-Revolutionary Age

The decades between, say, Harold Cruse's 1967 *The Crisis of the Negro Intellectual* and Hortense Spillers's 1994 "Postdate," to paraphrase Sonia Sanchez, fell like a stone on black lives.[81] Spillers argues that those decades witnessed an "epistemic shift" that allows consideration of "new facets of relationship between one [theoretical] object and another." This is a physical and cognitive re-remapping of the concept of community, and a remapping of the relationship between capitalism, nation-states, and (neo-)imperialism. Spillers is especially concerned with another outcome of Black Power's defeat or exhaustion: the institutionalization of black studies—the emergence of new institutional protocols of evaluation and norms of rigor—which accelerates black studies' instrumentalization and subordination to individual entrepreneurialism or careerism. Similar concerns certainly inform Baraka's criticism of fellow poets and musicians whom he sees as having capitulated to mainstream tastes for personal advancement without a broader account of how to help or be accountable to the people, save as a good role model. In this era, the black situation—encompassing the structure of racial feeling and the role race plays in particular antagonisms—alters, and with it alters the meaning of experimental techniques. My question, therefore, is how one makes art for "the people" when "the people" are neither what nor where one imagines them to be. How does one navigate the particularity of a post-revolutionary age without simply admitting defeat? How does one continue to focus on and cultivate areas of unorganizable free space and time from which to reimagine social forms that might follow from a ceaselessly deferred revolution? Baraka's solution is, partially, a return to earlier investments in reconstituting individuality, but he must now also reconstitute racial particularity against the prevailing or ascendant neoliberal, bourgeois terms.

One of the signals of Baraka's transition from cultural nationalism to Third World Marxism (ca. 1974) was a single he released in 1976 as a member of the Advanced Workers with the Anti-Imperialist Singers.[82] Featuring members of Kool and the Gang, the Commodores, Parliament, and other rhythm and blues bands, Side A was "You Was Dancin Need to Be Marchin So You Can Dance Some More Later On"; Side B, "Better Red Let Others Be Dead." This collaboration was a more successful—or at least more complete—merger of popular rhythms and radical politics than even Baraka's own 1968 *Black and Beautiful . . . Soul and Madness* (Jihad) or his 1972 *It's Nation Time/African Visionary Music* (Motown/Black Forum). As a record that might play at a party, it is on par with some of Gil Scott-Heron's collaborations with Brian Jackson. Referring to an "army of workers" in the street, Baraka says, "when they said party, they meant an anti-revisionist revolutionary Communist party." The contrast with extant black nationalist models is striking. "The people" here do not await political symbols and directives; they are self-led by "the science of revolution" (presumably grasped in and through revolutionary praxis) and a strong party structure. Baraka and others had long understood "marching" or "dancing" in the streets as veiled references to the urban uprisings throughout the later 1960s. We might think of those uprisings themselves as evidence of the mismatch between political leadership that sought to navigate existing institutions and inchoate anti-institutional longing, an extreme form of an anarchist- or communist-inflected imagination. Within the logic of "Dancing," in the absence of a party structure, "the people" need continued moral and spiritual support in their self-organization and self-definition through struggle. Here, that means understanding the nature of the struggle in which they find themselves. If aesthetics continues to have political value, its value will depend on the degree to which it can wrest forms forged from within the culture industries into a broader project of inventory and of invention through which the people produces itself anew.

I have pursued an account of avant-garde jazz and poetry to this point that largely reads the works in the context of the "now-swell" of the Black Power era, a familiar, even overdetermined pairing that relies on seeing both avant-garde aesthetics and Black Power politics emerging from progressively decentralized mechanisms of cultural and political authority. That the sources of decentralization differ—as I will discuss in this section in order to frame a reading of Baraka's 1982 collaboration with David Murray and Steve McCall, *In the Tradition*—is less significant for present purposes than the degree to which in each domain the rallying cry was "freedom." But how to consider the end of the Black Power era? The primary markers for my purposes are the dissolution of black political coalitions due to internal fragmentation and state repression, a broader public revision of the civil rights movements as having been primarily concerned with equal access to elite institutions (an aim that was putatively achieved), and a political climate that grew increasingly hostile to collective organizing. That dissolution corresponds with the reassertion of more centralized forms of cultural authority, declining profits for those forms of black music less hospitable to the tastes of a globally ascendant bourgeoisie, and intensified financialization aided by state and extra-state policies (e.g., "structural readjustment programs").

Stuart Hall's argument that cultural production is neither wholly resistant nor co-opted, but always bound up in the "double movement of containment and resistance" characteristic of popular culture as such, also gives us a way of considering the pace with which black rebellion simply became spectacle.[83] Indeed, Amy Abugo Ongiri details some of the ways the Black Panther Party, in particular, mobilized popular visual and media culture, arguing that the Party was "not only invested in influencing American popular culture ... but was also in the business of creating it."[84] Similar techniques and stances change valences over time, so that what is liberatory in one instance can become confining in another, which is one reason that socially contextualizing accounts of relatively stable aesthetic production are less useful for long periods. How might we read Baraka in a way that considers the aesthetic field's relative autonomy, its non-synchronism with underlying shifts that it registers or refracts in uneven ways across different actors and institutions? How might, in other words, we consider the aesthetic field as a space shaped by internal conflicts and forces that are not a proxy for or symptom of broader social and historical processes? We have relatively few models for considering the cultural production in the post–Civil Rights era of those who shaped its aesthetics, and fewer ways of considering how they confront the emergence of a new "cultural dominant" characterized by what Richard Iton terms a "sublative tendency in black politics: a commitment not to be 'rude' and to assimilate or approximate dominant narratives and practices energized paradoxically by an exhaustion with politics or, more precisely ... the 'political.'"[85]

During and immediately following the Black Arts era, evocations of the extra-terrestrial operated alongside new investments in the "inner-space" as counter-discourses of rural or premodern life (the oft-cited "African retentions"). These tropes index a desire to move beyond the "ideological universe through which the containment of the black population was mediated."[86] To say as much is not to evaluate their effectiveness, but to clarify their stakes. While these tropes sought to codify and direct new forms of community, they often took the form of nostalgia for "traditional African" forms of social organization. Too often, a paradoxical fantasy-as-nostalgia—seeking reconstitution of what did not exist as such—takes the place of necessary political work for which, according to thinkers such as Harold Cruse and Adolph Reed, it substitutes "banal symbols of 'blackness'" and "a new array of 'revolutionary' consumer goods."[87] Rather than facilitating mass politics by helping to imagine and build new affective or proto-political solidarities, commodity fetishism displaces truly mass politics as the horizon of collective being-together. Reed, though astute in his analyses of the ever-shrinking room to maneuver as the dominant ideology continues to privilege "the market" (itself a mystification) above all, refuses to see the class character of the romance of "African origins" or obsolete/fetishistic models of community. There are genuine, if obscure, anti-capitalist elements—even proto-revolutionary ideals—in such views, and attention to them might help index the uneven development of race alongside other forms of social antagonism that capitalism depends on and exploits. Focusing almost exclusively on the alliance between the black leadership strata ("comprised mainly of low-level state functionaries, merchants and 'professionals' servicing black markets, and the clergy")[88] and its narrow advancing of its own class interests, Reed tends to be too dismissive of "organic ideologies," everyday forms of sense making that interact with "practical and popular forms of consciousness."[89] Rather than interrogating how such leaders maintained legitimacy or how that legitimacy broke down, we're left without any analysis of collective agency or aspiration. Baraka's ambivalence toward the "middle class" or bourgeois norms that sustained him marks his privileging of those "organic ideologies" in ways that upheld their authentic (self-sustaining) separateness from the capitalist modernity that enfolded them. How could he oppose social domination when the only terms, concepts, languages, and political forms available to him were shaped by the same "ideological universe through which the containment of the black population was mediated"? On the one hand, Baraka's insistence on explaining the origins and thus contingent nature of domination is important—hence the inventory. But simply focusing on the origins of domination that nonetheless seems durable and ideologically permanent could well lead to despair—hence the need to invent perspectives that at least intend different ideological universes, overturning or rethinking bedrock assumptions of the bourgeois order (including the nation).

Throughout the 1960s, Baraka and other black aestheticians could argue for a "functional" art that linked aesthetic production with the production of a revolutionary present—linking heterogeneous people's intuitions about the unfolding, punctual now to the event of black liberation—in part thanks to the extra-cartographic trope of the "community." Community, as Hortense Spillers argues and as Langston Hughes seemed to have recognized, proved less homogeneous and stable than imagined, exceeding both the physical and political "coordinates on the map of the inner city."[90] Meanwhile, the rise of neoconservatism (an alignment of "disillusioned liberals and socialists turned Cold War hawks"[91]) and with it the emergence of what Stuart Hall and his comrades termed "authoritarian populism," helped shift the very terrain of politics itself. The changing significance of black alterity—the changing character and condition of what was once termed "the black community"—accompanied by the depoliticization and commodification of the signs and symbols of black solidarity, and the new fundamentally anti-political relations between capital, the state, and labor typically referred to as the neoliberal era, defines that age, our own.

From this perspective we might think of Baraka's poem "Against Bourgeois Art" as a distancing from—if not repudiation of—some of his 1970s phonographic poetry. If the end of the "sixties"—corresponding with the global economic crisis of 1973–74—"liberated" race and gender from social class, we can understand Baraka's investments in theorizing and creating an oppositional art as a partial response to that general theoretical crisis. He would criticize his black nationalist period—especially the tendency of the latter to use "*Black*, an impossibly diverse abstraction, as a definition for political direction."[92] Yet he tends to leave analysis of the relationship between race and class only implicit in his many critical and poetic texts. Instead he reframes earlier arguments, resuming a critique of "the suffocating arena of middle-class unseriousness" and attacking those musicians he sees as "deliberately trying to *declass* the music, transforming it into a secondary appendage of European concert music, rather than the heroic expression of the folk and classical music of the African-American majority as well as the spirit of a progressive and populist high art."[93] Putting aside the class implications of "classical music," to "declass" the music here means severing it from its mass sources—namely, the blues, as a "cultural insistence, a feeling-matrix, a tonal memory," and finally a "national consciousness."[94] Later Baraka argues that the new music "reinforces the most valuable memories of a people but at the same time creates new forms, new modes of expression, to more precisely reflect contemporary experience"; it "*uses* history, it is not paralyzed by it."[95] In other words, the new music resolves the crisis of experience by being that which, from the past, emerges in the present as an indication of "where we are or will be."

These claims are continuous with Baraka's earlier cultural nationalist claims about black culture, although they attempt to avoid the mystification of "the people" as a homogenous bloc who need political symbols and slogans. Baraka's effort, as he puts it, is "to link up what is direct with what is advanced," which he notes "requires another kind of skill, which I still have to develop."[96] He continued to understand blackness as an alternative to capitalist modernity, something that capital could not or would not wholly subsume, and as such he linked it "to the survival of a general *liberating intelligence*" that would prevent the culture's destruction.[97] Although his references to black culture are concrete and historical, they also function as an ideological anchor or "quilting point" in a broader hegemonic struggle whose first step is the construction—the re-collection—of the people who could respond to the call that his poem "S O S" puts forward to "all black people": "come / on in."[98] It is important, then, to take seriously the work of negativity in Baraka's thought: his opposition to "bourgeois art" implied a social alternative whose power derived from its opposition and apposition to what Stuart Hall terms "the culture of the power bloc."[99] Baraka enacted opposition to abstractions disconnected from the rhythms and concerns of everyday living. From this perspective, "black" in his work refers to a contingent but historically linked alliance of classes, strata, and social forces whose cohesion, like the cohesion of the social groups that comprise that alliance, is continually undone and remade in the course of struggle.

The tension between constituting the people by raising their "level of consciousness" and addressing "the people" where they are is a primary tension of his work during the 1980s, especially on his justly celebrated 1982 recording *New Music—New Poetry*.[100] Most of the analysis of that record has foregrounded the poem "In the Tradition," the title of which is taken from alto saxophonist Arthur Blythe's 1979 album of the same name.[101] Travis A. Jackson observes that Columbia Records signed Blythe and promoted him as part of an effort, ultimately less successful than its attempts with Wynton Marsalis, to "bring jazz powerfully back into the marketplace"—even as Blythe, for his part, thought of tradition as a "developing resource."[102] The idea of tradition as itself in development, even renewed by those acts of invention that inscribe it as contemporary, informs my reading of the poems "Against Bourgeois Art" and "Class Struggle in Music I and II," and indeed Baraka's later work more generally.

Although concerned with the producers of the music, "in the main the Afro-American workers and small farmers," it is clear that the "class struggle" Baraka has in mind is not primarily the rate of exploitation, the subsumption of traditional musical labor practices, or the affective relationship musicians have to their own product, but the ways they situate their culture against the mainstream.[103] "Class Struggle in Music" refers to "the battle between those of us who want to transform this society and those who have come up with the newer-sounding ways of supporting the status quo of racism and exploitation."[104] Baraka targets a very particular, and very old theoretical problem: capital's dissolution (and people's reconstitution) of group social life, which problematizes notions of aesthetic production and invention rooted in "the community." And he does so in the wake of the League of Revolutionary Black Workers, and other militant labor organizations. He does it in the wake of the expulsion of Communists from the American labor movement, which Fredric Jameson argues "consolidated the new anti-political 'social contract' between American business and the American labor unions, and created a situation in which the privileges of a white male labor force take precedence over the demands of black and women workers and other minorities."[105] The situation in the decolonizing world was, of course, worse. As Joy James observes, throughout the Cold War period, antagonisms of capitalist modernity "play[ed] out on Third World terrain where the casualties against bodies already dehumanized by Europe would not create significant political collateral damages in either democracies or dictatorships of the people."[106] Racial explanations shifted from the mystifications of biology to the mystifications of "culture," but some populations remained more proximate to death than others. Revolutionary times are chaotic, exhausting times, and one might see the domestication of black politics—the emergence of the African American rather than the black person—as an index of the exhaustion with the political to which Iton refers. Further, as Spillers implicitly argues, race itself comes to be depoliticized, and too often treated by the left as a non-class antagonism, or epiphenomenon. Reading together Iton's and Spillers's accounts, one can say that blackness itself comes to be subject to a fundamentally anti-political—because anti-solidaristic—social contract within which justifiable concerns over essentialism aligned with the large-scale shift of class attachment that the "gains of the sixties" brought.

Along these lines we can read "Class Struggle in Music" as articulation of race and class, and better specify Baraka's sense of class struggle, which does not take the characteristic forms or address the antagonisms one might expect. If "black" seemed too abstract owing to its unsuturable heterogeneity in actual practice, then class, and the figure of the unmarked "worker," was even less tenable since too few people globally fit that category, and without analysis of the state, imperialism, and ideology one is left with the heterogeneity of a depoliticized and increasingly marginalized class struggle. One point to underscore is that capitalist class dynamics dialectically reinforce and reproduce racialist logics and vice versa. This mutuality is essential to the apparently smooth integration of the state and economic domains such that bourgeois ideology seems inevitable, even sacrosanct.[107] If "new subjects of history" were to take the stage, then, Baraka seems to suggest that black people, given both historical and present forms of domination and alienation, would be good candidates from which to theorize new forms of solidarity and collective action. Moreover, music seemed to Baraka as likely a field as any through which to awaken a truly mass politics, since the changing political and aesthetic terrain required that the music continually reinvent itself, finding more resources to re-constellate into powerful new arrangements. Given its place in his thinking as a marker of organic ideologies, music is the most likely field, despite his continued investments in poetry, drama, and other literary modes. The historical nucleus of this vernacular avant-garde formation is the exclusion of the black creators from full civic membership. I argue above that this practice aims at creating a new collective subject rooted in a translocal notion of community that is enabled by sonic circulation, and by suspicion toward the inducements of the citizen and civil rights as the *telos* of black politics. Here, then, the sense of inventory—the inventories that (in)form the individual (subject is no less inadequate as a term)—can align with "invent."

Recorded in front of an audience in 1981 at Soundscape in New York City, and released on *New Music—New Poetry* in 1982, "Class Struggle in Music I" poses the haunting question, "What is the emotion?" against Steve McCall's mid-tempo shuffle-time rhythm and David Murray's blues-based riff and improvisation. At the word "vitality," the poem finds a new mood:

> beat beat beat beat beat
> boom buppa doompa doom
> boom buppa doompa doom
> boom buppa doompa doom
> boom buppa doompa doom
> yeh,
> that and
> boom buppa doompa doom
> boom buppa doompa doom
> boom buppa doompa doom[108]

Steve McCall plays faster, changing his rhythmic pattern to one compatible with but not simply imitative of the one Baraka speak-sings. Voice, liberated from semantic content, signifies, but does not lend itself to a stereotyped notion of "jazz." It is a remarkable moment, one that recalls some of the exciting avant-garde experiments of the 1970s.[109] But it works as a fusion of African American funk traditions with stereotyped views of "African" and Afro-Caribbean rhythms. It enacts the "we/us—eye," the collectivity still to be (re)searched and sought, that can combine "a blues emotion," "a factory girder reflection emotion," "an assembly line thing," and "a love heat."

"Class Struggle in Music II" is in free time, Murray's tenor sax wail accompanying Baraka's more assertive reading and McCall's tom-tom rolls. Recontextualized via this recording, it is difficult to hear this music as another instance of spectacularized black protest (e.g., Mingus's "Angry Man of Jazz" or Impulse! Records' "angry black tenor man" image). Instead, the phonopoem makes a sonic argument that the multiple streams of tradition are equally valid and contemporary with one another. The reappropriated sign of black rhythm here comes to figure the transcendental rootedness of black modernity. The musicians and Baraka effect a kind of counter-abstraction, which I read as analogous to the litany that concludes "Black Dada Nihilismus." No doubt, the tom-tom and insistent rhythms have been problematic markers of blackness throughout a long history of musicology and popular understandings of "Africa." But here reclaiming even the signifiers of a "premodern" past becomes a central component in imagining an art that (as the poem concludes, repeating):

> ... even reached you
>   & even reached you
>   reached you
>   you
>   you.[110]

(The dispersal of the words across the page, into the book's central fold, is especially vivid, but also a reminder that it still is difficult to know what such hard-won unity would look like or be in practice.) The poem is concerned with the precise fissure that Langston Hughes had already envisioned, where that which neither the power bloc nor popular classes can co-opt ("taken my blues and gone") will simply be erased, leading to ideological "invention" where new forms appear as though isolated from and not responsive to any past. In this context, Baraka's frequent invocations of the artist's "stance" suggest a historically conditioned but steady bulwark against the expanse of capitalism. To be avant-garde in this sense means trying to hold on to those parts of black experience that are appropriable without being directly consumable as commodities—a subtle, unstable project.

Anarchic Regard

I conclude this chapter considering Baraka's 1999 reunion with the NYAQ. I want to briefly sketch the work's intellectual and aesthetic context, defined in part by a central unresolved tension about the particularity of black cultural production. I have alluded to the ways the "success" of Baraka's and others' arguments for specialized norms of criticism become absorbed by the corporatizing university, making black distinctness a matter of professional advancement more than political urgency. Calls for the self-determination of the black community, which is no longer where or what it was imagined to be, become calls for empowerment, for black capitalism, for "enterprise zones."[111] Insofar as "community" cathects a range of political dreams, schemes, projects, propositions, and questions that no longer seem pertinent, those dreams become so many ruins to navigate.[112]

The crisis of temporality I identify in Baraka's early work comes to characterize his later untimely presence in an era chastened by its radical past. This shift corresponds with broader changes in the media landscape. Discussing the selective lionization of a handful of black thinkers in such publications as the *New Yorker* and the *Atlantic Monthly*, Hazel Carby notes the rhetorical tendency to "deny an organic relation between contemporary black intellectuals to a past of collective struggle."[113] A similar phenomenon shaped contemporaneous discourses of jazz. Record labels such as Columbia, Verve, and Blue Note championed "young lions," largely university-trained musicians positioned to pick up the neo-classicist gauntlet Wynton Marsalis, Albert Murray, and Stanley Crouch had thrown down, and become the new face of jazz.[114] Defining the music in opposition to the avant-garde and fusion, labels as well as the mainstream press helped shift the legitimate range of black aesthetics. That shift corresponded with similar processes in the fields of rhythm and blues and politics.[115] Platform change (the emergence of the compact disc as the dominant format for private music consumption) legitimized by digital remastering—with Columbia, Verve, and Blue Note helping to lead the charge—enabled the rerelease of every recording of bebop's key innovators, some never before heard. Fans and collectors could fashion themselves historians of the music, hearing its development take after take. When they were finished with their favorite Charlie Parker or Bud Powell records, consumers could easily find their way to new work that bore more than a passing resemblance to that of past "masters."

Sound recording may bear an indexical trace of whatever was proximate to the recording apparatus, but *records*, as consumer objects, have more variegated relations to time, tarrying with the definition of their time whether as history or the ever-expanding archive of ephemera, kitsch, the fashionable, or the outmoded. Soundwork, in this view, does not assume the solidarity of a tradition or radical stance but emerges from and through the processes by which aesthetics links one moment's affective solidarities and aesthetic commitments with another's, indexing along the way those formations that become outmoded in the face of broader social changes. The "young lions'" work was promoted as a musical renaissance. This effectively reified technical proficiency—liberated techniques from the situations in which they emerged—while rejecting the cultural nationalism of the 1960s and 1970s in favor of familiar arguments linking "jazz" to an idea(l) of American pluralism. Jazz could embody the ideals of a post–Civil Rights era by paradoxically rooting itself in the pre–Civil Rights and rhetorically distancing itself from the more unruly forms and claims of black nationalism and experimental music. Against such a backdrop, Baraka could not help appearing as a revenant, a person from another time whose very presence mocks and reminds of unfinished business.

Even as his faith in revolution itself waned ("I thought that revolution would be immediate, at one point. And I don't think that's so much mellowing but deepening your understanding to find that that's not reality, that it's not an event, that it's a process"[116]), Baraka continued to uphold "art as a weapon, and a weapon of revolution."[117] "Revolutionary" means both a refusal to separate art from the conditions that create it and an insistence on taking it as a totality, as his two-part "Class Struggle in Music" does. This view of revolution requires that the artist continue to draw out what is unresolved in the past as a spur to defining the now as the present. With popular political struggles waning in public consciousness if not in the streets, the signifiers and rhetoric of Black Power no longer worked to suture the differences of class, gender, sexuality, ideologies, and other social differences into theoretically and practically binding political solidarities. What remained were affective solidarities, spaces, and practices that seemed relatively free of capitalist regulation or exploitation, and proto-political stances and quotidian resistances that could still develop into strategies of collective liberation.

Baraka's work following *New Music—New Poetry* generally refuses the comforts and reassurances of the solitary subject and "bourgeois art"; he largely avoids the enclosure of experience behind the fiction of a first-person "I" that strains under the weight of the history it is tasked to carry. Instead, his work privileges improvisatory visions of collectivity rooted in and routed through a second-person address that underscores the degree to which black experience is not shared, whether across the broader society that continually resignifies and reifies racial difference as cultural, or among black people themselves. If this work is still avant-garde, it no longer presents itself as vanguard. Rather, it becomes more invested in the kind of difference blackness—as unassimilable historical experience—makes despite and across class differences. The language of class alternates between allowing Baraka to negotiate black heterogeneity, even as his castigation of the "middle class," as etho-political stance, occasionally reverberates with earlier attempts to align racial difference and objective ethico-political commitments.

Much of Baraka's "post-revolutionary" work, in other words, aims to reconstellate racial signifiers by investing them with associations that often run counter to commodity logic. His work continues to play between invention and inventory, trying to articulate visions of collectivity and individuality against the dominant understandings of the present. If his early work concerns itself with the texture and discontinuities of lived experience and the role of poetry in transforming the present, his later work is much more concerned with vernacular wit, which makes quotidian dislocations and discontinuities legible as urgently political problems related to a racial situation defined by assimilation. If the earlier work figures the poem as a space of referral, where meaning and sound overwrite and refer to one another and encourage a notion of subjective experience that prioritizes sound rather than sight, the more recent work—collaborations with woodwind players David Murray[118] and Billy Harper,[119] bassist William Parker (himself a poet),[120] trumpeters Hugh Ragin[121] and Malachi Thompson,[122] and others—moves closer to the modes of jeremiad, elegy, and Zen koan. The poem becomes a space of resonance, of what Fred Moten might call "interinanimation." It is, finally, conjuring work: articulating the past into new "association complexes" in order to create the sense of a syncope in habitual associations of black signifiers and black life.[123]

Baraka organized his 1999 phonopoem "Seek Light at Once," with the NYAQ, around his poem "Masked Angel Costume: The Sayings of Mantan Moreland." This poem recontextualizes the inventory that concludes "Black Dada Nihilismus." The phonopoem begins with Baraka saying "here on the ground," then haltingly asking, "Was it ever so quiet that the room started to ask you questions?" as Milford Graves and Reggie Workman—the latter replacing Lewis Worrell—play a low drum roll/bowed bass note. They build in intensity, Rudd and Tchicai occasionally adding soft, fluttering notes as Baraka begins counting "63, 64, 65 . . ." up to 99 (the year of the recording). He doubles back, invoking signifiers of the 1960s Black Liberation struggles (e.g., Birmingham, Watts, Black Power), then transitions to sounding syllables ("muh muh muh") and then to juvenile scatology ("pee pee," "doo doo"). This moment recalls his own description of Coltrane's music as evoking "a grown man learning to speak."[124] The intensity builds: Tchicai plays a series of short, generally descending chromatic figures while Rudd joins with a growling, muted trombone. The opening section, apparently a collective improvisation with voice featured among the other instruments, concludes with Baraka shouting, "Kill! Kill! Kill!"

Abruptly, they shift mood: Workman and Baraka are now in duet as the latter begins reading the printed poem, which consists of a numbered series of short, witty aphorisms presented in the supposed voice of the great comedic actor Mantan Moreland. For example, "Ghosts think they / good lookin / Never stay to find out!"[125] Moreland's most famous role—Charlie Chan's butler Birmingham Brown—recalls the minstrel figure Zip Coon, a verbose, malapropism-plagued dandy who mocked black class aspirations to freedom and improved social status. Like Zip Coon's, Birmingham Brown's clothes and tendency toward malapropism are like a grotesque bourgeois costume; his ready grin at once embodies and mocks go-along-to-get-along assimilationist entrepreneurialism.

The minstrel figure invokes an ideology of black inferiority whose function is to justify and make pleasurable the ascriptive hierarchies that structure the social, even as present ideological norms will consider her abjectness a sign of personal failing rather than systemic rot. In our "post-revolutionary" era, the convergence of conservative and liberal views that trace persistent racial inequalities to heteronormative and patriarchal assumptions about family structure rather than to exploitation and dispossession give Zip Coon and his avatars (e.g., President Barack Obama's "Cousin Pookie") a new function: securing consent for the current hegemonic regime, for which race continues to be a structuring component. In Baraka's poem, Birmingham Brown is wise, but not empowered; he is the normative political subject of post–Black Power politics: hard-working, uncomplaining, seeking a narrowly conceived self-advancement. Wrenched from his moment and plunged into a new historical conjuncture lacking mass mobilization or even public discourses opposing deep structural racism, he is another of Baraka's alienated subjects. Yet, the primary aim of "Seek Light at Once" is not to recover Moreland's agency or reveal his subversive use of the minstrel mask, even as the poem does offer, as opacity, a glimpse into a complex offstage life and professional exploitation (e.g., "I am never really / laughing / except / off / camera"). The phonopoem teases apart the life from the spectral, mocking, omnipresent figure of black abjection, the "something grinning" that "stalks" black life in a later poem[126]— that implicitly asks both his and subsequent generations about the psychic costs and compromises of integration without the greater social transformation he and others sought under the banner "revolution."

Here again, the personal commingles with the more broadly political: Moreland, known less for malapropism than virtuosic Black English, recalls Baraka's own insistent use of black-marked speech in his poetry and criticism. Black English functions in this regard less as a marker of authenticity than as an invitation to deciphering practice, asking readers-as-critics to consider their own investments or disavowals of this performance/production of blackness. Rather than embrace an otherwise abjected blackness, the poem (like "Heathens and Space/Time Projection" released the previous year with Malachi Thompson) refuses assimilation and its promises. Rather than "humanize" Moreland, making him legible within a racially marked regime of the human, "Seek Light at Once" thematizes the inhumanity of his role by making him (like the character he played) obsessed with ghosts, and haunted by something else. The poem exploits his ambivalent position vis-à-vis the bourgeois norms his characters imperfectly embodied. In this way, the poem performs a complicated operation of claiming and revision. The final stanza reads as follows:

14
  Birmingham
  Birmingham
was where
4 of my daughters
were killed

John Coltrane
composed
Alabama

It was the music
that moved
  my feet

  they never
failed.

At one level, Baraka's Moreland claims as daughters Denise McNair, Addie Mae Collins, Cynthia Wesley, and Carole Robertson, who were killed on September 15, 1963, by a terrorist firebomb at the 16th Street Baptist Church in Birmingham, Alabama. He claims them through John Coltrane's composition, "Alabama," included on *Live from Birdland* for which Baraka wrote the liner notes. Introducing this section, Baraka bellows "Birmingham," repeating it seven times, echoing the beginning of the phonopoem. Roswell Rudd joins him on the fifth repetition with a New Orleans–inspired trombone growl in the same register. Baraka repeats the term an eighth time, multiplying its grammatical and sonic functions. Once he finishes the words, he scat sings, John Tchicai joins him on tenor saxophone, playing freely. Baraka does not speak again, but adds handclaps to the group improvisation before the phonopoem ends.

    The poem gives Moreland both a personal and objective stake in the deaths of these children, one mediated and made possible through layers of mass mediation. It offers to link subjective and objective histories in the ways "Black Dada Nihilismus" fails to do. At another level, recalling that Birmingham Brown is Moreland's most famous character, the repetition of that word—a bellowing call both in the improvised opening of the poem and in this climactic section—allows the word to float, signifying minstrelsy, militancy, and mourning, intertwined and mutually informing. Insofar as anxiety over the disappearance of subservient Birmingham Browns and the social order they represented led to the church being targeted, one Birmingham calls to the other, and in the poem one cannot celebrate the first without mourning the second. Likewise, one cannot hear Moreland's catchphrase, to which Baraka alludes, "feets don't fail me now"—usually his response to encountering a ghost he then fled—without hearing Coltrane's song "Alabama," which here becomes the source of his moving feet. The poem upends ordinary temporality: Coltrane would not write his song "Alabama" until twenty years after Moreland's heyday, but Baraka has them haunt each other, making minstrel spectacle an inventory for modern art.

For Baraka, bourgeois racial liberalism—no less than black nationalism—represented a kind of cruel optimism (Lauren Berlant's phrase), misplacing faith in a formation or goal that is contrary to one's thriving. Here, it engenders political ambivalence. There are no cures for ambivalence, but there are consolations that need not be self-deceiving or flattering. Part of the question "Seek Light at Once" poses is how we might consider productive(ly) other forms of irresolution without lapsing into the cruel optimism of harmful attachment or partial blindness in the name of declaring a good outcome. How do we accept the "gains of the sixties" without forgetting the unfinished business that constitutes the present crisis of experience, suspended between an optimistic sense of progress and daily reminders of what has not changed but has only become harder to name? That optimism grew crueler as the 1980s and 1990s unfolded, as it became clear the degree to which most forms of official politics and culture were at best indifferent and at worst antithetical to black life *as such*, the spectacular success of a few individual black people notwithstanding. Moreland's cultural and aesthetic value lies in his over-representing, to the point of distortion, a segment of the black population as a permanent underclass whose mocking omnipresence becomes uneasy comedy. The repeated injunction to "seek light at once" is a call to critically reappraise the conditions that produced Mantan Moreland as abject.

Aesthetically, Baraka's project in this late phase is still defined by the call to "all black people" in "S O S," though he now calls them not just to gather but to think and desire differently. Considering his continued evocation of figures like Moreland, we might also think of it serving the function of an inventory, a close look at all the forces responsible for blackness in the present, rather than only acknowledging those one would valorize. This unfixes race from its apparent intractability, making racial (re)definition itself the site of political struggle. The project is to introduce standards of judgment and ways of thinking that allow for the redemption even of those arts and artists produced from within the depths of racist structures of thought and feeling. In this way, Baraka's later work starts to show what a real response to "S O S" might look like. "Seek Light at Once" becomes an instance of "anarchic regard," a lawless looking at the past: skeptical, situated "here in the world," and aiming, as I will argue in the next chapter, to reconceive the universal. Though legible as jeremiad, Baraka's post-revolutionary calls largely eschew authority in favor of using the vernacular and the second person to deconstruct the distinctions between the individual and the collective. They do not just unfold in this punctual moment but attempt to make now thinkable as a present, with new possibilities and obligations, new explanations and pathways forward rooted in new sound that can become a new basis for thought: the thought of a livable present, and of the "we" who conjure and live in that present.

Creating Music as sound within the whole body,
which must be brought to the level of total deperson-
alized realization, exciting various limbs, etc.
—CECIL TAYLOR, liner notes to *Air Above
Mountains, Buildings Within*

It's a love thing / If love is ever really
loved that way / The way they say
—JEANNE LEE, "Blasé"

. . . no named aggregate enclosed or could
encompass the supple oneness we felt.
—NATHANIEL MACKEY, *Bass Cathedral*

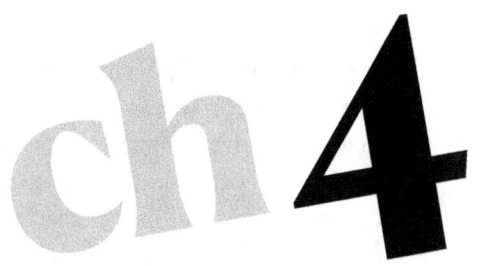

Body/Language
The Semiotics and Poetics of Improvisation and Black Embodiment

To Make Music Poetry

Players and audiences should not be the same when the play is finished. A casual review of song and album titles associated with free jazz uncovers countless references to oneness of the kind Nathaniel Mackey describes: unbound, all-encompassing, the result of a transformative encounter with free improvisation. Cecil Taylor, whose sonic experiments in music and poetry this chapter considers alongside those of Jeanne Lee, once said, "you must surrender whatever preconceptions you have about music if you're really interested in it. So that leads you to understand the really poetic essence of that music. And what I'm talking about is the spirit that informs those people as to what the music should be made of."[1] I take "poetic essence" to be a way of describing investment in the grammars, vocabularies, vernaculars, and impulses of collective thinking that comprise "free jazz," whose freedom I understand in terms of its relationship to the existing musical forms and genres whose eccentricity it reanimates. This chapter analyzes free improvisation as collective commitment to yet unrealized alternatives, within and beyond music. Central to that analysis are the claims that music and poetry make for forms of experience beyond those associated with the sovereign, intending subject that dominates Western philosophy. Oneness is not simply reducible to subjectivity, which is best understood as a grammatical principle that makes experiences legible and shareable at the expense of their open-ended abundance and play. Poetry and music both generate alternative grammars of experience, period arguments regarding the text and excitement in the possibilities of free improvisation, which tend to be cast in spiritual terms. To track that, this chapter puts free improvisation in conversation with contemporaneous poststructuralist accounts of the semiotics and/as an erotics.

In a parallel argument, Gayatri Chakravorty Spivak suggests that we think of translation as an erotics of surrender. I hear in that another term for the reciprocal attunement especially required of free improvisation: an erotics of surrender (rooted in the unmasterable, unencloseable intimacies engendered by the trace of the other in the self, rather than the self in the other) of the self to the ensemble and surrounding community.[2] Often, such erotics sound like ecstasy—not ego gratification but dispossessive, emptying out. Along these lines, I posit the freedom of "free" improvisation in terms of the drama of individuation—a "journey to the one" to borrow a phrase from Pharoah Sanders, to light out again into new configurations of singularities that are at once ante- and anti-subjection, prior to and excessive of the subject's narrativizing enclosure.[3] "Erotics," as it operates in Cecil Taylor and Jeanne Lee's respective sound practices, is not another cartography of desire spurred by what the subject lacks but a way of describing an embrace of the embodied, the sensuous, and the non-enclosed. In the introduction I describe reciprocal attunement as a form of play, a commitment to what may happen in the course of the event's unfolding, but also an openness to conceptual revisioning to make room for the forms of transformation of self and others that may come. Aesthetics, as a mechanism for sorting forms of sensuous experience, fundamentally refers to ways of relating self and other. Considering poetry and music together, Cecil Taylor's claim to be inventing a new language is paradigmatic of free music's alternative grammars and its radical challenge not only to extant musical orders and aesthetics.[4]

Taylor once said that "to feel is perhaps the most terrifying thing in this society." One version of the ecstatic is unsettling feeling for which we lack a name, unsettling feeling that calls existing names into question.[5] The era of his greatest prominence is defined in part by the possibilities and limits of the text, the possibilities and limits of a political aesthetic as many of the forms and signs of protest were commodified almost in the moment of their appearance. That era saw a temporary, vertiginous flux in the governing structures of social organization, aided by faster circulation of aesthetic concepts, new acknowledgment of the relationship between concepts and their mode of expression, and renewed attention to the capacities of the ecstatic, the irrational or para-rational, seized by some as potential models for the world to come. Older models of the artwork became insufficient. Black Arts, French poststructuralist, and other theorists conceived the experience of the artwork as production, and shared faith in what art might produce. Differentially positioned by race and geography, they responded to a common postcolonial context defined by transforming relations of domination, dispossession, and exploitation. In that transitional moment, emergent reconfigurations of power/knowledge gave the relationship between embodiment, subjectivity, and non-subjective forms of experience such as ecstasy renewed salience. The aesthetic became a site from which to reconceive the function of art, the experience of the beautiful, and subjective experience itself. For each, finally, we see a push against aesthetic models oriented around surface/depth models and a desire to forge new pathways to meaning by underscoring the material processes of signification—for example, intensifications of rhythm, timbre, and voice rather than speech, signification, or representation. If we conceive of them as equally involved in concerns over the status of the common as capitalism entered its contemporary phase, we can produce fuller accounts of their common pursuit of aesthetic and critical practices as permanent insurgency.

Julia Kristeva's account of the semiotic, Roland Barthes's account of the text, Larry Neal's account of the "destruction of the text,"[6] and Sylvia Wynter's call for the "reinvention of the concrete self" in her retrospective critique of Black Arts–era "ethnopoetics" are the primary coordinates of my analysis here, which seeks to describe an evolving set of concepts at play in free improvisation.[7] Hortense Spillers's critique of psychoanalysis informs my way of conceiving alternatives to the self through which we might better hear the music and understand its political potential. Emphasizing the implicit or explicit new modes of individuality and subjectivity at stake in the music, I pursue new ways to hear the ways musicians and poets conceived of music's communication function, favoring the dissociative and agonistic—the dissonant—and as such playing on the line between the semantic (poetry) and somatic (embodied sound) to suggest alternative phenomenologies rooted in non-subjective affects, that is, in forms of experience not comprehended by familiar psychoanalytic or phenomenological frames.

How might we simultaneously consider new aesthetics as a reflexive commitment to blackness and as a deorchestration of the narrativities (the texts and sign complexes) that subtend and suffuse race-specific forms of experience and consciousness? Margo Crawford reminds us that throughout the Black Arts era "black" itself referred to the unknown and unthought "dimensions of freedom and self-determination," as well as a "desire to reenchant black humanity as much more than an identity category."[8] To hear reenchantment requires attunement to the agonistic and open-ended search for alternatives we might call *playing*. In the absence of conventionally agreed-upon ways of generating and resolving tension, of moving from one idea to another, such playing gives individuals and ensembles maximum responsibility for each sound they make relative to other sounds or silence. Free playing takes chances through its models of ecstatic time, a responsibility and commitment to the trace of the other in the self (trumpeter Don Cherry referred to this as "complete communion"), and its exploration of alternative models of psychic and social constitution immanent to this world and its traditions.[9] Free playing is thus also the free de- and rearrangement of received materials—techniques, collective models, traditions—without the expectation or requirement of fidelity to a standard developed outside of its own context. I conceive those collective models and traditions as "the common," and here analyze the place of "free" improvisation in helping orient or articulate inchoate experiences, incoherencies, and undecidabilities that reveal the internal differentiations that defer every claim to community as an achieved phenomenon. Rather than serving as a model of pluralist society or exclusively serving as critique of what is existing, free improvisation creates a common space for imagining otherwise, gathering the fragments of experience that stand in surplus of identity. Proceeding in these terms, we might better grasp "outness" and "outsideness" as theoretical practice, not the fulfillment of teleological accounts of freedom but their disruption.

Free improvisation does not refer to specific style elements, but rather a commitment to ongoingness, to experimental open-endedness grounded in something other than the circularity and circulation of received forms, paired with the free manipulation of received aesthetic material in ways that at once unground the traditions of so-called "jazz" and reground it as the product and precondition of the common. Such manipulation and re-orchestration is "free" insofar as it does conform to pre-established formulas of value. Historically, it belongs to a set of ephemeral, insurgent strategies that operate in the not-yet-organized space-time between emergence of the new and its absorption by the dominant. I read the de- and reorchestration of modernist conceptual and harmonic dissonance in conjunction with semi-connected freedom struggles as part of a general desire for new politics, or at least see in its improvised new aesthetic modes a proto-politics. Beyond Ralph Ellison's "solo flight" of an individual among individuals within preconfigured socio-discursive space, "free jazz" requires re-theorizing the nature of the improvisatory act in terms that call into question the subject/object relation, and that therefore ask us to rethink the theoretical and practical place of singularity in our analyses. Appreciated at its most radical, its "outness" is best understood as the displacement and recontextualization of binaristic reference to African (or Afrological) and Euro-American (or Eurological) modernist modalities. What if, maintaining a place for the person or personality of its performers, we conceive "free jazz" as the pursuit of a freedom more fundamental and more difficult to name than those modes of freedom bound to the liberal form of the personal and the subject? What if, in other words, we took seriously its taking seriously the possibilities of play and playing?

This framing foregrounds the problem of the text and textuality, which serves as a hinge between jazz and poetry, improvisation and writing.[10] Attention to it allows us to avoid overstating their categorical distinctness or, worse, reinscribing a hierarchical relationship between music and text. More often, critics insist on poetry's adjacency to improvisation, on poetry as translation, reproduction, distribution, or representation of improvisation's "pure" performativity, which leaves as open question the points of practical and theoretical articulation between them. Meta DuEwa Jones, for example, stresses the "evanescent nature of a live jazz performance," which she argues "requires resuscitation through recordings, whether by a sound engineer's precise rendering or by a poet's lyrical translation."[11] Of course, both sound engineer and poet "read" (and different senses create) the sound, and textualization offers to transform it into a new text, which is to say they interpret, internalize, and transform it into the site of a new encounter.[12] Alternative accounts of the text—deconstruction of the most fundamental grammars of historical experience—and subjective experience are fundamental to free improvisation. At its most radical, it sits itself "at the limit of the rules of the speech-act [*énonciation*]," presenting itself as ecstatic expression that indicates something more fundamental than the self.[13] As such, it participates in both individual and collective struggles against prevailing aesthetic norms, which themselves refract social and political grammars. Texts are irreducibly plural, "not consumed by the reader but solicit[ing] collaboration on the part of the reader ... a practice of disruptive and self-disruptive *jouissance*."[14] To *experience* such *jouissance* as pleasure requires "finding the self, then killing it": exposing the self to what displaces the subjective identities upon which aesthetic pleasure relies. It is to conceive of a poetry whose implied speech embeds itself in a black positionality that cannot be fully subjectively experienced.

To recall Cecil Taylor's desire to "make music into poetry" is to recall that the relationship between the two fields is asymmetrical but reciprocal.[15] Rather than deconstruct the music/text binary with emphasis on the former's discursivity and the latter's unruly phonic excess, I highlight the practice of the outside, the production of outfulness, unsanctioned outs endemic to the music and the poetry that draw each other into tight weaves. Poetry, in both Cecil Taylor and Jeanne Lee's hands, refers to processes of relating individual and collective experience, including language and history, within the field of literature in order to mark and create spaces of encounter. Those spaces of encounter do not serve a predetermined ethical project or impulse, but instead name ways of improvising the common as culture, the generative, unstable ground of difference and differentiation. Poetry in this sense is where the subjective and intersubjective meet, and where the inherited abstraction of the self may be reworked and new selves and modalities of world-making conceived. Poetry can thus can refer to processes of de-subjection rooted in the de-composition of words into heterogeneous assemblages of sounds and impulses, of signifying and non-signifying elements that efface or defer the presumed stability of the self, race, culture, or "the body."[16] Accordingly, the emphasis is on that play on and with the surplus or margins of lyrical translation, or what eludes the embrace of "lyric reading" (generalizing subjective representation as the horizon or master code of all poetry) to re-situate other pathways of expression.

Improvisation: Journey to the One

To grasp free jazz improvisation in all of its radicalness requires taking seriously its implicit investments in embodiment—implied, among other ways, by the extended techniques and lengthy performances—to outline an alternative grounding conception of sociality, of the common of community. "Free jazz" designates the abandonment or loosening of the relationship between melody and harmony, as well as rearticulated understandings of recapitulation and swing.[17] Some critics and performers sought to link free improvisation to black nationalist politics or black consciousness, a legacy that persists, transformed, in accounts of the music as resistance or critique.[18] For all they reveal, those accounts tend to understate the radical potentiality of the music as a collaboration between listeners and players. Free improvisation is best understood in terms of social ecstasy (Ashon Crawley's term) whose improvisation of the common makes thinkable other ways of being, and being together. The new forms of intensity—and the structures, techniques, and critical perspectives that enable them—are a starting point from which to consider the dissolved boundaries between poetry and music.

New aesthetic practices expanded the range and intensity of expression, or made intensity itself—the deferral or rejection of traditional resolution, the emphasis on the jagged and agonistic over settled convention, or emphasis of the sensual aspects and embodied experience and practice of language—into an autonomous aesthetic value. Foregrounded, intensity can sound like an agonistic negation of tradition, but it is usually a dialectical re-sounding and transformation from within: new intensities, new ecstasies. Black ecstasy is a site of liberatory risk or chance that does not posit a unique, lived experience of blackness but instead insists on blackness as a disruption of prevailing accounts of phenomenological lived experience. "Social ecstasy" is a claim for subjective "undoneness as ontological priority," and a practice of "emptying oneself toward a social," a surrender to unanticipated, non-enclosed forms of oneness with otherness.[19] "Ecstasy" names forms of out experience not easily encompassed by the signs that usually allow us to make sense of whatever is happening. Reckoning with a tradition of outsideness requires attending to the subjective experience of art while also considering the objective organization of the social that grounds such experience. Putting these together may help us hear the broader postcolonial reverberations beyond the obvious ways musicians and musical traditions from the decolonizing world circulate in this period and nurture free jazz.

Considered in light of black experimental aesthetics, we should also emphasize the opening of selves to others in the course of improvising under- or not-yet-regulated forms of intense experience that only retrospectively will have been pleasurable.[20] Without conflating the erotic and the pleasurable, we should hear the erotic resonance of social ecstasy, even when emptied selves do not share physical space. Putting together social and erotic ecstasy, a picture emerges of the pursuit of ecstatic experience as a discomfiting and unassimilable encounter with the truth of the world not as transcendence but immanence, often grounded in specific communities and communal experience. This framing can help reattune us to the stakes of the spiritualism of "soul jazz" on the one hand and that of John Coltrane and others—the pursuit of "objectless love" and "selflessness" at the core of their music, on the other. It can also give us a different vocabulary for engaging the different modalities of intensity at work in Taylor, Lee, or Archie Shepp, to name a few. If my first chapter concerns itself with the continual drawing of Frederick Douglass's (hermeneutic) circle to accommodate the shifting meanings and practices of black sound, we take up those aural traditions that resist interpretation and indeed refuse the circle's enclosure in pursuit of elusive, eccentric outs.

My reference to pleasure as retrospective is a reminder that there is no "as such" to ecstasy. It does not exist as pure dispatch, even as it cuts and augments (borrowing Fred Moten's phrase) experience with what we habitually exclude. Social ecstasy, forms of collective experience that have no (proper) name, in this sense re-sign-ifies black embodied experience and practices, such as improvisation. Considering free improvisation in terms of the semiotic, which would be another way to frame the preceding, is not entirely new. John Corbett discusses improvisation as a "semiotic system without a semantic level," which positions it on the side of the "perpetual present" familiar to students of lyric theory.[21] Read alongside Julia Kristeva, a semiotic system without semantic level would be a realization of poetic language's emancipatory capacity in the wholesale reconstitution of culture through the fissures in the Symbolic—the latent, language-mediated and socially orchestrated sign complexes through which the world appears as stable, ordered, and coherent—it exploits. But the result of Corbett's argument is a thin sense of improvisation extending a "we" (via Roland Barthes, "ourselves writing") into a future detached from any past or tradition. It is improvisation as pure rupture, pure ecstasy, which misses, for example, claims by musicians like Cecil Taylor or Ornette Coleman on the centrality of the blues as signifier of the deeply historical traditions their musical practice drew on and extended. At stake, in other words, is not just the erosion of the Symbolic or the semantic, but new paths forward from the resources of the past. Polymath trumpeter and composer Jacques Coursil, positing "spoken language"—specifically, the "non-premeditation of common speech"—"as a theoretical horizon" addresses the issue of time and inheritance, the thicker sense of community-making at stake in most forms of musical improvisation. He writes, "What is happening now contains a part that has never been previously declared in the future tense in any past discourse."[22] (Yet, Taylor might add, "the statement becomes more finite as it grows, if it's growing.")[23] The irreducible possibility of errantry—parapraxis, babble, elisions, repetition, incidental sounds, and other material sonic excess—becomes the basis for improvisation's novelty in much the way that rhythm, assonance, sound play, and other emphases on the material practice of sounding inform Kristeva's account of the semiotic. But where Julia Kristeva's account turns on recovering a prediscursive (i.e., pre-Symbolic) plenitude figured by the maternal body and a *jouissance* that precedes the subject/object binary desire presupposes, Coursil suggests the irruption of something immanent, a "beyond" not yet named. Stressing the textual mediations of the Symbolic, the enclosure of intelligible "reality," Kristeva's semiotic undermines both object and enunciating subject, making room for what Sylvia Wynter terms the "reinvention of the concrete self" by allowing other possibilities for selfhood.

Kristeva's semiotic is a genre of irony that destabilizes the Symbolic by making its laws objects of analysis and aesthetic material to rework. Poetic language, she argues, would "wipe out sense through nonsense and laughter," specifically by accessing a pre-discursive, pre-subjective libidinal plenitude rooted in the mother's body.[24] It is a kind of non- or counter-representational intensity, a *jouissance* of the body rather than the subject, the unrepresentable pre-symbolic and potentially destructuring materiality of signification. Yet, as Judith Butler argues, Kristeva's "naturalistic descriptions of the maternal body effectively reify motherhood and preclude an analysis of its cultural construction and variability," and that reification is at once constitutive of the semiotic's power and an arbitrary limit.[25] Even if one accepts Kristeva's positing of female embodiment as unassimilable alterity and insurgent ground against the Symbolic's paternal law, one must also attend to the variable positioning of maternity *within* the Symbolic, which is not uniformly governed by one Law. Such is one of the lessons of Hortense Spillers's engagement with psychoanalysis. Among other things, this means different mothers access the signifiers of motherhood from meaningfully distinct positions, as is clear when one parses the nonalignment of the *mother* and the *mama*.

Yet, we can read Kristeva with Fanon's notion of "epidermalization"—a process of appropriating blackness as a sign complex whose lived experience dissolves the distinction between "outer" appearance and "inner" truth—and ask what would happen if we conceived Kristeva's semiotic as the embodiment of a surplus, as access to kinds of *jouissance* prohibited by bourgeois society. "Epidermalization" offers an account of embodiment as a social process, in this case one that produces the aporia between the bourgeois ideal of self-possession and the realities of dispossession and attenuated citizenship. Embodiment, that is, comes to be coded as the ground of difference rather than an effect of social organization. Fanon's genius is to suggest that bodies, in the way of texts, are the product of overlapping generative processes and thus belong to competing, incommensurate, even contradictory schemes of desire, myth, and meaning making. Epidermalization, then, is a name for the symbolic process that appropriates—semanticizes—its own surplus. Fanon outlines a distinctly modern process: the bourgeoisie wins individuality by figuring socially valued differences as natural—creating contingent but quasi-permanent typologies of otherness in order to manage the new forms of psychic excess industrial modernity creates. "When the whites feel over-mechanized, they turn to the black man for a little human sustenance."[26] In different terms, insistence on black alterity functions as the transcendental signification that subverts and displaces grammatical codes and textual play inherent in black texts, devolving self-assertion and self-definition into alienated symbols of enjoyment that reinscribe the black body's excessiveness.

Yet "the black body"—already a figure for desired and disavowed black personhood—is not simply a plenitude to recover. It is itself suffused with gendered signs, histories, and structures of feeling. To avoid the reification that limits Kristeva, we have to resist the lure of the abstract. The question of different bodies' relationships to the symbolic becomes especially pressing in Jeanne Lee's work, which thematizes black maternity and kinship between women. There, claims to the mother's body are in excess of the law (in multiple registers), playing on and against the historical processes that alienate black women from normative gender processes and from motherhood. Could we understand investment in instrumental or embodied voice as semiotic—not self-expression but a "slide away from the proposed," an erosion of the Symbolic from the position strategically unthinkable timelines of reclaimed, invented black maternity? Black mothering abounds, despite every social force and norm aligned against it and the many discourses that malign it. However, within the universalizing frame of psychoanalysis, where the Law's prohibition protects the mother's body from unwanted touch, black maternity is impossible. To the normative maternal time, black maternity exists as a series of stolen moments, stolen time with children apt to be taken either by the murderousness or punitive tendencies of the law. To inhabit that time, to hold open that space of encounter might help us conceive the stolen time of free improvisation on its way to producing what has truly "never been previously declared in the future tense in any past discourse": the freedom of black people whose basis is free black maternity. This is to listen beyond the liberationist and supersessionist narratives surrounding poetry and music for those zones of undecidability where an opening, a caesura, appears for reconceiving.

Social mediations—including race and class—differentially inscribe maternity as experience and category, differentially ascribe its legibility and legitimacy as a component of social reproduction. Judith Butler here is helpful: "the Symbolic remains hegemonic except when the semiotic disrupts its signifying process through elision, repetition, mere sound, and the multiplication of meaning through indefinitely signifying images and metaphors."[27] The semiotic plays in the Symbolic's irreducibly material surplus, running now with and against its grain to create ephemeral resting points from which new possibilities become thinkable. But Fanon teaches us that surplus has a tendency to be reappropriated, especially insofar as it can be posited as outside the Symbolic, as "nature." Despite Kristeva's reification of the maternal into a univocality that ultimately reinforces paternal law, her arguments help us understand embodiment as process, and potentially better hear the ways insistence on the body in music's production might bear political content. This is to conceive of Kristeva's belonging—however complicatedly—to a generation of French thinkers shaped by the Algerian War of Independence and global decolonization.[28]

The push against surface/depth models might reflect a greater push against—or desire to reframe—subjectivity as the province of the bourgeois, rights-having individual. At stake are alternative principles of aesthetic structuration governing both the practice and the theoretical object of black sound. Artists sought both poetics and aesthetic accounts, in Sylvia Wynter's terms, not governed "by the sociogenic principle or 'code' that is determining of our present mode of being and 'form of life,'" but that would trigger "awareness of the realm of 'unfreedom' that haunt[s] critical practice."[29] Wynter belongs to the Black Arts/black aesthetic generation, which means, in David Scott's terms, she shares a "*habitus* of temporal experience" and "lived experience of social time"[30] with her erstwhile Black Aesthetic movement colleagues, despite their divergent political and intellectual commitments. Wynter's attention to "the psycho-affective field of normative sentiments by which we are collectively *induced* to behave in specific *ways* able to bring our present global order and its role-allocated hierarchies into being"[31] resonates with Larry Neal's critique of the "white thing": "white ideas and white ways of looking at the world."[32] Wynter argues that aesthetics, as a political project, reifies whiteness and bourgeois norms as natural. She further argues that those norms condition the biochemical pleasure/punishment system. Unlearning those beauty ideals, produced in opposition with the permanent nonwhite abject, requires the pursuit of new pleasures.[33]

What Wynter refers to as the "reinvention of the self" offers an especially lucid conception of a black aesthetic project beyond the impulses of "ethnic" enclosure or the structured subordinativities reified by the concept of the universal, which she reveals to be historically contingent. Deciphering practice thus appears to be the name for semiotic analysis, or simply poetics: attention to the culturally and historically specific means by which a text produces meanings through the interplay of grammar and referentiality. Rather than parsing the degree to which particular practices are black or European (or affirm blackness or Europeanness), we might uncover truly transgressive aesthetic acts that not only violate preexisting codes but make new ones. This, then, is what I argue is ultimately at stake in free improvisation: the reinvention of the concrete self as adjacent to and in excess of the subject, whose coherence is a fiction that serves the interests of particular configurations of power and ways of ordering the social. The ecstatic is to the subject's fictional coherence as riots are to the fiction of social coherence vouchsafed by leadership. They form the limits and boundaries of aesthetic experience and theory.

I stress the continuities between Wynter and the earlier generation of black aesthetics theory in part to draw out the ways her critique of the sociogenic principles that condition subjectivity (the Symbolic) end up being concerned with the ideologically determined limits of semiotic capacity. Wynter's call for reinventing "the concrete self [by] first recogniz[ing] the abstraction of the self which, imposed on us, we have inherited"[34] echoes Amiri Baraka's programmatic definition of the New Black Music ("find the self, then kill it"), as well as Larry Neal's claim that "the text could be destroyed and no one would be hurt in the least by it."[35] What lies "beyond" or on the "outside" is the anarchic potential of that which, refused, remains immanent as destabilizing potentiality. Although Neal is most explicitly concerned with the effect of the commodity form on the production of culture (rather than the media of writing) and the effects adaptation of "universal" standards would have on the uncategorized and unruly in black culture, all three accounts imply some extra-discursive materiality and extra- or non-subjective agency in excess of conventional aesthetics. To "kill" the self requires a shift in the very terms under which one can imagine the agent of the self's dispatch. It requires considering forms of individuation that aren't necessarily reducible to the formal freedom and equality required for property ownership and taxation.

Free improvisation empties the self toward the social, and doing so reactivates immanently disruptive forms of individuation that cut and augment the Symbolic. But what does such individuation look like? For that, I draw on what Hortense Spillers, in her work on race and psychoanalysis, terms the "one":

> Before the "individual," properly speaking, with its overtones of property ownership and access, more or less complete, stands the "one," who is both a position in discourse—the spoken subject of *énoncé* that figures a grammatical instance and a consciousness of positionality—the speaking subject of the *énonciation*, the one in the act of speaking as consciousness of position.... In the meantime, who is this one? I am referring to a *structure* in this instance: the small integrity of the now that accumulates the tense of the presents as proofs of the past, and as experience that would warrant, might earn, the future.[36]

The one is a singularity rather than an individual or subject—it differs and defers the universal/particular binary. Its plural form is multiplicity rather than collectivity.[37] It is a name of conceiving of those excessive capacities and opacities suppressed to make a subject, through both *énoncés* (utterances whose meanings are relatively autonomous within established discursive chains) and enunciation (the production of meaning in specific times and places). It functions well as a term for the kinds of historically grounded intersubjective experiences that inscribe improvisation as both production and reproduction. In slightly different terms, the "one" is the trace of historical and social processes that precede (antedate and are logical preconditions of) and exceed possessive individualism, and makes thinkable in historical terms the limits of that conception of the human. As with her celebrated notion of the "flesh," Spillers urges us to think beyond or alongside familiar categories (e.g., the individual, the subject) in order to grasp the complex social practices that subtend, depend upon, and mobilize those categories. The "one" is in this sense "vestibular": between disorganized affects and impulses and culturally conditioned understandings of the subject that ultimately presuppose particular forms of social organization—those of Euro-American bourgeois society—as universal. The "one"—a placeholder for notions of experience and being subverted by the grammars of the self—is what remains after the self's "killing," what works toward the improvisatory production of the common. All of this is to point to other spaces and potentialities from within the Symbolic that erode and degrade it, recreating its own ground rather than imagining permanent exteriority as its goal. With these considerations in mind, I turn to Cecil Taylor's overdubbed poetry followed by Jeanne Lee's hybrid song-texts.

Form Is Possibility

One way to open oneself to the experience of listening to Cecil Taylor is to take seriously his desire "to make music into poetry"[38] or his claim, "I've always tried to be a poet more than anything else."[39] Statements like these, which he would often repeat even when not discussing his poetry, point beyond the political and aesthetic debates associated with members of his generation. I read them as commitment to ongoingness, as the enunciation of a discrepant relationship to signification, a commitment to annul and reconstitute sense through extra-subjective excess oriented around the one—ensemblic one, pre- and extra-individual one—rather than the subject and its dependencies. Considering that commitment in light of the ways his extended techniques refuse the distinction between physical and mental labor in and through (collective) play, the ensemble of his sounding marks an effort to reenchant embodied (black) being in the world. We might consider these two—reenchanting the laboring and ecstatic body—as two aspects of one reflexive process that negotiates the "utopian aspiration and political despair" characteristic of the confused temporalities of futures that never arrived and immanent possibilities blocked by extant configurations of power/knowledge. That is, we might read it in terms of the Kristevan semiotic, provided we adjust our understanding of the Symbolic to account for the differentially distributed antagonisms that structure limits of subjectivity and social forms. Poetic language, the work of the semiotic, could refer to extra-subjective libidinalities not rooted in unbarred access to the mother's body but in the erotics of social ecstasy. Such is more generally true of so-called "free jazz," whose relationship to the textually mediated problem space of "jazz" is as often orthogonal or appositional as oppositional. Cecil Taylor's approach to composition and improvisation as "sonic design" includes words and vocal sounds as part of a larger project he discussed in spatial terms, reinforced by frequent reference to dance as well as poetry. The resulting sound texts enact "methodologic fissures" between, and deconstruction of, the mutually constitutive aesthetic fields of literature and music, signifying and non-signifying, voice as self and other.[40] In the vein of Charles Mingus, Thelonious Monk, and others, Taylor taught ensemble members their parts aurally, singing their parts and allowing them maximum freedom to interpret and collectively produce an arrangement, in effect making their listening public. If he approached the piano as a set of "eighty-eight tuned drums," then we can say that he not only created space for fuller and more complex form of ensemble interplay, but that he changed the sound and function of the piano. He created a compositional language that develops but also remains strikingly consistent throughout decades of recorded performance, and his innovations extend into written and performed poetry. Taylor generated new pathways and new possibilities for ensemble interaction that, like his poetry, involves establishing the grounds of different kinds of ecstatic encounter—emptying or sidestepping the self in the interest of higher unities.

Taylor's relationship to language, mined for intensities and unexpected connections that illuminate an immanent outside, parallels his relationship to the piano and jazz traditions. Improvisation as a question of time, of gathering, links them. The provenance of his sound—the sources of and influences on his technique (which carries a long history of the racial coding of sound practice) is often the crux of listening or refusing to listen. Valerie Wilmer, one of the music's earliest advocates, dubbed him "the first musician of any importance to introduce atonality into so-called jazz": "This means music in which a key-centre, or note in the scale to which everything gravitates when it comes to rest, is absent."[41] What results is a "nonfunctional" approach to sound, where sounds abut one another according to a logic of color or texture unrelated to diatonic music. Because Taylor eschewed cadential resolution, tone clusters—"pile[s] or stack[s] of tones, created by simultaneously striking all or most of the chromatic steps within a certain area"—rather than chords are central to his practice.[42]

His preference for symmetrical scalar concepts (e.g., whole-tone or diminished scales), which he tended to play in both hands at tremendous speed, likewise allows maximal freedom for soloist and members of the ensemble. In both solo and ensemble performances, he played simultaneous melodies and countermelodies of dazzling density. Nonfunctional approaches (e.g., modal playing and other alternatives to diatonic music's harmonic gravity) abound in the history of jazz. Bebop had already introduced chromaticism. Taylor's generation carried those developments further. Making what may be an irresistible analogy, Wilmer argues that, by using notes without reference to a particular key, "the artist gains a richer harmonic vocabulary, rather like a language that has more words." Following that, one could say that in fact the relevant "vocabulary" stops being harmonic if harmony refers to conventional ways of building and resolving tension. It becomes rhythmic instead. As Taylor told A. B. Spellman:

> Music is the organization of sound existing in time, its dimensions hanging in space. The problem was reorganization of ingredients to discover surprise. Harmonic changes provide yesterday's dynamism. Additive technique, extended phrases, slowing down of harmonic motion, diads [sic], clusters replace chords built on thirds. Rhythmic possibilities are expanded, and knowledge of given time is understood. And the ecstatic compression of time's energy produces twelve, sixteen, and thirty-two measures—complete sketches, improvisation, content, and shape becoming one.[43]

The degree of autonomy each note has with respect to the others, and that each member of the ensemble has, paired with rhythm's centrality make Taylor's approach distinctive.

Although he was conservatory trained, Taylor insisted his apparent atonality derived primarily from implications of the blues, stride, and bebop piano conventions. He made what would have been passing tones the basis of a new approach that increases the allowable range of pitch possibilities to create a sense of resolution relative to the musical environment. He supplemented tone clusters and symmetrical concepts with arpeggios and motivic figures, all played, as Lynette Westendorf puts it, with "exquisite clarity of articulation at phenomenal speeds, with precise definition of tonal and dynamic shading, brilliant rhythmic control, flawless pedaling, and extraordinary endurance."[44] Moving through an implied set of tonal centers rather than keys or modes, Taylor fundamentally changed the sound of the piano in "jazz," moving far beyond traditional chord-based accompaniment or "comping," where the pianist spells out the harmonic structure and responds to the soloist. Instead, as he put it, "[t]he piano [works] as catalyst feeding material to soloists in all registers. . . . [M]otors become knowledge at once felt, memory which has identified sensory images resulting in social response."[45] Seizing on the idea of "motor responses," Andrew Bartlett emphasizes the degree to which "the body is the locus of [Taylor's] improvisatory process," and I would further emphasize the relationship between memory and the sensory in the resulting "social response."[46] *Text*, as compositor of time that connects listeners and performers in a sense of "lived time," mediates memory, sensory images, and motor response.

Tradition, a public way of mediating and appropriating fragments of time into narratives about self and nation, are central to conceiving Taylor's work for fans and detractors alike. As Fred Moten observes, anxieties about the "alienating, feminizing, homosexualizing, whitening" effect of European influence often animates critiques of a nominally "Euro-aesthetic absence of emotion and the concomitant hegemony of an inauthentic intellectualism disconnected from its home or origin."[47] This is one context in which to read Spellman's claim that Taylor "wishes people would listen to the essentially blues content of his music instead of to whatever forms and devices he may have brought over from the conservatory. Cecil believes that his problem is to utilize 'the energies of the European composers, their technique, consciously, and blend this with the traditional music of the American Negro, and to create a new energy. . . . This is what has always happened. [Duke] Ellington did it.'"[48] The conservatory, as synecdoche for Europe, figures aesthetic modes and concepts hostile to black thriving. But it also figures anxieties over the ethnographer-composer of the earlier twentieth century who, as Langston Hughes puts it, mixed "my blues" with symphonies.[49] Spellman apparently has that anxiety in mind when he refers to Taylor as "a kind of Bartók in reverse," citing his ability to "incorporate all that he wants to take from classical and modern Western composition into his own distinctly individual kind of blues without in the least compromising those blues."[50] Moten is right that notions of home, aesthetic, and sexual propriety, metonymically linked in the figure of the straight black male as ideal subject of the music, are at stake in criticism surrounding Taylor and the supposedly emotionless intellectualism of some performers. But Spellman's comment invites further thinking. More than the "prophet of the black musical outside" who "disrupts and allows the Black political unit and unity,"[51] Taylor is a figure (or prophet) of black communism, where the improvisation of the common reconditions the ground of blackness and its constitutive components (e.g., tradition) itself.

Béla Bartók was an ethnomusicologist as well as a composer, celebrated for his incorporation of "folk" or vernacular material into cosmopolitan modernism, where that material was "refined." His project is recognizably modernist insofar as it transforms spatial distance into temporal distance in order to appropriate the Other's cultural forms and inject new energy into a set of codes and aesthetic procedures that had lost vitality. Although "refinement" is one way to conceive of the abstraction and translation of musical elements from one musical domain to another, it becomes possible to show, as Taylor does, that "refinement" is a name for the improvisatory (self-analytical) reworking of what Amiri Baraka termed "old forms and old nightmares" in order to make new music.[52] On one level, reverse movement here is deconstructive movement that engages the vernacular, common aesthetic practices, without recourse to the frame of refinement. It is a formalist procedure for framing a "we" and revealing what that "we" has in common, of interrogating, perhaps, what it means to say "we." Taylor's procedure does not just add "classical" elements to vernacular stock, or vice versa; it engages the idea of tradition "from the outside" in the interest of producing the common as something divided and distributed but not owned. Simultaneously, as Aldon Nielsen argues, "as Free Jazz became a self-organizing radical activity it began to gather an ever widening and appreciative audience," and greater absorption and neutralization by state cultural apparatuses (e.g., the US State Department's anti-communist articulation of "freedom" in the music).[53] The dispersal of that audience, already lamented by Harold Cruse in *The Crisis of the Negro Intellectual*, has as much to do with economics—the onset of mid-1970s recession and corresponding shifts in the funding priorities of governmental and nongovernmental philanthropic organizations—as with aesthetics.

If we take "methodologic fissures" to be a description of Taylor's formal procedures, his free working of musical material in order to rework traditions, those procedures improvise the common by deviating from—reversing or otherwise altering—existing identity categories and, stretching a bit, deviating from compulsory norms of social reproduction. Moten refers to this as "a free and out negation of identity—lingering emergences in and from the fissure between and outside as well as in groups."[54] Emphasizing "lingering emergences" that mark the non-self-identity of groups is a means of improvising the common. To move in reverse—to elevate the "primitive" tone cluster over to the "refined" chord or mode or, better, to treat the chord or mode *as* tone cluster (which it surely is)—is to pass into a different mode of musical presentation whose end is neither allegorical representation nor social reproduction. Pausing over Taylor's controversial claim regarding audience preparation ("The absolute choices an artist must have are not to be bargained with. You prepare and you present. The audience, whether it knows it or not, also prepares"[55]), we can understand improvisation itself as a set of exchanges structured by the previously agreed-upon arrangement of musical and other materials that creates the context in which agency takes on dimension. Improvisation is about the dispersal of self, an emanation without immanence that moves into and back out of the extra- or infra-subjective one. This is another way of conceiving the inescapable discussion of "outness" when discussing Taylor. Improvisation binds "the player" to the area's "unknown totality" through "self analysis (improvisation)."[56] It participates in the process of individuation discussed above, as well as the inter-subjective negotiations of environment (milieu and social context) and received musical materials that precede and ground subjectivity in the first place.

The abstractness of the music and its improvisation of the common beyond given social identities creates ambiguities, which Phillip Brian Harper has recently addressed, in part by stressing music as non-conceptual and nonrepresentational. Musical "material," he reminds us, is not immediately given but is constitutively imbricated in a complex weave of social relations that form or participate in a greater totality, and as such calls for dialectical analysis and engagement. Part of Harper's aim is to emphasize traditions of black poetic and visual abstraction that celebratory accounts of the music can obscure. Music's overemphasis as model or reference requires its idealization, suppressing what is most potentially productive about sound, the habits of listening that create sound objects (relatively autonomous fragments of sound whose value exceeds referentiality or indexicality alone, as discussed in chapter 1) and the material heterogeneity of sound events. For Harper, music's blackness does not derive from the internal arrangement of material but from the coordination of sound object and its paratext. While "sonic phenomena achieve their aesthetic effects in the same modality in which they sustain their objective existence," he argues, "the means by which music accedes to blackness . . . consists not in a specifically sonic modality but in a narrative discursivity that is not properly musical at all."[57] Black sound becomes the technical-textual index of an underlying desire to make sound media, and sound itself, work a certain way. Yet Harper's own method—notational transcription from an early recording—is itself a way of narrativizing a certain *listening*, and listening is always productive. Musical notation is itself a kind of idealization that presents sounds as discrete, unidimensional, and universal (i.e., assumes that the timbral and spatial differences between different soundings of "C" are epiphenomenal to the "whatness" of "C"). More profoundly, anyone who has produced or tried to play a transcribed improvised solo quickly becomes aware that transcription is the document of accumulated and embodied listening, subject to another's choices and interpretations of a recording that is itself the product of an engineer's interpretation of the sound event. A transcription is the production of a *narrative* of listening according to conventions external to the sound itself—it is no more "properly musical" than any other text. Rather, it activates a paradigm of music as representation that Taylor's practice—engaging members of the Unit to learn and shape their parts by interpreting a single hummed line, his occasional recourse to pounding the keyboard with his fist, his commitment to out poetics open to the other's listening—subverts. That subversion may not be "inherently," but the forms of active listening Taylor invites are often rooted in black-marked traditions.

Listening, as practice and as trope, helps us remain attuned to the social texture of sound practices, and helps us remember the multiple conflicting, even mutually exclusive, impulses at play in the network of sound and its reception. Terms like "jazz" generate and manage textual excess through a chain of equivalences that attempt to make race a structural or inherent component of the sound text's signifying structure rather than a fundamentally intuitive critical stance. Harper helps us recall the degree to which "music proper," an idealization of music as self-identical and self-referential, is actually an effect of inscriptions and counter-inscriptions that precede and exceed it, just as idealizations of The Music are. One solution, suggested by Taylor and other artists, is to relinquish claims to the "properly musical," and thereby to relinquish teleological understandings of form in favor of "an alternative, modular approach, in which the structural content of music is located in the free play of smaller constituent units."[58] Although Vijay Iyer in the preceding citation does not directly refer to Cecil Taylor, that free play of smaller constituent units is an apt description of Taylor's project beyond the generous and attentive analyses Harper offers of Taylor's early recordings. We might add time to the list of music's media and conceive of Taylor's new music, for which the removal of conventional harmonic markers encourages the gradual loosening of time (most dramatically in the role drummers, especially Sunny Murray and Andrew Cyrille, play in the Unit); we might hear this and other instances of the New Black Music as an orchestration of time.

In both music and poetry, abstraction produces meaning precisely by engaging complex cultural weaves of sonic phenomena, semantic and syntactical innovation, and extrinsic discourses that disrupt or undermine the conventions and narratives that define them. The respective abilities of poetry and music to revolutionize their own modes and norms of affective and discursive production—convert noise to music, convert music to noise, or otherwise alter the line between the sensuous and the sensible—best suit them to engage a project of reconceiving the political even when they don't engage politics as currently existing. Free jazz's recontextualization of existing Western and African

American traditions is as important (and as black) as its citation of existing traditions.[59] Such a conclusion is inescapable if one grants the textuality of music itself, and if one allows a greater range of black expressivity. Each generates a text that is not obliged to be representative or even communicative, but is simultaneously productive of and enmeshed in the production of broader social meanings.

Listening to Cecil Taylor otherwise will mean taking seriously, on the one hand, his claims about common, racially coded technique ("We in black music think of the piano as a percussive instrument: we beat the keyboard, we get inside the instrument. . . . But the physical force going into the making of black music—if that's misunderstood, it leads to screaming")[60] and his related desire to "make music into poetry." If "form is possibility," analysis should proceed by showing some of the ways Taylor and his ensemble rework musical material *including* media, indeed the ways they work the art/non-art boundary in ways that invent new forms. The condition of songfulness results when sound's surplus materiality develops a relatively autonomous significance independent of simple utility.[61] The question of what exactly it means to make music poetry, then, might require what Fred Moten in a related context termed an "*a*calculation of that function whose upper limit is reading and whose lower limit is transcription."[62] Acalculation here either names a refusal to calculate (or choose) between the two poles or integral limits, instead lingering in the uncertain zone between the two, or emphasizes the spaces such an integral function leaves unmeasured. Through attention to what remains incalculable, acalculation might also indicate the limits of calculation as a tool of analysis when faced with forms that insistently undermine their own intelligibility within only one domain.

In the following sections, I read Taylor's phonographic poetry as reenchantment and play with the multiplicity of social norms and structures, taking what is suppressed within the social order as the basis for its transformation. Taylor developed the possibilities of working from the impulses sedimented in musical material that, through "instant composing" he and members of his different ensembles could reorganize to a practice of the outside, not as simple opposition to the interiority of traditions of "society" but something subtending and escaping the oppositions that usually animate it. This practice, in other words, is an improvisation of the common as the material "outside" to the organic ideologies of existing power relations. This, after all, is what is at stake in Spillers's "one," which does not oppose the subject/object or interiority/exteriority binary so much as comprehend them in order to better conceive the complexities of social organization—hence the importance of temporality. The cultivation of intensity and multiplication of harmonic, rhythmic, and melodic possibilities, the production of generous, self-opening forms in the project of "creating Music as sound within the whole body" ultimately foregrounds sound as a matter of energy-in-time.[63]

Taylor's poetry invests the quotidian and referential—especially African American, West African, and other colonial histories from the perspective of the oppressed—with an anarchic, de-orchestrating energy that allows him to move between material/spiritual concerns ("poets live to eat / spirits commingle"). The poems tend at once to offer programmatic statements—as with this chapter's epigraph, or his most-cited writing, "Sound of Subculture Becoming Major Breath/Naked Fire Gesture," the liner notes to his 1966 Blue Note album *Unit Structures*—and subvert that function. As his poetry generally does, "Naked Fire Gesture" startlingly mixes registers, producing metaphors, as he says in another context, "to confound the senses": metaphors invoke the music, but just as quickly trope and re-signify it into dense weaves of history, mythology, and aesthetic theory.[64] This tendency toward semiotic ongoingness, as we will see, is the closest point of contact between his poetic and musical practice, which similarly sets up expectations of harmonic movement only to undermine them, refusing the lure of cadential closure. Taylor's rhetorical and tropic fluidity marks an especially compelling conversion of the in-time process-oriented art of improvisation into the over-time production of poetry on the page or on record.[65] Considering his commitment to "the possibility of using language to move outside of the self," that notion of improvisation would require the kind of critical reframing I have been discussing around the one, a singular imagining of all that exists within and alongside what we have settled names for.

Taylor's involvement with poetry is coextensive with his work as a professional musician. He worked with Diane di Prima and Amiri Baraka to mimeograph copies of *Floating Bear*,[66] participated in the Umbra Workshop,[67] and printed his poetry in small journals. However, he did not formally integrate his poetry and music practices until the 1970s, when he began to publish poetry as liner notes for his own Unit Core albums. His use of poetry as liner notes itself blurs lines between discursive modes in ways that underscore a more primary textuality. Rather than explain, provide personal or aesthetic context for the music, they enhance the music in ways only comprehensible through the medium of the album, which thus becomes something other than simple document. For example, poems first published in 1965 reappear in the liner notes to his 1977 solo performance *Indent*. If the improviser generally orchestrates time, these albums present Taylor as an orchestrator on a very large scale, as if to suggest that something of the mid-1960s persists as the pressure of something to be done, or understood. With the 1982 album *Garden*, a recording of a 1981 solo performance in Basel, Switzerland, he began to issue recordings of the poetry, adding yet another textual layer to his practice, another way of bridging or falsifying the gap between music and poetry, while still refusing to let the latter stand as explanation for the former. Music and poetry become one another's complicating reference, one another's interior inter-subjectivity.

An examination of his recorded poetry will test, amend, and complicate the preceding claims. *Chinampas*, featuring Taylor solo on voice, recitation, and percussion, holds an unusual place in his discography. His poetry typically falls into two categories: recorded "live" as part of performances that also included dance, and recorded as after-the-fact extension and complication of a "live" solo or ensemble performance. As an example of the first, I will share my listening to the poem and music of "Elell" on *Garden*. For the second, I will offer comments on the poem cycle "Squash People/Eyes Within the Voice/Eucalyptus Intersection and Failure to Appear/Feather Upon Brow/Roses," recorded nine years later and released as *Double Holy House*. Recalling Fred Moten's argument that "the unit [Taylor's name for the ensembles, which outwardly resembled traditional jazz configurations but often operated as modular, autonomous sub-units] is present in Taylor's 'solo' performances as surely as he 'leads' (structures or feeds) the performance of the unit," my ways of reading the interactions within the sound text hold for larger ensembles as well.[68] Music and poetry stand in relation to one another as fragments that refuse belonging to a whole and in so doing calls for new understandings of the whole.

A. GARDEN

   Rhythm every where
     in every place
       is
     every thing
        not think that
       writing this
         read it
        what
       then never over
   start[69]

The recording captures Taylor's 1981 performance of words and piano in Basel, Switzerland. "Ah he dé" and long variable "o's," distant at first, approach. Moaning finds the microphone on a prepared stage. Moaning refuses words, skirts them, becomes tune, melodic minor if it is a mode, sung or wrested from an unwilling throat. Wordless tune becomes tuneless words, then song again, as before, agonized in the throat, wrestling:

> about the thrasher
> death comes too soon
> about the thrasher
> and we will go into the field to plow
> [percussive sound: hands clapping, foot stomping
> moaning, sub-semantic phonemes]
> Ah he dé
> Ah he dé
> Ah he dé
> Ah he dé
> thrash, thrash
> [moan]
> [percussive "eh" sound becoming growl; repeats][70]

Applause. About two minutes have lapsed. Taylor, now apparently seated at the piano, begins to play. First, a descending syncopated motif played slowly with both hands separated by an octave, G-E-G-E-G-E, answered by the same figure, played with a less halting rhythm, up an octave. The shift offers to resolve the tension by being apparently more regular. Keeping the notes and their sequence constant shifts attention to rhythm—there is not enough harmonic information yet to speak of tonality. He plays a very low note followed by the same note at the opposite end of the keyboard, then begins to repeat the sequence with differences of accent or "attack." When he finally modulates (if the term makes sense in this context) and changes the sequence to B♭-G, one almost wants to hazard a guess about tonality (a diminished scale?). He abandons that, briefly flirting with an abstracted stride piano line, heavy with left hand, before returning to develop the motivic theme that dominates this performance. One of his most observant critics argues that the "ability to think structurally at great speed . . . along with a kind of spontaneous constructionism that occurs as the music unfolds in real time comprise the real foundation of Taylor's music."[71] "Spontaneous," here, is a tell: it reinscribes a split between composition/improvisation and structure/play that haunts criticism of the music. If Taylor is indeed "thinking structurally at great speed," then some new paradigm of play, a paradigm that could displace the predicates of traditional musical analysis, is needed. It's a continual process of establishing and destabilizing structures whose logic is the refusal of a transcendental term like *music* or *poetry* to anchor the play of significations. Its discipline points to an order immanent to the work itself. One does not so much listen as surrender to it.

A similar paradigm of play is apparently at stake in the poetry.[72] Semi- and sub-semantic sounds hold the same status as words, whose value is as much rhythmic as motivic or ritual, which is to say their function is semiotic, or melodic. "It's all melody," Taylor replied to his father's challenge that he should play more melodically, which is the same as saying it needs to be conceived along the diachronic rather than synchronic axis.[73] Melody with a discrepant relationship to underlying harmony is play in the boundlessness of rhythmic and tonal variation, where tonal variation itself becomes another element of rhythm. But reading is the question: "Elell," which is not unambiguously the title of the poem, most likely comes from the Tamasheq language (a variant of the Tuareg language spoken throughout the Western Sahara region), referring to "nobility." Readers may convince themselves of the relationship, ironic or otherwise, of the theme of nobility and the explicit invocations on thrashers, but the remaining words (I have been unable to arrive at a plausible reading or translation of "ah he dé") do not provide any obvious clues for interpretation. Both transcription and a certain notion of reading remain unavailable. How the text of the poem, transcribed from the recording, speaks to the music—again, ironically or otherwise—remains a question.

Taylor's practices of ecstatic voicing—emphasizing a destabilizing or corrosive desire for language—touching on language as communal while insisting on its passage through the cavities of an irreducibly singular body—trouble the distinction between poetry and music, musicalizing language and insisting on sound's semantic remit. In Taylor's practice, bodies, inscribed and made legible by race, become loci, implicitly and explicitly, for grounding the thought of the universal through demanding, attentive interaction. Insofar as embodied voice stresses text's destination and situation rather than origin, Taylor's soundwork amounts to a deconstruction of the performance/text binary by shifting attention to text as active address for which the model might be something other than an exchange between sovereign individuals in a contemplative stance. Voice, as Brandon Labelle characterizes sound poetry more generally, engages "sonorous excess so as to unsettle subjectivity and its reliance on linguistic coding," but without becoming a (Kristevan?) "ritualistic celebration and restaging of the primal (maternal) scene."[74] Voice's juxtapositionality need not be thought in terms of fantasmatic "recovery" of some primal self, but rather recalls Spillers's one, a figure for what is antecedent to subjection, and the surplus subjection artificially suppresses insofar as subjection is a putting-to-work of the fundamental tropes of social reproduction. The *one* is to the *subject* as the *flesh* is to the *body*. *Body* in each case is a term for social coding mapped onto nature. *Flesh* is not recoverable as plenitude; however, it might tune us to the production of the common as a remapping of potential social relations, starting with aesthetics in the broadest sense. Cecil Taylor's sound/poetry implicates "the body" as well as "the flesh"; it condenses and displaces questions of race, which is also to say gender—the supplement to sex understood, as Foucault emphasized, as a technology of control and regulation of sexuality—to make thinkable the un- or underregulated, the immanent outside. This is not so much a "reading" of the poem as an attempt to understand what it does with and against meaning.

Rhythm ("life the space of time danced thru") connects Taylor's disparate claims to play the piano as if it were "eighty-eight tuned drums" and to "try to imitate on the piano the leaps in space a dancer makes." It is Taylor's most general term for what I have been terming a philosophy of the outside, a term for movement that links the subjective and objective beyond the predicates of energy (as Ekkerhard Jost would have it).[75] It perhaps can serve as a name for meaning as movement rather than destination, and from that perspective re-energize our listening—the constitutive aesthetics that makes a "we"—beyond the binaries that typically mark a refusal or inability to listen: European or black, composition or improvisation, jazz or not jazz.

B. DOUBLE HOLY HOUSE

> What I'm interested in in my music is the variety of pulses that exist in a given moment. I'm very conscious of body movement when I play. I apply it to the piano in ways never seen before. I sing inside me, and I sing out loud. I write poems and I recite them in the middle of my pieces.[76]

Double Holy House is the product of a live solo performance at the Bechsten Concert House in Berlin and an overdubbed poetry recitation, recital's after-the-fact extension and revision. Taylor actually recorded the poem cycle ("Squash People," "Eyes within the Voice," "Eucalyptus Intersection and Failure to Appear," "Feather Upon Brow," "Roses") on September 22, 1990, the day before the piano performance, and one wonders whether his plan was always to merge them into one final recording. As it stands, the two recitals draw each other into co-implicating technological echo. Cecil Taylor's desire to "create metaphors that confound the senses" and his disturbance of the line between audience and performer—between "of" and "beyond"—points to an ecstatic potential, a disorganization "of one's whole [sensory] apparatus," the possibility of "surpris[ing] yourself."[77] The self is ecstatic, self-excessive; the minimal integrity of the now that limns accumulated paths and promises the future. The body's centrality—especially in Taylor's emphasis on the throat and difficult-to-reproduce guttural sound—also foregrounds time.

"Squash People" begins with an exhalation, a nonrepresentational rustle at the back of the throat: "Ahh!" The sound of discovery, of release, of easefulness—closely followed by the trill of the tongue behind the palate. This is a performance of the voice as a product of mouth, throat, and lungs; in Kristeva's vocabulary, this might be an instance where the "genotext" takes priority.[78] Taylor uses all of the facilities of his voice across octaves; syllables spaced far apart that only gradually find their home in words; words that decompose back into syllables or function as rhythmic rather than semantic units. Again the approach to the microphone and the opening of the throat. The sound of heavy footfalls and the body's percussion. Taylor repeats the English words *blue* and *black*, alternating, shortening the period between them until they make a novel but familiar compound, the color of the sea or a bruise. This gives way to "avast," the nautical term commanding "Hold!" "Stop!" or "Cease!"—or "a vast," the marker of an indeterminate territory. Suspended, palimpsestic space informs the central figures "double double house of the horizon" or "dual equinox." This alternation gives way to what may be the Latin *ōriri-* (to rise, to be born; the rising sun, east; to rise, become visible, appear), etymon of *aboriginal*, *abort*, *origin*, *orient*, and so on, or Yoruba *orirí* (have you seen it?), an expression of astonishment, or a promise that you're going to see something.[79] He intersperses recitation of *ōriri/orirí* with idiosyncratic sound patterns such as "ee-ohs" whose value as far as I can tell is their sound. *Orirí/ōriri* repeats as an alternate rhythmic refrain (the other being *double holy house* or *double double house*), less nonsense than not-yet-sense.

Taylor's improvisatory performance implies the inverse of John Corbett's definition: not a "semiotic system without a semantic level," but a semiotic system that traverses several semantic structures without translating. Kofi Agawu, typologizing differences between music and "natural language," argues, "A musical segment (phrase, period, sentence, paragraph, section, movement) exists in two interdependent planes, the plane of succession ('melody') and the plane of simultaneity ('harmony'). Language lacks the plane of simultaneity."[80] Puns and figurative language notwithstanding, this is true to the extent that in order to enter into the processes of differentiation from which meaning derives, language must organize itself into "temporally bounded or 'closed'" texts. To make sense at all requires reading texts in ways that select against the simultaneous significations upon which poetry thrives. "[O]nce we move beyond the ontological specificity of the work, our attempts to decode it necessarily reconfigure it as an open text."[81] That move "beyond" involves taking seriously what I have been calling the practice of outside, those levers that dislodge or interrupt the presumed naturalness of meaning production, in this case by introducing a "plane of simultaneity" as irresolvable discord. Taylor's poetry, no less than the ephemeral harmonies and harmonic structures that appear and dissolve in his improvisations, differs and defers a "semantic level" to reveal and revel in the ineluctable processes of play—the "essence of music"—that undermine the ideology of the "work," the oeuvre as finished, commodifiable object. Commingling languages, the poem produces a dispersal: "the double woes of tongue." Eventually his reading gives way to solo piano, which seems to build out of the poetry, respond to it, rather than accompany or replace it. At 35:41, his reading resumes, accompanied by his voice, on another track, making guttural sounds from the back of the throat, a wavering pitch running additional interference with the words, perhaps pointing to the coexistence of the pre-lingual within the lingual, the co-implication of genotext with phenotext, the way that improvisation is never fully unforeseen despite the word's etymology.

The spoken words, invoking Nathaniel Mackey, seem as much formed by as torn from his mouth, "advanc[ing] the exponential potency of dubbed excision—plexed, parallactic articulacy, vexed elevation, vatic vacuity, giddy stilt."[82] Rooted in the co-implicating materialities of music, sound, language, and medium (*dubbed* excision), this phonographic poetry is an out inhabitation of language. The mixed temporalities of the composite text constitute not *one* statement, even as repetition suggests it is, somehow, *only* one statement. The album as a whole implies further crossings. Discussing folk culture in 1899, an anonymous formerly enslaved Georgia Sea Island woman said, "Dese spirituals am de best moanin' music in de world, case dey is de whole Bible sung out and out. Notes is good enough for you people, but us likes a mixtery," both a mixture and a mystery, a mixture greater than the sum of its component parts, the contrapuntal interaction of different lines of articulation without reducing one to another.[83] On one level, she's referring to the processes of gathering and transmitting the spirituals aurally, where different songs and Biblical references could fuse into unexpected new wholes, their meaning vouchsafed by the Word. On another, she also refers to the sonic textures and formal innovations of African American performance, which often seemed to whites to be mere noise. In the case of Taylor, dissonances and inconclusiveness of both poetry and music interact, inflect, and redirect one another. Invoking Mackey again, the result is not harmony but "an unruly, agonistic sound in which it seems that the two lines of articulation are wrestling, that they are somehow each other's contagion or contamination."[84] In chapter 1, I suggested the term "rebel voice," a compensatory vocality that refers to broken collectivity rather than serving as the sign of a subject. It is, we might say, the "voice" of a *one*.

Taylor similarly produces "mixtery," two recordings that anticipate one another, each the other's revenant shadow, as the ecstatic *now* of encounter. Throughout Taylor's poem cycle, initially recognizable terms give way to one another and to terms from other languages, especially those of West Africa, without producing any stable meaning apart from the thought of a "connective tissue / intersecting / light of / a transatlantic consciousness" whose purposeful arrangement is invoked by the repetition of the Chinese concept-metaphor "feng shui." Phonography appears as another form of inscription, one rooted in an embodied, sonic materiality invested in the full possibilities of words as units of sound and sense. The formal presentation, the multi-track recording of the voice (one track of which consists of guttural sounds of the sort that begin the performance) layered with the piano performance along with the multilingual play and homophony, presents the ineluctable risk of language and sense-making inherent in the invitation to listen. The non-signifying necessarily coexists with the signifying, like noise within communication, the risk or fall from meaning necessary to any meaning, or changed meanings. Latin and Yoruba specify different ways of considering the origins of race-delimited standards of civilization, of orature and poetry, of regimes of the Word. They each imply racial discourses and rhetorics of attachment, of alienation and disalienation. The realization of racial discourses in the body becomes the starting point of a way of reading these practices that insist on the real, historical effects of racial discourse, the discursive nature of which becomes the tenuous ground of aesthetic invention.

Yeh Come T'Be: For Jeanne Lee

One important aspect of the "free" of "free jazz" as I've been discussing it is the liberation and regrounding of aesthetic techniques in the interest of initiating new insurgent traditions that have a dissonant relationship to the existing order. These traditions exist in uneasy relationship to dominant aesthetic modes and understandings without being purely oppositional or resistant. They forge new spaces and modalities of sense making or, more simply, new aesthetics. I have referred to this process as the improvisation of the common: not a recuperation of the past but its rearticulation, its regrounding for future invention. This chapter in particular has so far discussed the ways Cecil Taylor creates disjunction in his poetry between vocalization and voice, deploying a full range of guttural sounds, grunts, vocal timbres, and other vocal effects at once related to speech and abstracted, creating the effect of expression without representation or semiotics without a semantic alibi. As critics and historians write Taylor's legacy as pianist, composer, and bandleader, the followers they name will primarily be men, with potential exceptions made for Geri Allen, Marilyn Crispell, and Angelica Sanchez. However, I would situate his vocal practice, which roots itself as much in sound poetry as in jazz, in a lineage defined primarily by women,[85] starting with Abbey Lincoln and extending through Amina Claudine Myers, Jeanne Lee, and more recently Terry Jenoure and Matana Roberts.[86] In an unsung tradition, Jeanne Lee is at once the most important and perhaps the least heralded. In many ways, however, she embodies the strain of free jazz I have been outlining, not least because of her commitment to the idea that aesthetic modes provide "point[s] of reference for people to be able to move into the energy of this time," the present.[87] The ways she foregrounds embodied experience—as a black woman and a black mother—are central to her overall project, which I read less as a vindication of black maternity and black women's sexuality than as an attempt to claim what Hortense Spillers has termed the "insurgent ground" of gendered difference beyond inclusion or reconciliation.[88] In this, we might find in Lee's practice, rooted concretely and materially in *a* mother's body ("There is great joy / in being / Naima's mother"), a way of conceiving text and the semiotic as generative and open-ended in their recombinatory capacities without reifying the mother's body within the Symbolic's patriarchal coding that simultaneously produces the black mama's vulnerability.[89] Her practice (like Taylor's) is insurgent, emerging from specific contexts that may not be generalizable, that may not be available as a general strategy. Yet it encodes a way of belonging to a moment in transition, a moment of flux, so that the value perhaps isn't the aesthetics themselves but the ways she mobilizes an aesthetic project toward a broader political aim of reimagining collectivity and the universal.

Lee's "multidisciplinary" soundwork exemplifies and complicates the arguments this chapter makes for improvisation as text, especially with her investment with the voice "in itself" and as a medium of emotional content. Her vocal art loosens the relationship between emotion and content, and thereby opens onto genres of quotidian experience for which we lack adequate names. Eric Porter, in one of the few scholarly accounts of her work, argues, "Lee conceived of a new social imaginary that was attuned to human liberation. Her vision . . . maintained an ethical and political commitment stemming from her immersion in her artistic communities, foregrounding the role that improvisation could play in building new social groups."[90] She played a key role on a number of groundbreaking recordings by such politically and aesthetically diverse musicians as Andrew Cyrille, Anthony Braxton, Marion Brown, and Archie Shepp. Her contributions were integral to the success of those projects, yet she rarely receives attention in the histories of "free jazz." Apart from a general difficulty among jazz critics to recognize vocalists—who are usually women—as key innovators, the neglect may stem from her decision to devote time to "raising [her] children," which took her off of performing and recording circuits.[91]

Eric Porter also stresses her engagement with European collaborators, and reads Lee as a vanguard of a modernism defined (drawing on George Lewis) by a "hybrid [e.g., combining the Euro- and African American avant-gardes] aesthetic orientation," which he argues belongs to both a post-nationalist and post-cultural nationalist "social imaginary that informed the creative and intellectual work of other African American improvisers during the 1970s and that has helped define experimental, improvised music through the present."[92] The idea of a "pure" aesthetic orientation describes less a practice than a position within an aesthetic field. Marion Brown's paradigmatic insistence, for example, that "the creation and learning of music in traditional African society is primarily an aural experience" amounts to an anxious claim for the distinctness of black aesthetic practice in a moment of generic and stylistic promiscuity.[93] Still, emphasizing the active pursuit of alternatives to cultural forms that embody fundamental antagonisms, "hybrid aesthetic orientation" might designate an aesthetic practice of re-constellating past practices into new forms and structures of feeling, a practice of expression without representation that defines free jazz as the improvisation of the common for a people yet to emerge.

Lee's soundwork is avant-garde insofar as it asks us to orient our affective investments in aesthetic techniques toward a day when the conditions of alienation from which those techniques emerged no longer hold. Rather than "When Will the Blues Leave," as Ornette Coleman asks, what will become of the blues when we have reorganized society to eliminate the forms of privation of which the blues is witness and cure? Porter's implicit claim, I take it, is that Lee's practice somehow "transcends" overt claims to a politicized blackness associated, for example, with Archie Shepp, with whom Lee created the proto-feminist "Blasé" where the avowal of blackness doubles as a contest over its meaning. I am less interested in parsing musicians' ideological commitments than observing the degree to which Lee's commitment to both Euro- and Afro-modernist techniques (sound poetry is a major touchstone for Lee) finds them ambivalently "liberated" once class processes render invalid any imputed isomorphism between aesthetics and politics subtended by "the black community" as a transcendental signified. If blackness is no longer the source, goal, and object of the black text, then those techniques thought to express blackness take on new functions. "Post-cultural nationalist," that is, more accurately names a historical situation or affective relation to a new political context than a coherent political stance. It designates a way of navigating the aporias between history itself and the cultural and political paradigms through which one understands and relates to history.

Rather than a term of praise for Jeanne Lee, I propose "post-cultural nationalist" as the name for a crisis of temporality resulting from artists' and critics' failure or inability to negotiate the terms of the world that would follow the dissolution of the post–World War II liberal racial order. As electoralism became the almost exclusive terrain of black freedom struggles (or when black power and black art severed owing to political necessity), the adaptation of nationalism as cover for bourgeois or even anti-black politics ultimately proved demobilizing. Lee's work is rarely overtly political in these terms, which is instructive. The recording that best captures the moment's temporal disorder is Gil Scott-Heron's oft-cited "The Revolution Will Not Be Televised" (1970). That phonopoem's famous diagnoses of black imbrication in what Guy Debord termed "spectacle" (the universal commodification of aspects of social life—including attachments and desire—previously imagined and lived as distinct) makes its implicit diagnosis of a class dynamic where "black liberation" becomes image—a set of "revolutionary" slogans, symbols, and consumer goods (the "red, black, and green liberation jumpsuit"). Adapting Fredric Jameson, the red, black, and green liberation jumpsuit is "essentially an image for other people to have of us, and we consume less the thing itself, than its abstract idea, open to all the libidinal investments ingeniously arrayed for us by advertising."[94] Scott-Heron's parallel critique of the bourgeois media's juxtaposition of images of (male-identified) urban uprising, prestige programming ("brought to you by Xerox / in four parts without commercial interruption"), and (female-identified) melodrama suggests the processes that delegitimate, make undesirable, or distract from the project of black liberation. In this poem, cultural nationalism, insofar as it primarily stimulates desire for "revolutionary" consumer goods without being able to pierce reification's veil or produce new forms of the common, becomes an impediment rather than facilitator of authentically revolutionary consciousness. In such a situation, the emergent black bourgeoisie could proclaim fealty to a black-working-class-identified "revolution" while negotiating a shifting political terrain that co-opted the already flawed premises of "black capitalism." Scott-Heron diagnoses a situation in which people seem able to relate only through "popular culture," which now encompasses the signifiers of cultural nationalist "militancy."[95] The Revolution, spoken only in the future tense, will have been an event, a partition of time into a before and after. It will have dissolved reification and "false consciousness" to reveal the fundamental class character (with class understood to be a relationship between exploiter and exploited) of racial antagonism. More profoundly, it would create an unstable shard of space-time dividing experience into a "hitherto" and, in terms derived from Joy James's engagement with Frantz Fanon, a *"henceforward"* in which new solidarities are formed and fought for.[96] Released first in 1970 on *Small Talk at 125th and Lenox* and then set in a different musical context (featuring Hubert Laws, Ron Carter, and Bernard "Pretty" Purdie) and rereleased on *Pieces of a Man* in 1971, the poem's ambivalence toward a female- and bourgeois-identified popular culture and anxious injunction to "brothers" situates it comfortably adjacent to cultural nationalism and revolutionary nationalism alike. However, similar to "free jazz" in the terms I've been discussing, it probes and re-situates the roots of black vernacular culture. It is "post-cultural nationalist," where the point is more the "post"—the opening onto new collective political possibilities—than the "cultural nationalist."

Lee's practice occupies the space-time of the "henceforward," with all the uncertainties and potential for dramatic reversals it names. Like Taylor, Lee has insisted on the interrelation of music, dance, and poetry: "It's energy ... it's all one thing."[97] Her poems tend to thematically emphasize gendered embodiment, the particular challenges and promises of the female body. Her phonopoem "Angel Chile," from *Conspiracy*, her 1975 debut as leader, takes the reified sign of black maternity, the cornerstone and crisis of those accounts of the incipient black nation, and transforms intergenerational love between mother and daughter into the aural sign of alternate forms of social organization. The phonopoem features Lee unaccompanied performing variations on the syllables of "Naima," her daughter's name, that emerge from what initially seems to be an embarrassed laugh and proceed through breathy syllables and humming, as of a child learning to speak and sing.[98] Her collaborative reading of Elouise Loftin's "Sunni" declares Sunni's mother's "womb had a window / so she know [sic] exactly what she / was coming into."[99] In contrast with a freedom oriented only with the production of an event ("the revolution will be live"), Lee's emphasis on maternity draws attention to the reproductive labor that accompanies the improvisation of the common, yet it avoids making her daughter into mere allegory. This is to read her as avant-garde for the ways she sought to make desirable alternative possibilities immanent within the present order but selected against, belonging to versions of "the people" who didn't know to answer to that name.

Both activity and object, improvisation-as-text is at once a generative, non-referential system and a non-figural system that operates by subverting the grammars of performance and tradition to which it owes its legibility.[100] The acts of invention generate new meanings to "surprise the self" and entice us to "improper" attachments, while the framing and limiting function of jazz as transcendental signifier that makes improvisatory acts legible also limits their power. Surprising the self strongly implies the detaching work of medium, whether print, recording, or performance. Both openings to enchantment and surprise and foreclosure by reification appear as history. We might therefore reframe Eric Porter's discussion of Lee and her "aesthetics of excess"—a faithful infidelity to African American and Euro-international avant-garde practices, on the one hand, and her play in the semiotic spaces between signification and sheer sensuous sound on the other. Porter indexes Lee's "excess" to her illegibility in the Euro-international avant-garde tradition and orthogonal relation to the African American avant-garde tradition. Rather than a "recuperative humanism that would reclaim black people merely as national citizen-subjects or participants in a triumphant multiculturalism," however, I hear a much more specific claim to women's solidarity as a particular, irreducible relationship to "meaning located in the body."[101] Self-disclosing and concealing, conventional and innovative in the same gesture, Jeanne Lee's textuality touches on the processes of collective formation not through reflecting and avowing belonging to unfolding group experience but through the ways it produces and genders the common.

A vivid, if also more ambiguous, example of her poetics of black women's embodiment is her performance with Marion Brown on a piece called "Djinji's Corner," named for Brown's son, and featured as the B-side of his 1970 recording *Afternoon of a Georgia Faun* (the title recalls Claude Debussy's *Afternoon of a Faun*). Both of Brown's compositions have collective improvisation as a key component, and in Lee's general assessment Marion Brown is "almost like a tone poet, you know, he creates an environment."[102] The ensemble features Brown, Anthony Braxton and Bennie Maupin on reeds, Gayle Palmore and Lee on vocals, Chick Corea on piano, Jack Gregg on bass, and Andrew Cyrille, Larry Curtis, William Green, and Benny Malone on percussion. The woodwind players play multiple reeds; they switch at loosely determined intervals (one reviewer writes, "each performer should spend between thirty and forty seconds at each station, during which time each player sets up a phrase on an instrument of his choice. These phrases may be developed at other stations, or new phrases may be played").[103] This approach distributes the roles of thematic development across members of the ensemble and emphasizes timbres and textures over pitch and unifying rhythm, effectively dislodging instruments from their more familiar ensemble functions. Percussion, piano, and woodwinds create a spacious sonic enclosure through and within which Lee and Palmore's vocals weave, scat lines chasing each other as might the lustful gods from whom the suite gets its name. Abruptly, Lee transitions from wordless scat vocables to a poem, the hint of a poem, enjoining, "listen to it" or "listen to it sing" and asking, "can you hear?" Around 7:20, she sing-whispers the startling question, "Have you heard the blood of my sister?" Without pausing, she repeats the word "sister," extending the initial syllable of "sister" into a long cry joined by the woodwinds, which now enfold her vocals, somewhere between support and concealment. She returns to scat syllables, but the expectation of further comment or elaboration lingers. (At about 16:45 the question returns, this time cast, "Did you hear? Did you hear her?") We might hear these words as an instance of her using (apparently extemporized) poetry as the basis for improvisation, and, intriguingly, speech appears to be her secondary "instrument." The words ultimately sound an invitation to listen, an invitation that in the context of the suite as a whole includes attending to small differences, such as the difference between fawn (a baby deer) and faun (mythical goat-god), and thus to imaginatively remap Georgia. Her synesthetic question calls for intensified listening to hear even the sound of blood in veins or spilling from them, to hear the violence at the edges of or memorialized in serious play. This, too, we might hear against Brown's more romantic view of African society, as we might also hear it as a call to attend to the relationship between myth and the material violence from which myth is in flight. The myth of African (or Georgian) social order requires that a past of violence be silenced. Listen for it.

The differentiating effects of gender prove to be another important thematic concern throughout her other work, perhaps most famously in the phonopoem "Blasé," released on Archie Shepp's album of the same name. Recorded for BYG Actuel two weeks after *Live at the Pan-African Festival*, which featured Shepp with poets Ted Joans and Don L. Lee and a number of Algerian and Tuareg drummers, this album strikes a tone of struggle and striving as if to answer for or correct the earlier work's optimism. "Blasé" uses the elements of popular songs and song forms as a springboard for its sonic experimentation. The title piece, anchored by pianist Dave Burrell and bassist Malachi Favors's vamp, alternates between minor (B♭ minor 6) and major (E♭ major 9) modes. Burrell plays the same piano voicing, and Favors changes its tonality by concluding the ostinato he plays with either F or E♭. Rather than playing time, Philly Joe

Jones plays impressionist figures to spur or support the ensemble. Its dirgelike tempo, impressive for the players' discipline, focuses attention primarily on the other musicians. It builds by accretion. Shepp states the theme, then improvises in the first section, his sound warm and dark, informed by the blues, a sense of the causes and cures of loss, an articulacy, in my hearing, beyond or beside speech. Jeanne Lee's voice, whose singsong rhythms signify a performative play adjacent to the personal's consolations, is melancholic: it suggests less the desire to recover a lost object than a before-the-fact mourning for the object or home that concludes the search. "Blasé, ain't you, daddy? You, who shot your sperm into me / But never set me free" are her opening lines. She follows them with her most frequently cited qualification "this ain't a hate thing, it's a love thing," followed by an extended qualification worthy of Langston Hughes: "if love is ever really love that way / the way they / say." It's worth printing the rest of the poem:

> I give you a loaf of sugar
> You tilt my womb 'til it runs
>
> All of Ethiopia awaits you
> My prodigal son
>
> [Shepp interlude]
>
> Blasé, ain't you big daddy?
>
> But mama loves you
>
> She
> always has

"All of Ethiopia," after the exuberance of *Live at the Pan-African Festival*'s "We Have Come Back," seems mocking, especially in light of the tone of rebuke with which Lee recites it. Following the interlude noted in square brackets, Shepp accompanies her in a manner familiar from other styles of vocal performance in jazz. When she gets to the final line, she elongates "she," with Shepp softly overblowing to match her pitch. As on "Djinji's Corner," it seems that she has deconstructed the line between speech and song, showing the ways the signifying depends on the non-signifying and the apparent inevitability that some code will be imposed to semanticize "pure" sound or voicing. Harmonica players Chicago Beau and Julio Finn enter next, building a riff off the first notes of the C blues scale (C, E♭, F), adding a D♮ (a semitone above the D♭ in Burrell's voicing). Shepp rejoins, improvising; the dissonance against Burrell and Favors's vamp creates a ghostlike, almost-there sonority, deferring what would otherwise be a satisfactory irruption of the blues implied throughout. A discrepant blues if not the discrepancy blues, a blues over inevitable discrepancy, inevitable inaptness, inevitable lapse. Discrepancy and unexpected joining are themes; lapsed possibility and new horizons are themes; asymmetrical and conflicting desires are themes; sexual ecstasy as exposure and vulnerability is a theme; love, both a matter of semiotic excess and communist regrounding of community, is finally a theme.

Shepp is the only credited composer of "Blasé," but the poem is more consistent with Lee's poetry than his own. It seems likely that Shepp gave his collaborators material to shape and develop in a manner recalling Cecil Taylor. It's possible that Shepp wrote the lines "You shot your sperm into me / but never set me free," but Lee elevates them, discrepantly merging the sermonic and street corner palaver, public harangue and bedroom purr. The poem itself joins discrepant claims to and refusal of black women's bodies—more precisely claims to and refusal of a black *mama*'s body—through the figures of potential and/or symbolic motherhood. The gap between potentiality and the symbolic is part of the point. Moving in reverse, the phonopoem weds an older fantasy of Pan-African unity ("all of Ethiopia awaits you") and the practical disjunction of mutually constitutive sexual, anti-colonial, and black liberation movements, whose radicalness often stopped short of reimagining forms of social organization beyond the patriarchal family ("never set me free").[104] The "love thing" at the poem's rhetorical center stands as a "subversive gift," a corrosive offering that should make its recipient question his attachments to a (masculine) fantasy that he is the object that will complete the *mama*, whose love exists outside of time ("always has").[105] It's a conditional gift: "if love was ever really loved that way," then "this is a love thing, not a hate thing." It's a call for self-reorientation if not reinvention, an invitation to desire mama beyond the conditions of fungibility, alienation, and abjection that mark her, a call to reimagine and enact affective solidarities and attachments to the world that make black love possible in its full, radical sense.

What Amiri Baraka describes as "[t]he freedom to (of) Love," of love "without object," requires de-cathecting attachment to the position "big daddy" or "mama."[106] It requires their radical revision and regrounding in the common, which can make "out" sounds seem to come to us from the future, even as that future entails tracing new paths forward from the past. The semantic overdetermination of "mama," its approximation of but adjacency to psychoanalysis's "mother," the play in the seam and the semiotic (both the material excess to signification and the networks of signs that produce meaning) between those two is a necessary component of the project.

Free jazz, as soundwork, is not just about recreating the ear, although it is explicitly about reshaping aesthetic sensibilities—new somatic-affective responses to sense experience that, many believed, could form the basis for new communities. Free jazz is also about forging the kinds of affective solidarities—shared sensibilities and compatible attachments and orientations to the past and future—that are a necessary (but not sufficient) precondition to collective effort. Political solidarities rooted in concrete struggles and theoretical articulations across national boundaries enabled broader imaginative and practical collective possibilities, even as "Blasé" and, in a different register, the cycle "Double Holy House" point to imaginative and practical limits of such imagining. Above, I suggested that critics should understand free jazz's de- and reorchestration of modernist conceptual and harmonic dissonance alongside a general desire for a new politics of the word, a new politics of the text and of writing. Those new politics might lead listeners to surrender, to cross the threshold of a self and, invoking Lauren Berlant, to "try a new incoherence."[107] That will be the incoherence of what resists translation or recoding, what withholds itself even as it seems to give itself over. "What I'm doing," Cecil Taylor claimed, "is creating a language" that refuses a distinction between intellect and emotion—an embodied language that moves toward the ecstatic.[108] We can better hear the new forms of incoherence as strenuous effort to escape conceptual apparatuses that hear for us, compelling the reproduction of the understanding of "jazz" the music challenges us to hear otherwise. Taylor and Lee enfold poetry into their respective sounds of love, sounds that root themselves—and root around in—the ruins of misnamed experience for new ways of being free.

Coda

No Simple Explanations

Working with the music has provided me with a lot of freedom. I don't feel restricted.
My whole respiratory system is involved in an assemblage of free tones.
—JAYNE CORTEZ, quoted in Melhem, *Heroism in the New Black Poetry*

Since I began writing this book, the voice has taken on renewed significance in black experimental music. Writing in 1975, reviewing Jayne Cortez's debut recording, June Jordan prophesied a moment of synthesis, even chiasmus, where "the poet is a musician of words, and the musician is a poet of his sounds."[1] Recent years have seen a resurgence of phonographic poetry, with poets and poetry featured on high-profile recordings from artists including William Parker, Terri Lyne Carrington, Nicole Mitchell, Ben LaMar Gay, Mike Reed, and others. This shift corresponds with the past decade or so—since, say, David Murray, Jamaaladeen Tacuma, and Amiri Baraka offered ambiguous praise of Barack Obama's 2008 election.[2] During that time, the fog of melancholy posts (e.g., post-Civil Rights, post-black, postcolonial, postnationalist—the ruins of past teleological schema) and requisite celebrations of the "gains of the sixties" has given way to stark new configurations and practices of realpolitik, including a dramatic increase of mass protest and unsanctioned, "spontaneous" uprising. Without positing causality, the mainstream hegemony of quieter modes in black poetry and music—terse epiphany, well-turned developments in the vein of bebop—also break in this period, allowing room for an efflorescence of experimental approaches.[3] Also continuous with the Black Arts era is a desire to use the voice not only to say something but to bring about epistemological shift and rupture. Both poets and musicians, in their respective domains, enjoy a privileged relationship to truth telling, to wrenching the familiar to reveal what would otherwise remain unthinkable. In a moment characterized by euphemism, code words, and other evasions (e.g., "officer involved shooting"), unequivocally naming a situation takes on new value. But given the history I've touched on throughout *Soundworks*, we might see an endeavor, invoking Rahsaan Roland Kirk, to build a new vibration society, radiating from affinities between aesthetic forms to new shared understandings and critical attunements to the everyday.[4]

Forming vibration societies, (re-)forming the sense of a "we," is what black soundwork does most generally. Blackness, understood as index of epistemic rupture and reformation of troubled ipseity (troubled, partial, or denied individuation and incomplete subjection), accrues meaning only in the wake of chattel slavery and the historically novel social forms that develop alongside it. But those social forms alone do not adequately explain the development of new aesthetics or ways of understanding and experiencing, of converting sensuous experience into meaning or the sense of something to be done. Understanding that process requires attention to instances of musical engagement in which aesthetic possibilities come to be renegotiated *and* to the processes that shape and reshape the meanings of those practices as they circulate. These together comprise black soundwork. Without making collaboration a figure for established social forms, I continue to hear in it minimal resources for imagining, feeling, and knowing the world on other terms.

I came to this project thinking about pianist Jason Moran's use of untranslated Turkish and Chinese, as well as English-language, speech as rhythmic and melodic source material for compositions. He repeats that experiment by way of virtual collaboration with artist Adrian Piper, who admonishes that "artists ought to be writing" in order to refuse the distinction between artist and consumer.[5] That sampled speech (from Peter Kennedy's 1975 film *Other than Art's Sake*) appears twice on the 2006 album *Artist in Residence*. In the first instance, Moran manipulates the sequence so that Piper calls for a "breakdown" of the art world, the artist, the society, and the general public. As Moran's composition draws out the musicality of spoken language in those compositions (does the abstraction and repurposing of everyday speech or the news make them poems?), the voice functions as blunt instrument, whereby its function as medium is secondary to its materiality, its pitch, its rhythm. Its use of medium was the initial hook, but as the project developed, I have found myself returning to Piper's injunction, "artists ought to be writing," which touches on the relationship between the popular and the common that informs *Soundworks*. Moran's work helped me listen to collaborations I thought I knew well. As I've developed the argument that phonographic poetry, as black experimental sound practice, rearticulates past techniques and styles in the interest of improvising the common for an emergent people, Jayne Cortez's work has been in the back of my mind. Her work, especially with her band the Firespitters, exemplifies the relationships among the subaltern, the popular, and the common at stake throughout this book. I conclude listening to her.

Some might fairly wonder where rap music (or spoken word poetry) belong in this critical narrative. I have been analyzing the emergence of phonographic poetry in the context of the dis- and reorganization of the cultures surrounding "jazz," and the ideas of race, nation, sound, and media upon which it depends. Stressing the internal differentiations and debates in and around the music, its articulations of and responses to problems of form and audience, and its engagement with parallel forms from its moment and the past, I have also sought to trouble supersessionist arguments rooted in an idea of black vernacular music's linear or progressive development, which would have made rap the logical terminus of these arguments. Such developmental arguments tacitly assume that as the dominant culture ideologically or materially absorbs and neutralizes liberatory aesthetic forms (i.e., as jazz becomes "mainstream"), new forms emerge that better speak to working-class (or mass) impulses and values. Such arguments assume a natural relationship between cultural and class processes, while neglecting the commodity form itself—the text, the record, the copyrighted song. Insofar as teleological arguments describe cultural transitions as quasi-"natural" developments, they obscure the operation of power Stuart Hall describes:

> Sometimes we can be constituted as a force against the power bloc: that is the historical opening in which it is possible to construct a culture which is genuinely popular. But, in our society, if we are not constituted like that, we will be constituted into its opposite: an effective populist force, saying "Yes" to power. Popular culture is one of the sites where this struggle for and against a culture of the powerful is engaged: it is also the stake to be won

or lost in that struggle. It is the arena of consent and resistance. It is partly where hegemony arises, and where it is secured.⁶

Techniques and genres are neither inherently subversive nor compromised; instead, subversion or reinforcement of a norm involves culturally conditioned practices of reading or interpretation. Rap music is a good example of an increasing misfit between avant-garde sonic techniques, including vocal techniques, and a discursive tendency to make bodily freedom coextensive with freedom as such, in effect making saying "yes" to power feel like subversion because of the racism that polices bodily expression. One sees something similar in the tendency to make personal guilt a sufficient response to the forms of exploitation that allow some to "get over" and escape the physical bounds of "the community," which in turn allows individual charity to replace meaningful structural change. As rap music and its ability to foster opposition to existing states of affairs emerged as a popular music in the late 1980s, experiments in jazz have increasingly used poetry not only to reflect present conditions but to offer genuinely popular visions of freedom.

Hall goes on to argue that "cultural change" entails both a selection for something new or newly compelling *and* a selection against something already in place.⁷ That process is one vantage point from which to study the operation of power, but also from which to consider jazz as aesthetic and political form selected against. In the case of black vernacular avant-garde, we would have to relate succession from jazz to R&B/soul and then to hip-hop (a common teleological scheme), and we could point to unforeseen consequences. Economic conditions forced many community-based artists to perform in Europe or work in universities. The corresponding promotion of jazz as "America's classical music" arguably did more to alienate working-class listeners than any aesthetic development or tendency. The music became popular—part of the symbolic forms and practices of the dominant classes—but the players generally remained subaltern. We should understand "jazz," newly promoted to "high" art, to "share a social and aesthetic situation" with rap music as both "low" art and the expression of authentic, autonomous subaltern culture.⁸ Yet during rap's "golden age," rap DJs and producers eagerly sampled a relatively wide range of jazz recordings, insisting on a complementary response to the problems of form and audience, and a counter-articulation of jazz as black rather than American music. The reinscription and evaluation of jazz as self-conscious high art co-opts midcentury claims to aesthetic autonomy, to cultivating audiences and critical norms adequate to its innovations, which I have argued are one place in which black communism could become thinkable. The claim to "cultivate" audiences is always ambiguous, and easily decomposes into mere connoisseurship, the sense that listening to the music requires training or deep involvement. While the claims that audiences needed special attunement have at different moments been part of larger strategies of advancing a particular race project, they also threaten to mystify the consumption of culture as a social hygiene project—this was the failure of Black Swan records, the first black-owned label.[9] The class politics of hip-hop's apparent eclipse of jazz lie in the nature of the cultural industries and the state cultural apparatuses that shape the larger situation in which both operate. This is to emphasize political economy and the ways race mediates the relatively autonomous aesthetic field, the ways texts and techniques produce and subvert the grammars of race and racial formation. Finding moments of subversion or resistance within cultural texts is necessary, but insufficient. The more difficult and more pressing task is to find those spaces where true alternatives become thinkable and desirable.

Jayne Cortez, who would experiment with hip-hop aesthetics (sampling and DJ effects) on her 1990 album *Everywhere Drums*, reminds us that effective subversion requires adequate analysis of the situation, and of the limitations of vernacular forms whose communicative function the reifying logic of capital eventually erodes. Cortez's sound practice calls together the disparate aesthetic traditions of the African diaspora and the Global South into a common vernacular avant-garde practice. Cortez would claim that music was "another dimension with which to compose," but her unusual commitment to it, going so far as to maintain a working band, is one cue that we should pay more attention to her collaboration.[10] Melba Joyce Boyd pushes June Jordan's observation, cited earlier, further. She argues that Cortez "constructs thematic constellations that explode and interact on several planes simultaneously as the poems progress through thought and the Cortez cosmos."[11] Cortez's use of refrain and repetition alongside her clear political commitment has caused some reviewers to miss the profundity of her associative leaps and vivid juxtapositions. Stressing her affirming use of the vernacular, we might miss the ways her work prompts careful attention to those modes of expression that exceed or otherwise fail to align with representation. We might ask what in addition to poetry she composed.

Cortez came of age during the struggle for black political and aesthetic autonomy. She underwent a political awakening organizing alongside Ella Baker and the Student Non-Violent Coordinating Committee before going on to co-found the Watts Repertory Theater Company and decades later, with Ama Ata Aidoo, the Organization of Woman Writers of Africa. The institution that most concerns me here is her cooperative ensemble the Firespitters (whose nucleus—Bern Nix, guitar; Al MacDowell or Jamaaladeen Tacuma, bass;

Denardo Coleman, drums—all contributed to Ornette Coleman's Prime Time ensembles). She recorded and released six albums with them, most of them released by her own Bola (short for the Yoruba "oyebola," meaning "successful") Press.[12] Cortez's sound practice is equally informed and influenced by Langston Hughes, the Négritude poets' Afro-surrealism, and Fanon's reminder that "there is no question of a return to Nature," no moment of non-alienated past to recover, only a future to invent.[13] Fanon continues, "It is simply a very concrete question of not dragging men towards mutilation, of not imposing upon the brain rhythms that very quickly obliterate it and wreck it." Cortez and her ensemble created irresistible counter-rhythms to domination, brazenly constructed from available cultural materials and discordantly assembled.

Like others of her generation, Cortez saw the line between aesthetics and politics as permeable by acts of willful commitment,[14] which rather than refusing exchange per se emphasizes other forms of exchange and circulation. "If you're a political person and a poet," she said in an interview, "you will write political poetry. You make political decisions. At some point, your work will represent your political thought."[15] (There are, from this perspective, no truly nonpolitical people: to fail to make political decisions is to affirm hegemonic power.) In this, she stands against some of the quieter tendencies of some of her poetic and musical contemporaries, on the one hand, and the more austere forms of abstraction that characterize some others. Hers is a raucous abstraction that marshals poetry's estranging relationship to language and experience to give names for liminal or novel experiences, feelings, thought, and association-complexes. Some modes, similar to popular music, are more easily appropriated to the project of covering over the anxieties attendant to passing time by creating a kind of subjective mask, adopting a posture of immediacy available for others to adapt. Cortez and the Firespitters' experimental modes of poetry and music heighten and make volatile the tensions, contradictions, and aporias of contemporary life and its idealized monadic subjectivity, helping break the conventional isomorphism between expression and representation (i.e., of a subject). "I use dreams, the subconscious, and the real objects," she said in an interview. "I open up the body and use organs, and I sink them into words, and I ritualize them and fuse them into events. I guess the poetry is like a festival. Everything can be transformed."[16]

The political modernism of the kind Theodor Adorno and others in his wake imagined transforms; the distinction between revolutionary and reactionary transgressions of a norm is obscured by the jargon of "lifestyle" on the one hand and "resistance" on the other. This, for all of its shortcomings (discussed in chapter 3), is what I think Baraka was after in his attacks on the (black) middle-class or "bourgeois art," and as we'll see is a problem Cortez addresses in sonic practice. Without that kind of analysis, criticism is compelled to make intuitive links between form and politics, among race, gender, and class (social relations rather than identities), between ideology and multinational capital. We might collect these broadly sketched tendencies—the co-optation and neutralization of modernist aesthetics even as those are increasingly promoted as "progressive," as with the "Young Lions" and "New Black Aesthetic" of the late 1980s; the dissolution or hollowing out of collective structures and institutions, including citizenship, that interfere with the mobility and proliferation of capital; a global post–Cold War order defined by the promotion of a thin, procedural democracy as the only and happiest end of history. The dissolution of collective structures and institutions makes a general problem of modernism—the relation of art to its public(s)—more acute. Here the emphasis on recording, rather than the tour or community concert (often more lucrative for working musicians), is one index of that shift even as, especially in Cortez's case, control of her work's circulation through independent production and circulation is one progressively oriented act of resistance. Like Cecil Taylor, Cortez appeared at large public concerts and forums. Many of them, however, were under the auspices and management of corporate or university sponsorship to a degree unseen in prior moments, even with government underwriting of many arts projects, which itself we should understand as an aggressive depoliticization of an explicitly political practice.

All of these are so many scattered speculations toward conceiving the poetic and musical practice Cortez termed "supersurrealist"[17] within a broader situation that, I think, better reveals the stakes and effectiveness of her transformative invocations and re-politicization of black vernacular forms such as the blues and jazz. In her hands, these invocations become again something other than style or self-legitimation. Cortez stressed her desire "to move this combination of poetry, music and technology to a higher poetic level . . . the poetic orchestration of it all."[18] Poetry's orchestration, in her hands, is simultaneously the de-orchestration of the Symbolic in terms discussed in the fourth chapter. If we understand realism as an aesthetic and epistemological process that makes a totality of social relations and class antagonisms perceivable and thinkable, "supersurrealism" re-presents irrationality as the culturally logical contradictions that comprise the lived experience of daily life. Drawing on Aimé Césaire, Tony Bolden describes Cortez's method as one of "disalienation," which I read somewhat against the grain of his argument that she incarnates a "secular priesthood" through which she "assume[s] the role of the ancestral healer."[19] In the Marxist tradition, alienation refers to processes of dissociation—workers from their labor, from each other, from the very predicates of living—and those processes often entail shaping the "practical and popular forms of consciousness" by which alienation is lived and justified, even forming a set of affectively necessary and life-organizing attachments.[20] Disalienation asks what it would mean to live otherwise, to live free.

Although I want to avoid making the Firespitters into an allegory, one cannot fully understand Cortez's sound practice without considering the importance of performing (beginning in 1964) and recording with musicians (she formed the Firespitters with her son Denardo Coleman in 1980) to her overall concept. Asked about the difficulties in pairing music and poetry, she quickly moves from aesthetic concerns (e.g., "The definition and implication of words. The definition and implication of harmony and rhythm. The effort to combine speech and music. Finding the key set of words, the pitch, the direction, the tempo.") to material ones, including having "enough money to pay for the space and time needed to experiment."[21] Her candor about these matters substantiates her poetry's tough-minded and incisive topical references and political analyses: if surrealism is a fundamentally modernist engagement with the structuring illogic or fundamental contradictions of the capitalist order whose playful juxtapositions ultimately figure the imagination's non-alienated production, supersurrealism reflexively situates that fantasy of liberation in its material context.

The title work on *There It Is*, a boogie-woogie blues, begins by denying the salience of familiar political positioning:

> My friend
> They don't care
> if you're an individualist
> a leftist a rightist
> a shithead or a snake
> They will try to exploit you
> absorb you confine you
> disconnect you isolate you
> or kill you.

On this phonopoem and throughout the album, deep irony mingles with pathos and deadly seriousness that, in performance, Cortez holds together largely through her deliberate delivery as much as by her keen compositional eye and ear. Part of Cortez's genius was to hear in common phrases like "what's happening" or "there it is" a point of departure for radical thought. The phrase "there it is" speaks to a logic of unmasking, a plain reckoning with social reality primarily composed of antagonisms whose class character reification obscures. "The ruling class will tell you that / there is no ruling class," and in a familiar dynamic the fight over political labels convinces people to align with their oppressors. The mode of the poem is not jeremiad. Lines such as "the old folks dying of starvation" closely follow "the enemies polishing their penises between / oil wells at the Pentagon." "Supersurrealism" refers to the juxtaposition of the rhetorically and the morally grotesque, to vulgar shock opening awareness of the shock of everyday vulgarity.

A somewhat ragged transition from the song's instrumental solo section to its concluding stanza betrays difficulty of the performance conditions and of the getting together the poem calls for:

And if we don't fight
if we don't resist
if we don't organize and unify and
get the power to control our own lives
Then we will wear
the exaggerated look of captivity
the stylized look of submission
the bizarre look of suicide
the dehumanized look of fear
and the decomposed look of repression
forever and ever and ever
And there it is

Syllepsis—in this case yoking multiple phrases to one verb ("wear")—is the poem's controlling trope. It functions rhetorically, suggesting dissonant unity between disparate outcomes, and allegorically, insofar as the poem asks how much "we," the vibration society of speaker and readers/listeners hailed as "my friend," will bear before finally organizing and fighting back. The poem asks us to consider the figurative and literal ways the somatic, erotic, extractive, and militarized comprise the absurd banality of everyday life. "U.S. policies concerning Third World countries are designed to destabilize—they cripple and destroy independence. I'm opposed to those policies that promote death of people, death of land, death of culture."[22] The intimacy of familiar address— "my friend"—is part of a strategy to disrupt the processes of isolation and reification the poem diagnoses. Sonically and epistemologically—and part of the point is her refusal of that distinction—she returns to the root to de-sediment practices, and meanings, without an outcome guaranteed in advance.

Her vocal virtuosity is a key element of her phonopoetics. D. H. Melhem describes her voice as "shimmering from silk to steel";[23] Aldon Nielsen describes the "melodic effects" she achieves "within the chosen tonal range of the individual line";[24] while Renee M. Kingan emphasizes her timbral imagination and emotional complexity.[25] Cortez described her own performance in these terms: "my whole respiratory system is involved in an assemblage of free tones."[26] Across her work, one hears this as intensification that frees vocal tonality from semantic function (e.g., using rising inflection without signaling the interrogative mood—a technique she frequently uses, perhaps to best effect in her poem "No Simple Explanations") in order to allow her to blend into the ensemble.[27] In performance, the voice becomes a sign of something other than the individual subject.

Here, we might ask about the relationship between timbre, the irreducibly singular and historical aspects of vocal and instrumental sound, and tone, which Sianne Ngai describes as a text's "global or organizing affect" through which "one understands the text as a totality within an equally holistic matrix of social relations."[28] What is the relationship between tone and tonality (by which I want to invoke both functioning within a diatonic framework and the affective states habitually associated with certain harmonic and rhythmic configurations)? A first pass would be to say that the strident, bracing tone (organizing affect) of the poem is at variance with the tone (habitually associated affect) of twelve-bar blues. Yet, despite and because of the apparent discrepancy, her use of the blues is inspired, beyond the ways it signals racial affinity. Syllepsis functions as an analogue for skilled musicians' ability to find in the structural predictability of twelve-bar blues an endless resource for invention. In this context, too, it allows her to draw out the grammar of daily life of the early 1980s, where the soundtrack to atrocity was likely to be a song that sounded like celebration. Rather than a poem to which music is added or vice versa, the phonopoem demands attention to processes of making meaning from inherited structures whose apparent outmodedness conceals revolutionary potential.

Cortez emphasizes the difficulties of making art under capitalist relations, which might dampen the tendency one might otherwise have to read her performance of joy—non-appropriable excess, submerged potentiality, enhanced capacity. Her poems' thematic focus on dispossession and oppression remind us that black soundwork refers to a tradition of trouble, of the struggle between freedom and compulsion. Cortez makes investment in non-alienated labor, despite all we know, not only plausible or desirable, but irresistible in Toni Cade Bambara's sense.[29] In Cortez's work black sound is the thought, feeling, and untimely anticipation of the coming world, for which one must resist, organize, and fight. It is a poetry for the living and for life yet to be imagined, of navigating situations defined the ubiquity of intense affects for which older epistemic categories no longer suffice. Cortez and the Firespitters carry out the work always implied by the label "free jazz": creating new genres that belong to forms of social life that will have been.

I am especially interested in the destabilizing effects of repetition on the page and as mediated by their great inventive ear/feel for improvisation. This requires considering her engagement with popular forms such as the blues and R&B upon which the Firespitters, like Coleman's Prime Time band, build.[30] But it also requires, again, listening not just for triumph but trouble, for her music draws on and draws out both. Critics ought to conceive jazz and its others in the same frame, responding to common aesthetic and political problems. Without unduly stereotyping popular music, we should consider its function libidinizing the dead time of retail experiences, distracting by turn from the dead time of working, commuting, shopping, and waiting. I am thinking of the music that, in Audre Lorde's terms, "emphasizes sensation without feeling," an essentially pornographic music where subjectivity appears as a mask of clichés, and empty virtuosity supplements the "chaos of our strongest feelings."[31]

Cecil Taylor once asserted that "To feel is perhaps the most terrifying thing in this society," not least because genuine feeling could "make somebody else lose all sense of time, all sense of his [sic] own existence."[32] Taylor's solution is to reject repetition—harmonic recapitulation, playing standards, or developing a repertoire. Cortez and the Firespitters invite us to consider other (libidinal and affective) uses of repetition that, rather than stifling the force of the erotic, awaken us to the force of repetition as a practice of the outside. Taylor pushes abstraction to the point that it undermines referentiality in its emphasis on the excessive materiality of language and bodies to advance a holistic aesthetic practice that makes time for encounters. Cortez, abstract in a different way, is more apt to consider the arrangements and disarrangements of time that constitute the quotidian, directly and explicitly pushing us to consider the world as the total of our wounded attachments. In this, she's closer to poet, composer, improviser, and vocalist Jeanne Lee, who insisted on "poetry as a point of departure for improvisation" and stressed the "the natural rhythms and sonorities or the emotional content of words."[33] Their openness and opening to play is perhaps (tone) parallel to Adorno's autonomous art: a historically grounded art that creates the conditions for its autonomy. If we understand the Black Arts era as a still unfolding set of arguments and positions against the backdrop of the new aesthetic possibilities implied by the dissolution of the old racial liberal order, we might retrospectively frame its aesthetic insurgency as ante- or proto-political. Doing so allows us to read claims of the moment's revolutionary character as belonging to an attempt to remediate black art and life.

In her justly celebrated poem "U.S./Nigeria Relations," Cortez repeats the line "They want the oil but they don't want the people" twenty times (twenty-four times in an initial read with the Firespitters released on 1982's *There It Is*). In print, one can read this as a refrain, which Cortez calls "a device to add the next layer of sound, next metaphor, next transformation."[34] This line is a refrain for a poem to be written, a before-the-fact elegy and psalm for the end of the world. As recorded, we must also think in terms of rhythm—a way of relating events in time. In fact, "they" *do* want some version of the people and their pain as a kind of proof that dehumanization is not total, which then facilitates relatively guiltless exploitation. That is the rhythm of domination.

Throughout her initial twenty-four repetitions on the recording, Cortez builds in pace and intensity. Maintaining a relatively constant tone—starting low and declarative and gradually building in intensity owing to a subtle accelerando as the other members of the ensemble embroider her lines—she finishes the series and the other musicians collectively improvise. At times she shifts out of phase with the other musicians. One reason for this rhythmic dis-ease is technical. As she explained, "The setup in the studio was negative. There were no isolation spaces. I had to scream my lungs out in the middle of the room so the musicians could hear the words and respond."[35] One can hear the way Cortez herself "sits down on notes and intensifie[s]," playing with the tonality of her voice especially when she starts another twenty-four-line series, which has now become a de facto "head" or theme.[36] The effect of her repetition is semi-mimetic: the phrase implies ritualistically repeated and euphemistically reported ("relations" registers as one such euphemism) horrors it does not name, conveying both the sameness and the varieties of violent domination. ("I sink them into words, and I ritualize them into events.") Yet, the phonopoem also insists on listening ("everything can be transformed"), which in this context doubles as an act of witness to the processes of alienation, ecocide, and accumulation by dispossession. Additionally, the phono poem uses a black sonic practice that intends black listeners. The abstract "they" refers to both the US state and actions carried out in "our name," and "the people," which historically excludes most black folk. "U.S./Nigeria Relations" asks listeners to consider the connection between the United States' historical treatment of black people domestically and in Nigeria, naming with devastating precision a concrete antagonism and ongoing accumulation by dispossession. Sound isn't necessarily "resistance" to those processes of reifying abstraction, but a counter-abstraction grounded in a different set of historical and political imperatives. This is a counter-rhythm to domination.

In its conclusion, "U.S./Nigeria Relations" transitions from free time to a stricter 4/4 that initially sounds paradoxical. It initially seems to relieve the tension of the free-time section, which climaxes with an accelerando, but very quickly generates its own tension. Cortez repeats "they don't want the people" with a very gradual group decelerando whose conclusion has "people" as almost two words. "They" bears the weight of abstraction, but "the people" is now a shorthand for a process of subalternization, the elimination of institutionally legitimated or legible actions and collectivities. For what forms of institutionally legible action will register as legitimate in this context? At stake is something more expansive than postcolonial disillusion with the limitations of (black) sovereignty as political goals: framing extractive capital as a conflict between nation-states mystifies the actual processes unfolding. Here the most profound effect of "U.S./Nigeria Relations" is clearest, and most difficult to hear if one cannot think through the distancing that the bourgeois media—from the *New York Times* to *National Geographic*—fetishizes in its production of a *there* and a *here*, its production of the human of "human interest." I refer to the coincidence of "democratized" social institutions, the expansion of self-rule, and the ascendance of neoliberal forms of governmentality that have effectively narrowed the range of legitimate demands and actions for the citizen.

Yet, Cortez and the Firespitters *play*. Throughout *Soundworks* I have tried to balance concerns such as the above with analysis of performance style, the sounding of sound, as an important site of artistic self-fashioning and artistic production, and as such merits analytic attention. Cortez's shifting approach to the lines—deeply resonant in her chest ranging up into her falsetto register—creates an alternative sound aesthetic akin to that Bill Cole's unorthodox shehnai technique achieves. As with rhythm, tone and timbre shape sound's signature resonance. By making audible the inter-resonation of bodies and, more metaphorically, the vibration of the self and of one self in another, it suggests a model of individuation that necessarily draws on a thick sense of context.

Barbara Christian notes that Cortez's "skill with words and rhythm demands that we listen."[37] Soundwork is material practice shaped by practices handed down across generations in person and through recordings. Listening is a proto-political, ante-ethical sensuous activity of entanglement with others. Listening might also be a way, analytically, to break down the sender/receiver models and help us conceive the ways the interaction of media and social mediation make sound a collaborative project. Transmission, in Cortez's practice and throughout *Soundworks*, mediates temporal and spatial distance: it figures or witnesses the continually evolving and contingent forms of tradition and community from which livable futures may yet be fashioned. Conceiving sound *as* work, and attending to the historical mediations that shape our ability to associate timbre and other techniques of sound—rhythm, in this instance—opens further pathways for considering the ways race shapes aesthetics as a social formation, making it difficult to hear, for example, the forms of theoretical reflection and reflexivity at stake in black soundwork

Cortez and the other poets in this study draw on phonography in a context defined by new plasticity in our social arrangements, which enabled new ways of conceiving poetry's media. Phonographic poetry emerges in a context in which the phonographic took on meanings beyond the illusion that sound itself is the source of knowledge. Knowledge exists among members of communities, and communities organize themselves around particular aesthetic practices, including ways of listening. Phonographic poetry emerges as part of a broader effort to change the ways we listen, what we listen for, what we can hear. The outcome Adorno seemed to at once predict and fear—that music would "become" writing—has not happened.[38] Rather than "relinquish[ing] its being as mere signs," phonography emerged from overlapping ethnographic and commercial processes that had already racialized—sign-ified—sound, and thus enabled new grammars of listening, and new modes of signification in excess of those grammars.[39] Each citation of a sonic "truth" of race also plays in the interstitial zone between restatement or reinscription and potential resignification or transformation. Phonographic poetry is among the new forms electric sound recording makes available, transforming and extending music's productive force rather than extinguishing it. Phonography, even with the most carefully planned recording session or reading, ineluctably creates the conditions for overhearing—hearing more than the performers know to be there, unauthorized hearing that confuses or willfully confuses text and subtext.[40] Phonography thus never entails the simple transmission of a message, the translation of sound from one medium (air, built environments) to another (durable storage media): textuality's inevitable surplus always also bears along what is not yet communicable. Black soundwork is a modality of disalienation, which entails radical forms of dissociation and regrounding tradition, ultimately manifesting attempts to address vibration societies that no longer exist or are not yet constituted as one, while seeking alternative forms and practices of the self. Disalienation is a strategy of rejecting false alternatives and generating a sense of productive dis-ease about the present whose aim is not the symbolic reconstitution of a whole sundered by processes of capitalist alienation but the production of new ways of being together. And there it is.

Notes

INTRODUCTION

1 "We Are on the Edge," Art Ensemble of Chicago, *We Are on the Edge* (Pi Recordings, 2019).
2 Amiri Baraka, *Black Music* (1967. New York: Da Capo Press, 1998), 64.
3 Nathaniel Mackey, *Late Arcade* (San Francisco: City Lights Press, 2017), 182.
4 Robin Kelley argues for this periodization: "If we can agree that the Black Arts Movement is not defined by race riots and dashikis but by a self-conscious collective effort to promote black art for black communities, art about liberation and freedom, then we should push our chronology back to the mid-1950s. For instance, radical black musicians formed collectives for both economic security and artistic collaboration in the 1950s and early 1960s, developing structures for cooperative work that anticipated the Black Arts Movement's efforts of the late 1960s" (Robin D. G. Kelley, "Dig They Freedom: Meditations on History and the Black Avant-Garde," *Lenox Avenue: A Journal of Interarts Inquiry* 3 [1997]: 18).
5 Lauren Berlant, *Cruel Optimism* (Durham, NC: Duke University Press, 2012), 4.
6 Gérard Genette defines *paratext* as a "threshold" or "vestibule," an "'undefined zone' between the inside and the outside, a zone without any hard and fast boundary on either the inward side (turned toward the text) or the outward side (turned toward the world's discourse about the text)" (Gérard Genette, *Paratexts: Thresholds of Interpretation*, trans. Jane E. Lewin [Cambridge: Cambridge University Press, 1997], 2).
7 Quoted in Ronald Sukenick, *Down and In: Life in the Underground* (New York: William Morrow, 1987), 221. George Lewis's treatment of this moment in the formation of experimental jazz is indispensable. See George Lewis, *A Power Stronger Than Itself: The AACM and American Experimental Music* (Chicago: University of Chicago Press, 2008), 29–54.
8 Aldon Nielsen, "Now Is the Time: Voicing Against the Grain of Orality," in *People Get Ready: The Future of Jazz Is Now!*, eds. Ajay Heble and Rob Wallace (Durham, NC: Duke University Press, 2013), 34. Richard Iton in a similar vein urges attention to "the conjunctions made possible by the artist-activist, and efforts to sustain infrastructures that might support more extended and intensive forms of creative expression such as

the band, the collective, workshops, and live performances," which he analogizes to "the struggle for room within language itself" (Richard Iton, *In Search of the Black Fantastic: Politics and Popular Culture in the Post–Civil Rights Era* [Oxford: Oxford University Press, 2008], 287).

9   I refer especially to Gayatri Chakravorty Spivak, "Scattered Speculations on the Subaltern and the Popular," *Postcolonial Studies* 8, no. 4 (2005): 475–86.

10 Iton, *Black Fantastic*, 200. Iton's later gloss is helpful: "It is this ethical lack of commitment—this anarchist-inflected imagination—that enables subaltern subjects to push for inclusion among those protected by the prophylactic state while at the same time recognizing the limitations of this recognition" (202).

11 Quoted in John Szwed, *Space Is the Place: The Lives and Times of Sun Ra* (New York: Pantheon Books, 1997), 365.

12 Richard Iton, "Still Life," *Small Axe* 40 (March 2013): 27.

13 Samuel Floyd, *The Power of Black Music: Interpreting Its History from Africa to the United States* (Oxford: Oxford University Press, 1996), 6.

14 Stuart Hall, "When Was 'the Post-colonial'?" 254. "It does not mean," Hall cautions, "that what we have called the 'after-effects' of colonial rule have somehow been suspended. It certainly does *not* mean that we have passed from a regime of power-knowledge into some powerless and conflict-free time zone. Nevertheless, it does also stake its claim in terms of the fact that some other, related but as yet 'emergent' new configurations of power-knowledge relations are beginning to exert their distinctive and specific effects. This way of conceptualizing the shift between these paradigms—not as an epistemological 'break' in the Althusserian/structuralist sense but more on the analogy of what Gramsci called a movement of deconstruction-reconstruction or what Derrida, in a more deconstructive sense, calls a 'double inscription'—is characteristic of all the 'posts.'"

15 For an excellent summary account of Benjamin's understandings of medium and apparatus, I recommend Antonio Somaini, "Walter Benjamin's Media Theory: The *Medium* and the *Apparat*," *Grey Room* 62 (Winter 2016): 6–41.

16 I develop this distinction between the "real" or empirical object and the theoretical one from Hortense Spillers, by way of Louis Althusser. Spillers argues that "the 'purest' object that the black creative intellectual always imagined as the unmediated 'thereness' is situated in his/her concept of natal community," which she urges us to reconsider for reasons practical, political, and theoretical (Hortense Spillers, *Black, White, and in Color: Essays on American Literature and Culture* [Chicago: University of Chicago Press, 2003], 458). Most germane to my argument here is that the black creative intellectual's "raw material" does not conform to an empiricist conception of knowledge but refers instead to a "structure of intuition or 'representation' which combines in a peculiar '*Verbindung*' [complex structure] the mode of production, sensuous, technical and ideological elements." In other words, the real object, as raw material, is not a given but already *produced* within a "historically constituted system of an *apparatus of thought*, founded on and articulated to natural and social reality" (Louis Althusser and Étienne Balibar, *Reading* Capital, trans. Ben Brewster [London: Verso 1997], 44). A black sound studies adequate to its concept must consider "the imposition of the complex (sensuous-technical-ideological) structure

which constitutes it [black sound and blackness] as an *object of knowledge*" (*Reading Capital*, 46).
17 Alexander Weheliye, *Phonographies: The Grooves of Sonic Afro-Modernity* (Durham, NC: Duke University Press, 2005), 22.
18 Weheliye, *Phonographies*, 205, 32.
19 Stuart Hall, "What Is This 'Black' in Black Popular Culture?" in *Black Popular Culture*, ed. Gina Dent (Seattle: Bay Press, 1992), 21.
20 George Lewis offers a telling account of the difficulties journeyman recording engineers faced when his colleagues in the Association for the Advancement of Creative Musicians first began recording (*Power*, 141–43).
21 I draw the "upworking of revolutionary ideals" from Saidiya Hartman, *Wayward Lives, Beautiful Experiments: Intimate Histories of Riotous Black Girls, Troublesome Women, and Queer Radicals* (New York: W. W. Norton, 2019), 93.
22 I find persuasive Cynthia Young's argument in *Soul Power: Culture, Radicalism, and the Making of a U.S. Third World Left* (Durham, NC: Duke University Press, 2006) that black artists, intellectuals, and activists found inspiration in international struggles, effectively imagining new internationals between African Americans and other black and brown intellectuals throughout what was called the Third World. For that reason I am wary about overemphasizing the CPUSA in particular. In his essay "A Movement of Movements: The Definition and Periodization of the New Left" (in *A Companion to Post-1945 America*, eds. Jean-Christophe Agnew and Roy Rosenzweig [London: Wiley-Blackwell, 2006], 277–302), Van Gosse helpfully recovers the complexity and transnational character of the social movements for socialism and radical democracy of the post–World War II era, recovering those voices subsequently grouped and dismissed under the sign of "identity politics."
23 Miriam Bratu Hansen, "The Mass Production of the Senses: Classical Cinema as Vernacular Modernism," *Modernism/Modernity* 6, no. (1999): 59.
24 Ralph Ellison defined *vernacular* "as a dynamic *process* in which the most refined styles from the past are continually merged with the play-it-by-eye-and-ear improvisations which we invent in our efforts to control our environment and entertain ourselves." Ralph Ellison, *The Collected Essays of Ralph Ellison*, ed. John F. Callahan (New York: Modern Library, 2003), 612. While I reject the notion of refinement, Ellison usefully outlines the ways individual artists might act with indifference toward, and thus redefine, the racializing logics associated with particular styles. Grant Farred extends this line of thinking, using "vernacular" to modify intellectual practice "[d]eeply grounded in the ways in which the cultural shapes and reshapes the political impact" of black intellectual labor in a postcolonial and anti-colonial context. Grant Farred, *What's My Name?: Black Vernacular Intellectuals* (Minneapolis: University of Minnesota Press, 2003), 2.
25 Christopher Small, *Music of the Common Tongue: Survival and Celebration in Afro-American Music* (London: John Calder Publishers, 1987), 8–9.
26 James Smethurst, *The Black Arts Movement: Literary Nationalism in the 1960s and 1970s* (Chapel Hill: University of North Carolina Press, 2006), 59. Smethurst's conception of a "popular avant-garde" tracks with Martha Biondi's discussion of the Black Popular Front in *To Stand and Fight: The Struggle for Civil Rights in Postwar New York City* (Cambridge, MA: Harvard University Press, 2003).

27 Smethurst, *The Black Arts Movement*, 59.
28 Amiri Baraka, *The Amiri Baraka Reader*, ed. William J. Harris (New York: Basic Books, 2009), 174. For more on this era and the one immediately following, see Robin D. G. Kelley, *Race Rebels*; Dayo F. Gore, *Radicalism at the Crossroads*; and Michael Dawson, *Blacks In and Out of the Left*. Smethurst's *New Red Negro* details African American literary engagements with the left during the Depression and World War II, while Mary Helen Washington's *The Other Black List* joins scholarship by William Maxwell and Bill V. Mullen in excavating the many complex interactions between African Americans and the communist left.
29 Jerrold Hirsch's influential "Modernity, Nostalgia and Southern Folklore Studies: The Case of John Lomax," *Journal of American Folklore* 105.416 (Spring 1992): 183–207, notes the relationships between romantic nationalism, genocidal colonial policies, and the processes of legitimating imperialism and segregation (by reifying violent social transformations under the sign of "disappearing culture"). Jonathan Sterne, drawing on Hirsch and Erika Brady, underscores the coincidence between the rise of sound media cultures in the late nineteenth century, romantic nationalism, the rise of ethnography, modernity's territorial expanse, and the genocidal effects of the policies that supported that expansion in the United States. The more Native Americans (and other cultures) "disappeared" through death or assimilation, the more sound technologies fit and promoted new social constructs of sound's reproducibility and preservation. Moreover, as a somewhat unitary popular culture diffused through records spread, the homogenization of American culture as a truly national culture accelerated the conditions of the disappearance of local folk cultures—the disappearance of the "folk" illuminated and selected for the use of sound media to preserve the languages and songs of colonial others almost as a fetish. The fetishization of "folk spirit"—a term for original community—is a key component of romantic nationalism, promoting a view of all those cultures and peoples on modernity's periphery as living reliquaries whose cultures can be adopted as an alternative to an increasingly mechanized, overdeveloped modern world. Arguments on the analogous function of "primitivism" in literature, often figured through music, are too numerous to cite. As one example, Jean Toomer calls *Cane* the "swan song" of a Negro folk spirit "walking in to die on the modern desert" in the context of the Great Migration (Jean Toomer, *The Wayward and the Seeking: A Collection of Writings by Jean Toomer*, ed. Darwin M. Turner [Washington, DC: Howard University Press, 1980], 123).
30 For African American participation in what will become the music industries, see Tim Brooks, *Lost Sounds: Blacks and the Birth of the Recording Industry, 1890–1919* (Urbana: University of Illinois Press, 2004). Andre Millard discusses the relationship of sound recording to the rise of ethnography as a separate branch of anthropology, and, at least initially, as a consumer object recorded by Emile Berliner, Victor, and Gennett in *America on Record: A History of Recorded Sound* (Cambridge: Cambridge University Press, 2003).
31 Jonathan Sterne, *The Audible Past: Cultural Origins of Sound Reproduction* (Durham, NC: Duke University Press, 2003), 182.
32 Michael Denning, *Noise Uprising: The Audio Politics of a World Musical Revolution* (London: Verso, 2015).

33　I am drawing on Weheliye, *Phonographies* and Denning, *Noise Uprising*.
34　Aldon Nielsen discusses recordings by Duke Ellington, Jack Kerouac, Lawrence Ferlinghetti, Kenneth Rexroth, and Kenneth Patchen in *Black Chant: The Languages of Black Postmodernity* (Cambridge: Cambridge University Press, 1997), 173–233. Jacob Smith writes about the ways the circulation of poetry on record extended the "verse-recitation movement" in Victorian England and record companies' attempts to appeal to middle-class and middle-class-aspirant listeners, foregrounding Caedmon Records' poetry recordings in *Spoken Word: Postwar American Phonograph Cultures* (Berkeley: University of California Press, 2011). And Peter D. Goldsmith offers a comprehensive account of Folkways Records, famous in the postwar era for recording black and other poets, musicians, and public figures in *Making People's Music: Moe Asch and Folkways Records* (Washington, DC: Smithsonian Institution Press, 1998).
35　Theodor W. Adorno, *Essays on Music*, ed. Richard Leppert, trans. Susan H. Gillespie et al. (Berkeley: University of California Press, 2002), 280.
36　Adorno, *Essays on Music*, 280.
37　Fred Moten, *In the Break: The Aesthetics of the Black Radical Tradition* (Minneapolis: University of Minnesota Press, 2005), 1. "Paraontological" is Nahum Chandler's way of describing the conceptual disturbances blackness enacts within and against positivism on one hand and phenomenology on the other, insofar as the former's things-as-they-are neglects the social forces that shape existence (naturalizing racist outcomes as "facts" about race) and the latter's intending subject always at least implies a European subject.
38　Jacques Rancière, *The Politics of Aesthetics: The Distribution of the Sensible*, trans. Gabriel Rockhill (London: Continuum, 2004), 12.
39　Jacques Rancière, *Disagreement: Politics and Philosophy*, trans. Julie Rose (Minneapolis: University of Minnesota Press, 1999), 6. Translation modified.
40　Rancière, *The Politics of Aesthetics*. Rockhill explains that "*le commun*," variously translated, "is strictly speaking what makes or produces a community and not simply an attribute shared by all of its members" (102n5).
41　Michael Hardt, "Production and Distribution of the Common: A Few Questions for the Artist," *open! Platform for Art, Culture & the Public Domain*. February 6, 2006. http://www.onlineopen.org/production-and-distribution-of-the-common. Accessed May 9, 2018.
42　Rancière, *Disagreement*, 12.
43　Saidiya V. Hartman, *Scenes of Subjection: Terror, Slavery, and Self-Making in Nineteenth-Century America* (Oxford: Oxford University Press, 1997), 115.
44　Moten, *In the Break*, 86.
45　I derive the notion of "relative autonomy" from Louis Althusser, who deployed it as an alternative conceptual framework through which to conceive the relationship between economic, political, ideological, and theoretical "levels" articulated into a "complex unity" for which the economic, notoriously, proves "determinant in the last instance." The economic, in other words, is a kind of theoretical vanishing point, a necessary but not sufficient reference for conceiving unity between otherwise discrete social formations. The argument is related to Lukacs's notion of "phantom objectivity," but attempts to conceive the relationship between these

"levels" as imperfect correspondence rather than Hegelian expression. See Althusser and Balibar, *Reading Capital*, 91–101. For an account of the mutual inflection of class and race—notably absent from Althusser's account—see Stuart Hall, "Race, Articulation, and Societies Structured in Dominance," in *Black British Cultural Studies: A Reader*, eds. Houston Baker Jr., Manthia Diawara, and Ruth H. Lindeborg (Chicago: University of Chicago Press, 1996), 16–60.

46 Sherrie Tucker's work, especially her essay "Bordering on Community: Improvising Women Improvising Women-in-Jazz" (*The Other Side of Nowhere: Jazz, Improvisation, and Communities in Dialogue*, eds. Daniel Fischlin and Ajay Heble [Middletown, CT: Wesleyan University Press, 2004]: 244–67), is especially helpful. Her insistence on considering "improvising women" as "a working condition of 'improvising women'" underscores that, while the power gender norms exercise may produce resistance, the exercise of resistance threatens to erode the very footholds the women worked to make for themselves.

47 Sherrie Tucker, "Deconstructing the Jazz Tradition," in *Jazz/Not Jazz: The Music and Its Boundaries*, eds. David Ake, Charles Hiroshi Garrett, and Daniel Goldmark (Berkeley: University of California Press, 2012), 279.

48 Here I draw on and synthesize several sources. Though largely silent on African American practices, Joan Shelley Rubin, *Songs of Ourselves: The Uses of Poetry in America* (Cambridge, MA: Harvard University Press, 2010), and Mike Chasar, *Everyday Reading: Poetry and Popular Culture in Modern America* (New York: Columbia University Press, 2012), offer compelling arguments about the place of verse in the formation of quotidian US life, from advertising jingles and scrapbooking to church bulletins, family gatherings, and beyond. Lesley Wheeler's attention to the practicalities of voice, poetry, and performance is a welcome focus in *Voicing American Poetry: Sound and Performance from the 1920s to the Present* (Ithaca, NY: Cornell University Press, 2008). Tyler Hoffman, *American Poetry in Performance: From Walt Whitman to Hip Hop* (Ann Arbor: University of Michigan Press, 2011), offers an expansive view of the "civics of American performance poetry and the nexus of its oral and print modalities in the light of shifting political and cultural formations in the nation over the last century and a half" (4). His attention to a broad range of performance practices and cultural identities is in line with such studies as Julia Novak, *Live Poetry: An Integrated Approach to Poetry in Performance* (Amsterdam: Rodopi, 2011), and Susan B. A. Somers-Willett's indispensable *The Cultural Politics of Slam Poetry* (Ann Arbor: University of Michigan Press, 2009).

49 Don Ihde, *Listening and Voice: Phenomenologies of Sound*, 2nd ed. (Albany: State University of New York Press, 2007), 4. I adapt the term "songful" from Lawrence Kramer's discussion of "songfulness," an excess materiality of words in performance that can extend or contradict semantic meanings, in "Beyond Words and Music: An Essay on Songfulness," in *Word and Music Studies Defining the Field: Proceedings of the First International Conference on Word and Music Studies at Graz, 1997*, eds. Walter Bernhart, Steven Paul Scher, and Werner Wolf (Amsterdam: Rodopi, 1999).

50 Sterne, *The Audible Past*, 182.

51 Gayatri Chakravorty Spivak, "Scattered Speculations on the Question of Value," in *In Other Worlds: Essays in Cultural Politics* (New York: Routledge, 1988), 162.

52 Jacques Attali, *Noise: The Political Economy of Music*, trans. Brian Massumi (Minneapolis: University of Minnesota Press, 1985), 101.
53 Attali, *Noise*, 101.
54 Peter Szendy, *Listen: A History of Our Ears*, trans. Charlotte Mandell (New York: Fordham University Press, 2008), 142.

CHAPTER 1. VOICE PRINTS

1 Adorno, letter to Walter Benjamin, November 10, 1938, in Theodor W. Adorno and Walter Benjamin, *The Complete Correspondence, 1928–1940*, trans. Nicholas Walker, ed. Henri Lonitz (Cambridge, MA: Harvard University Press, 1999), 283.
2 Alexander Weheliye, *Phonographies: Grooves in Sonic Afro-Modernity* (Durham, NC: Duke University Press, 2005), 39. I refer to Moten who in *In the Break* cites Frederick Douglass's citation, in his 1845 *Narrative*, of his Aunt Hester's cry as anti- and ante-origin of black phonic materiality, implicitly calling for analysis in terms of media. I draw the specific sense of textuality from Gayatri Chakravorty Spivak's "Scattered Speculations on the Question of Value," where textuality is a name for those moments of the dialectic (in the context of referring to Marx's critique of utopian socialists) that, in rejecting a positive origin, lend themselves to an open-endedness analogous to post-structuralist accounts of textuality.
3 I'm drawing on John Guillory, whose "annotations on a linked set of evolving terms"—in my case *expression, text, experience*, and *embodiment*—inspire my method here. John Guillory, "Genesis of the Media Concept," *Critical Inquiry* 36, no. 2 (Winter 2010): 326.
4 Weheliye, *Phonographies*, 7.
5 Spivak, "Scattered Speculations on the Relation between the Subaltern and the Popular."
6 Fred Moten, *In the Break: The Aesthetics of the Black Radical Tradition* (Minneapolis: University of Minnesota Press, 2005), 212.
7 I'm thinking of Sylvia Wynter who, summarizing Frantz Fanon's *Black Skin, White Masks*, writes that "The true leap . . . consists in bringing invention into existence. The buck stops with us." "Unsettling the Coloniality of Being/Power/Truth/Freedom: Towards the Human, After Man, Its Overrepresentation—An Argument," *CR: The New Centennial Review* 3, no. 3 (Fall 2003): 331.
8 Steve Coleman, *Sonic Language of Myth: Believing, Learning, Knowing* (CD, RCA Victor 74321 64123 2, 1999).
9 Sylvia Wynter, "Rethinking 'Aesthetics': Notes Toward a Deciphering Practice," in *Ex-Iles: Essays on Caribbean Cinema*, ed. Mbaye M. Cham (Trenton, NJ: Africa World Press, 1992), 237–79. While her reliance on biological research makes it difficult to interrogate the ways the biological sciences participate in and shore up normative notions of the human, her account of the public value of criticism remains valuable.
10 Simone White, *Dear Angel of Death* (Brooklyn, NY: Ugly Duckling Presse, 2019), 100.
11 The latest version of this occurs in a May 22, 2018, conversation with Jonathan Capehart of the *Washington Post*. Marsalis posted Capehart's write-up on his professional website: https://wyntonmarsalis.org/news/entry/wynton-marsalis-rap-hip-hop-more-damaging-tha-robert-lee.

12. Fred Moten, "Blackness and Nothingness (Mysticism in the Flesh)," *South Atlantic Quarterly* 112.4 (2013): 757.
13. Sherley Ann Williams's analysis of the place of music in literature from the Harlem Renaissance to her contemporary moment is one potential addition. See *Give Birth to Brightness: A Thematic Study in Neo-Black Literature* (New York: Dial Press, 1972), esp. 135–67.
14. Frederick Douglass, *Autobiographies*, ed. Henry Louis Gates Jr. (New York: Library of America, 1994), 24, 185.
15. Jon Cruz, *Culture on the Margins: The Black Spiritual and the Rise of American Cultural Interpretation* (Princeton, NJ: Princeton University Press, 1999).
16. I'm drawing on Jonathan Sterne's argument that the changed status of the voice promoted new uses of sound recording technologies, and on Stephen Best's arguments about the relationship between slavery, commodities, and intellectual property. See Sterne, *The Audible Past*, 289–99; and Stephen Best, *The Fugitive's Properties: Law and the Poetics of Possession* (Chicago: University of Chicago Press, 2004), especially his discussion of "fugitive sound," which informs my own conception of the fugitive voice.
17. Moten, *In the Break*, 15.
18. David Suisman details this process in *Selling Sounds: The Commercial Revolution in American Music* (Cambridge, MA: Harvard University Press, 2012).
19. W. E. B. Du Bois, *Writings*, ed. Nathan Huggins (New York: Library of America, 1986), 536–37.
20. Du Bois, *Writings*, 536–37. I am also extending Spivak's argument in "Scattered Speculations on the Subaltern and the Popular," 480.
21. Farah Jasmine Griffin, "When Malindy Sings: A Meditation on Black Women's Vocality," in *Uptown Conversation: The New Jazz Studies* (New York: Columbia University Press, 2004), 114. David Levering Lewis argues that Du Bois is thinking of a Wolof song of captivity, and that "gene ma" roughly translates as "get me out." David Levering Lewis, *W. E. B. Du Bois: Biography of a Race, 1868–1919* (New York: Henry Holt and Company, 1993), 14.
22. Zora Neale Hurston, "Spirituals and Neo-Spirituals," *Folklore, Memoirs, and Other Writings*, ed. Cheryl A. Wall (New York: Library of America 1995), 869.
23. Hurston, "Spirituals and Neo-Spirituals," 870.
24. Hurston, "Spirituals and Neo-Spirituals," 870.
25. Hurston, "Spirituals and Neo-Spirituals," 871.
26. Moten, *In the Break*, 6.
27. Moten, *In the Break* 16.
28. Amiri Baraka, *Blues People: Negro Music in White America* (1963. New York: Perennial, 2002), viii.
29. Amiri Baraka, "You Think This Is About You?," liner notes to Albert Ayler, *Holy Ghost: Rare and Unissued Recordings (1962–1970)* (Revenant 213, 2004), 40, Baraka's emphasis.
30. Baraka, "You Think This Is About You?"
31. Baraka, *Blues People*, 152.
32. Amiri Baraka, "Screamers," in *The Fiction of LeRoi Jones/Amiri Baraka* (Chicago: Lawrence Hill Books, 2000), 184.
33. Baraka, *Black Music*, 67.

34 Baraka, *Blues People* 28–29, Baraka's emphasis.
35 Larry Neal, in Hoyt Fuller, ed., "Writers Symposium," *Negro Digest* 17, no. 3 (January 1968): 81.
36 Larry Neal, "Black Revolution in Music: A Talk with Drummer Milford Graves," *Liberator* (September 1965), 14.
37 Archie Shepp, "An Artist Speaks Bluntly," *Down Beat* (December 1965): 11. Eric Porter cites this passage in the midst of a longer discussion detailing the differences between Karenga, Shepp, and Baraka (Eric Porter, *What Is This Thing Called Jazz?: African American Musicians as Artists, Critics, and Activists* [Berkeley: University of California Press, 2002], 203). Larry Neal would resist the characterization of the music as "revolutionary," declaring that labeling it such was an "abuse of terms" because it had failed to "extend itself into the black community" (Larry Neal, *Negro Digest* 16, no. 5 [March 1967]: 56). I mention these simply to underscore the important disagreements among theorists of black sound. Ronald Radano argues that these thinkers ultimately undermined the movement: "By taking on the role of spokespersons who declared free jazz a sonic expression of black power, they oversimplified the ideological dimensions of the music [which] permitted aesthetically conservative writers [who had since the 1960s been labelling any black musician who appeared sympathetic to Black Nationalism 'reverse racist' or 'Crow Jim'] to ridicule the music while maintaining a seemingly objective stance" (Ronald Radano, *New Musical Figurations: Anthony Braxton's Cultural Critique* [Chicago: University of Chicago Press, 1993], 69). Linking the music to a reified notion of black power meant that as Black Power and black radicalism waned and a new, less assertive black politics became ascendant, the music, already only tenuously connected to its communities, was now "liberated" from any non-aesthetic concerns.
38 Karenga, of course, would be an important influence on Baraka and others of his generation. Extending his argument, he called for "our art [to] remind us of our distaste for the enemy, our love for each other, and our commitment to the revolutionary struggle that will be fought with the rhythmic reality of a permanent revolution." Ron Karenga, "Ron Karenga and Black Cultural Nationalism: A Response," *Negro Digest* 17, no. 3 (January 1968): 5, 9.
39 Frantz Fanon, *Black Skin, White Masks*, trans. Charles Lam Markmann (New York: Grove Press, 1962), 112.
40 Tony Bolden, *Afro-Blue: Improvisations in African American Poetry and Culture* (Urbana: University of Illinois Press, 2004), 33.
41 Jed Rasula's observations about the construction of a jazz canon are especially pertinent here. See Jed Rasula, "The Media of Memory: The Seductive Menace of Records in Jazz History," in *Jazz Among the Discourses*, ed. Krin Gabbard (Durham, NC: Duke University Press, 1995), 134–62.
42 Margo Natalie Crawford, "The Poetics of Chant and Inner/Outer Space," in *The Cambridge Companion to American Poetry Since 1945*, ed. Jennifer Ashton (Cambridge: Cambridge University Press, 2013), 106.
43 I draw the phrase "sound for sounding" from Amiri Baraka's preface to Larry Neal, *Black Boogaloo: Notes on Black Liberation* (San Francisco: Journal of Black Poetry Press, 1969), i.

44 I refer to Mladen Dolar, *A Voice and Nothing More* (Cambridge: MIT Press, 2006), 14. Thank you to the anonymous reader for pushing me to think more carefully about voice throughout this project.

45 Reading Nikki Giovanni's description of Aretha Franklin, Emily Lordi theorizes the term "signature voice"—as "the artist's self-assertion and her extension of authority toward others." It encodes a notion of the artist as "singular . . . without being insular" and inscribes performance within a signifying tradition that belongs to all who will claim it. Emily J. Lordi, *Black Resonance: Iconic Women Singers and African American Literature* (New Brunswick, NJ: Rutgers University Press, 2013), 175.

46 Lewis offers an invaluable account of the Jazz Composer's Guild and similar associations in *A Power Stronger than Itself*, 92–95. For an account of organizations such as the Jazz Composer's Guild in the ideological context of the Cold War, see Bernard Gendron, "After the October Revolution: The Jazz Avant-garde in New York, 1964–65," in *Sound Commitments: Avant-Garde Music and the Sixties*, ed. Robert Addington (Oxford: Oxford University Press, 2009), 211–53. Eric Porter offers the fullest account of the intellectual context of Archie Shepp in this period in *What Is This Thing Called Jazz?*

47 The contrast with his later performance of the phonopoem "Poem for Malcolm" (*Poem for Malcolm*, BYG Actuel, 1969), which features a full-throated delivery just short of a yell, is striking.

48 Nielsen, *Black Chant*, 203.

49 Nat Hentoff, liner notes to Archie Shepp, *Fire Music* (Impulse!, 1965).

50 Sterne, *The Audible Past*, 299.

51 Sterne, *The Audible Past*, 182.

52 Baraka, "Screamers," 184.

53 Ornette Coleman, quoted in A. B. Spellman, *Four Lives in the Bebop Business* (New York: Limelight Editions, 1994), 130.

54 Archie Shepp, cited in Lewis, *A Power Stronger than Itself*, 43.

55 Brent Hayes Edwards, *Epistrophies: Jazz and the Literary Imagination* (Cambridge, MA: Harvard University Press, 2017), 16. I am also drawing on Nathaniel Mackey's argument that "everybody talks about the speech-like qualities of instruments as they are played in African American music. Built into that is some kind of dissatisfaction with—if not critique of—the limits of conventionally articulate speech, verbal speech. One of the reasons the music so often goes over into nonspeech—moaning, humming, shouts, nonsense lyrics, scat—is to say, among other things, that the realm of conventionally articulate speech is not sufficient for saying what needs to be said. We are often making the same assertion in poetry." Nathaniel Mackey, *Paracritical Hinge: Essays, Talks, Notes, Interviews* (Madison: University of Wisconsin Press, 2005), 193.

56 Baraka, Preface to Larry Neal, *Black Boogaloo: Notes on Black Liberation* (San Francisco: Journal of Black Poetry Press, 1969); Larry Neal, "And Shine Swam On," in *Black Fire: An Anthology of Afro-American Writing*, ed. Amiri Baraka and Larry Neal (1968; Baltimore: Black Classic Press, 2007), 653.

57 Lewis, *A Power Stronger than Itself*, 90.

58 Hentoff, liner notes to *Fire Music*.

59 Amy Obugo Ongiri, *Spectacular Blackness: The Cultural Politics of the Black Power Movement and the Search for a Black Aesthetic* (Charlottesville: University of Virginia Press, 2010), 128–29.
60 Karl Marx, *Capital, Vol. 1*, trans. Ben Fowkes (London: Penguin, 1976), 786.
61 Lawrence P. Neal, "A Conversation with Archie Shepp," *Liberator* 5, no. 11 (November 1965): 24.
62 Porter, *What Is This Thing Called Jazz?*, 205.
63 Neal, "The Black Arts Movement," 29.
64 Shepp quoted in Neal, "A Conversation with Archie Shepp," 25.
65 Jacqueline Dowd Hall, "The Long Civil Rights Movement and the Political Uses of the Past," *Journal of American History* 91, no. 4 (March 2005): 1233–63.
66 I'm thinking here and throughout these comments of Adolph Reed's indictment of Black Power politics in his essay "Black Particularity Reconsidered" (*Telos* 1979.39 [March 1979]: 71–93), which is especially unsparing in its criticism of black leadership from the mid-1960s to the mid-1970s. Acute though it is, one wishes for more analysis of, or at least attention to, other forces that determine how that moment's crisis would be understood—what kind of crisis people faced—and thus which solutions could have been won.
67 Ongiri, *Spectacular Blackness*, 129.
68 Spillers, *Black, White, and in Color*, 432. Her point is that black studies should consider "the community" as an object of knowledge, our understanding of which is inextricable from shifting relations of production rather than an empirical or stable "real object."
69 Michael Denning, "The End of Mass Culture," *International Labor and Working-Class History* 37 (Spring 1990): 4.
70 That, of course, is not the whole story. Ongiri details some of the ways the Black Panther Party, in particular, mobilized popular visual and medial culture, arguing it was "not only invested in influencing American popular culture . . . but was also in the business of creating it" (Ongiri, *Spectacular Blackness*, 18–19). Angela Y. Davis makes complementary arguments in "Afro Images: Politics, Fashion, and Nostalgia," *Critical Inquiry* 21, no. 1 (Autumn 1994): 37–45.
71 Porter, *What Is This Thing Called Jazz?*, 206.
72 Pierre Bourdieu, *Distinction: A Social Critique of the Judgment of Taste*, trans. Richard Nice (Cambridge, MA: Harvard University Press, 1984), 32.
73 James C. Hall, "The African American Musician as Intellectual," *Harold Cruse's the Crisis of the Negro Intellectual Reconsidered*, ed. Jerry Watts (London: Routledge, 2004), 115.
74 Phillip Brian Harper, "Nationalism and Social Division in Black Arts Poetry of the 1960s," *Critical Inquiry* 19, no. 2 (Winter 1993): 247.
75 Harper, "Nationalism and Social Division," 250.
76 Hentoff, liner notes to *Fire Music*.
77 Baraka, "A Conversation with Archie Shepp," 24–25.
78 Cecil Taylor, "Sound Structure of Subculture Becoming Major Breath/Naked Fire Gesture," liner notes to *Unit Structures* (Blue Note, 1966).
79 Michael Denning, *The Cultural Front: The Laboring of American Culture in the Twentieth Century* (London: Verso, 1997), 22.

80 Walter Benjamin, "The Medium through Which Works of Art Continue to Influence Later Ages," trans. Rodney Livingstone, in *Selected Writings*, trans. Edmund Jephcott et al., ed. Marcus Bullock et al., 4 vols. (Cambridge, MA: Harvard University Press, 2002), 1: 235.
81 Phil Freeman, "Matana Roberts," *Wire-London* 328 (June 2011): 20.
82 Matana Roberts, "Artistic Statement," Matanaroberts.com. Based in part on this description, David Rando compellingly reads *Coin Coin* as Matana Roberts's aesthetic analogue to Walter Benjamin's unfinished *The Arcades Project*. David Rando, *Hope and Wish Image in Music Technology* (Basingstoke, UK: Palgrave Macmillan, 2017), 16.
83 Matana Roberts and Jason Moran, "Coin Coin Recollections," *Loop* 1 (2016): 60.
84 Matana Roberts, "Keeping on . . . ," *Critical Studies in Improvisation/Études critiques en improvisation* 6, no. 2 (2010): 1.
85 Matana Roberts, quoted in Daniel Spicer, "Chains of the Heart," *Wire-London* 356 (October 2013): 34.
86 Roberts, quoted in Daniel Spicer, "Chains of the Heart."
87 Roberts, quoted in Daniel Spicer, "Chains of the Heart."
88 Roberts, "Artistic Statement." In another comment, she avers her fascination with "ephemeral decay. Decay in memory, decay in a good life lived . . ." (Matana Roberts, "Below the Radar," *Wire-London*, https://www.thewire.co.uk/audio/btr/below-the-radar-15/15, ellipses in original).
89 Katherine McKittrick, "Mathematics Black Life," *Black Scholar* 44, no. 2 (Summer 2014): 16.
90 Matana Roberts, *Coin Coin Chapter One: Gens de couleur libres* (Constellation Records, 2011).
91 Moten, *In the Break*, 22.
92 Roberts, liner notes, *Coin Coin Chapter One*.
93 Iton, *In Search of the Black Fantastic*, 9.

CHAPTER 2. COMMUNITIES IN TRANSITION

1 *Epistrophies: Jazz and the Literary Imagination* (Cambridge, MA: Harvard University Press, 2017), 17.
2 Langston Hughes, "The Negro Artist and the Racial Mountain," *The Nation* 122 (June 23, 1926): 692–94. Reprinted in *The Collected Works of Langston Hughes: Essays on Art, Race, Politics, and World Affairs*, vol. 9, ed. Christopher C. De Santi (Columbia: University of Missouri Press, 2002), 32.
3 Nathaniel Mackey, *Bass Cathedral* (New York: New Directions, 2008), 11.
4 Fred Moten, *A Poetics of the Undercommons* (Butte, MT: Sputnik & Fizzle, 2016), 24.
5 Charles Mingus, "What Is a Jazz Composer?" in *Charles Mingus: More Than a Fake Book* (New York: Jazz Workshop, 1991), 119. Mingus initially published this essay as the liner notes to his 1971 album *Let My Children Hear Music* (Columbia KC 31039).
6 Vera M. Kutzinski, *The Worlds of Langston Hughes: Modernism and Translation in the Americas* (Ithaca, NY: Cornell University Press, 2012), 10.
7 I refer to the title work of Jeanne Lee's 1975 album *Conspiracy*. The interplay of the musicians (Sam Rivers, flute; Jack Gregg, bass; Gunter Hampel, woodwinds and

vibraphone; Steve McCall, percussion; and Lee, vocals) exemplifies the intersection of breathing room and breathing together.
8 Arnold Rampersad, noting Hughes's overcommitment and resultant diffusion of energies across many obligations, suggests that Hughes's assessment of Duke Ellington's "indiscriminate pursuit of the money and prestige denied him in the past" applies to Hughes himself. Arnold Rampersad, *The Life of Langston Hughes, Vol. II: 1941-1967: I Dream a World* (Oxford: Oxford University Press, 2002), 287.
9 This is not to deny Mingus's volatility or to gloss over his many famous altercations. In the wake of essays like Norman Mailer's "The White Negro," which figured a certain African American masculinity as an alternative to mechanized white Americanism, it is worth being cautious about characterizing Mingus's outsized public displays of emotion as anger alone. As he wrote in an open letter to Miles Davis, "My music is alive and it's about the living and the dead, about good and evil. It's angry yet it's real because it knows it's angry." Charles Mingus, "An Open Letter to Miles Davis," *Down Beat* (November 30, 1955): 12–13.
10 Anthony Dawahare, "Langston Hughes's Radical Poetry and the 'End of Race,'" *MELUS* 23, no. 3 (Fall 1998): 21–41. For all his insights, Dawahare's strong antinationalist argument at times leads him to conflate Hughes's contemporary reception with Hughes's more evocative—and elusive—poetry.
11 Hughes, Smethurst argues, "was a typical Cold War African-American radical artist, rather than former Leftist, in his occasional evasiveness and denials." James Smethurst, "'Don't Say Goodbye to the Porkpie Hat': Langston Hughes, the Left, and the Black Arts Movement," *Callaloo* 24, no. 4 (Fall 2002): 1227.
12 Maryemma Graham, "The Practice of a Social Art," in *Langston Hughes: Critical Perspectives Past and Present*, eds. Henry Louis Gates Jr. and Kwame Anthony Appiah (New York: Amistad, 1993), 218.
13 Graham, "The Practice of a Social Art," 232.
14 Spivak, "Scattered Speculations on the Subaltern and the Popular," 475–76. Spivak reminds us that "subalternity is a position without identity," and that what is at stake is agency: "institutionally validated action, assuming collectivity, distinguished from the formation of the subject, which exceeds the outlines of individual intention" (476). "Sonic color line" is Jennifer Stoever's phrase. See *The Sonic Color Line: Race and the Cultural Politics of Listening* (New York: New York University Press, 2016).
15 Stefano Harney and Valentina Desideri, "A Conspiracy Without a Plot," in *The Curatorial: A Philosophy of Curating*, ed. Jean-Paul Martinon (London: Bloomsbury Press, 2013), 128.
16 Langston Hughes, "The Influence of Negro Music on American Entertainment" (April 25, 1952), in *The Collected Works of Langston Hughes, vol. 9, Essays on Art, Race, Politics, and World Affairs*, ed. Christopher C. De Santi (Columbia: University of Missouri Press, 2002), 208.
17 Robert Young, "Red Poetics and the Practice of 'Disalienation,'" *Montage of a Dream: The Art and Life of Langston Hughes*, eds. John Edgar Tidwell and Cheryl Ragar (Columbia: University of Missouri Press, 2007), 141.

18 Richard Iton, *In Search of the Black Fantastic: Politics and Popular Culture in the Post-Civil Rights Era* (Oxford: Oxford University Press, 2010): 133.
19 Moten, *A Poetics of the Undercommons*, 39.
20 Moten, *A Poetics of the Undercommons*, 14.
21 Kutzinski, *The Worlds of Langston Hughes*, 184–220.
22 Elizabeth Davey, "Building a Black Audience in the 1930s: Langston Hughes, Poetry Readings, and the Golden Stair Press," in *Print Culture in a Diverse America*, eds. James P. Danky and Wayne A. Wiegand (Urbana: University of Illinois Press, 1998), 223.
23 Davey, "Building a Black Audience in the 1930s," 234.
24 Charles Mingus, *Blues and Roots* (Atlantic Records, 1960). "Better Git It in Your Soul" from *Mingus Ah Um* (Columbia Records, 1959) may be a more celebrated instance.
25 Mingus quoted in Nat Hentoff's liner notes to Charles Mingus, *A Modern Jazz Symposium of Music and Poetry with Charlie Mingus* (Bethlehem, 1957).
26 Miles Davis quoted in Gene Santoro, *Myself When I Am Real: The Life and Music of Charles Mingus* (Oxford: Oxford University Press, 2000), 113.
27 Moten, *A Poetics of the Undercommons*, 24.
28 Gene Santoro, *Myself When I Am Real: The Life and Music of Charles Mingus* (Oxford: Oxford University Press, 2000), 128.
29 Aldon Nielsen writes: "Rexroth and Kerouac certainly knew a lot about musicians and listened with a keen ear to jazz, but they evidenced little clear understanding of how the music was put together, and thus their approach to locating their own lines within the music was generally intuitive. The music was, as [David] Meltzer says [in *Reading Jazz* (San Francisco: Mercury House, 1993)], more frequently background (or even distraction) than equal partner in a new genre." Aldon Nielsen, *Black Chant: The Languages of African-American Postmodernity* (Cambridge: Cambridge University Press, 1997), 178.
30 Mingus quoted in Santoro, *Myself When I Am Real*, 130.
31 Arnold Rampersad, Hughes's biographer, argues that Hughes was an innovator of jazz-poetry collaborations (Arnold Rampersad, *The Life of Langston Hughes, Vol. II: 1941–1967: I Dream a World* [Oxford: Oxford University Press, 2002], 279). In a 1958 *Chicago Defender* article, however, Hughes writes, "the reading of poetry to jazz began about a year ago on the Coast and now seems to be achieving popularity all across the country. In San Francisco poets Kenneth Rexroth and Kenneth Patchen started it, and in Los Angeles Lawrence Lipton, Saul White and others carried it on. . . . But so far as I know, the first Negro college to sponsor a poetry-and-jazz program was Fisk University" in 1956 (Langston Hughes, "Poetry, Jazz and Nightclubs," *Chicago Defender*, May 17, 1958 10). It is possible that in the *Defender* article Hughes wants to distinguish the current practice rooted in bebop from earlier practices. His relationship to the Beats is less important for my purposes than his divergent sense of improvisation, and his divergent sense of the relationship of poetry to jazz. Like the Beats, Hughes wanted the musicians to be equal partners in a reciprocal procedure: "Whatever they bring of themselves to the poetry is welcome to me. I merely suggest the mood of each piece as a general orientation. Then I listen to what they say in their playing, and that affects my own rhythms with I read. We listen to each

other." Hughes quoted in Nat Hentoff, "Langston Hughes: He Found Poetry in the Blues," *Mayfair* (August 1958): 27. Steven C. Tracy cites this same passage (178).

32 As Josh Kun argues, "America" for Hughes is hemispheric rather than contained by the geopolitical or ideological borders of the United States. See Josh Kun, *Audiotopia: Music, Race, and America* (Berkeley: University of California Press, 2005), 143-83. Along similar lines, Fred Moten, noting the importance of a trip to Tijuana for Mingus's development of his concept of "rotary perception," argues that a similar hemispheric disruption offers a necessary lens through which to read his work. See Fred Moten, "The New International of Rhythmic Feeling(s)," in *Sonic Interventions*, eds. Sylvia Mieszkowski, Joy Smith, and Marijke de Valck (Amsterdam: Editions Rodopi, 2007), 31-56.

33 Scott Saul analyzes this dynamic in *Freedom Is, Freedom Ain't: Jazz and the Making of the Sixties* (Cambridge, MA: Harvard University Press, 2003).

34 Jacques Derrida, "Freud and the Scene of Writing," in *Writing and Difference*, trans. Alan Bass (Chicago: University of Chicago Press, 1978), 225. I am also thinking here and throughout this chapter with Gayatri Chakravorty Spivak, *A Critique of Postcolonial Reason: Toward a History of the Vanishing Present* (Cambridge, MA: Harvard University Press), especially 37-67.

35 Keith Leonard, *Fettered Genius: The African American Bardic Poet from Slavery to Civil Rights* (Charlottesville: University of Virginia Press, 2006), 82.

36 Hughes, "The Negro Artist and the Racial Mountain," 32.

37 "Actually, 'jazz accompaniment' is not an adequate term to describe Hughes's performances. Given his emphasis on mutually attentive listening and responding as the catalyzing ingredients of effective collaboration, jazz interaction or jazz communication more suitably denotes what, ideally, occurs between poet and musician." Meta DuEwa Jones, *The Muse Is Music: Jazz Poetry from the Harlem Renaissance to Spoken Word* (Urbana: University of Illinois Press, 2011), 49.

38 Small insisted that critics should understand "music" as a verb for the ways people "take part, in any capacity, in a musical performance, whether by performing, by listening, by rehearsing or practicing, by providing material for performance (what is called composing), or by dancing. We might at times even extend its meaning to what the person is doing who takes the tickets at the door or the hefty men who shift the piano and the drums or the roadies who set up the instruments and carry out the sound checks or the cleaners who clean up after everyone else has gone. They, too, are all contributing to the nature of the event that is a musical performance." Christopher Small, *Musicking: The Meanings of Performing and Listening* (Middletown, CT: Wesleyan University Press, 1998), 8.

39 Scott Saul, *Freedom Is, Freedom Ain't*, 158. Mingus describes the Workshop in the liner notes to *Town Hall Concert, 1964, Vol. 1* (Jazz Workshop 1964).

40 Charles Mingus, *Beneath the Underdog: His World as Composed by Mingus* (1971. New York: Vintage, 1991), 351.

41 Jacqueline Dowd Hall, "The Long Civil Rights Movement and the Political Uses of the Past," *Journal of American History* 91, no. 4 (March 2005): 1239, 1250.

42 Carles Mingus, liner notes for *Pithecanthropus Erectus* (Atlantic, 1956).

43 Brian Priestley, *Mingus: A Critical Biography* (New York: Da Capo Press, 1982), 66.

44 Eric Porter details Mingus's ambivalence toward the term *jazz* in the third chapter of *What Is This Thing Called Jazz?* Mingus's impulse to distinguish his art from a music that, from advertising to US State Department–sponsored tours, was becoming a global token of "freedom" is worth taking seriously as one indicator of at least a "juxtapolitical" or proto-political stance, with the function of the music itself suggesting a positive concept he did not always elaborate.

45 Ingrid Monson succinctly explores the ideology of the jazz musician as "untutored, instinctual, nonverbal, and immoral rather than knowledgeable," owing in part to the dominance of early jazz criticism by French critics "with strong relationships to the primitivist movement." Ingrid Monson, "Doubleness and Jazz Improvisation: Irony, Parody, and Ethnomusicology," *Critical Inquiry* 20, no. 2 (Winter 1994): 286.

46 Brent Hayes Edwards and Jed Rasula, "The Ear of the Behearer: A Conversation in Jazz," *New Ohio Review* 3 (Spring 2008): 46.

47 In the liner notes to the 2001 reissue of Mingus's 1957 *Tijuana Moods*, Ben Young notes the importance of post-production editing techniques such as overdubbing, "composite editing (using the best parts of parallel takes); shuffling segments; editing out parts of the score; and splicing-in overdubbed parts" (6).

48 Priestley notes that Mingus's *The Black Saint and the Sinner Lady* (Impulse! 1963) "marks the first occasion where the combination of overdubbing and creative editing actually determined the nature of the product," that is, the realized composition (Priestley, *Mingus*, 147).

49 Mingus, "What Is a Jazz Composer?," 155.

50 Charles Mingus, "An Open Letter to the Avant-Garde," in *More Than a Fake Book*, 119. Originally published in Sue Graham Mingus's *Changes Magazine* (June 1973).

51 The title change plays on Morris West's Cold War–era novel *The Shoes of the Fisherman* (1963), adapted into a film of the same title in 1968.

52 Gérard Genette defines *paratext* as a "threshold" or "vestibule"; an "'undefined zone' between the inside and the outside, a zone without any hard and fast boundary on either the inward side (turned toward the text) or the outward side (turned toward the world's discourse about the text)." Gérard Genette, *Paratexts: Thresholds of Interpretation*, trans. Jane E. Lewin (Cambridge: Cambridge University Press, 1997), 2.

53 One can trace the roots of concretism through such earlier composers as Carol-Bérard, who in 1929 proposed using sound media to capture ambient sounds from nature and the city (Carol-Bérard, "Recorded Noises—Tomorrow's Instrumentation," *Modern Music* 6 [January-February 1929]: 26–29; reprinted in *Music, Sound, and Technology in America: A Documentary History of Early Phonograph, Cinema, and Radio*, eds. Timothy D. Taylor, Mark Katz, and Tony Grajeda [Durham, NC: Duke University Press, 2012], 110–13). In his work on radio, Rudolf Arnheim lauded the "rediscovery of the musical note in sound and speech, the welding of music, sound and speech into a single material" and sought the liberation of sound as an aesthetic object in its own right (Rudolf Arnheim, *Radio*, trans. Margaret Ludwig and Herbert Read [London: Faber & Faber, 1936], 30–31). As Marc Battier notes, Schaeffer developed his musique concrète from these and other theorists' and composers' interest in electronic media and the blurred line between noise and musical notes. See Marc Battier, "What the GRM Brought: From Musique Concrète to Acousmatic Music,"

Organized Sound 12, no. 3 (December 2007):189–202. The ultimate emergence of technologically mediated sound in its own right, and sounds as aesthetic objects to be arranged like the different timbres of musical instrumentation, can arguably be traced to Edgard Varèse, a favorite of Charlie Parker, and his 1958 *Poème Electronique* composed for magnetic tape. Thom Holmes details that early history starting with Elisha Gray, a contemporary of Alexander Graham Bell, and his "music telegraph" in 1874 (*Electronic and Experimental Music*, 6). Robin Kelley stresses that "[t]hese historical developments clearly shaped black modernism in the postwar period, but it was not limited to black people," and sees in their practice an articulation of recent and ancient past, as well as "modernist experiments in sound" that one could date back to the dawn of sound recording. Robin D. G. Kelley, "'Dig They Freedom': Meditations on History and the Black Avant-Garde," *Lenox Avenue: A Journal of Interarts Inquiry* 3 (1997): 24.

54 Charles Mingus, liner notes to *Pithecanthropus Erectus* (Atlantic, 1956). Though Mingus claims to have "collected these sounds from the Bay Area," hence the subtitle "in San Francisco," Brian Priestley notes that the sound effects were in fact produced live with small percussion instruments and détourned instruments such as detached saxophone mouthpieces, anticipating the Art Ensemble of Chicago's celebrated use of "little instruments" (Priestley, *Mingus*, 69).

55 On *The Charles Mingus Quintet Plus Max Roach* (Debut, 1955), Mingus recorded and released an earlier version of the song featuring tenor saxophonist George Barrow and trombonist Eddie Bert simulating the car and foghorn sounds on his trombone, confirming that those sounds are compositional elements that occur at specific moments in the statement of the theme and during solos.

56 Langston Hughes Papers, Beinecke Library, Yale University, Box 442. Hughes would also collaborate with Randy Weston on his 1961 album *Uhuru Afrika* (Roulette, 1961), writing the liner notes and two poems performed by Tuntemeke Sanga, Martha Flowers, and Brock Peters.

57 Elder is best known for his play *Ceremonies in Dark Old Men*. He and co-writer Suzanne de Plesse were the first African Americans nominated for a screenwriting Academy Award for their adaptation of *Sounder* (1972). The text of "Scenes in the City" marked Elder's first work as a professional (i.e., paid) writer.

58 Stewart played Hughes's Jesse B. Semple character in the play *Simply Heavenly* (1957), and substituted for Hughes reading with Mingus at the Half Note and other jazz clubs in Greenwich Village. He eventually reprised the role of Jesse B. Semple for *Langston Hughes' The Best of Simple* (Folkways 1961).

59 Mingus, *More Than a Fake Book*, 110. The editors incorrectly state that Mingus made only one recording of this composition, and transcribe only what they see as the main theme. Both versions I have found consist of two sections—an up-tempo blues and a slower section played with a two feel—establishing the basic emotional framework of the piece.

60 Priestley, *Mingus*, 89.

61 Santoro, *Myself When I Am Real*, 134

62 Stressing the relation of their coinage to the English *witchcraft*, Barbara and Karen Fields define "racecraft" as "one among a complex system of beliefs, also with

combined moral and cognitive content, that presuppose invisible, spiritual qualities underlying, and continually acting upon, the material realm of beings and events.... Marking the terms ["racecraft" and "witchcraft"] linguistically with *-craft* announces that the workings of those phenomena are not open to objective or experimental demonstration, that is to say, by anyone, anywhere, and independent of doing or believing" (*Racecraft: The Soul of Inequality in American Life* [London: Verso Books, 2012], 202–3).

63 I am drawing here on David Schwarz's psychoanalytic account of the relationship between music and subject formation in order to outline a different way one participates subjectively in the musical act. He argues that one either experiences music as a "fantasy thing" (that "reminds" us of an event only imagined to have happened), or a "fantasy space," a site that connects "such fantasies to a wide variety of theoretical, historical, and personal contexts," including "an emergence of conventionality." David Schwarz, *Listening Subjects: Music, Psychoanalysis, Culture* (Durham, NC: Duke University Press, 1997), 15.

64 I refer to his simulated club chatter on his studio recording *Charles Mingus Presents Charles Mingus*, released in 1961 on Nat Hentoff's Candid Records (CJM 8005). This album, of course, features his famous, apparently improvised lyrics to "Fables of Faubus." The piece, linking the Ku Klux Klan and "Nazi Fascist supremists [sic]," was controversial. Brian Priestley wryly comments, "whether or not it played any part in the speedy discontinuation of the Candid label must be left to conjecture" (Priestley, *Mingus*, 119–20).

65 This moment recalls Gene Santoro's descriptions of Hughes reading an apparent warm-up with Mingus, where lines of the poem ("Hear my old piano on the way") become musical cues (Santoro, *Myself When I Am Real*, 140).

66 Eve Kosofsky Sedgewick, *Between Men: English Literature and Male Homosocial Desire* (New York: Columbia University Press, 1993), 5.

67 Schwarz, *Listening Subjects*, 16.

68 Suzan-Lori Parks, *The America Play and Other Plays* (New York: Theater Company Group, 1994). I draw "nonplace" from Stefano Harney and Fred Moten, *The Undercommons: Fugitive Planning and Black Study* (New York: Minor Compositions, 2013), 39.

69 Ekkerhard Jost, *Free Jazz* (New York: Da Capo Press, 1994), 39–40.

70 Mingus, *Beneath the Underdog*, 351.

71 Moten, "The New International of Rhythmic Feeling(s)," 33ff.

72 Charles Mingus, Interview with Leonard Feather, *Down Beat*, May 26, 1960. Quoted in Priestley, *Mingus*, 109–10. Ellipses in original.

73 Thomas Carmichael, "*Beneath the Underdog*: Charles Mingus, Representation, and Jazz Autobiography," *Canadian Review of American Studies* 25, no. 3 (Winter 1995): 29–41.

74 This text is on the dedication page of Langston Hughes's *Montage of a Dream Deferred*, reprinted in *The Collected Poems of Langston Hughes*, eds. Arnold Rampersad and David Roessel (New York: Alfred Knopf, 2004), 387.

75 Mingus, "What Is a Jazz Composer?," 156.

76 Karl Hagstrom Miller makes a related argument in *Segregating Sounds: Inventing Folk and Pop Music in the Age of Jim Crow* (Durham, NC: Duke University Press, 2010).

I draw "alter-native" from Michel-Rolph Trouillot, who argues that capitalist modernity produces forms of alterity central to its material and ideological functioning: "As part of the geography of imagination that constantly recreates the West, modernity always required an Other and an Elsewhere. It was always plural, just like the West was always plural. This plurality is inherent in modernity itself, both structurally and historically. Modernity as a structure requires an other, an alter, a native—indeed, an alter-native" ("The Otherwise Modern: Caribbean Lessons from the Savage Slot" in *Critically Modern: Alternatives, Alterities, Anthropologies*, ed. Bruce M. Knauft [Bloomington: Indiana University Press, 2002], 224). The process necessarily produces surpluses, consumed as pleasurable.

77 Mackey, *Paracritical Hinge*, 239.
78 Langston Hughes, "Ten Ways to Use Poetry in Teaching," in *The Collected Works of Langston Hughes: Vol. 9, Essays on Art, Race, Politics, and World Affairs*, ed. Christopher C. De Santi (Columbia: University of Missouri Press, 2002), 319.
79 Hughes, "Ten Ways to Use Poetry in Teaching," 319.
80 Spillers, *Black, White, and in Color*, 20.
81 Rampersad, *The Life of Langston Hughes*, Vol. II, 199.
82 Horace Parlan is the credited leader, but Mingus, who wrote the music, actually led the group. Aldon Nielsen suggests that contractual issues artificially elevated Parlan's stature in the Workshop for purposes of this recording (Nielsen, *Black Chant*, 178).
83 Jones, *The Muse Is Music*, 68. Seth Rothstein, who prepared the LP for reissue, may have had a hand in this decision. In passing, Althea Loglia's new design features Roy DeCarava's photograph of a chain that immediately invokes slavery, and whose shape suggests a human figure kneeling, her arms pulled back. The original LP cover features a door and inset black and white photographs, flush with the right edge, of Hughes reading from a book and members from both bands holding their instruments and listening.
84 Langston Hughes, "Consider Me," *American Scholar* 21, no. 1 (Winter 1951-52): 100.
85 Robin D. G. Kelley, *Race Rebels: Culture, Politics, and the Black Working Class* (New York: Free Press, 1994), 47.
86 Kelley, *Race Rebels*, 47.
87 Hazel V. Carby, "The Politics of Fiction, Anthropology, and the Folk: Zora Neale Hurston," in *New Essays on Their Eyes Were Watching God*, ed. Michael Awkward (New York: Cambridge University Press, 1991), 32.
88 Aimé Césaire, *Discourse on Colonialism*, trans. Joan Pinkham (New York: Monthly Review Press, 2000), 52.
89 Walter Benjamin, *The Arcades Project*, trans. Howard Eiland and Kevin McLaughlin (Cambridge, MA: Belknap Press of Harvard University Press, 1999), 10. Benjamin later offers this definition: "Dialectical images are constellated between alienated things and incoming and disappearing meaning, are instantiated in the moment of indifference between death and meaning. While things in appearance are awakened to what is newest, death transforms the meanings to what is most ancient" (466).
90 Anita Haya Patterson, "Jazz, Realism, and the Modernist Lyric: The Poetry of Langston Hughes," *MLQ: Modern Language Quarterly* 61, no. 4 (December 2000): 678n54.

91 *Weary Blues* was recorded March 18, 1958; Mingus and his Workshop recorded *Blues and Roots* (Atlantic 1960) February 4, 1959. Brian Priestley notes that owing to the 6/4 compound meter of "Wednesday Night Prayer Meeting" and the later "Better Git It in Your Soul," "Mingus did the most to crystallize the influence of gospel on what became known as soul-jazz" as distinct from the soul identified with Aretha Franklin, traceable back to artists such as Ray Charles, Dinah Washington, and Solomon Burke. Priestley, *Mingus*, 88.

92 Praising this work in the *Journal of Negro History*, historian Carter G. Woodson heard and read in this poem "evidence of the self-assertion of the subordinated Negro." Carter G. Woodson, "Jim Crow's Last Stand by Langston Hughes," *Journal of Negro History* 28, no. 4 (October 1943): 493–94.

93 Arthur P. Davis, "The Harlem of Langston Hughes's Poetry," *Phylon* 13, no. 4 (4th Qtr. 1952): 280.

94 Davis, "The Harlem of Langston Hughes's Poetry," 282.

95 Hughes, "Good Morning," *Collected Poems*, 427. Hughes reads this poem with Red Allen's group on the other part of *Weary Blues*.

96 John Lowney, *History, Memory, and the Literary Left: Modern American Poetry, 1935–1968* (Iowa City: University of Iowa Press, 2006), 127.

97 Hughes would pursue this theme further in *Ask Your Mama: 12 Moods for Jazz*, included in *Collected Poems*, making a theme of the woman's silence and desired speech. Rather than being excluded from the production of the history of domination, she is an important resource, the person who manages the space into which records and knowledge of the world flows, and the person expected to unravel the speaker's puzzles. The mama is at once the rhetorical figure over whose imagined body communities of men are made in improvisatory verbal games ("the dozens"), but also the key to whatever world is in emergence. From this perspective, it does not seem coincidental that in an encyclopedic poem keen to specify and name its heroes and villains that Leontyne Price is the first performer named. In keeping with the themes of the phonopoems analyzed here, the "quarter of the Negroes" becomes a pun when we discover show fare is thirty cents. The basic economic constraints remain firmly in place.

98 Hazel V. Carby, *Race Men* (Cambridge, MA: Harvard University Press), 138, Carby's emphasis. She is specifically reading the ways Miles Davis constructs a spiritual/material divide in his autobiography, with the oppressive world of women on the side of the material.

99 Audre Lorde, "Age, Race, Class, and Sex," in *Sister Outsider: Essays and Speeches* (Freedom, CA: Crossing Press, 1984), 123.

100 Here I draw on Salim Washington, "'All the Things You Could Be by Now': Charles Mingus Presents Charles Mingus and the Limits of Avant-Garde Jazz," *Uptown Conversation: The New Jazz Studies*, eds. Robert G. O'Meally, Brent Hayes Edwards, and Farah Jasmine Griffin (New York: Columbia University Press, 2004), 27–49.

CHAPTER 3. TOMORROW IS THE QUESTION!

1. Amiri Baraka, "We Are the Blues," *Funk Lore: New Poems (1984-1995)*, ed. Paul Vangelisti (Los Angeles: Littoral Books, 1996), 95-96.
2. Amiri Baraka, *The Music: Reflections on Jazz and Blues* (New York: Morrow, 1987), 177.
3. Amiri Baraka, *Home: Social Essays* (New York: William Morrow, 1966), 211. Thank you to Ashley James for reminding me of this essay.
4. Black social life did indeed transform, but in unanticipated ways. An emergent black "middle class," some drawn from the ranks of the former revolutionaries, would serve as fig leaves for ongoing dispossession, itself framed by familiar political slogans (e.g., community empowerment) now evacuated of their original meanings.
5. The chant/slogan "Marxism, Leninism, Mao Tse-Tung Thought" is the refrain of "You Was Dancin Need to Be Marchin So You Can Dance Some More Later On" (45 rpm, People's War, 1976). Komozi Woodard, *A Nation Within a Nation: Amiri Baraka (LeRoi Jones) and Black Power Politics* (Chapel Hill: University of North Carolina Press, 1999), offers an excellent account of the relationship between CAP and the black convention movement of the 1970s, emphasizing their embrace of electoralism as strategy but downplaying Baraka's Marxism. His analysis stops short of CAP's transformation into the Revolutionary Communist League. Cedric Johnson, *Revolutionaries to Race Leaders: Black Power and the Making of African American Politics* (Minneapolis: University of Minnesota Press, 2007), contextualizes that transformation within a broader set of changes, but similarly looks past Baraka's Marxism. Robeson Taj P. Frazier fills in some of those gaps in "The Congress of African People: Baraka, Brother Mao, and the Year of '74," *Souls* 8, no. 3 (2006): 142-59. Max Ebaum offers a very helpful account of Baraka's involvement with CAP and the New Communist Movement in *Revolution in the Air: Sixties Radicals Turn to Lenin, Mao and Che* (2002. London: Verso, 2018). The fullest account of Baraka's post-nationalist politics, including his affiliation with the New Communist movement of the 1970s, is Michael Simanga, *Amiri Baraka and the Congress of African People: History and Memory* (New York: Palgrave, 2015).
6. Exceptions include Kathy Lou Schultz, who treats his poem cycle *Wise, Why's, Y's: The Griot's Song Djeli YA* in her monograph *The Afro-Modernist Epic and Literary History: Tolson, Hughes, Baraka* (New York: Palgrave Macmillan, 2012). In an insightful article, Jeremy Matthew Glick argues that a "pragmatist longing" in recent Baraka scholarship and criticism focuses primarily on critical assessments of the transition from LeRoi Jones in the Village to Amiri Baraka of the Black Arts Movement ("'All I Do Is Think about You': Some Notes on Pragmatist Longing in Recent Literary Study of Amiri Baraka," *Boundary 2* 37, no. 2 [Summer 2010]: 107-32).
7. "An Interview with Amiri Baraka," *Greenfield Review* 8, no. 324 (Fall 1980): 27; reprinted in William J. Harris, *The Poetry and Poetics of Amiri Baraka: The Jazz Aesthetic* (Columbia: University of Missouri Press, 1985), 147.
8. Hoyt Fuller, ed., "Writers Symposium," *Negro Digest* 17, no. 3 (January 1968): 81.
9. Simone White urges attention to Baraka's citation practice alongside his many published reviews, essays, and interviews. The title essay of her collection *Dear Angel of Death* (Brooklyn, NY: Ugly Duckling Presse, 2019), 71-150, offers a compelling meditation on Baraka's citation of W. E. B. Du Bois.

10   Referring to a performance of the John Coltrane Quintet, featuring Eric Dolphy augmenting his "classic" quartet (McCoy Tyner on piano, Jimmy Garrison on bass, and Elvin Jones on drums), *Down Beat* magazine's then-associate editor John Tynan wrote: "[t]hey seem bent on pursuing an anarchistic course in their music that can but be termed anti-jazz" (November 23, 1961). Few go so far as to term Baraka's post-1972 output "anti-poetry." Werner Sollors's argument that Baraka's "postnationalist, Maoist work admits only occasional flashes of poetry" and that "what Baraka perceives as a political strength in his new commitment may well be a crucial poetic weakness; he knows exactly what he wants to say at all times" could stand as consensus of much of the later work (*Amiri Baraka/LeRoi Jones: The Quest for a "Populist Modernism"* [New York: Columbia University Press, 1979], 236–7). Jerry Gafio Watts, whose 2001 polemic *Amiri Baraka: The Politics and Art of a Black Intellectual* (New York: New York University Press, 2001) dismisses Baraka's 1972 *Hard Facts* as "embarrassing," declares the 1979 *Poetry for the Advanced* "equally banal," and concludes by unfavorably comparing Richard Wright's and Baraka's investments in communism (459–61).

11   Watts, *Amiri Baraka: The Politics and Art of a Black Intellectual*, 458. This criticism is valid (if not particularly illuminating) regarding the poem Watts considers, "When We'll Worship Jesus." But even then, some acknowledgment is due of the ways Baraka is affiliating himself with a tradition of African American poems including Langston Hughes's "Goodbye, Christ," or at least that it is a revolutionary call to "sing about, creation, our creation, the life of the world and / fantastic / nature." Amiri Baraka, *S O S: Poems 1961–2013* (New York: Grove Press, 2014), 171.

12   Amiri Baraka, "Ka 'Ba," *The LeRoi Jones/Amiri Baraka Reader*, ed. William J. Harris (New York: Basic Books, 2009), 222.

13   Amiri Baraka, *Black Music* (New York: Da Capo Press, 1998), 71.

14   Fumi Okiji offers a good account of the ways foregrounding the bourgeoisie limits Theodor Adorno's account in the first chapter of *Jazz as Critique: Adorno and Black Expression Reconsidered* (Stanford: Stanford University Press, 2018).

15   Baraka, *The Music*, 243.

16   Walter Benjamin, "On Some Motifs in Baudelaire," trans. Harry Zohn, in *Walter Benjamin: Selected Writings, Vol. 4: 1938–1940*, eds. Howard Eiland and Michael W. Jennings (Cambridge, MA: Harvard University Press, 2006), 317.

17   Benjamin, "On Some Motifs in Baudelaire," 314.

18   I'm drawing on Lauren Berlant's description of the present as a political project in *Cruel Optimism* (Durham, NC: Duke University Press, 2011). "We understand nothing about impasses of the political without having an account of the production of the present," she argues (4). Discrepant or divergent accounts of the present inform Baraka's many political transformations, and his relative marginalization within accounts of American and global avant-garde poetry.

19   Richard Iton, *In Search of the Black Fantastic: Politics and Popular Culture in the Post-Civil Rights Era* (Oxford: Oxford University Press, 2010), 200.

20   Baraka, *Black Music*, 200.

21   Nielsen, *Black Chant*, 180.

22   Komozi Woodard details Baraka's effective and tireless political organizing, which included his work alongside Jesse Jackson and other black liberals, radicals, and

cultural nationalists in the national Black Convention Movement. The CAP was instrumental in mobilizing the city of Newark to elect Kenneth Gibson as its first African American mayor, although Gibson did not and could not bring about the kind of radical change they wanted. Woodard, *A Nation Within a Nation*, 219-54.

23 Baraka, *The Music*, 180.

24 Amiri Baraka, A. B. Spellman, and Larry Neal co-founded and edited the *Cricket*; Roger Riggins, James T. Stewart, and Ron Welburn edited the *Grackle*. For an account of those journals and a broader argument for the centrality of jazz to the Black Arts Movement as part of "the creation of a socially conscious aesthetic standard that proved difficult for both musicians and audiences to maintain," see Lorenzo Thomas, "Ascension: Music and the Black Arts Movement," in *Jazz Among the Discourses*, ed. Krin Gabbard (Durham, NC: Duke University Press, 1995). For a fuller account of the importance of independent publishing to the Black Arts Movement, I recommend James Smethurst's *The Black Arts Movement: Literary Nationalism in the 1960s and 1970s* (Chapel Hill: University of North Carolina Press, 2005); and Howard Rambsy II's *The Black Arts Enterprise and the Production of African American Poetry* (Ann Arbor: University of Michigan Press, 2013). On musical institutions, see Eric Porter, *What Is This Thing Called Jazz? African American Musicians as Artists, Critics, and Activists* (Berkeley: University of California Press, 2002); Benjamin Looker, *"Point from which Creation Begins": The Black Artists' Group of St. Louis* (Chicago: University of Chicago Press, 2004); and George E. Lewis, *A Power Stronger Than Itself: The AACM and American Experimental Music* (Chicago: University of Chicago Press, 2008).

25 Fredric Jameson, "Periodizing the 60s," *Social Text* 9/10 (Spring-Summer 1984): 182. Michael Dawson discusses "the sundering" of black and white left political organizations, owing largely to the communist left, in particular, treating racial struggles as secondary or epiphenomenal to a more fundamental class struggle. Michael Dawson, *Blacks In and Out of the Left* (Cambridge, MA: Harvard University Press, 2013), 47-49.

26 Fredric Jameson, "Reification and Utopia in Mass Culture," in *Signatures of the Visible* (1979. New York: Routledge, 1990), 23.

27 Amiri Baraka, *Black Music* (1967. New York: Da Capo Press, 1998), 64.

28 Baraka, *Black Music*, 65.

29 Saidiya V. Hartman, *Scenes of Subjection: Terror, Slavery, and Self-Making in Nineteenth-Century America* (Oxford: Oxford University Press, 1997), 115.

30 Ralph Ellison, *The Collected Essays of Ralph Ellison*, ed. John F. Callahan (New York: Modern Library, 2003), 267.

31 Hartman, *Scenes of Subjection*, 117.

32 Baraka, *Black Music*, 65.

33 Baraka, *Blues People*, 152.

34 Amiri Baraka, "You Think This Is About You?," liner notes to Albert Ayler, *Holy Ghost: Rare and Unissued Recordings (1962-1970)* (Revenant 213, 2004), 40.

35 Baraka, *Black Music*, 65.

36 Theodor Adorno, "On the Social Situation of Music," in *Essays on Music*, ed. Richard Leppert, trans. Susan H. Gillespie et al. (Berkeley: University of California Press, 2002), 391, 392. The literature in jazz studies on Adorno is too extensive to cite. Michael Denning persuasively situates Adorno among his contemporaries, noting:

"Adorno began from the ambiguity of the term 'jazz,' and used it to sum up all of the modern dance musics that emerged in the wake of the Great War.... For Adorno, as for many listeners and many musicians, jazz, rhumba, hula and tango were part of the same musical world." Michael Denning, *Noise Uprising: The Audiopolitics of a World Musical Revolution* (London: Verso, 2015), 90.

37 Baraka, *Blues People*, 225.
38 Julian Mayfield, "You Touch My Black Aesthetic and I'll Touch Yours," in *The Black Aesthetic*, ed. Addison Gayle Jr. (New York: Anchor Books, 1971), 29.
39 As Lorenzo Thomas observes, the problem, for Baraka in that period, "was *class* identification" (Thomas, "Ascension: Music and the Black Arts Movement," 266). On this view, middle-class critics on either side of the color line failed to consider or appropriately value the sources of the music, the "attitude, the stance ... the Negro's peculiar way of looking at the world" (Baraka, "Jazz and the White Critic," *Black Music*, 185). Though resonant with the concerns of an earlier romantic nationalism, Baraka's attention to the forms of historical and cultural isolation that define black people's experience of modernity and made possible such a stance allow him to consider race as practice rather than essence.
40 Amiri Baraka, *Digging: The Afro-American Soul of American Classical Music* (Berkeley: University of California Press, 2009), 1.
41 Baraka, *Blues People*, 182.
42 John Gennari, "Baraka's Bohemian Blues," *African American Review* 37, no. 2/3 (Summer-Autumn 2003): 256. Gennari reads *Blues People* in the context of Dwight McDonald's "Masscult and Midcult" and Norman Mailer's "The White Negro," although he does not consider the ways Baraka's ambivalent valorization of black difference departs from and perhaps critiques Mailer's.
43 Paul Gilroy, *The Black Atlantic: Modernity and Double Consciousness* (London: Verso, 1993), 111.
44 Baraka, *Blues People*, 225.
45 Ralph Ellison, *Living with Music*, ed. Robert G. O'Meally (New York: Modern Library Classics, 2002), 127.
46 Baraka, *Blues People*, 229.
47 Baraka, *Blues People*, 229.
48 Ellison, *Living with Music*, 70. In contrast with Ellison's apparent investment in carefully maintained boundaries between genres, Baraka argues that "the techniques of European classical music can be utilized by jazz musicians, but in ways that will not subject the philosophy of Negro music to the less indigenously personal attitudes of European-derived music" (Baraka, *Blues People*, 229).
49 In his essay "Afro-American Literature and Class Struggle," Baraka summarizes their argument as follows: "Ellison says that the 'black aesthetic crowd' 'buys the idea of total cultural separation between blacks and whites, suggesting that we've been left out of the mainstream. But when we examine American music and literature in terms of its themes, symbolism, rhythms, tonalities, idioms and images it is obvious that those reject 'Negroes' have been a vital part of the mainstream and were from the beginning.'" He rejoins, "We know we have been exploited, Mr. Ralph, sir, what

we's arguing about is that we's been exploited! To *use* us is the term of our stay in this joint, but being left out of the mainstream means that Bird died scag [heroin], Jelly Roll had to play in a whorehouse, Duke played one-night stands till he died, the Beatles make millions and cite some blood [black man] running an elevator in Jackson." Amiri Baraka, "Afro-American Literature and Class Struggle," in *Daggers and Javelins: Essays, 1974-1979* (New York: William Morrow, 1984), 321-22. As with his critique of Black Swan Records, Baraka critiques the ideal of incorporation into white society rather than its wholesale reconstitution in ways that acknowledge historic and persistent forms of exploitation.

50 Hartman, *Scenes of Subjection*, 116-17.
51 Baraka, *The Music*, 273.
52 Amiri Baraka (as LeRoi Jones), *Black Magic: Poetry 1961-1967* (Indianapolis: Bobbs-Merrill, 1969), 117.
53 Howard Rambsy II, *The Black Arts Enterprise and the Production of African American Poetry* (Ann Arbor: University of Michigan Press, 2013), 91.
54 Baraka, *Home*, 212.
55 Baraka, *Black Music*, 178.
56 Carter Mathes, *Imagine the Sound: Experimental African American Literature after Civil Rights* (Minneapolis: University of Minnesota Press, 2015), 56.
57 Mingus, "An Open Letter to the Avant-Garde," 119.
58 Harris, *The Poetry and Poetics of Amiri Baraka*, 76.
59 Harris, *The Poetry and Poetics of Amiri Baraka*, 75, my emphasis.
60 Raymond Williams, *Politics and Letters: Interviews with* New Left Review (London: Verso, 2015), 232.
61 Sollors, *Amiri Baraka/LeRoi Jones*, 199.
62 Carby, *Race Men*, 159, my emphasis. Ricky Vincent and Tony Bolden have each provided exemplary analyses of funk. The most sustained attention to the practice and implications of free time as practiced by Sunny Murray and Milford Graves remains Valerie Wilmer's 1977 *As Serious as Your Life: The Story of the New Jazz*, reprinted with the subtitle *John Coltrane and Beyond* (London: Serpent's Tail, 1992).
63 Nielsen observes that "Baraka's rendition of the poem is nearly identical to his cool and suspense-filled performance, without music, recorded at an August 1964 Asilomar conference taped by Pacifica radio" that William J. Harris also refers to (Harris, *Black Chant*, 191). Harris argues that "Baraka's reading is virtually indistinguishable from any other mainstream literary writer of the time—he manifests no black ethnic markers: in essence, he reads just like a white man, the literary model of the period." William J. Harris, "How You Sound??: Amiri Baraka Writes Free Jazz," in *Uptown Conversation: The New Jazz Studies*, eds. Robert G. O'Meally, Brent Hayes Edwards, and Farah Jasmine Griffin (New York: Columbia University Press, 2004), 314.
64 Baraka, *Black Music*, 119.
65 Nielsen, *Black Chant*, 191.
66 Baraka, quoted in Jason Weiss, *Always in Trouble: An Oral History of ESP-Disk, the Most Outrageous Record Label in America* (Middletown, CT: Wesleyan University Press, 2012), 229.

67 Moten, *In the Break*, 93.
68 Moten, *In the Break*, 94.
69 Moten, *In the Break*, 96.
70 DJ Spooky, in his 1996 re-envisioning of the phonopoem, creates a dub that loops John Tchicai's first two notes, treated with reverb effect (and other effects), against three repeated notes from Lewis Worrell's bass and Milford Graves's skittish snare drum figure from the 1965 recording. Baraka's reading is more animated as he moves to the poem's climax, but generally retains the much-discussed reticence of the prior reading. DJ Spooky would include the instrumentals, without Baraka's vocals, on his 1996 *Songs of a Dead Dreamer* (Asphodel 0961).
71 Amiri Baraka (as Leroi Jones), *The Dead Lecturer: Poems* (New York: Grove Press, 1964), 64.
72 Nielsen, *Black Chant*, 195. His reading (190–95) tracks the interactions between musicians and poet in more detail than I do here.
73 *The Lone Ranger*'s Tonto's inclusion in the list reinforces his concern with racially specific forms of reification and complicity, made more complicated by the ways the TV show positions viewers and listeners to identify with the Lone Ranger, and thus with white supremacist expansion, but also to appreciate the loyal Tonto, a native informant and race traitor. From this perspective, he seems to be an analogue for the poet. Daniel Won-gu Kim offers a compelling reading along these lines of the list of civilizations destroyed by Western civilization—"Byzantium, Tenochtitlan, Comanch"—in his essay "'In the Tradition': Amiri Baraka, Black Liberation, and Avant-Garde Praxis in the U.S.," *African American Review*, 37, no. 2/3 (Summer-Autumn 2003): 345–63.
74 Hartman, *Scenes of Subjection*, 115.
75 Nielsen, *Black Chant*, 196.
76 I refer to *In Search of the Black Fantastic*, Richard Iton's assessment of Baraka's first collection *Preface to a Twenty-Volume Suicide Note*, his play *The Toilet*, and his novel *The System of Dante's Hell*. In *The Dead Lecturer*, the project of crafting a literary "transgressive interiority" becomes a more difficult meditation on racial reification.
77 Cynthia Young, *Soul Power: Culture, Radicalism, and the Making of a U.S. Third World Left* (Durham, NC: Duke University Press, 2006), 18–53.
78 Baraka explains to Harris that "your friends" in "Black Dada Nihilismus" refers to his "Bohemian" circle: "Most of the people who lived in the Village and the Lower East Side, who I saw all the time, who I had some commonality with but at the same time felt estranged from since most of them were running around saying that poetry and politics had nothing to do with each other, and I was getting much more political" (Harris, *The Poetry and Poetics of Amiri Baraka*, 145). In a prior interview with Kimberly Benston, he explained: "A lot of the poetry in *The Dead Lecturer* is speaking out against the political line of the whole Black Mountain group, to which I was very close. That was a very interesting mélange of folks in New York at the time.... I hung out with all of them; but the overwhelming line was always antipolitical. Or, when politics did emerge, as in Olson's work, I didn't

agree with it." Kimberly Benston, "Amiri Baraka: An Interview," *Boundary 2* 6, no. 2 (Winter 1978): 306.
79 Benston, "Amiri Baraka: An Interview," 218.
80 Harris, *The Poetry and Poetics of Amiri Baraka*, 145.
81 Sonia Sanchez, "A Letter to Dr. Martin Luther King, Jr.," *Homegirls and Handgrenades* (New York: Thunder's Mouth Press, 1984), 69.
82 "You Was Dancin Need to Be Marchin So You Can Dance Some More Later On"/"Better Red Let Others Be Dead," 45rpm, People's War, 1976. I use his essay "Some Questions About the Sixth Pan-African Congress" (*The Black Scholar* 6, no. 2 [October 1974]: 42–46) and the events that occasioned it to mark the shift.
83 Stuart Hall, "Notes on Deconstructing 'the Popular,'" *Cultural Theory and Popular Culture: A Reader*, ed. John Storey (Upper Saddle River, NJ: Pearson/Prentice Hall, 1998), 443.
84 Ongiri, *Spectacular Blackness*, 18–19.
85 Iton, "Still Life," 35. Iton is drawing on a distinction political theorist Chantal Mouffe and others make between politics ("le politique"), referring to the quotidian forms of administration and engagement when all the important decisions shaping possible futures have been made, and the political ("la politique"), referring to the theoretical determination of the possible and the quotidian themselves.
86 Adolph Reed, "Black Particularity Reconsidered," *Telos* 1979.39 (March 1979): 85.
87 Reed, "Black Particularity Reconsidered," 85.
88 Reed, "Black Particularity Reconsidered," 78.
89 Stuart Hall, "Gramsci's Relevance for the Study of Race and Ethnicity," *Journal of Communication Inquiry* 10, no. 2 (1986): 20. Reed's relative neglect of ideology is surprising because his analysis of the interaction of the state and capital is so astute, as is his compelling argument that spontaneous urban uprisings reveal the limits of the leadership models through which the state sought to manage them. Certainly, however, the inspiration many drew from freedom struggles throughout the decolonizing world ought to inspire, at least, some curiosity about the ways emergent forms of globalization impacted both popular and dominant ideologies as we moved into a new epoch.
90 Spillers, *Black, White, and in Color*, 432.
91 Dowd Hall, "The Long Civil Rights Movement and the Political Uses of the Past," *Journal of American History* 91, no. 4 (March 2005): 1237.
92 Baraka, "You Think This Is About You?," 48.
93 Baraka, *The Music*, 260.
94 Baraka, *The Music*, 263.
95 Baraka, *The Music*, 267.
96 C. W. E. Bigsby, "The Theatre and the Coming Revolution," in *Conversations with Amiri Baraka*, ed. Charlie Reilly (Jackson: University Press of Mississippi, 1994), 141.
97 Baraka, *The Music*, 261, Baraka's emphasis.
98 Baraka, *Black Magic*, 115.
99 Stuart Hall, "Notes on Deconstructing 'the Popular,'" 452.

100 Amiri Baraka with David Murray and Steve McCall, *New Music—New Poetry* (LP, India Navigation, 1982).
101 Arthur Blythe, *In the Tradition* (LP, Columbia, 1979). Travis A. Jackson and Daniel Won-gu Kim offer convincing readings of that poem—the former with sensitive attention to the oral and musical performance traditions Baraka, Murray, and McCall collectively draw on, the latter with a keen eye for the ways Baraka negotiates the tensions between aesthetic and political radicalism. See Jackson, "'Always New and Centuries Old': Jazz, Poetry, and Tradition as Creative Adaptation," in *Uptown Conversation: The New Jazz Studies*, eds. Robert G. O'Meally, Brent Hayes Edwards, and Farah Jasmine Griffin (New York: Columbia University Press, 2004): 357–72; and Kim, "'In the Tradition': Amiri Baraka, Black Liberation, and Avant-Garde Praxis in the U.S."
102 Jackson, "Always New and Centuries Old," 359–60.
103 Baraka, *The Music*, 317.
104 Baraka, *The Music*, 261.
105 Jameson, "Periodizing the 60s," 182.
106 Joy James, "Concerning Violence: Frantz Fanon's Rebel Intellectual in Search of a Black Cyborg," *South Atlantic Quarterly* 112, no. 1 (Winter 2013): 61–62.
107 Here, I am thinking after Adolph Reed, "Unraveling the Relation of Race and Class in American Politics," in *Political Power and Social Theory* 15, no. 264 (2002): 265–74, and his "Rejoinder" in the same volume, 301–15.
108 Baraka, *The Music*, 98.
109 When I first encountered the poem on the page, this section immediately reminded me of alto saxophonist Julius Hemphill's "Skin 1" from his 1975 album *Coon Bid'ness* (Arista Freedom), which also featured alto saxophonist Arthur Blythe, baritone saxophonist Hamiet Bluiett, cellist Abdul Wadud, drummer Barry Altschul, and percussionist Daniel Zebulon. Eventually they move into free time, but even in that context, it is clear that they are seeking a rhythmic alternative to swing.
110 Baraka, *The Music*, 103.
111 Taking a narrower view, Cedric Johnson argues that desegregation played a more decisive role in "the transformation of black politics from radical protests [aimed at] systemic change toward a politics of insider negotiation and incremental payoffs within the established political order." Cedric Johnson, *Revolutionaries to Race Leaders: Black Power and the Making of African American Politics* (Minneapolis: University of Minneapolis Press, 2007), 218. One might supplement Johnson's argument by considering more carefully the spontaneous uprisings and other mass mobilizations that in effect announced the illegitimacy of the state rather than appealing to it. Johnson's arguments complement Michael Dawson's *Blacks In and Out of the Left*, and Dawson's more wide-ranging *Black Visions: The Roots of African American Political Ideologies* (Chicago: University of Chicago Press, 2003), which offer a broader view of the variety of black political organizations and their interactions with the white Left. More focused on literary arts, James Smethurst's *New Red Negro: The Literary Left and African American Poetry, 1930–1946* (Oxford: Oxford University Press, 1999) and his indispensable *The Black Arts Movement* give a sense of the ways artist-intellectuals

traverse the mid-twentieth century. Finally, Houston Baker's account of how black intellectuals (including himself) confronted new intellectual demands owing to ambiguities around their theoretical object (blackness) and shifts in the industrial substructure of knowledge production remains a vital if underutilized resource on the post–Black Arts moment. Houston Baker, *Blues, Ideology and Afro-American Literature* (Chicago: University of Chicago Press, 1984).

112 I'm thinking of David Scott, "The Temporality of Generations: Dialogue, Tradition, Criticism," *New Literary History* 45.2 (Spring 2014):159–60.

113 Carby, *Race Men*, 127. Writing polemically, Adolph Reed argues that early-1990s black public intellectuals (e.g., Michael Eric Dyson, Cornel West, bell hooks) are in a lineage reaching back to Booker T. Washington, a "trusted informant" who could "communicate to whites what the Negro thought, felt, wanted, needed," particularly in the context of "white liberals' retreat from the Reconstruction era's relatively progressive racial politics" (Adolph Reed, "What Are the Drums Saying Booker?: The Current Crisis of the Black Intellectual," in *Class Notes: Posing As Politics and Other Thoughts on the American Scene* [New York: The New Press, 2001], 779). It seems to me, however, that Carby's framing, focusing on the terms under which one could be black, public, and intellectual in that moment, is more generative. With the benefit of hindsight, the issue was not white liberals' retreat but the emergence of black liberalism, promoting the interests of the petit-bourgeoisie, as hegemonic. Whatever validity Reed's criticisms may have, disparaging an arbitrary group of thinkers anointed "black public intellectuals" mistakes symptom—an emergent sublative tendency in black politics—with cause, understanding in individual, even voluntaristic terms what I take to be a broader phenomenon.

114 In *What Is This Thing Called Jazz?* Eric Porter offers an account of the economic and intellectual environment of this conservative turn, especially 287–334.

115 Paul Gilroy was among the first critics to observe this shift. See "'After the Love Has Gone': Bio-Politics and Etho-Poetics in the Black Public Sphere," *Public Culture* 7 (1994): 49–76.

116 Quoted in D. H. Melhem, *Heroism in the New Black Poetry: Introductions and Interviews* (Lexington: University Press of Kentucky, 1990), 235.

117 Quoted in Harris, *The Poetry and Poetics of Amiri Baraka*, 149.

118 See especially *Fo Deuk Revue* (Justin Time, 1997).

119 *Blueprints of Jazz, Vol. 2* (Talking House Records, 2008).

120 *I Plan to Stay a Believer: The Inside Songs of Curtis Mayfield* (AUM Fidelity, 2010).

121 *An Afternoon in Harlem* (Justin Time, 1999).

122 *Freebop Now!* (Delmark Records, 1998).

123 Amiri Baraka and Kalamu ya Salaam, "Amiri Baraka Analyzes How He Writes," *African American Review* 37, no. 2/3 (Summer/Autumn 2003): 216. Baraka retrospectively describes the process of composing *System of Dante's Hell*, but the sense of indirection ("What I thought of—and this is really a musical kind of insistence—I thought I'm going to get something in my mind but I'm not going to talk about it directly") also characterizes the late work's references to music and history.

124 I quote Baraka's account of a 1963 John Coltrane performance (Baraka, *Black Music*, 59).
125 Baraka, *Funk Lore*, 11.
126 I refer to Baraka's collaboration with the Roots, "Something in the Way of Things (In Town)" on *Phrenology* (MCA, 2002).

CHAPTER 4. BODY/LANGUAGE

1 Robert D. Rusch, *Jazztalk: The Cadence Interviews* (Secaucus, NJ: Lyle Stuart, 1984), 57.
2 Gayatri Chakravorty Spivak, *Outside in the Teaching Machine* (London: Routledge, 1993): 183.
3 Pharoah Sanders, *Journey to the One* (Theresa, 1980).
4 Chris Funkhouser, "Being Matter Ignited . . . : An Interview with Cecil Taylor," *Hambone* 12 (Spring 1992): 17–39.
5 Giddins, "The Avant-Gardist Who Came in from the Cold," in *Riding on a Blue Note: Jazz and American Pop* (New York: Da Capo, 2000), 282.
6 Neal, "And Shine Swam On," 653. Composer and saxophonist Marion Brown would make a similar argument: "The true spirit of the music (ragtime) was lost when pianists began relying on sheet music (notes), and not upon its spontaneity." Marion Brown, "Improvisation and the Aural Tradition in Afro-American Music," *Black World* 23, no. 1 (November 1973): 16. Both seek to frame black sound as communal property at risk of alienation and commodification.
7 Sylvia Wynter, "Ethno or Socio Poetics," in *Alcheringa: Ethnopoetics*, eds. Michael Benamou and Jerome Rothenberg (Boston: Boston University, 1976), 86. Wynter, like Larry Neal and Stephen E. Henderson, ultimately comes to favor a more empirical approach to criticism, but in later work Wynter goes further in considering the relationship between aesthetics, sociogeny, texts, and the self. See Larry Neal, "The Black Contribution to American Letters: Part II The Writer as Activist 1960 and After" in *The Black American Reference Book*, ed. Mabel M. Smythe (Englewood Cliffs, NJ: Prentice Hall, 1976), 767–90; and Stephen E. Henderson, "The Question of Form and Judgment in Contemporary Black American Poetry: 1962–1977," in *A Dark and Sudden Beauty: Two Essays in Black American Poetry*, ed. Houston A. Baker Jr. (Philadelphia: University of Pennsylvania Press, 1977), 19–36. For a fuller account of these essays, see Baker, *Blues, Ideology and Afro-American Literature*, 64–112. Alison Donnell offers a helpful account of Wynter's critical activity around the Caribbean Artists Movement—co-founded in London by John La Rose, Andrew Salkey, and Kamau Brathwaite—in her *Twentieth-Century Caribbean Literature: Critical Moments in Anglophone Literary History* (London: Routledge, 2005).
8 Margo Crawford, *Black Post-Blackness: The Black Arts Movement and Twenty-First Century Aesthetics* (Urbana: University of Illinois Press, 2017), 3.
9 Don Cherry, *Complete Communion* (Blue Note, 1966). Period interviews, album reviews, and essays remain the best sources to engage the complexity of the period. Valerie Wilmer's pivotal account of community forces and formation in *As Serious as Your Life: John Coltrane and Beyond* (New York: Da Capo Press, 1977) provides an indispensable overview. Eric Porter engages some of these projects at length in the fifth and sixth chapters of *What Is This Thing Called Jazz?*

10 Albert Murray's term for this mutually constitutive relationship is "reciprocal 'voicing,'" a metaphor whose incidental effacement of writing gives me pause (Albert Murray, *Stomping the Blues* [New York: Da Capo, 1976], 108). Recently, Brent Hayes Edwards has paired Murray's concept with Theodor Adorno's notion of "pseudomorphosis"—conceptually reworking one medium in the shape or shadow of another. Edwards posits pseudomorphosis as the paradigm of innovation in black art—"a motor of artistic innovation, defined in the words of Nathaniel Mackey as the 'pursuit of a more complex accommodation between technique and epistemological concerns, between ways of telling and ways of knowing.'" Brent Hayes Edwards, *Epistrophies: Jazz and the Literary Imagination* (Cambridge, MA: Harvard University Press, 2017), 17. He refers to Nathaniel Mackey, "Expanding the Repertoire," *Tripwire* 5 (Fall 2001): 7.
11 Jones, *The Muse Is Music*, 212.
12 For an elaboration of this argument, see Alan Williams, "Is Sound Recording Like a Language?" *Yale French Studies* 60 (1980): 51–66.
13 Roland Barthes, "From Work to Text," in *Image, Music, Text*, ed. and trans. Stephen Heath (New York: Hill and Wang, 1977), 58.
14 Jonathan Culler, "Text—Its Vicissitudes," in *The Literary in Theory* (Stanford, CA: Stanford University Press, 2007), 106. This essay, a review of poststructuralist accounts of the notion of "text" and their usefulness for interdisciplinary thinking, is in the background of my thinking in this section.
15 Kevin Lynch, "Cecil Taylor and the Poetics of Living," *Down Beat* 53, no. 11 (November 1986): 67.
16 I'm thinking in part about the overlapping interests between Taylor's practice and sound poetry in Steven McCaffery's paradigmatic account: "the liberation and promotion of phonetic and sub-phonetic features of language to the state of a *material prima* for creative, subversive endeavors." Steven McCaffery, "Voice in Extremis," in *Close Listening: Poetry and the Performed Word*, ed. Charles Bernstein (Oxford: Oxford University Press, 1998), 163. Any such "liberation" is only partial and ambiguous. Though anxious to move beyond what he perceives as naïveté in earlier formulations, McCaffery insists on sound poetry as avant-garde practice, and we might helpfully understand it as the dialectical flipside of the lyrical—where typically nonexpressive or surplus elements signify something conventionally held to be deeply personal or idiosyncratic—or "speech-based" poetics to which the avant-garde is usually contrasted. A certain understanding of race and racial alterity is central to both lyric poetry, primarily theorized through speech, and the avant-garde, generally routed through suspicion toward "speech-based poetics." In this way, sound poetry's implication of "the body" also condenses and displaces questions of race, which is also to say gender—the supplement to sex understood, as Foucault emphasized, as a technology of control and regulation of sexuality. But it also draws our attention to other forms of resonance that inform relationships between bodies, to "the body" as a relationship between form and matter, as a point of mediation between "inside" and "outside" in specific and extended senses.
17 These are the criteria David Such specifies as the "major ingredients to hard bop (and a number of other styles of jazz)" in his valuable *Avant-Garde Jazz Musicians: Performing*

Out There (Iowa City: University of Iowa Press, 1993), 4. Ekkerhard Jost highlights new "heterogeneous principles" of composition and form, shifting meanings of simultaneous playing from solo/accompaniment to collective improvisation, a "negation of traditional norms," and the emergence of autonomously developing approaches in Europe, Japan, and elsewhere. Jost, *Free Jazz*, 9–12. Jost's polemical "Instant Composing as Body Language," liner notes to Cecil Taylor, *The Complete Cecil Taylor in Berlin '88* (FMP, 2015), has greatly informed my understanding of Taylor's art, even where I read some of Jost's arguments—especially regarding composition—against the grain.

18 See Frank Kofsky, *John Coltrane and the Jazz Revolution of the 1960s* (New York: Pathfinder Press, 1998) (previously released as *Black Nationalism and the Revolution in Music* [1971]); and Carles and Comolli, *Free Jazz/Black Power* (Paris: Galilée, 1971). For more on the French reception and support of experimental black music in this period, see Eric Drott, *Music and the Elusive Revolution: Cultural Politics and Political Culture in France, 1968–1981* (Berkeley: University of California Press, 2011); and Lewis, *A Power Stronger Than Itself*, 215–58.

19 Ashon Crawley, *Blackpentecostal Breath: The Aesthetics of Possibility* (New York: Fordham University Press, 2016), 99.

20 Alongside much of the queer theoretical work around the erotic as self-shattering, Jennifer Nash, *The Black Body in Ecstasy: Reading Race, Reading Pornography* (Durham, NC: Duke University Press, 2014), is invaluable for keeping the particulars of race in the frame.

21 John Corbett, "Ephemera Underscored: Writing around Free Improvisation," in *Jazz Among the Discourses*, ed. Krin Gabbard (Durham, NC: Duke University Press, 1995), 217. Corbett is anxious about the status of sound recording, "the post-facto selection, editing, organization, sequencing and packaging" that interrupts his notion of improvisation as a "writerly" text without writing or repetition.

22 Jacques Coursil, "Hidden Principles of Improvisation," in *Arcana III: Musicians on Music*, ed. John Zorn (New York: Hips Road/Tzadik, 2008), 64.

23 "Being Matter Ignited."

24 Julia Kristeva, *Desire in Language: A Semiotic Approach to Literature and Art*, ed. Leon S. Rudiez, trans. Thomas Gora and Alice A. Jardine (New York: Columbia University Press, 1982), 142.

25 Judith Butler, *Gender Trouble: Feminism and the Subversion of Identity* (London: Routledge, 1990), 101.

26 Fanon, *Black Skin, White Masks*, 108, translation modified.

27 Butler, *Gender Trouble*, 82.

28 Eric Drott argues for the salience of this context in understanding that the French critical celebration of free jazz required reading "local" African American liberation struggles as synecdochially related to "global" anticolonial struggles (111–54).

29 Wynter, "Rethinking 'Aesthetics,'" 261. She critiques the Black Aesthetics theorists for falling into a trap of mere "ethno-aesthetics": "claim[ing] and identify[ing] an 'ethnic' and cultural-indigenous tradition inherent to" particular texts and modes of signification, and "suppress[ing], thereby, all awareness of the dialectical nature" of such distinctness (265). While many of the arguments in the 1970s were concerned with rooting black aesthetic practices in vernacular culture, many of the thinkers

were intensely aware of the degree to which black culture emerged in response to the historical upheavals imposed on people of African descent and the forms of life they had no choice but to build in order to survive. Houston Baker, summarizing the shift in focus for the black aesthetic generation (to which he belongs), argues that while "it would be incorrect to assert that the mid- and later seventies witnessed a total revisionism on the part of former advocates of the Black Aesthetic," its "defensive inwardness" and "manifest appeal to a racially conditioned, revolutionary, and intuitive standard of critical judgment—made the new paradigm an ideal instrument for those wishing to usher into the world new and *sui generis* Afro-American objects of investigation" (Baker, *Blues, Ideology, and Afro-American Literature*, 86). In this, Black Arts theorists' notion of the text "as an occasion for transactions between writer and reader, between performer and audience," and the related notion of "destruction of the text," implied "an open-endedness of performance and response that created conditions of possibility for the emergence of both new meanings and new strategies of verbal transaction" that need not be tied to the notions of blackness each would subsequently revise (102).

30 Scott, "The Temporality of Generations," 160–61.
31 Wynter, "Rethinking 'Aesthetics,'" 259.
32 Neal, "The Black Arts Movement," 30.
33 Wynter, "Rethinking 'Aesthetics,'" 244.
34 Sylvia Wynter, "Ethno or Socio Poetics," in *Alcheringa: Ethnopoetics*, eds. Michael Benamou and Jerome Rothenberg (Boston: Boston University, 1976), 86.
35 Baraka, *Black Music*, 176; Neal, "And Shine Swam On," 653.
36 Spillers, *Black, White, and in Color*, 395, 396.
37 I'm drawing again on Spivak, "Scattered Speculations on the Subaltern and the Popular," 480.
38 Lynch, "Cecil Taylor and The Poetics of Living," 67.
39 Spencer Richards, liner notes, Cecil Taylor, *Live in Vienna* (CD, Leo, 1988).
40 The phrases "sonic design" and "methodologic fissures" come from Cecil Taylor's liner notes to his album *Air Above Mountains (Buildings Within)* (Enja, 1976).
41 Wilmer, *As Serious as Your Life*, 46.
42 Jost, *Free Jazz*, 74.
43 A. B. Spellman, *Four Lives in the Bebop Business* (1966. New York: Limelight Editions, 1985), 38. Taylor cites the liner notes to *Unit Structures* (1966). Spellman's text is invaluable, yet one should also recall what Taylor would later tell Robert D. Rusch about Spellman's book: "Essentially when he interviewed me my feeling is that he never really saw me at all . . . and the information he obtained was of a particular kind. You can't separate . . . a person's being most privately from what it is they're saying they're doing." Rusch, *Jazztalk*, 58.
44 Lynette Westendorf, "Cecil Taylor: Indent—'Second Layer,'" *Perspectives of New Music* 33, no. 1/2 (Winter-Summer 1995): 295.
45 Cecil Taylor, "Sound of Subculture Becoming Major Breath/Naked Fire Gesture," liner notes for *Unit Structures* (Blue Note, 1966).
46 Andrew Bartlett, "Cecil Taylor, Identity Energy, and the Avant-Garde African American Body," *Perspectives of New Music* 33, no. 1/2 (Winter-Summer 1995): 279.

47 Moten, *In the Break*, 160–61. Moten specifically discusses Baraka's writing about and around Taylor, but the many references to Taylor's "fluttering hands," small stature, cigarette smoking, and eating habits in journalistic accounts similarly perform "veiled and submerged distancings, critiques, outings" (161).
48 Spellman, *Four Lives in the Bebop Business*, 28.
49 Langston Hughes, "Note on Commercial Theater," *The Collected Poems of Langston Hughes*, eds. Arnold Rampersad and David Roessel (New York: Alfred Knopf, 2004), 215.
50 Spellman, *Four Lives in the Bebop Business*, 5.
51 Moten, *In the Break*, 161.
52 Baraka, *Black Music*, 111.
53 Aldon Nielsen, "Now Is the Time: Voicing Against the Grain of Orality" in *People Get Ready: The Future of Jazz is Now!*, eds. Ajay Heble and Rob Wallace (Durham, NC: Duke University Press, 2013), 35.
54 Moten, *In the Break*, 162.
55 Giddins, "The Avant-Gardist Who Came in from the Cold," in *Riding on a Blue Note: Jazz and American Pop* (1981, New York: Da Capo, 2000), 276.
56 Taylor, "Naked Fire Gesture."
57 Phillip Brian Harper, *Abstractionist Aesthetics: Artistic Form and Social Critique in African American Culture* (New York: New York University Press, 2015), 73.
58 Vijay Iyer, "Improvisation, Temporality, and Embodied Experience," *Journal of Consciousness Studies* 11, nos. 3-4 (2004): 162.
59 "In comparing Cecil to this pianist [Arthur "Montana" Taylor] from the preceding generation, rather than to any then-current practitioner, Baraka invests him with a condition of lineal descendancy that mitigates the extent to which he might register as musically original. . . . These effects are of a piece with the overall objective of Baraka's essay, which is in fact wholly committed to establishing not the thoroughgoing *originality*, but the inarguable *precedentedness* of Taylor's music." Harper, *Abstractionist Aesthetics*, 106, Harper's emphases.
60 Quoted in Wilmer, *As Serious as Your Life*, 49–50.
61 This is Lawrence Kramer's term for "a fusion of vocal and musical utterance judged to be both pleasurable and suitable independent of verbal content: it is the positive quality of singing-in-itself: just singing," or in this case, the surplus of sound to sense (Kramer, "Beyond Words and Music: An Essay on Songfulness," 305).
62 Moten, *In the Break*, 45.
63 Taylor, liner notes to *Air Above Mountains (Buildings Within)*.
64 This and the following quotations appear in Chris Funkhouser's invaluable "'Being Matter Ignited.'" Referring to the influence of Robert Creeley, Charles Olson, and especially Bob Kaufman on his poetry, Taylor tells Funkhouser: "the thing that allows me to enter into what they do is the feeling that I get. It's the way they use words. It's the phraseology that they use, much the way the defining characteristic of men like Charlie Parker or Johnny Hodges is the phraseology. And in the phraseology would be the horizontal as well as the vertical. In other words, the harmony and the melodic."
65 I draw this helpful framing from Iyer, "Improvisation, Temporality, and Embodied Experience."
66 Nielsen relates this anecdote in "Now Is the Time," 37.

67 David Grundy, in a tribute to Taylor, notes that most of Taylor's work with Umbra was undocumented. David Grundy, "'... And Not Goodbye': Cecil Taylor (Part 2—Taylor as Poet)," Streams of Expression (blog), April 29, 2018. http://streamsofexpression.blogspot.com/2018/04/and-not-goodbye-cecil-taylor-part-2.html. Accessed November 25, 2019.
68 Moten, *In the Break*, 159.
69 Cecil Taylor, liner notes to *Garden* (CD, Hat ART 6050, 1990).
70 I have elected to maintain a justified left margin in the absence of any printed version of the poem to avoid inadvertently introducing further textual complication.
71 Jost, "Instant Composing as Body Language," 92.
72 Moten, *In the Break*, 45.
73 Cecil Taylor, "With Cecil Taylor," https://issueprojectroom.org/news/cecil-taylor.
74 Brandon Labelle, "Raw Orality," in *Voice: Vocal Aesthetics in Digital Arts and Media*, eds. Norie Neumark, Ross Gibson, and Theo van Leeuwen (Cambridge, MA: MIT Press, 2010), 150.
75 Jost, in 1975, argues that Taylor "does not refashion swing by placing it in a new setting, but replaces it entirely by a new quality, energy," which he defines in terms of "impulse density" (Jost, *Free Jazz*, 71, 73). A little over a decade later Jost complains: "The extreme energy- and density-levels ... ultimately lead to a uniform and homogeneous musical result. A constantly turbulent texture tells no stories, creates no formal connections, refers neither to the past nor the future, but simply *is*" (Jost, "Instant Composing as Body Language," 100). The terms initially recall Mingus and attempt to impose a normative framework on Taylor. However, the notion that the music is all matter without spirit, without development or self-consciousness, recalls Hegel's racist philosophy of history. This is not deafness, but a refusal to listen. Perhaps Jost fully heard the radical potentiality of what he calls turbulent and refused it.
76 Cecil Taylor, quoted in Whitney Balliett, *American Musicians: 56 Portraits in Jazz* (New York: Oxford University Press, 1986), 414.
77 Funkhouser, "Being Matter Ignited."
78 For Kristeva, the *genotext* is a "process, which tends to articulate structures that are ephemeral ... and non signifying," as opposed to the *phenotext*, which is "language that serves to communicate." See Julia Kristeva, *Revolution in Poetic Language*, trans. Margaret Waller (New York: Columbia University Press, 1985), 86–87.
79 Thank you to Tejumola Olaniyan for suggesting this translation.
80 Kofi Agawu, "The Challenge of Semiotics," *Rethinking Music*, eds. Nicholas Cook and Mark Everist (Oxford: Oxford University Press, 1999), 143.
81 Agawu, "The Challenge of Semiotics," 142.
82 Nathaniel Mackey, *Atet A.D.* (San Francisco: City Lights Books, 2001), 118.
83 Recounted in Jeanette Robinson Murphy, "The Survival of African Music in America," *Popular Science Monthly* 55 (September 1899): 662.
84 Mackey, *The Paracritical Hinge*, 193.
85 There's an antic-ecstatic tradition of sui generis male baritone vocalists that would include Andy Bey, Leon Thomas, and K. Curtis Lyle's sublime collaborations with Julius Hemphill. While each in his way is a master of tremulous moan, wail, and yodel, for each, vocal techniques enhance rather than compete with semantic meaning.

86 See especially Jenoure's work with John Carter and Roberts's *Coin Coin* series.
87 David Lewis, "Interview: Jeanne Lee and David Eyges," *Cadence* 4, no. 23 (1997): 8.
88 Hortense Spillers, "Mama's Baby, Papa's Maybe," in *Black, White, and in Color*, 229.
89 This phrase comes from "In These Last Days," which Lee recorded with Andrew Cyrille and Jimmy Lyons on the cooperative album *Nuba* (Black Saint 1979).
90 Eric Porter, "Jeanne Lee's Voice," in *People Get Ready: The Future of Jazz Is Now!*, eds. Ajay Heble and Rob Wallace (Durham, NC: Duke University Press, 2013), 97.
91 Lewis, "Interview: Jeanne Lee and David Eyges," 9.
92 Porter, "Jeanne Lee's Voice," 89.
93 Brown, "Improvisation and the Aural Tradition in Afro-American Music," 15.
94 Fredric Jameson, "Reification and Utopia in Mass Culture," *Signatures of the Visible* (London: Routledge, 1990), 12.
95 In *Noise Uprising*, Michael Denning details the complex relationship popular culture itself has to creating alternate modes of sociality by attuning us to the function of phonography in a nascent anticolonial sensibility in which vernacular recordings would be central *even as* they also normalized by what Jonathan Sterne calls the "fetish of distant listening" intrinsic to the popularization of imperialism (*Audible Past*, 209).
96 Joy James, "'Concerning Violence': Frantz Fanon's Rebel Intellectual in Search of a Black Cyborg," *South Atlantic Quarterly* 112, no. 1 (Winter 2013): 58. James's article meditates on the solidaristic implications of Fanon's claim in *Wretched of the Earth* for the revolution as that moment when "Henceforward, the interests of one will be the interests of all."
97 Lewis, "Interview," 7.
98 Jeanne Lee, "Angel Chile," *Conspiracy* (LP, Earthforms 815, 1975).
99 Elouise Loftin, *Jumbish* (New York: Emerson Hall Publications, 1972), 40. Lee and Loftin recorded the poem with Andrew Cyrille on his album *Celebration* (LP, IPS Records, 1975).
100 I'm here modifying an argument Paul De Man makes in *Allegories of Reading: Figural Language in Rousseau, Nietzsche, Rilke, and Proust* (New Haven, CT: Yale University Press, 1979), 270.
101 Porter, "Jeanne Lee's Voice," 108, 92.
102 Lewis, "Interview," 11.
103 David Ernst, "Record Review: Afternoon of a Georgia Faun, Djinji's Corner," *Black Perspective in Music* 2, no. 1 (Spring 1974): 95–97.
104 This point will require patient elaboration in a separate context, including a frame that acknowledges the extent to which the institutions of liberal democracy absorbed the energies, rhetoric, and institutions of the left without transforming its basis in property relations, or patriarchal relations of production.
105 Iton, *In Search of the Black Fantastic*, 9.
106 Referring to "without object" I'm suggesting that Baraka may be linking his notion of sound in this instance to his description of John Coltrane's "objectless" love as an ideal of black music: "The rise, the will *to be* love. The contemplative and the expressive, side by side, feeding each other. . . . The change to Love. The freedom to (of) Love. And in this constant evocation of Love, its need, its demands, its birth,

its death, there is a morality that shapes such a sensibility, and a sensibility shaped by such moralizing." Baraka, *Black Music*, 200.
107 Lauren Berlant, "A Properly Political Concept of Love: Three Approaches in Ten Pages," *Cultural Anthropology* 26, no. 4 (2011): 685.
108 "Being Matter Ignited."

CODA

1 Review of *Celebrations and Solitudes* by Jayne Cortez and Richard Davis, *Black World* 26, no. 5 (March 1975), 63.
2 "Yes We Can" on *Rendezvous Suite* (Jazzwerkstatt, 2011).
3 As I don't want to ahistorically claim there were not mass protests before, say, 2012, so do I not want to minimize previous or ongoing efforts such as, for example, clarinetist Don Byron's 1990s collaborations with poet Sadiq Bey.
4 I refer to Kirk's 1970s band, whose name Nathaniel Mackey cites in the preface to *Blue Fasa*.
5 The first experiments, "Ringing My Phone (Straight Outta Istanbul)" and "Infospace," appear on Jason Moran, *The Bandwagon* (Blue Note, 2003); the collaborations with Piper appear on Jason Moran, *Artist in Residence* (Blue Note, 2006).
6 Stuart Hall, "Notes on Deconstructing the 'Popular,'" in *Cultural Theory and Popular Culture: A Reader*, ed. John Storey (Upper Saddle River, NJ: Pearson/Prentice Hall, 1998), 453.
7 "'Cultural change' is a polite euphemism for the process by which some cultural forms and practices are driven out of the centre of popular life, actively marginalized" (Hall, "Notes on Deconstructing the 'Popular,'" 443).
8 Michael Denning, "The End of Mass Culture," *International Labor and Working-Class History* 37 (Spring 1990): 6.
9 Amiri Baraka identified Harry Pace's company as "[o]ne of the funniest and most cruelly absurd situations to develop because of the growth and influence of a definable black middle class in America"; Pace's attempt to cultivate middle-class tastes in his listeners failed because they "did not care as much about the *dignity* of its musical tastes as the Negro business community" (Baraka, *Blues People*, 128–29). David Suisman provides a more detailed account of Black Swan's demise in *Selling Sounds: The Commercial Revolution in American Music* (Cambridge, MA: Harvard University Press, 2009), but Baraka's core argument—that Pace and company failed to attract black listeners because of the ways they wanted to police those listeners' tastes—holds.
10 D. H. Melhem, "MELUS Profile and Interview: Jayne Cortez." *MELUS* 21, no. 1 (Spring 1996): 77.
11 Melba Joyce Boyd, Review of *Coagulations: New and Selected Poems* by Jayne Cortez. *The Black Scholar* 16, no 4 (July/August 74. 1985): 65.
12 Renee Kingan credits Cortez with "creating a collaborative environment in which all members had vital input" (Renee Kingan, "Taking it Out!: Jayne Cortez's Collaborations with the Firespitters," in *Black Music, Black Poetry: Blues and Jazz's Impact on African American Versification*, ed. Gordon E. Thompson (Farnham, UK: Ashgate, 2014), 150.

13 Fanon, *Wretched of the Earth*, 314-15. Kingan goes as far as to argue that Cortez draws on Hughes and "Négritude surrealists" to create a fundamentally activist poetics (Kingan, "Taking it Out!," 150). This is correct, but from my perspective only constitutes one level of her work.
14 Jayne Cortez, "Commitment," *There It Is* (LP, Bola Press, 1986).
15 D. H. Melhem, *Heroism in the New Black Poetry: Introductions and Interviews* (Lexington: University Press of Kentucky, 1990), 202.
16 Melhem, "MELUS Profile and Interview: Jayne Cortez," 74.
17 Melhem, *Heroism in the New Black Poetry*, 181.
18 Melhem, "MELUS Profile and Interview: Jayne Cortez," 79.
19 Tony Bolden, "All the Birds Sing Bass: The Revolutionary Blues of Jayne Cortez," *African American Review* 35, no. 1 (Spring 2001): 65.
20 Stuart Hall, "Gramsci's Relevance for the Study of Race and Ethnicity," 20.
21 Feinstein, "Returning to Go Some Place Else," 54.
22 Melhem, *Heroism in the New Black Poetry*, 210.
23 Melhem, *Heroism in the New Black Poetry*, 191.
24 Nielsen, *Black Chant*, 222.
25 Kingan, "Taking it Out!" 156.
26 Melhem, *Heroism in the New Black Poetry*, 204.
27 "No Simple Explanations," Jayne Cortez, *Maintain Control* (LP, Bola Press, 1986).
28 Sianne Ngai, *Ugly Feelings*, 28.
29 Kay Bonetti, "An Interview with Toni Cade Bambara," *Conversations with Toni Cade Bambara*, ed. Thabiti Lewis (Jackson: University Press of Mississippi, 2012), 35-47.
30 Aldon Nielsen discusses Ornette Coleman's harmolodics in this light in his essay "Capillary Currents: Jayne Cortez," in *We Who Love to Be Astonished: Experimental Women's Writing and Performance Poetics*, eds. Laura Hinton and Cynthia Hogue (Tuscaloosa: University of Alabama Press, 2002).
31 Audre Lorde, "Uses of the Erotic: The Erotic as Power," in *Sister Outsider: Essays and Speeches* (Freedom, CA: Crossing Press, 1984), 54.
32 Nat Hentoff, liner notes, Cecil Taylor, *Cecil Taylor: In Transition* (LP, Blue Note, 1975).
33 Roger Riggins, "Jeanne Lee," *Coda* 1 (February 1979): 4.
34 Sasha Feinstein, "Returning to Go Some Place Else: Jayne Cortez," *Ask Me Now: Conversations on Jazz and Literature*, ed. Sasha Feinstein (Bloomington: Indiana University Press, 2007), 50.
35 Feinstein, "Returning to Go Some Place Else: Jayne Cortez," 52.
36 Melhem, *Heroism in the New Black Poetry*, 196.
37 Barbara Christian, "There It Is: The Poetry of Jayne Cortez," *Callaloo* 26 (Winter 1986): 239.
38 "If, however, notes were the mere signs for music, then, through the curves of the needle on the phonograph record, music approaches decisively its true character as writing. Decisively, because this writing can be recognized as true language to the extent that it relinquishes its being as mere signs: inseparably committed to the sound that inhabits this and no other acoustic groove. If the productive force of music has expired in the phonograph records, if the latter have not produced a

form through their technology, they instead transform the most recent sound of old feelings into an archaic text of knowledge to come" (Theodor Adorno, "The Form of the Phonograph Record," trans. Susan H. Gillespie, in *Essays on Music*, ed. Richard Leppert [1934. Berkeley: University of California Press, 2002], 279–80).

39 Adorno, "The Form of the Phonograph Record," 280.
40 Rosalind Morris, in a conversation with the author, suggested this way of conceiving "overhearing."

Bibliography

Adorno, Theodor W. *Essays on Music*. Ed. Richard Leppert. Trans. Susan H. Gillespie et al. 1934. Berkeley: University of California Press, 2002.
Adorno, Theodor W. "The Form of the Phonograph Record." Trans. Susan H. Gillespie. *Essays on Music*. Ed. Richard Leppert. 1934. Berkeley: University of California Press, 2002. 277–82.
Adorno, Theodor W. "On the Social Situation of Music." Trans. Susan Gillespie. *Essays on Music*. Ed. Richard Leppert. 1931. Berkeley: University of California Press, 2002. 391–436.
Adorno, Theodor W., and Walter Benjamin. *The Complete Correspondence, 1928–1940*. Trans. Nicholas Walker. Ed. Henri Lonitz. Cambridge, MA: Harvard University Press, 1999.
Agawu, Kofi. "The Challenge of Semiotics." *Rethinking Music*. Eds. Nicholas Cook and Mark Everist. Oxford: Oxford University Press, 1999. 138–60.
Althusser, Louis, and Étienne Balibar. *Reading Capital*. Trans. Ben Brewster. 1965. London: Verso, 1997.
Arnheim, Rudolf. *Radio*. Trans. Margaret Ludwig and Herbert Read. 1913. London: Faber & Faber, 1936.
Attali, Jacques. *Noise: The Political Economy of Music*. Trans. Brian Massumi. Minneapolis: University of Minnesota Press, 1985.
Bailey, Derek. *Improvisation: Its Nature and Practice in Music*. New York: Da Capo Press, 1992.
Baker, Houston A. *Blues, Ideology and Afro-American Literature: A Vernacular Theory*. Chicago: University of Chicago Press, 1984.
Balliett, Whitney. *American Musicians: 56 Portraits in Jazz*. New York: Oxford University Press, 1986.
Baraka, Amiri. *Black Magic: Poetry 1961–1967*. Indianapolis: Bobbs-Merrill, 1969.
Baraka, Amiri. *Black Music*. 1967. New York: Da Capo Press, 1998.
Baraka, Amiri. *Blues People: Negro Music in White America*. 1963. New York: Perennial, 2002.
Baraka, Amiri. *Daggers and Javelins: Essays, 1974–1979*. New York: William Morrow, 1984.
Baraka, Amiri. *Digging: The Afro-American Soul of American Classical Music*. Berkeley: University of California Press, 2009.

Baraka, Amiri. *The Fiction of LeRoi Jones/Amiri Baraka*. Chicago: Lawrence Hill Books, 2000.

Baraka, Amiri. *Funk Lore: New Poems (1984-1995)*. Ed. Paul Vangelisti. Los Angeles: Littoral Books, 1996.

Baraka, Amiri. *Home: Social Essays*. New York: William Morrow, 1966.

Baraka, Amiri. *The LeRoi Jones/Amiri Baraka Reader*. Ed. William J. Harris. New York: Basic Books, 2009.

Baraka, Amiri. Preface. *Black Boogaloo: Notes on Black Liberation*, by Larry Neal. San Francisco: Journal of Black Poetry Press, 1969.

Baraka, Amiri. *S O S: Poems 1961-2013*. New York: Grove Press, 2014.

Baraka, Amiri. "Some Questions about the Sixth Pan-African Congress." *Black Scholar* 6, no. 2 (October 1974): 42-46.

Baraka, Amiri, and Amina Baraka. *The Music: Reflections on Jazz and Blues*. New York: Morrow, 1987.

Baraka, Amiri, and Kalamu ya Salaam. "Amiri Baraka Analyzes How He Writes." *African American Review* 37, nos. 2/3 (Summer/Autumn 2003): 211-36.

Barthes, Roland. *Image, Music, Text*. Trans. and ed. Stephen Heath. New York: Hill and Wang, 1977.

Bartlett, Andrew. "Cecil Taylor, Identity Energy, and the Avant-Garde African American Body." *Perspectives of New Music* 33, nos. 1/2 (Winter-Summer 1995): 274-93.

Battier, Marc. "What the GRM Brought: From Musique Concrète to Acousmatic Music." *Organized Sound* 12, no. 3 (December 2007): 189-202.

Benjamin, Walter. *The Arcades Project*. Trans. Howard Eiland and Kevin McLaughlin. Cambridge, MA: Belknap Press of Harvard University Press, 1999.

Benjamin, Walter. "The Medium through Which Works of Art Continue to Influence Later Ages." Trans. Rodney Livingstone. *Selected Writings*. Trans. Edmund Jephcott et al., ed. Marcus Bullock et al., 4 vols. Cambridge, MA: Harvard University Press, 2002). 1:235.

Benjamin, Walter. "On Some Motifs in Baudelaire." Trans. Harry Zohn. *Walter Benjamin: Selected Writings, Volume 4: 1938-1940*. Eds. Howard Eiland and Michael W. Jennings. Cambridge, MA: Harvard University Press, 2006.

Benston, Kimberly. "Amiri Baraka: An Interview." *boundary 2* 6, no. 2 (Winter 1978): 303-18.

Bérard, Carol. "Recorded Noises—Tomorrow's Instrumentation." *Music, Sound, and Technology in America: A Documentary History of Early Phonograph, Cinema, and Radio*. Eds. Timothy D. Taylor, Mark Katz, and Tony Grajeda. 1929. Durham, NC: Duke University Press, 2012. 110-13.

Berlant, Lauren. *Cruel Optimism*. Durham, NC: Duke University Press, 2012.

Berlant, Lauren. *The Female Complaint: The Unfinished Business of Sentimentality in American Culture*. Durham, NC: Duke University Press, 2008.

Berlant, Lauren. "A Properly Political Concept of Love: Three Approaches in Ten Pages," *Cultural Anthropology* 26, no. 4 (2011): 683-91.

Bernstein, Charles, ed. *Close Listening: Poetry and the Performed Word*. Oxford: Oxford University Press, 1998.

Best, Stephen. *The Fugitive's Properties: Law and the Poetics of Possession*. Chicago: University of Chicago Press, 2004.

Biondi, Martha. *To Stand and Fight: The Struggle for Civil Rights in Postwar New York City*. Cambridge, MA: Harvard University Press, 2003.

Bolden, Tony. *Afro-Blue: Improvisations in African American Poetry and Culture.* Urbana: University of Illinois Press, 2004.

Bolden, Tony. "All the Birds Sing Bass: The Revolutionary Blues of Jayne Cortez." *African American Review*, 35, no. 1 (Spring 2001): 61–67.

Bonetti, Kay. "An Interview with Toni Cade Bambara." *Conversations with Toni Cade Bambara.* Ed. Thabiti Lewis. Jackson: University Press of Mississippi, 2012. 35–47.

Boyd, Melba Joyce. Review of *Coagulations: New and Selected Poems* by Jayne Cortez. *Black Scholar* 16, no 4 (July/August 1985): 65–66.

Brady, Erika. *A Spiral Way: How the Phonograph Changed Ethnography.* Jackson: University Press of Mississippi, 1999.

Brooks, Tim. *Lost Sounds: Blacks and the Birth of the Recording Industry, 1890–1919.* Urbana: University of Illinois Press, 2004.

Brown, Marion. "Improvisation and the Aural Tradition in Afro-American Music." *Black World* 23, no. 1 (November 1973): 14–19.

Butler, Judith. *Gender Trouble: Feminism and the Subversion of Identity.* London: Routledge, 1990.

Carby, Hazel V. "The Politics of Fiction, Anthropology, and the Folk: Zora Neale Hurston." *New Essays on* Their Eyes Were Watching God." Ed. Michael Awkward. New York: Cambridge University Press, 1991.

Carby, Hazel V. *Race Men.* Cambridge, MA: Harvard University Press, 1998.

Carles, Philippe, and Jean-Louis Comolli. *Free Jazz/Black Power.* Trans. Grégory Pierrot. 1971. Jackson: University Press of Mississippi, 2015.

Carmichael, Thomas. "Beneath the Underdog: Charles Mingus, Representation, and Jazz Autobiography." *Canadian Review of American Studies* 25, no. 3 (Winter 1995): 29–41.

Césaire, Aimé. *Discourse on Colonialism.* Trans. Joan Pinkham. New York: Monthly Review Press, 2000.

Chandler, Nahum Dimitri. *X: The Problem of the Negro as a Problem for Thought.* New York: Fordham University Press, 2014.

Chasar, Mike. *Everyday Reading: Poetry and Popular Culture in Modern America.* New York: Columbia University Press, 2012.

Christian, Barbara. "There It Is: The Poetry of Jayne Cortez." *Callaloo* 26 (Winter 1986): 235–39.

Coleman, Ornette, and Jacques Derrida. "The Other's Language: Jacques Derrida Interviews Ornette Coleman, 23 June 1997." Trans. Timothy S. Murphy. *Genre* 36 (Summer 2004): 319–29.

Corbett, John. "Ephemera Underscored: Writing around Free Improvisation." *Jazz among the Discourses.* Ed. Krin Gabbard. Durham, NC: Duke University Press, 1995. 217–40.

Crawford, Margo Natalie. *Black Post-Blackness: The Black Arts Movement and Twenty-First-Century Aesthetics.* Urbana: University of Illinois Press, 2017.

Crawford, Margo Natalie. "The Poetics of Chant and Inner/Outer Space." *The Cambridge Companion to American Poetry Since 1945.* Ed. Jennifer Ashton. Cambridge: Cambridge University Press, 2013.

Crawley, Ashon. *Blackpentecostal Breath: The Aesthetics of Possibility.* New York: Fordham University Press, 2016.

Cruse, Harold. *The Crisis of the Negro Intellectual: From Its Origins to the Present*. New York: William Morrow, 1967.

Cruz, Jon. *Culture on the Margins: The Black Spiritual and the Rise of American Cultural Interpretation*. Princeton, NJ: Princeton University Press, 1999.

Culler, Jonathan D. "Text—Its Vicissitudes." *The Literary in Theory*. Stanford, CA: Stanford University Press, 2007: 99–116.

Davey, Elizabeth. "Building a Black Audience in the 1930s: Langston Hughes, Poetry Readings, and the Golden Stair Press." *Print Culture in a Diverse America*. Eds. James P. Danky and Wayne A. Wiegand. Urbana: University of Illinois Press, 1998. 223–43.

Davis, Angela Y. "Afro Images: Politics, Fashion, and Nostalgia." *Critical Inquiry* 21, no. 1 (Autumn 1994): 37–45.

Davis, Arthur P. "The Harlem of Langston Hughes's Poetry." *Phylon* 13, no. 4 (4th Qtr. 1952): 276–83.

Dawahare, Anthony. "Langston Hughes's Radical Poetry and the 'End of Race.'" MELUS 23, no. 3 (Fall 1998): 21–41.

Dawson, Michael. *Blacks in and Out of the Left*. Cambridge, MA: Harvard University Press, 2013.

Dawson, Michael. *Black Visions: The Roots of Contemporary African-American Political Ideologies*. Chicago: University of Chicago Press, 2001.

De Man, Paul. *Allegories of Reading: Figural Language in Rousseau, Nietzsche, Rilke, and Proust*. New Haven, CT: Yale University Press, 1979.

Denning, Michael. *The Cultural Front: The Laboring of American Culture in the Twentieth Century*. London: Verso, 1997.

Denning, Michael. "The End of Mass Culture." *International Labor and Working-Class History* 37 (Spring 1990): 4–18.

Denning, Michael. *Noise Uprising: The Audio Politics of a World Musical Revolution*. London: Verso, 2015.

Derrida, Jacques. "Freud and the Scene of Writing." *Writing and Difference*. Trans. Alan Bass. Chicago: University of Chicago Press, 1978. 196–231.

Dolar, Mladen. *A Voice and Nothing More*. Cambridge, MA: MIT Press, 2006.

Donnell, Alison. *Twentieth-Century Caribbean Literature: Critical Moments in Anglophone Literary History*. London: Routledge, 2005.

Douglass, Frederick. *Autobiographies*. Ed. Henry Louis Gates Jr. New York: Library of America, 1994.

Drott, Eric. *Music and the Elusive Revolution: Cultural Politics and Political Culture in France, 1968–1981*. Berkeley: University of California Press, 2011.

Du Bois, W. E. B. *Writings*. Ed. Nathan Huggins. New York: Library of America, 1986.

Ebaum, Max. *Revolution in the Air: Sixties Radicals Turn to Lenin, Mao and Che*. 2002. London: Verso, 2018.

Edwards, Brent Hayes. *Epistrophies: Jazz and the Literary Imagination*. Cambridge, MA: Harvard University Press, 2017.

Edwards, Brent Hayes, and Jed Rasula. "The Ear of the Behearer: A Conversation in Jazz." *New Ohio Review* 3 (Spring 2008): 42–64.

Ellison, Ralph. *The Collected Essays of Ralph Ellison*. Ed. John F. Callahan. New York: Modern Library, 2003.

Ellison, Ralph. *Living with Music*. Ed. Robert G. O'Meally. New York: Modern Library Classics, 2002.

Ernst, David. "Record Review: Afternoon of a Georgia Faun, Djinji's Corner." *Black Perspective in Music* 2, no. 1 (Spring 1974): 95–97.

Fanon, Frantz. *Black Skin, White Masks*. Trans. Charles Lam Markmann. New York: Grove Press, 1962.

Fanon, Frantz. *Wretched of the Earth*. Trans. Constance Farrington. 1961. New York: Grove Press, 1963.

Farred, Grant. *What's My Name?: Black Vernacular Intellectuals*. Minneapolis: University of Minnesota Press, 2003.

Feinstein, Sasha. "Returning to Go Some Place Else: Jayne Cortez." *Ask Me Now: Conversations on Jazz and Literature*. Ed. Sasha Feinstein. Bloomington: Indiana University Press, 2007.

Fields, Barbara, and Karen Fields. *Racecraft: The Soul of Inequality in American Life*. London: Verso Books, 2012.

Floyd, Samuel. *The Power of Black Music: Interpreting Its History from Africa to the United States*. Oxford: Oxford University Press, 1996.

Frazier, Robeson Taj P. "The Congress of African People: Baraka, Brother Mao, and the Year of '74." *Souls* 8, no. 3 (2006): 142–59.

Freeman, Phil. "Matana Roberts." *Wire-London* 328 (June 2011): 20.

Fuller, Hoyt, ed. "Writers Symposium." *Negro Digest* 17 no. 3 (January 1968): 10–45.

Funkhouser, Chris. "Being Matter Ignited . . . : An Interview with Cecil Taylor." *Hambone* 12 (Spring 1992): 17–39. https://writing.upenn.edu/epc/authors/funkhouser/ceciltaylor.html. Accessed May 28, 2019.

Gendron, Bernard. "After the October Revolution: The Jazz Avant-Garde in New York, 1964–65." *Sound Commitments: Avant-Garde Music and the Sixties*. Ed. Robert Addington. Oxford: Oxford University Press, 2009. 211–53.

Genette, Gerard. *Paratexts: Thresholds of Interpretation*. Trans. Jane E. Lewin. Cambridge: Cambridge University Press, 1997.

Gennari, John. "Baraka's Bohemian Blues." *African American Review* 37, nos. 2/3 (Summer-Autumn 2003): 253–60.

Giddins, Gary. "The Avant-Gardist Who Came in from the Cold." *Riding on a Blue Note: Jazz and American Pop*. 1981. New York: Da Capo, 2000.

Gilroy, Paul. "After the Love Has Gone": Bio-Politics and Ethno-Poetics in the Black Public Sphere." *Third Text* 8, nos. 28/29 (1994): 25–46.

Gilroy, Paul. *The Black Atlantic: Modernity and Double Consciousness*. London: Verso, 1993.

Glick, Jeremy Matthew. "'All I Do Is Think about You': Some Notes on Pragmatist Longing in Recent Literary Study of Amiri Baraka." *boundary 2* 37, no. 2 (Summer 2010): 107–32.

Goldsmith, Peter D. *Making People's Music: Moe Asch and Folkways Records*. Washington, DC: Smithsonian Institution Press, 1998.

Gore, Dayo F. *Radicalism at the Crossroads: African American Women Activists in the Cold War*. New York: New York University Press, 2011.

Gosse, Van. "A Movement of Movements: The Definition and Periodization of the New Left." *A Companion to Post-1945 America*. Eds. Jean-Christophe Agnew and Roy Rosenzweig. London: Wiley-Blackwell, 2002. 277–302.

Graham, Maryemma. "The Practice of a Social Art." *Langston Hughes: Critical Perspectives Past and Present*. Eds. Henry Louis Gates Jr. and Kwame Anthony Appiah. New York: Amistad, 1993. 213-35.

Gramsci, Antonio. *Selections from the Prison Notebooks*. Eds. and trans. Quintin Hoare and Geoffrey Nowell Smith. New York: International, 1985.

Green, Adam. *Selling the Race: Culture, Community, and Black Chicago, 1940-1955*. Chicago: University of Chicago Press, 2007.

Griffin, Farah Jasmine. "When Malindy Sings: A Meditation on Black Women's Vocality." *Uptown Conversation: The New Jazz Studies*. Eds. Robert G. O'Meally, Brent Hayes Edwards, and Farah Jasmine Griffin. New York: Columbia University Press, 2004. 102-25.

Grundy, David. "'. . . And Not Goodbye': Cecil Taylor (Part 2—Taylor as Poet)." Stream of Expression (blog), April 29, 2018. http://streamsofexpression.blogspot.com/2018/04/and-not-goodbye-cecil-taylor-part-2.html. Accessed November 25, 2019.

Guillory, John. "Genesis of the Media Concept." *Critical Inquiry* 36, no. 2 (Winter 2010): 321-62.

Hall, Jacqueline Dowd. "The Long Civil Rights Movement and the Political Uses of the Past." *Journal of American History* 91, no. 4 (March 2005): 1233-63.

Hall, James C. "The African American Musician as Intellectual." *Harold Cruse's the Crisis of the Negro Intellectual Reconsidered*. Ed. Jerry Watts. London: Routledge, 2004. 109-19.

Hall, Stuart. "Gramsci's Relevance for the Study of Race and Ethnicity." *Journal of Communication Inquiry* 10, no. 2 (1986): 5-27.

Hall, Stuart. "Notes on Deconstructing 'the Popular.'" *Cultural Theory and Popular Culture: A Reader*. Ed. John Storey. Upper Saddle River, NJ: Pearson/Prentice Hall, 1998. 442-53.

Hall, Stuart. "Race, Articulation, and Societies Structured in Dominance." *Black British Cultural Studies: A Reader*. Eds. Houston Baker Jr., Manthia Diawara, and Ruth H. Lindeborg. Chicago: University of Chicago Press, 1996. 16-60.

Hall, Stuart. "What Is This 'Black' in Black Popular Culture?" *Black Popular Culture*. Ed. Gina Dent. Seattle: Bay Press, 1992. 21-33.

Hall, Stuart. "When Was 'the Post-colonial'? Thinking at the Limit." *The Post-colonial Question: Common Skies, Divided Horizons*. Eds. Iain Chambers and Lidia Curti. London: Routledge, 1995. 242-60.

Hansen, Miriam Bratu. "The Mass Production of the Senses: Classical Cinema as Vernacular Modernism." *Modernism/Modernity* 6, no. 2 (1999): 59-77.

Hardt, Michael. "Production and Distribution of the Common: A Few Questions for the Artist." *open! Platform for Art, Culture & the Public Domain*. February 6, 2006. Online http://www.onlineopen.org/production-and-distribution-of-the-common. Accessed May 9, 2018.

Harney, Stefano, and Valentina Desideri. "A Conspiracy Without a Plot." *The Curatorial: A Philosophy of Curating*. Ed. Jean-Paul Martinon. London: Bloomsbury Press, 2013. 125-36.

Harper, Phillip Brian. *Abstractionist Aesthetics: Artistic Form and Social Critique in African American Culture*. New York: New York University Press, 2015.

Harper, Phillip Brian. "Nationalism and Social Division in Black Arts Poetry of the 1960s." *Critical Inquiry* 19, no. 2 (Winter 1993): 234-55.

Harris, William J. "How You Sound??: Amiri Baraka Writes Free Jazz." *Uptown Conversation: The New Jazz Studies*. Ed. Robert G. O'Meally, Brent Hayes Edwards, and Farah Jasmine Griffin. New York: Columbia University Press, 2004.

Harris, William J. *The Poetry and Poetics of Amiri Baraka: The Jazz Aesthetic*. Columbia: University of Missouri Press, 1985.

Hartman, Saidiya V. *Scenes of Subjection: Terror, Slavery, and Self-Making in Nineteenth-Century America*. Oxford: Oxford University Press, 1997.

Henderson, Stephen E. "The Question of Form and Judgment in Contemporary Black American Poetry: 1962-1977." *A Dark and Sudden Beauty: Two Essays in Black American Poetry*. Ed. Houston A. Baker Jr. Philadelphia: University of Pennsylvania Press, 1977: 9-36.

Hentoff, Nat. "Langston Hughes: He Found Poetry in the Blues." *Mayfair* (August 1958): 27.

Hirsch, Jerrold. "Modernity, Nostalgia and Southern Folklore Studies: The Case of John Lomax." *Journal of American Folklore* 105, no. 416 (Spring 1992): 183-207.

Hoffman, Tyler. *American Poetry in Performance: From Walt Whitman to Hip Hop*. Ann Arbor: University of Michigan Press, 2011.

Holmes, Thom. *Electronic and Experimental Music: Technology, Music, and Culture*. London: Routledge, 2015.

Hughes, Langston. "Consider Me." *American Scholar*, 21, no. 1 (Winter 1951-52): 100.

Hughes, Langston. "The Influence of Negro Music on American Entertainment." April 25, 1952. Reprinted in *The Collected Works of Langston Hughes. Vol. 9, Essays on Art, Race, Politics, and World Affairs*. Ed. Christopher C. De Santi. Columbia: University of Missouri Press, 2002. 208.

Hughes, Langston. "Jazz as Communication." *The Collected Works of Langston Hughes. Vol. 9, Hughes: Essays on Art, Race, Politics, and World Affairs*. Ed. Christopher C. De Santi. Columbia: University of Missouri Press, 2002. 370.

Hughes, Langston. "The Negro Artist and the Racial Mountain." *The Nation* 122 (June 23, 1926): 692-94. Reprinted in *The Collected Works of Langston Hughes. Vol. 9, Essays on Art, Race, Politics, and World Affairs*. Ed. Christopher C. De Santi. Columbia: University of Missouri Press, 2002. 32.

Hughes, Langston. "Note on Commercial Theater." *The Collected Poems of Langston Hughes*. Eds. Arnold Rampersad and David Roessel. New York: Alfred Knopf, 2004: 215.

Hughes, Langston. "Poetry, Jazz and Nightclubs." *Chicago Defender*, May 17, 1958, 10.

Hughes, Langston. "Ten Ways to Use Poetry in Teaching." *The Collected Works of Langston Hughes. Vol. 9, Essays on Art, Race, Politics, and World Affairs*. Ed. Christopher C. De Santi. Columbia: University of Missouri Press, 2002. 319.

Hurston, Zora Neal. "Spirituals and Neo-Spirituals." *Folklore, Memoirs, and Other Writings*. Ed. Cheryl A. Wall, 1934. New York: Library of America, 1995. 869-74.

Ihde, Don. *Listening and Voice: Phenomenologies of Sound*. 2nd ed. Albany: State University of New York Press, 2007.

Iton, Richard. *In Search of the Black Fantastic: Politics and Popular Culture in the Post-Civil Rights Era*. Oxford: Oxford University Press, 2008.

Iton, Richard. "Still Life." *Small Axe* 40 (March 2013): 22-39.

Iyer, Vijay. "Improvisation, Temporality, and Embodied Experience." *Journal of Consciousness Studies* 11, nos. 3-4 (2004): 159-73.

Jackson, Travis A. "'Always New and Centuries Old': Jazz, Poetry, and Tradition as Creative Adaptation." *Uptown Conversation: The New Jazz Studies*. Eds. Robert G. O'Meally, Brent Hayes Edwards, and Farah Jasmine Griffin. New York: Columbia University Press, 2004. 357–73.

James, Joy. "Concerning Violence: Frantz Fanon's Rebel Intellectual in Search of a Black Cyborg." *South Atlantic Quarterly* 112, no. 1 (Winter 2013): 57–70.

Jameson, Fredric. "Periodizing the 60s." *Social Text* 9/10 (Spring-Summer 1984): 178–209.

Jameson, Fredric. "Reification and Utopia in Mass Culture." *Signatures of the Visible*. New York: Routledge, 1990. 9–34.

Johnson, Cedric. *Revolutionaries to Race Leaders: Black Power and the Making of African American Politics*. Minneapolis: University of Minneapolis Press, 2007.

Jones, Meta DuEwa. *The Muse Is Music: Jazz Poetry from the Harlem Renaissance to Spoken Word*. Urbana: University of Illinois Press, 2011.

Jordan, June. "Review of *Celebrations and Solitudes*, by Jayne Cortez and Richard Davis." *Black World* 26, no. 5 (March 1975): 53, 63.

Jost, Ekkerhard. *Free Jazz*. New York: Da Capo Press, 1994.

Kane, Brian. *Sound Unseen: Acousmatic Sound in Theory and Practice*. Oxford: Oxford University Press, 2014.

Karenga, Ron. "Ron Karenga and Black Cultural Nationalism: A Response." *Negro Digest* 17, no. 3 (January 1968): 5–9.

Kelley, Robin D. G. "Dig They Freedom: Meditations on History and the Black Avant-Garde." *Lenox Avenue: A Journal of Interarts Inquiry* 3 (1997): 13–27.

Kelley, Robin D. G. *Race Rebels: Culture, Politics, and the Black Working Class*. New York: Free Press, 1994.

Kim, Daniel Wong-gu. "'In the Tradition': Amiri Baraka, Black Liberation, and Avant-Garde Praxis in the U.S." *African American Review* 37, nos. 2/3 (Summer-Autumn 2003): 345–63.

Kingan, Renee. "Taking It Out!: Jayne Cortez's Collaborations with the Firespitters." *Black Music, Black Poetry: Blues and Jazz's Impact on African American Versification*. Ed. Gordon E. Thompson. Farnham, UK: Ashgate, 2014. 149–62.

Kofsky, Frank. *John Coltrane and the Jazz Revolution of the 1960s*. 1971. New York: Pathfinder Press, 1998.

Kramer, Lawrence. "Beyond Words and Music: An Essay on Songfulness." *Word and Music Studies: Defining the Field: Proceedings of the First International Conference on Word and Music Studies at Graz, 1997*. Eds. Walter Bernhart, Steven Paul Scher, and Werner Wolf. Amsterdam: Rodopi, 1999.

Kristeva, Julia. *Desire in Language: A Semiotic Approach to Literature and Art*. Trans. Thomas Gora and Alice A. Jardine. Ed. Leon S. Rudiez. New York: Columbia University Press, 1982.

Kristeva, Julia. *Revolution in Poetic Language*. Trans. Margaret Waller. New York: Columbia University Press, 1985.

Kun, Josh. *Audiotopia: Music, Race, and America*. Berkeley: University of California Press, 2005.

Kutzinski, Vera M. *The Worlds of Langston Hughes: Modernism and Translation in the Americas*. Ithaca, NY: Cornell University Press, 2012.

Labelle, Brandon. "Raw Orality." *Voice: Vocal Aesthetics in Digital Arts and Media*. Eds. Norie Neumark, Ross Gibson, and Theo van Leeuwen. Cambridge, MA: MIT Press, 2010. 147–72.

Leonard, Keith. *Fettered Genius: The African American Bardic Poet from Slavery to Civil Rights*. Charlottesville: University of Virginia Press, 2006.

Lewis, David. "Interview: Jeanne Lee and David Eyges." *Cadence* 4, no. 23 (April 1997): 5–13.

Lewis, David Levering. *W. E. B. Du Bois: Biography of a Race, 1868–1919*. New York: Henry Holt, 1993.

Lewis, George. *A Power Stronger Than Itself: The AACM and American Experimental Music*. Chicago: University of Chicago Press, 2008.

Loftin, Elouise. *Jumbish*. New York: Emerson Hall, 1972.

Looker, Benjamin. *"Point from Which Creation Begins": The Black Artists' Group of St. Louis*. Chicago: University of Chicago Press, 2004.

Lorde, Audre. "Age, Race, Class, and Sex: Women Redefining Difference." *Sister Outsider: Essays and Speeches*. Freedom, CA: Crossing Press, 1984. 114–23.

Lorde, Audre. "Uses of the Erotic: The Erotic as Power." *Sister Outsider: Essays and Speeches*. Freedom, CA: Crossing Press, 1984. 53–59.

Lordi, Emily J. *Black Resonance: Iconic Women Singers and African American Literature*. New Brunswick, NJ: Rutgers University Press, 2013.

Lowney, John. *History, Memory, and the Literary Left: Modern American Poetry, 1935–1968*. Iowa City: University of Iowa Press, 2006.

Lynch, Kevin. "Cecil Taylor and the Poetics of Living." *Down Beat* 53, no. 11 (November 1986): 22–24, 67.

Mackey, Nathaniel. *Atet A.D.* San Francisco: City Lights, 2001.

Mackey, Nathaniel. *Bass Cathedral*. New York: New Directions, 2008.

Mackey, Nathaniel. *Blue Fasa*. New York: New Directions, 2015.

Mackey, Nathaniel. "Expanding the Repertoire." *Tripwire* 5 (Fall 2001): 7–10.

Mackey, Nathaniel. *Late Arcade*. San Francisco: City Lights, 2017.

Mackey, Nathaniel. *Paracritical Hinge: Essays, Talks, Notes, Interviews*. Madison: University of Wisconsin Press, 2005.

Mackey, Nathaniel. *Splay Anthem*. San Francisco: City Lights, 2006.

Marx, Karl. *Capital, Vol. 1*. Trans. Ben Fowkes. London: Penguin, 1976.

Mathes, Carter. *Imagine the Sound: Experimental African American Literature after Civil Rights*. Minneapolis: University of Minnesota Press, 2015.

McCaffery, Steven. "Voice in Extremis." *Close Listening: Poetry and the Performed Word*. Ed. Charles Bernstein. Oxford: Oxford University Press, 1998. 162–77.

McKittrick, Katherine. "Mathematics Black Life." *Black Scholar* 44, no. 2 (Summer 2014): 16–28.

Melhem, D. H. *Heroism in the New Black Poetry: Introductions and Interviews*. Lexington: University Press of Kentucky, 1990.

Melhem, D. H. "MELUS Profile and Interview: Jayne Cortez." *MELUS* 21, no. 1 (Spring 1996): 71–79.

Millard, Andre. *America on Record: A History of Recorded Sound*. Cambridge: Cambridge University Press, 2003.

Miller, Karl Hagstrom. *Segregating Sounds: Inventing Folk and Pop Music in the Age of Jim Crow*. Durham, NC: Duke University Press, 2010.

Mingus, Charles. "An Open Letter to the Avant-Garde." *Charles Mingus: More Than a Fake Book*. 1973. New York: Jazz Workshop, 1991.

Mingus, Charles. "An Open Letter to Miles Davis." *Down Beat*, November 30, 1955, 12–13.

Mingus, Charles. "What Is a Jazz Composer?" *Charles Mingus: More Than a Fake Book*. 1971. New York: Jazz Workshop, 1991.

Monson, Ingrid. "Doubleness and Jazz Improvisation: Irony, Parody, and Ethnomusicology." *Critical Inquiry* 20, no. 2 (Winter 1994): 283–313.

Moten, Fred. "Blackness and Nothingness (Mysticism in the Flesh)." *South Atlantic Quarterly* 112, no. 4 (2013): 737–80.

Moten, Fred. *In the Break: The Aesthetics of the Black Radical Tradition*. Minneapolis: University of Minnesota Press, 2005.

Moten, Fred. "The New International of Rhythmic Feeling(s)." *Sonic Interventions*. Eds. Sylvia Mieszkowski, Joy Smith, and Marijke de Valck. Amsterdam: Editions Rodopi, 2007. 31–56.

Moten, Fred. *A Poetics of the Undercommons*. Butte, MT: Sputnik & Fizzle, 2016.

Moten, Fred, and Stefano Harney. *The Undercommons: Fugitive Planning and Black Study*. New York: Minor Compositions, 2013.

Mouffe, Chantal. *On the Political*. London: Routledge, 2005.

Murphy, Jeanette Robinson. "The Survival of African Music in America." *Popular Science Monthly* 55 (September 1899): 660–72.

Murray, Albert. *Stomping the Blues*. New York: Da Capo, 1976.

Nash, Jennifer C. *The Black Body in Ecstasy: Reading Race, Reading Pornography*. Durham, NC: Duke University Press, 2014.

Neal, Larry. "The Black Arts Movement." *Drama Review: TDR* 12, no. 4 (Summer 1968): 28–39.

Neal, Larry. "The Black Contribution to American Letters: Part II, The Writer as Activist 1960 and After." *The Black American Reference Book*. Ed. Mabel M. Smythe. Englewood Cliffs, NJ: Prentice Hall, 1976. 767–90.

Neal, Larry. "Black Revolution in Music: A Talk with Drummer Milford Graves." *Liberator* (September 1965): 14–15.

Neal, Larry. "And Shine Swam On." *Black Fire: An Anthology of Afro-American Writing*. Eds. Amiri Baraka and Larry Neal. 1968. Baltimore: Black Classic Press, 2007. 638–56.

Neal, Lawrence P. "The Black Musician in White America." *Negro Digest* 16, no. 5 (March 1967): 53–57.

Neal, Lawrence P. "A Conversation with Archie Shepp." *Liberator* 5, no. 11 (November 1965): 24–25.

Ngai, Sianne. *Ugly Feelings*. Cambridge, MA: Harvard University Press, 2005.

Nielsen, Aldon Lynn. *Black Chant: The Languages of Black Postmodernity*. Cambridge: Cambridge University Press, 1997.

Nielsen, Aldon Lynn. "Capillary Currents: Jayne Cortez." *We Who Love to Be Astonished: Experimental Women's Writing and Performance Poetics*. Eds. Laura Hinton and Cynthia Hogue. Tuscaloosa: University of Alabama Press, 2002. 227–35.

Nielsen, Aldon Lynn. "Now Is the Time: Voicing Against the Grain of Orality." *People Get Ready: The Future of Jazz Is Now!* Eds. Ajay Heble and Rob Wallace. Durham, NC: Duke University Press, 2013. 31–43.

Novak, Julia. *Live Poetry: An Integrated Approach to Poetry in Performance*. Amsterdam: Rodopi, 2011.

Okiji, Fumi. *Jazz as Critique: Adorno and Black Expression Reconsidered*. Stanford, CA: Stanford University Press, 2018.

Ongiri, Amy Abugo. *Spectacular Blackness: The Cultural Politics of the Black Power Movement and the Search for a Black Aesthetic*. Charlottesville: University of Virginia Press, 2010.

Parks, Suzan-Lori. *The America Play and Other Plays*. New York: Theater Company Group, 1994.

Parry, Sarah. "The LP Era: Voice-Practice/Voice Document." *ESC* 33, no. 4 (December 2007): 169–80.

Patterson, Anita. "Jazz, Realism, and the Modernist Lyric: The Poetry of Langston Hughes." *MLQ: Modern Language Quarterly* 61, no. 4 (December 2000): 651–82.

Porter, Eric. "Jeanne Lee's Voice." *People Get Ready: The Future of Jazz Is Now!* Eds. Ajay Heble and Rob Wallace. Durham, NC: Duke University Press, 2013. 88–110.

Porter, Eric. *What Is This Thing Called Jazz?: African American Musicians as Artists, Critics, and Activists*. Berkeley: University of California Press, 2002.

Priestley, Brian. *Mingus: A Critical Biography*. New York: Da Capo Press, 1982.

Radano, Ron. *New Musical Figurations: Anthony Braxton's Cultural Critique*. Chicago: University of Chicago Press, 1993.

Rambsy II, Howard. *The Black Arts Enterprise and the Production of African American Poetry*. Ann Arbor: University of Michigan Press, 2013.

Rampersad, Arnold. *The Life of Langston Hughes, Vol. II: 1941–1967 I Dream a World*. Oxford: Oxford University Press, 2002.

Rancière, Jacques. *Disagreement: Politics and Philosophy*. Trans. Julie Rose. Minneapolis: University of Minnesota Press, 1999.

Rancière, Jacques. *The Politics of Aesthetics: The Distribution of the Sensible*. Trans. Gabriel Rockhill. London: Continuum, 2004.

Rando, David. *Hope and Wish Image in Music Technology*. Basingstoke, UK: Palgrave Macmillan, 2017.

Rasula, Jed. "The Media of Memory: The Seductive Menace of Records in Jazz History." *Jazz Among the Discourses*. Ed. Krin Gabbard. Durham, NC: Duke University Press, 1995: 134–62.

Reed, Adolph. "Black Particularity Reconsidered." *Telos* 39 (March 1979): 71–93.

Reed, Adolph. "Unraveling the Relation of Race and Class in American Politics." *Political Power and Social Theory* 15, no. 264 (2002): 265–74.

Reed, Adolph. "What Are the Drums Saying, Booker?: The Current Crisis of the Black Intellectual." *Village Voice*, April 11, 1995, 31–36. Reprinted in *Class Notes: Posing As Politics and Other Thoughts on the American Scene*. New York: New Press, 2001.

Reed, Anthony. *Freedom Time: The Poetics and Politics of Black Experimental Writing*. Baltimore: Johns Hopkins University Press, 2014.

Riggins, Roger. "Jeanne Lee." *Coda* 1 (February 1979): 4-5.
Roberts, Matana. "Artistic Statement." Matanaroberts.com. Accessed June 8, 2019.
Roberts, Matana. "Below the Radar 15." *Wire.* https://www.thewire.co.uk/audio/btr/below-the-radar-15/15. Accessed June 8, 2019.
Roberts, Matana. "Keeping on . . ." *Critical Studies in Improvisation/Études critiques en improvisation* 6, no. 2 (2010): 1.
Roberts, Matana, and Jason Moran. "Coin Coin Recollections." *Loop* 1 (2016): 46-60.
Robinson, Cedric. *Black Marxism: The Making of the Black Radical Tradition*. 1983. Chapel Hill: University of North Carolina Press, 2000.
Rubin, Joan Shelley. *Songs of Ourselves: The Uses of Poetry in America*. Cambridge, MA: Harvard University Press, 2010.
Rusch, Robert D. *Jazztalk: The Cadence Interviews*. New York: Lyle Stuart, 1984.
Sanchez, Sonia. "A Letter to Dr. Martin Luther King, Jr." *Homegirls and Handgrenades*. New York: Thunder's Mouth Press, 1984. 69.
Santoro, Gene. *Myself When I Am Real: The Life and Music of Charles Mingus*. Oxford: Oxford University Press, 2000.
Saul, Scott. *Freedom Is, Freedom Ain't: Jazz and the Making of the Sixties*. Cambridge, MA: Harvard University Press, 2003.
Schultz, Kathy Lou. *The Afro-Modernist Epic and Literary History: Tolson, Hughes, Baraka*. New York: Palgrave Macmillan, 2012.
Schwarz, David. *Listening Subjects: Music, Psychoanalysis, Culture*. Durham, NC: Duke University Press, 1997.
Scott, David. *Conscripts of Modernity: The Tragedy of Colonial Enlightenment*. Durham, NC: Duke University Press, 2004.
Scott, David. "The Temporality of Generations: Dialogue, Tradition, Criticism." *New Literary History* 45, no. 2 (Spring 2014): 157-81.
Sedgwick, Eve Kosofsky. *Between Men: English Literature and Male Homosocial Desire*. New York: Columbia University Press, 1993.
Shepp, Archie. "An Artist Speaks Bluntly." *Down Beat* (December 1965): 11.
Simanga, Michael. *Amiri Baraka and the Congress of African People: History and Memory*. New York: Palgrave, 2015.
Small, Christopher. *Music of the Common Tongue: Survival and Celebration in Afro-American Music*. London: John Calder Publishers, 1987.
Small, Christopher. *Musicking: The Meanings of Performing and Listening*. Middletown, CT: Wesleyan University Press, 1998.
Smethurst, James. *The Black Arts Movement: Literary Nationalism in the 1960s and 1970s*. Chapel Hill: University of North Carolina Press, 2006.
Smethurst, James. "'Don't Say Goodbye to the Porkpie Hat': Langston Hughes, the Left, and the Black Arts Movement." *Callaloo* 24, no. 4 (Fall 2002): 1224-37.
Smethurst, James. *The New Red Negro: The Literary Left and African American Poetry, 1930-1946*. Oxford: Oxford University Press, 1999.
Smith, Jacob. *Spoken Word: Postwar American Phonograph Cultures*. Berkeley: University of California Press, 2011.
Sollors, Werner. *Amiri Baraka/LeRoi Jones: The Quest for a "Populist Modernism."* New York: Columbia University Press, 1979.

Somaini, Antonio. "Walter Benjamin's Media Theory: The *Medium* and the *Apparat.*" *Grey Room* 62 (Winter 2016): 6–41.
Somers-Willett, Susan B. A. *The Cultural Politics of Slam Poetry.* Ann Arbor: University of Michigan Press, 2009.
Spellman, A. B. *Four Lives in the Bebop Business.* 1966. New York: Limelight Editions, 1994.
Spicer, Daniel. "Chains of the Heart." *Wire* 356 (October 2013): 34–41.
Spillers, Hortense, J. *Black, White, and in Color: Essays on American Literature and Culture.* Chicago: University of Chicago Press, 2003.
Spivak, Gayatri Chakravorty. *A Critique of Postcolonial Reason: Toward a History of the Vanishing Present.* Cambridge, MA: Harvard University Press, 1999.
Spivak, Gayatri Chakravorty. "Scattered Speculations on the Question of Value." In *Other Worlds: Essays in Cultural Politics.* New York: Routledge, 1988. 154–75.
Spivak, Gayatri Chakravorty. "Scattered Speculations on the Subaltern and the Popular." *Postcolonial Studies* 8, no. 4 (2005): 475–86.
Sterne, Jonathan. *The Audible Past: Cultural Origins of Sound Reproduction.* Durham, NC: Duke University Press, 2003.
Stewart, Susan. *On Longing: Narratives of the Miniature, the Gigantic, the Souvenir, the Collection.* Durham, NC: Duke University Press, 1993.
Stoever, Jennifer. *The Sonic Color Line: Race and the Cultural Politics of Listening.* New York: New York University Press, 2016.
Such, David. *Avant-Garde Jazz Musicians: Performing Out There.* Iowa City: University of Iowa Press, 1993.
Suisman, David. *Selling Sounds: The Commercial Revolution in American Music.* Cambridge, MA: Harvard University Press, 2009.
Sukenick, Ronald. *Down and In: Life in the Underground.* New York: William Morrow, 1987.
Szwed, John. *Space Is the Place: The Lives and Times of Sun Ra.* New York: Pantheon Books, 1997.
Taylor, Cecil. "With Cecil Taylor." April 2012. https://issueprojectroom.org/news/cecil-taylor. Accessed November 25, 2019.
Thomas, Lorenzo. "Ascension: Music and the Black Arts Movement." *Jazz Among the Discourses.* Ed. Krin Gabbard. Durham, NC: Duke University Press, 1995. 256–74.
Toomer, Jean. *The Wayward and the Seeking: A Collection of Writings by Jean Toomer.* Ed. Darwin M. Turner. Washington, DC: Howard University Press, 1980.
Tracy, Steven C. *Langston Hughes and the Blues.* Urbana: University of Illinois Press, 1988.
Trouillot, Michel-Rolph. "The Otherwise Modern: Caribbean Lessons from the Savage Slot." *Critically Modern: Alternatives, Alterities, Anthropologies.* Ed. Bruce M. Knauft. Bloomington: Indiana University Press, 2002. 220–37.
Tucker, Sherrie. "Bordering on Community: Improvising Women Improvising Women-in-Jazz." *The Other Side of Nowhere: Jazz, Improvisation, and Communities in Dialogue.* Eds. Daniel Fischlin and Ajay Heble. Middletown, CT: Wesleyan University Press, 2004. 244–67.
Tucker, Sherrie. "Deconstructing the Jazz Tradition." *Jazz/Not Jazz: The Music and Its Boundaries.* Eds. David Ake, Charles Hiroshi Garrett, and Daniel Goldmark. Berkeley: University of California Press, 2012.
Tynan, John. "Take Five." *Down Beat,* November 23, 1961, 40.

Washington, Mary Helen. *The Other Black List: The African American Literary and Cultural Left of the 1950s*. New York: Columbia University Press, 2014.

Watts, Jerry Gafio. *Amiri Baraka: The Politics and Art of a Black Intellectual*. New York: New York University Press, 2001.

Weheliye, Alexander. *Phonographies: The Grooves of Sonic Afro-Modernity*. Durham, NC: Duke University Press, 2005.

Weiss, Jason. *Always in Trouble: An Oral History of ESP-Disk, the Most Outrageous Record Label in America*. Middletown, CT: Wesleyan University Press, 2012.

Westendorf, Lynette. "Cecil Taylor: Indent—'Second Layer.'" *Perspectives of New Music* 33, nos. 1/2 (Winter-Summer 1995): 294–326.

Wheeler, Lesley. *Voicing American Poetry: Sound and Performance from the 1920s to the Present*. Ithaca, NY: Cornell University Press, 2008.

White, Simone. *Dear Angel of Death*. Brooklyn, NY: Ugly Duckling Presse, 2019.

Williams, Alan. "Is Sound Recording like a Language?" *Yale French Studies* 60 (1980): 51–66.

Williams, Raymond. *Politics and Letters: Interviews with New Left Review*. London: Verso, 2015.

Williams, Sherley Anne. *Give Birth to Brightness: A Thematic Study in Neo-Black Literature*. New York: Dial Press, 1972.

Wilmer, Valerie. *As Serious as Your Life: John Coltrane and Beyond*. New York: Da Capo Press, 1977.

Woodard, Komozi. *A Nation Within a Nation: Amiri Baraka (LeRoi Jones) and Black Power Politics*. Chapel Hill: University of North Carolina Press, 1999.

Woodson, Carter G. "*Jim Crow's Last Stand* by Langston Hughes." *Journal of Negro History* 28, no. 4 (October 1943): 493-94.

Wynter, Sylvia. "Ethno or Socio Poetics." *Alcheringa: Ethnopoetics*. Eds. Michael Benamou and Jerome Rothenberg. Boston: Boston University Press, 1976. 78–94.

Wynter, Sylvia. "Rethinking 'Aesthetics': Notes Toward a Deciphering Practice." *Ex-Iles: Essays on Caribbean Cinema*. Ed. Mbaye M. Cham. Trenton, NJ: Africa World Press, 1992. 237–79.

Wynter, Sylvia. "Unsettling the Coloniality of Being/Power/Truth/Freedom: Towards the Human, After Man, Its Overrepresentation—An Argument." *CR: The New Centennial Review* 3, no. 3 (Fall 2003): 257–337.

Young, Cynthia. *Soul Power: Culture, Radicalism, and the Making of a U.S. Third World Left*. Durham, NC: Duke University Press, 2006.

Young, Robert. "Red Poetics and the Practice of 'Disalienation.'" *Montage of a Dream: The Art and Life of Langston Hughes*. Eds. John Edgar Tidwell and Cheryl Ragar. Columbia: University of Missouri Press, 2007. 135-46.

RECORDINGS AND LINER NOTES

Art Ensemble of Chicago. *We Are on the Edge*. Pi Recordings, 2019. CD.

Baraka, Amiri. Liner notes. John Coltrane, *Live from Birdland*. Impulse!, 1964. LP.

Baraka, Amiri. "You Think This Is About You?" Liner notes. Albert Ayler, *Holy Ghost: Rare and Unissued Recordings (1962-1970)*. Revenant, 2004. CD.

Baraka, Amiri, with David Murray and Steve McCall. *New Music—New Poetry*. India Navigation, 1982. LP.

Blythe, Arthur. *In the Tradition*. Columbia, 1979. LP.

Brown, Marion. *Afternoon of a Georgia Faun*. ECM, 1970. LP.
Cherry, Don. *Complete Communion*. Blue Note, 1966. LP.
Coleman, Steve. *Sonic Language of Myth: Believing, Learning, Knowing*. RCA Victor, 1999. CD.
Cortez, Jayne. *Maintain Control*. Bola Press, 1986. LP.
Cortez, Jayne. *There It Is*. Bola Press, 1986. LP.
Cyrille, Andrew, Jimmy Lyons, and Jeanne Lee. *Nuba*. Black Saint, 1979. LP.
Cyrille, Andrew. *Celebration*. IPS Records, 1975. LP.
Harper, Billy. *Blueprints of Jazz, Vol. 2*. Talking House Records, 2008. CD.
Hemphill, Julius. *Coon Bid'ness*. Arista Freedom, 1975. LP.
Hentoff, Nat. Liner notes. Archie Shepp, *Fire Music*. Impulse!, 1965. LP.
Hentoff, Nat. Liner notes. Cecil Taylor, *Cecil Taylor: In Transition*. Blue Note, 1975. LP.
Hughes, Langston. *Weary Blues*. 1958. Verve, 1990. CD.
Jost, Ekkerhard. "Instant Composing as Body Language." Liner notes. Cecil Taylor, *The Complete Cecil Taylor in Berlin '88*. FMP, 2015. CD.
Lee, Jeanne. *Conspiracy*. Earthforms Records, 1975. LP.
Mingus, Charles. *A Modern Jazz Symposium of Music and Poetry with Charlie Mingus*. Bethlehem, 1957. LP.
Mingus, Charles. *Ah Um*. Columbia, 1959. LP.
Mingus, Charles. *Blues and Roots*. Atlantic, 1960. LP.
Mingus, Charles. *Charles Mingus Presents Charles Mingus*. Candid, 1961. LP.
Mingus, Charles. *Pithecanthropus Erectus*. Atlantic, 1956. LP.
Mingus, Charles. *The Charles Mingus Quintet Plus Max Roach*. Debut, 1955. LP.
Mingus, Charles. *Town Hall Concert, 1964, Vol. 1*. Jazz Workshop, 1964. LP.
Moran, Jason. *Bandwagon*. Blue Note, 2003. CD.
Murray, David. *Fo Deuk Revue*. Justin Time, 1997. CD.
New York Art Quartet. *New York Art Quartet*. ESP-Disk, 1964. LP.
New York Art Quartet. *Reunion*. DIW Records, 2000. CD.
Parker, William. *I Plan to Stay a Believer: The Inside Songs of Curtis Mayfield*. AUM Fidelity, 2010. CD.
Ragin, Hugh. *An Afternoon in Harlem*. Justin Time, 1999. CD.
Richards, Spencer. Liner notes. Cecil Taylor, *Live in Vienna*. Leo, 1988. CD.
Roberts, Matana. *Coin Coin Chapter One: Gens de couleur libres*. Constellation Records, 2011. CD.
Roberts, Matana. *Coin Coin Chapter Two: Mississippi Moonchile*. Constellation Records, 2013. CD.
Roberts, Matana. *Coin Coin Chapter Three: River Run Thee*. Constellation Records, 2015. CD.
Sanders, Pharoah. *Journey to the One*. Theresa, 1980. LP.
Shepp, Archie. *The Cry of My People*. Impulse!, 1972. LP.
Shepp, Archie. *Live at the Pan-African Festival*. BYG Actuel, 1969. LP.
Shepp, Archie. *The Magic of Ju-Ju*. Impulse!, 1967. LP.
Shepp, Archie. *Poem for Malcolm*. BYG Actuel, 1969.
Shepp, Archie. *Rufus*. Fontana, 1963. LP.
Taylor, Cecil. "Sound of Subculture Becoming Major Breath/Naked Fire Gesture." Liner notes. Cecil Taylor, *Unit Structures*. Blue Note, 1966. LP.
Taylor, Cecil. *Double Holy House*. FMP, 1993. CD.

Taylor, Cecil. Liner notes. Cecil Taylor, *Air Above Mountains (Buildings Within)*. Enja Records, 1976. LP.

Taylor, Cecil. Liner notes. Cecil Taylor, *Garden*, vol. 1. Hat ART, 1990. CD.

The Roots featuring Amiri Baraka. "Something in the Way of Things (In Town)." *Phrenology*. MCA, 2002. CD.

Thompson, Malachi. *Freebob Now!* Delmark, 1998. CD.

Weston, Randy. *Uhuru Afrika*. Roulette, 1961. LP.

Young, Ben. Liner notes. Charles Mingus, *Tijuana Moods*. 1957. Bluebird, 2001. CD.

Index

abjection, racial, 12, 74, 108, 125, 138, 140, 153, 178
abolition/abolitionism, 16-17, 32-34
Abrams, Muhal Richard, 35, 54
abstraction, 90, 152, 159-61; "black" as, 66, 130-31; counter-abstraction, 133; of the self, 148, 154
Adams, Brooks, 38
Adorno, Theodor W., 24, 111, 119, 186, 191, 217n36, 225n10; music as writing, concern about, 13, 194, 232n38
Advanced Workers, 126
aesthetic production, 3, 41, 75, 128-29, 131; Baraka's periods of, 104-5, 107, 114
aesthetics, 3-7; autonomy of, 18; constitutive, 167; excess, 6, 12, 175; hybrid orientation of, 172; Marxist, 7, 106, 107; neutralization of, 69, 74, 106-7, 159, 183, 187; surface/depth models of, 145, 153; values and, 39, 114, 140, 149; Western, 7, 39-40, 111. *See also* black aesthetics
affiliation, 32, 57-58, 89, 110
affirmation, 8, 59, 66, 71, 78, 112-13, 117
Africa, popular understandings of, 134
African ancestrality, 34-35
African music, survival of as system, 37-38
"African retentions," 128
afro-modernity, 8, 27
Agawu, Kofi, 168-69
agency, 64, 89-90, 129, 138; context for, 159-60; extra- or non-subjective, 154; institutions and, 5, 24, 207n14
agonistic, the, 6-7, 74, 108, 145-46, 149, 169-70
Aidoo, Ama Ata, 185
Alexander, Elizabeth, 27

Algerian War of Independence, 153
alienation, 96-100, 187-88; of black women from motherhood, 152; church and, 99-100; dialectical images and, 96, 213n89; and disalienation, 68, 170, 187-89, 194
allegory, 4, 32, 62, 79, 114-15, 159, 174, 188-89
Allen, Henry "Red," 92
alterity, 29, 129, 151, 213n76, 225n16
alter-native, 90, 213n76
Althusser, Louis, 196n16
ambivalence, 6-7, 12, 174; Baraka and, 36-38, 104, 109, 119, 121, 123, 125, 129, 138-40, 218n42; celebration as method for managing, 59; of "liberation," 45, 109, 172-73; Mingus and, 88-91, 210n44; political, 140; in relationship of black sound with capitalism, 32-33; toward domestic institutions, 56
America, as hemispheric, 209n32
Amram, David, 72, 74
analogy, 3-4, 91, 196n8, 198n29, 201n2, 206n82; Baraka and, 111, 114; "exchange-time," 21; gendered, 86; and syllepsis, 189-90; of writing to recording, 33
"anarchic regard," 141
anarchist-inflected imagination, 6, 107, 113, 127, 196n10
Anderson, Fred, 54
antagonisms, 15, 19-20, 24, 38; and "antagonistic cooperation," 74; and "antagonistic liberation," 74; class-related, 10, 106, 188-89; individualism as solution to racial, 113, 126; in-group, 66; management of, 26; racial, 113, 118, 126, 174; social, 24, 26, 97, 129; and Third World, capitalist casualties, 131-32

anticipatory, the, 17, 121–22, 124, 190; jazz as, 61, 75, 91; and poetics of black communism, 75
anti-collective politics, 28, 30, 50
anti-colonial movements, 67, 178, 197n24
Anti-Imperialist Singers, 126
anti-institutional practices, 66–67, 72, 95, 126–27
appropriation: of neutralized aesthetic content, 69; reappropriation, 10–11, 34, 69, 133, 152; of slave song, 32–34
Armstrong, Louis, 78, 97
Art Ensemble of Chicago, 1–2, 21, 120, 211n54
articulacy, 45
Artist in Residence (Moran), 182–83
art/non-art boundary, 162
association complexes, 137
Association for the Advancement of Creative Musicians (AACM), 49, 54
Atlantic Records, 70, 76
Attali, Jacques, 21
Attica Prison uprising, 79
audience, 30–34, 47; black, 19, 70; cultivation of, 183–85, 221n9; line between performer and, 167; middle-class, female-identified, 50–51, 53; nonsynchronous, 52–53; and pedagogical introduction to jazz, 84–85; vibration societies, 182, 189; and "we," 2, 141, 150, 159, 167, 182, 189
authenticity, 36, 40, 49, 55, 70, 129; Mingus and, 89–90
authoritarian populism, 129
autonomy: aesthetic and political, 18, 109, 183–85; of listening, 21, 84; relative, 18, 118, 128, 199n45; of voice, 46
avant-garde, 5–6; black art as permanent, 113; Euro-international tradition of, 175; "intervernacular," 53; neutralized aesthetic content and, 69; popular, 10–11, 197n26; white, 5, 116. *See also* vernacular avant-garde
Ayler, Albert, 37, 115, 116, 118

Baker, Ella, 185
Baker, Houston, 223n111, 227n29
Baldwin, James, 27
Bambara, Toni Cade, 190
Banjo (McKay), 35
Baraka, Amiri, 2, 6, 103–41; and alternative black institution-building projects, 106–10; artist's stance, view of, 108, 134; "Beat" period of, 104, 105, 124; and black sound as unified whole, 37–38; critiques of, 216nn10–11; Cuba, trip to, 116, 124; cultural nationalist period of, 104, 106, 126, 130, 135; dimensions of invention in, 119–25; Ellison, debate with, 113–15, 218n49, 218n48; "here in the world" concept of, 115–19, 141; jazz criticism by, 110–12; middle class, view of, 107–8, 117–19, 136, 186–87, 218n39; Moten's discussion of, 17, 212, 228n47; nation-state, view of, 108, 110, 112, 114, 118–19, 126; Obama, commentary on, 181; optimism in, 125, 140; and poetics of liberation, 109–15; political activism of, 216n22, 220n78; reading style of, 120, 124; recorded sound, commitment to, 36–37, 105, 115; reification, concern with, 119–20, 122, 124–25; as revenant, 118, 135; revolutionary in thought of, 103–6, 111, 115, 117–19, 122–25, 135–36; temporality in work of, 103–4, 106–8, 118, 121, 123, 134–35, 140; Third World Marxist period and, 104–6, 126; voice, view of, 23, 27–28, 45–46; wit, use of, 136–37; work of negativity in thought of, 130–31; Works: "Afro-American Literature and Class Struggle," 218n49; "Against Bourgeois Art," 130, 131; *Black and Beautiful . . . Soul and Madness*, 126; "Black Art," 106, 115–20; "Black Dada Nihilismus," 115, 119–25, 137, 139, 220n78; *Black Magic: Poetry 1961–1967*, 106; *Black Music*, 23, 117; *Blues People*, 37, 110–14, 117, 218n42, 218n48; 231n9; "The Changing Same," 103; "Class Struggle in Music," 119, 131–34, 136; *The Dead Lecturer*, 120, 124; "Funk Lore," 103–4; "Heathens and Space/Time Projection," 138; "In the Tradition," 131, 222n101; *It's Nation Time/African Visionary Music*, 126; "Jazz and the White Critic," 111; "Ka 'Ba," 106; "Masked Angel Costume: The Sayings of Mantan Moreland," 137–38; *New Music—New Poetry*, 131–34, 136; "A Poem for Willie Best," 125; "The Revolutionary Theatre," 104, 105; "Seek Light at Once," 137–41; "S O S," 130, 140–41; *In the Tradition*, 105, 127; "You Was Dancin Need to Be Marchin So You Can Dance Some More Later On," 126, 215n5, 221n82. *See also* revolutionary, the
Barthes, Roland, 41, 145, 150
Bartlett, Andrew, 158
Bartók, Béla, 158–59
Baudelaire, Charles, 107
Beats, 5, 12, 208n31, 208n31; Baraka and, 104, 105
Beau, Chico, 177
bebop, 65, 72, 88
Beneath the Underdog (Mingus), 73, 87–89
Benjamin, Walter, 7, 32, 53–54, 107, 206n82, 213n89; and "dialectical images," 96
Bennett, Gwendolyn, 35
Benston, Kimberly, 124

Berlant, Lauren, 3, 140, 179, 216n18
"Bid 'em In" (Brown), 59
Birmingham, 16th Street Baptist Church bombing, 139
black aesthetics, 3, 9, 172, 218n49, 226–27n29; aesthetic component of, 51; as generation, 153–54; idealist vs. materialist, 20; institutions and, 45; integration arguments and, 36, 51–52; mainstream press and legitimate range of, 135; meanings and obligations of, 114; New Black Aesthetic, 187, 203n37; as political project, 153; radical, 60, 107, 129; riotous within, 9–10, 16–17, 20, 22, 90; as thingliness, 68, 117
"Black Art" (Baraka/Murray), 106, 115–20; invention and inventory in, 115, 117; norms decentered in, 115–16; "reflection" in, 116–17; sociality and the invaluable in, 117–18
Black Arts era (late 1950s through mid-1970s), 3, 39, 47, 195n4; collectivity, commitment to, 58, 153, 171–73, 185–86; contemporary turn to, 5, 182; freedom in context of, 109–10; leadership, critiques of, 205n66; poetry of, 51; processes within texts, 41; shifts in social organization, 144–45; simplification of black power, 60, 203n37; as "undisciplined," 26. *See also* Baraka, Amiri; Black Power; Hughes, Langston; Lee, Jeanne; Mingus, Charles; Shepp, Archie
black communism, 17, 184; poetics of, 67–69, 68, 71, 72–76, 93, 102; property, critique of, 67; Taylor as figure of, 158; undercommons and, 67–72. *See also* Hughes, Langston; Mingus, Charles
black convention movement, 215n5, 216n22
"Black Dada Nihilismus" (Baraka/New York Art Quartet), 115, 119–25, 137, 139, 220n78; anticipatory loss in, 121; "free time" in, 123; inventory in, 119, 122–23, 125; printed version of, 120; sections of, 121–23; subjectivity in, 122–25
"black excellence," 74
Black Liberation struggles, 24, 67, 129, 137, 173, 178
Black Music (Baraka), 23, 117
blackness: aesthetic component of, 51; as alternative to capitalist modernity, 130; anti-political social contract and, 132; commitment to, 145–46; commodification of, 128; as commodity, 36; destabilizing capacity of, 3, 13, 67, 154; as form of racialization, 17; heterogeneity of, 136; intuitive accounts of, 38; life evacuated from, 55; limitations of as parapolitical formation, 60; lived experience of, 3, 149, 151; market, proximity to of, 117; meanings of, 9, 13, 34–39, 67, 119; mystification and, 96; as name or site,

106; postwar class reorganization and, 39; revaluation of, 5, 30, 125; revolutionary, 39, 54–55, 58–60; rhythm as problematic marker of, 133–34; as social relation, 13–14, 187; as unassimilable, 71, 112, 136; uncertain status of, 115
Black Panther Party, 128, 205n70
Black Power, 173, 205n66; Baraka and, 126–27, 136–38; defeat/exhaustion of, 6, 126, 128, 132; opening provided by, 110; Shepp and, 47–49, 203n37. *See also* Black Arts era (late 1950s through mid-1970s)
black sound, 196–n16; affirmation and, 59; alternative principles of aesthetic structuration in, 153; ambiguous position of, 68; appropriation of, 32–33; circulation of, 4, 8, 12, 20, 22, 31–36; as concept, 23; definitions, 31; disarticulated from media, 35; as discrete object, 46; discursively and textually mediated, 52, 58; discussions within, 31; ethnographic recording, 11; as extra-discursive, 23; fetishization of, 22, 24; freedom, drive toward, 30; genealogy of, 31–41; as historically specific, 5, 8–9; learning to listen to, 2–3; legitimation of, 32; meaning borne by, 32, 39, 60; as medium of transformative energy, 38; as negotiation of "feeling of unwanted feeling," 30; obscured colonial relations in, 12, 107–8; as occult knowledge, 31, 43; as outside Western logic of "thing," 38; persistence of, 10, 25, 31; practices of, 3, 8, 14, 18–20, 23, 32; as proxy for thinking about black community, 32–39; reactive interpretations of, 24; as set of aesthetic practices, 3, 30; as set of relations, 14, 59; textuality of, 23–26; as theoretical object, 8, 32, 194; trouble, tradition of, 190; as unified whole, 37–38; "vibration societies," 182, 189. *See also* circulation of black sound; experimental sound practices; New Black Music; soundwork
black studies, 212n68, 67, 126
black (sound) studies, 22, 67, 196n16
Black Swan Records, 112, 185, 219n49, 231n9
Blanton, Jimmy, 84
"Blasé" (Shepp/Lee), 176–79
blues, 50, 61, 70, 81–83, 177–78; affect, organizing vs. habitually associated, 190; bad luck theme in, 83; as resource, 150
Blues and Roots (Mingus), 70, 98–99, 214n91
Blythe, Arthur, 131
body, 225n16; centrality of body to time, 168; language and singularity of, 166; mother's, 150–51, 178–79; as text, 40; voice and, 167–68. *See also* embodied practice; embodiment

INDEX / 253

Bolden, Tony, 40, 187–88
bossa nova, 50, 53
Bourdieu, Pierre, 50
bourgeois ideology and values, 6, 49; "equal access," 48, 76; masculinity, 94, 101; property and propriety, 16–17; transmitted through recordings, 12, 21
Boyd, Melba Joyce, 185
Brown, Birmingham (character), 137–40
Brown, James, 40
Brown, Marion, 172; Works: *Afternoon of a Georgia Faun*, 175–76; "Djinji's Corner," 175–76
Brown, Oscar, Jr., 59
Brown, Sterling, 36
Brubeck, Dave, 83
Burrell, Dave, 176, 177–78
Butler, Judith, 151, 152
Byrd, Donald, 45

"Call It Stormy Monday" (Walker), 95
capitalism: accumulation by dispossession, 49; alternative forms of value, 20, 117; "black," 173–74; black performance in context of, 113–14; black protest as spectacle of, 50, 127–28; black sound in ambivalent relationship with, 32–33; black sound in opposition to, 38; circuit of production in, 27; community dissolution due to, 121, 129, 131; as dependent on social antagonism, 10, 129, 131–32; and freedom, forms of, 16–17; genres of experience and politics excluded from, 68–69; institutions and, 45; personhood and, 16–17, 123–24; and social organization, 6. *See also* modernity
capitalist modernity, 20, 38, 71, 106, 130, 213n76
Carby, Hazel V., 95–96, 118, 135, 214n98, 223n113
Carmichael, Thomas, 89
celebration of black life, 53–60
Césaire, Aimé, 96, 187
Chandler, Nahum, 199n37
Cherry, Don, 115, 116, 118, 146
Chicago Defender, 67, 70, 72, 208n31
Christian, Barbara, 193
church, black, 99–100, 117
circle, 32–36, 58, 87–88, 149
circulation of black sound, 4, 8, 12, 20, 22, 31–36, 199n34; collective subject created by, 132–33; hermeneutic, 35; speed of, for recorded material, 42. *See also* black sound
Civil Rights Movement, 3, 24, 48, 73, 99; and contingent coalitions, 75–76; as Freedom Movement, 110, 114

class essentialism, 50–51, 132
"classical" music, 113
class issues, 7, 10, 39, 46–48, 68. *See also* middle class
"Class Struggle in Music I and II" (Baraka), 119, 131–34, 136
Coincoin, Marie Thérèse, 55–56, 59
Coin Coin series (Roberts), 53–60, 206n82; *Gens de couleur libres*, 54–60; "I Am," 57; and "panoramic sound quilting" approach, 55; phonopoems in, 57; "Pov Piti," 57, 58–59; "Rise," 56–57; storytelling as concern in, 58
Cold War, 65, 69–70, 129, 187, 207n11; and legitimate politics, mapping of, 108, 114; and Third World as site of capitalist antagonisms, 131–32
Cole, Bill, 193
Coleman, Denardo, 186, 188
Coleman, Ornette, 1, 16, 44, 116, 150; Mingus's view of, 88, 89; Prime Time band, 186, 191; Works: *Free Jazz*, 109; "When Will the Blues Leave," 172
Coleman, Steve, 29–30
collaborations between poets and musicians, 4–5, 17–18; alternative forms of value created by, 20, 69, 107–8, 143–48. *See also* phonographic poetry; *and specific artists*
collection, 20–22
collectivity: aesthetic projects of, 14; aspirational/ aspirations to, 3, 8; Black Arts/black aesthetic generation's commitments to, 153, 171–73, 185–86; black counter-public sphere and, 109; calls to as metonymic, 28; contemporary hostility to, 52; enabled by the sonic, 12; first- and second-person address, 136; in henceforward, 28, 174, 230n96; improvisation as commitment to, 143–46, 155, 161, 163; independent labels and artist collectives, 46, 48–49; individuality within, 7; mass culture as, 90; memory of, 107, 108; and "the people," 1; validation by, 89
colonialism: anti-colonial movements, 67, 178, 197n24; neocolonialism, 49, 76, 108; obscured, 12, 107–8; postcolonial context, 7, 145, 149, 181, 193, 197n24
Coltrane, Alice, 116
Coltrane, John, 29, 42, 57, 106, 116; Baraka on, 137; Works: "Alabama," 139; *Live at Birdland*, 110, 139; *A Love Supreme*, 45; *Om*, 45
commodification, 38, 72, 182; Baraka's view of, 119–20, 124–25, 128–29, 134, 136; of black nationalism, 173; reification and, 119–20

commodity: authenticity as, 89; belonging and, 90; blackness as, 36; labor as, 21; minstrel sounds as, 34; records as, 31; time as, 72
commodity culture, 11, 20–21, 67
commodity form, 7, 71, 154, 183
common, the, 199n40; abstractness and, 160; gendering of, 175; improvisation and, 14–17, 41, 71, 145–48, 158–60, 162, 170, 172, 174; "outside," 67; undercommons, 67–72
communal sensibility/spirit, 68, 97, 118
communism: defined, 14; as essence of black radicalism, 17; racial struggles seen as secondary, 109, 217n25; as refusal of bourgeois normativity, 68–69; as speculative frame, 69; as world-making project, 71. *See also* black communism; left
communist-inflected imagination, 6–7, 68, 71, 127
Communist Party of the United States of American (CPUSA), 69
communist poetics, 68, 73, 93, 102
"communities in transition," 62, 75–76
community: artistic, 54–55; as call for abolition of segregation, 69; as conceptual, sociospatial, and sonic space, 69; de- and re-formation, 3–4; enslaved people as, 33–34; historical situation and, 101; Hughes's sense of, 5, 90–94; "imagined," 121; as improvisation, 63; as material and conceptual space, 64; in post-revolutionary age, 126; in Roberts' work, 57–58; textuality and, 13–14; in transition, 62, 75; tropes of, 128–29. *See also* social organization; solidarity
community, black: Baraka's view, 37–38; dissolution of, 10, 129, 131–32; fetishization of, 46, 128–29; as gendered concept, 49; as marginal social life, 14; working-class, 46–47
Complete Communion (Cherry), 116
composition: as framework for interpretive action, 75; improvisation, relationship to, 76–77, 79, 165; "instant composing," 162; Mingus and, 63–64, 76–78; "pencil composers," Western, 78, 79; solos as, 78; sonic structures as, 29–30; spontaneity in, 63–65, 73, 77–80, 83–84, 90, 97–98, 224n6
concrete self, reinvention of, 30, 145, 150, 153–54, 178
concretism, 80, 210n53
Congress of African People (CAP), 104, 215n5, 217n22
consciousness, black, 4, 9, 20, 27–28, 35–36, 100; in Baraka's work, 107, 117, 122; Hughes and, 95–96; practical and popular forms of, 129; Shepp's view of, 42; sound as bearer of, 35; underlying social relationships and material practices of, 27; vernacular avant-garde aesthetics as expression of, 50–51
consciousness, false, 174
"Consider Me" (Hughes), 92, 93–97
conspiracy, 64
"Constructing the Jazz Tradition" (Deveaux), 19
contingency, 19–20
continuity/ongoingness, 13–14, 17, 56, 91, 119, 125, 146; African ancestrality and, 34–35, 52; as illusory, 98; in Mingus's project, 116; of revolutionary aesthetic techniques, 104; semiotic, 163; Taylor's commitment to, 155, 163
"cool jazz," 77
Corbett, John, 150, 168, 226n21
Cortez, Jayne, 181, 185–95; repetition, use of, 191–92; vocal virtuosity of, 189–90, 193; Works: "No Simple Explanations," 190; "There It Is," 188–89, 192; "U.S./Nigeria Relations," 192–93
counter-knowledge, project of, 22
Coursil, Jacques, 150
Crawford, Margo Natalie, 41, 146
Crawley, Ashon, 148
The Crisis of the Negro Intellectual (Cruse), 127, 159
Crouch, Stanley, 135
Cruse, Harold, 126, 128, 159
Cruz, Jon, 32
cultural nationalism, 41–42, 104–6, 126, 130, 172–74, 216n22; rejection of, 135
culture: homogenization of, 198n29; "mass" vs. "high," 10; mystifications of, 132; women's centrality to transmission of, 36
culture, black: as historical, 68; and line between synecdoche and metonymy, 8, 28, 34, 52, 54; as protection against mainline American culture, 113–14
culture industries, 4, 8, 10, 66–67, 121; contradiction of, 63; rap music and, 185; reification and, 119–20, 122, 124–25; space created beyond reach of, 12–13, 46, 49–50, 119, 127; vernacular avant-garde in communication with, 9, 11–12; white commentary class and, 124
Cunard, Nancy, 35
Curson, Ted, 88–89
Cyrille, Andrew, 103, 161

Davey, Elizabeth, 70
Davis, Angela, 50
Davis, Arthur P., 99

INDEX / 255

Davis, Miles, 48, 70, 84
Debord, Guy, 173
Debut Records, 65
decolonization of African world, 5, 87, 131, 149, 153, 221n89
democracy, 99, 230n104; *demos*, black people excluded from, 15, 92; rejection of jazz as resource for, 111; thin, procedural, 187
Denning, Michael, 12, 35, 50, 53, 230n95
Dennis, Kenny, 92
de-orchestration, 39, 163, 187
Derrida, Jacques, 73
destabilization: blackness as, 3, 67, 94, 119; of composition and improvisation, 77, 79; ecstatic voicing and, 166; as intent of U.S. policies, 189; intertextual, 25; repetition and, 191; of Symbolic, 150-51
destructionist approaches, 145
Deveaux, Scott, 19
dialectical images, 96, 213n89
diaspora, African, 100, 112
Dickenson, Vic, 92
disalienation, 68, 187-89
"disappearing culture," 198n29
dispossession, 22, 63, 145, 151, 190; accumulation by, 49, 192; black middle class and, 215n4; social order based on, 71, 81, 107; of unfreedom, 12, 108; voice as sign of, 29
dissemination, 40
dissonance, 6, 28-29, 35, 38, 169-70, 177-79, 189; de-orchestration and reorchestration of, 145, 146
Dixon, Bill, 42
DJ Spooky, 220n70
Dolphy, Eric, 88-89
domination, 51; accumulation by dispossession, 49, 192; counter-rhythms to, 186; direct, erosion of, 6-7, 49; origins of, 129; rap's socio-symbolic, 30; resistance to, 15, 35
Double Holy House (Taylor), 164, 167-170, 179
Douglass, Frederick, 31, 32-34, 35, 49, 149, 201n2; collective metonymized by, 34, 38-39
Du Bois, W. E. B., 31, 34, 47; on nationalism, 34

economic crisis of 1973-74, 130, 159
ecstasy, 9, 144-50, 153, 155-57, 170, 178-79, 229n85; centrality of body and, 166-68; pleasure as retrospective, 149-50; social, 148-49
Edwards, Brent Hayes, 45, 77, 225n10
Elder, Lonne, III, 80-81, 211n57

electoralist politics, 60, 173
elitism, 46, 48, 50
Ellington, Duke, 74, 76, 77, 88, 158
Ellison, Ralph, 27, 97; and "antagonistic cooperation," 74; Baraka, debate with, 113-15, 218n48, 218n49,; nation-state, view of, 114; vernacular, definition of, 10, 197n24
embodied practice, 6, 16, 77, 87; ecstasy and, 144-45; listening as, 99; in musical production, 152-53. *See also* body
embodiment, 143-79; and black alterity, insistence on, 151-52; and black women's bodies, 171; bourgeoisie and, 151; and flesh, concept of, 155, 166-67; and form as possibility, 155-70; and *jouissance*, 147; as process, 152-53; of racial discourses, 170; and reciprocal attunement as a form of play, 144; as social process, 151; of voice, 152, 168. *See also* body
emergence: of African and Caribbean forms of socialism, 6; as ambivalent, 48, 117; of black sound, 4, 24, 27; of conventionality, 86; as inventory, 117; lingering, non-self-identity of groups and, 159; of new technologies, 11-13; processes of, 13, 19-20; of world-making projects, 6-7
énoncé/énonciation, 154
ensemble, 16, 63-64, 73, 110; agonistic forms of, 108-9; as ideal sociality, 4; "solo flight" model of, 110, 146-47
entertainment, logic of rejected, 39
enunciation, 31, 154-55
epidermalization, 151
equal access, 48, 76
Ertegun, Nesuhi, 70, 89
ethnopoetics, 145
Evers, Medgar, 42, 46
Everywhere Drums (Cortez), 185
excess, 29, 75, 144, 151; aesthetic, 6, 12, 175; extra-subjective, 155-56
exchange-time and exchange-value, 20-21, 41
exclusion: of black creators from full civic membership, 132-33; of black people from *demos*, 15, 92; of black people vs. black culture, 67-69; conditions for possibility within, 18-19; in jazz studies, 18-19; masculinity and, 94; of non-refinable forms, 7; of "part that has no part," 15-16; strategic, 18-21, 71, 74; structured, of history, 86; "universality" and, 68; of women, 18, 85, 214n97
exhaustion, black, 6, 25, 55, 126, 128, 132
experience, reimagining of, 143-44

experimental sound practices, 2, 5, 7, 17–18; commercial success and, 48–49; in current era, 182; new audiences for, 50–51; processes within texts, 41; of Roberts, 30. *See also* black sound; soundwork; *and specific artists*

extra-terrestrial, tropes of, 128

Fabio, Sarah Webster, 45
familiar, potentiality within, 2, 9, 50
Fanon, Frantz, 28, 40, 151, 174, 186, 230n96
Farred, Grant, 197n24
Favors, Malachi, 176, 178
Feather, Leonard, 88, 92
feeling, as musico-tactile metaphor, 63
fetishization: of black community, 46, 128–29; of black sound, 22, 24; bourgeois, 193; of "distant listening," 230n95; of "folk," 198n29; of music, 82, 86; of "real woman," 86; of text, 41; of voice, 8
Fields, Barbara, 211n62
Fields, Karen, 211n62
figuration, 3–4
Finn, Julio, 177
Firespitters, 183, 185–95
Fisk Jubilee Singers, 34
Floyd, Samuel, 7
"Foggy Day, A" (Gershwin/Mingus), 80
folk, 12, 87, 90–91, 112, 130; alternative/counter-circulation of, 35–36; Bartók and, 158–59; disappearance of, 36, 198n29; fetishization of, 198n29; Hughes's focus on, 62–63, 66, 68, 90–91
formal strategies, 35, 43, 48–51, 66, 87, 97, 124, 159; innovation, 29, 51, 53, 169
Foucault, Michel, 167, 225n16
freedom, 15–17; and "antagonistic liberation," 74; black maternity as figure for, 152; conceptual dependencies of, 16–17, 123–24; contingent practices of, 110; of free jazz, 45, 144, 146–47, 156–57; human defined in opposition to black, 59; international struggles, 51, 99, 197n20; mainstream interpretations, 6; play as practice of, 74–75; poetics of liberation and, 109; refusals and, 58; unfreedom shapes black life, 12, 30, 55–56, 108, 153; in *Weary Blues*, 91–92. *See also* invention
"Freedom" (Mingus), 75, 99
Freedom Movement (Civil Rights Movement), 110, 114
Freedom Suite (Rollins), 109

free jazz, 10–11, 18, 25–26, 115–16, 118, 143–79; affective solidarities formed from, 174–75, 178–79; criticisms of, 48–49; freedom in, 45, 144, 146–47, 156–57; insurgent traditions, aesthetic techniques for, 170; play in, 143–47, 193; as radical activity, 159. *See also* improvisation
French poststructuralist theorists, 145, 153, 226n28
Freud, Sigmund, 73
fugitive voice, 28–29, 42, 49, 51, 54, 202n16; genealogy of black sound and, 34, 39
funk, 113, 118, 133
Funkhouser, Chris, 228n64
"Funk Lore" (Baraka), 103–4
fusion, 113

Gale, Eddie, 45
gatekeepers, cultural, 39, 44
gender, 36, 75, 225n16. *See also* women
genealogy of black sound, 31–41; and "circle"/circulation, 32–36; no singular origin, 31–32; production of value and meaning in, 32–33; slavery and, 33–35, 38–39
generations: Baraka's, 112, 203n38; Black Arts/black aesthetic, 153–54; black sound reinvented across, 5, 23, 25, 32; Mingus's, 65; Moreland's, 138; New Negro, 35, 112–13; Roberts's, 53–55, 58; Shepp's, 25, 46, 49, 53–55; Taylor's, 155, 157, 228n59; Wynter's, 153–54
Genette, Gérard, 195n6, 210n52
Gennari, John, 112
genotext, 168–69, 229n78
genre, 3–4, 10, 32, 68–69
Gens de couleur libres (Roberts), 54–60
gift, 29, 59, 74, 174, 178
Gillespie, Dizzy, 84–85
Ginsberg, Allen, 12, 120
Giovanni, Nikki, 45, 204n45
"Girl from Ipanema, The" (Jobim/Shepp), 50, 53
Graham, Maryemma, 65–66
graphic scores, 77
Graves, Milford, 118, 120–23, 137, 220n70
Great Migration, 34, 36
Greenwich Village clubs, 64
Griffin, Farah Jasmine, 34
Grimes, Henry, 115, 116
Guillory John, 201n3

Hadi, Shafi, 82, 84, 92, 93, 97, 100
Hall, Jacqueline Dowd, 76
Hall, James C., 51
Hall, Stuart, 8, 127, 129, 131, 183–84, 196n14, 231n7

INDEX / 257

Hamer, Fannie Lou, 58
Hammer, Bob, 84
Hancock, Herbie, 48
Hansen, Miriam Bratu, 10
Hardt, Michael, 15
Harlem, 62, 64, 73–75, 90, 93–98; and class-conscious, 99; in "Double G Train," 98–100; as site of listening, 84
Harlem Renaissance, 74
Harlem Writers Group, 80
Harney, Stefano, 67, 71
Harper, Billy, 137
Harper, Phillip Brian, 51, 160–61
Harris, William J., 104, 105, 116–17, 124, 219n63
Hartman, Saidiya, 14, 16, 17, 110, 114, 123–24
Harvey, David, 49
haunting, 138, 139, 140
Hawkins, Coleman, 78
Hayes, Brent, 62
"he(a)rded"/herding, 2–3, 9, 13, 18, 21–22, 100
Heath, Percy, 113
hegemonic order, 12, 24, 63, 73, 89, 130, 138, 186, 223n113; rhetoric of spontaneity reinforces, 9; Symbolic and semiotic in, 152
Hemphill, Julius, 222n109
henceforward, the, 28, 174, 230n96
Hentoff, Nat, 42, 43, 46
hermeneutics, 33, 35, 39, 122, 149
Hermes Trismegistus, 122
Herodotus, 15
Hill, Andrew, 45
Hinton, Milt, 92
historical context, 2–5; Mingus's, 87; and periods of political and aesthetic flux, 4–5; of phonopoem, 86; uncertainty and, 11, 28, 39, 87, 118
history: black sound's relationship to, 5, 8–9; Great Hole/"nonplace" of, 86, 212n68; mediation of, 38, 54; records bear and distort, 37; structured exclusions of, 86
"hokum" techniques, 80
homogenization, social, 49–50, 52, 198n29; Baraka's views of, 112, 114, 119, 129–30
Horkheimer, Max, 119
Hughes, Langston, 5, 27, 129, 186; Cold War and, 69–70, 207n11; community, sense of, 5, 90–94; criticism of, 65, 207n8; improvisation, sense of, 208n31; literary politics of, 65–66; lyric address in, 90, 96–98, 101; Mingus, collaboration with, 61–102; as in permanent exile, 64; revolutionary method of, 66; urban vernacular speech patterns used by, 77; and vernacular sources, 62–63, 65–66; *Works:* "The Cat and the Saxophone," 91; "Consider Me," 92, 93–97; "Dead in There," 97–98; "Double G Train," 98–100; "I Live on Music," 80; "Island," 99, 100; "Jazz as Communication," 61; *Jim Crow's Last Stand*, 99, 214n92; *Montage of a Dream Deferred*, 66–67, 72–73, 90, 93–98; "Motto," 97–98; "Same in Blues," 101; "Scenes in the City" (with Mingus), 80–90; *Selected Poems*, 92; "The Stranger," 97–98; "Warning: Augmented," 97–98, 99; *The Weary Blues*, 61, 90–102; "The Weary Blues," 61–63, 68; "Wednesday Night Prayer Meeting," 98–100, 214n91. *See also* Mingus, Charles
Hurston, Zora Neale, 31; *Works:* "How It Feels to Be Colored Me," 35; "Spirituals and Neo-Spirituals," 35–36

ideologies: of New Black Music, 7–8; organic, 129, 132; sound technologies influenced by, 7–8. *See also* bourgeois ideology and values; capitalism; commodification; commodity
Ihde, Don, 19
imperialism, 11–12, 24, 47, 88, 99, 230n95
improvisation, 143–79; collective, 86–87, 137, 175–76, 226n17; as collective commitment, 143–44; of the common, 14–17, 41, 71, 148, 158–60, 162, 170, 172, 174; community as, 63; composition, relationship to, 76–77, 79, 165; concept-metaphor of, 16; as disavowal of self, 102; "free," 146; future and, 101–2; Hughes and, 93–94; journey to one, 148–55; relation to social world of, 89; as "semiotic system without a semantic level," 150, 168, 171; and subject/object relation, 147; surprise and, 17, 175; as text, 174–75; verbal, 79. *See also* free jazz
Impulse! Records, 25, 42, 45, 133
incomprehensibility, 96–97
individualism: alternative models of, 106, 126, 154; liberal, 67, 69; "one" as prior to, 154–55; racial, 73; singularity vs., 154; as solution to racial antagonisms, 113, 126
individuation, 44, 117, 144, 154–55, 160, 182, 193
"inner-space," 128
innovation, 64, 88–90, 118, 156, 161, 184, 225n10; formal, 29, 51, 53, 169; as purposeful agency, 89
institution-building, alternative, 5–6, 14, 69, 107–10; anti-institutional practices, 66–67, 72, 95, 127; church as counter-institutional space, 99. *See also* social organization
institutions, 5–6; agency and, 5, 24, 207n14; authenticating, 109; poetry and music as, 45

insurgent practices, 3, 5, 113, 145–46, 151, 170–71, 191. *See also* revolution
integration, 22, 51–52, 69, 79, 92, 132; as ideological cover, 48; integration-as-incorporation, 113; limits of, 73, 90, 138
integration-as-incorporation, 113
intellectuals, black, 38, 135, 197n24, 222n111, 223n113
intelligibility, 7, 15, 90, 123, 162
intensity, forms of, 148–49
"interinanimation," 137
interiority, 7, 27, 162; "transgressive," 124, 220n76; voice as sign of, 29, 44
international freedom struggles, 51, 99, 197n20, 22
internationalism, 5, 101, 105, 175, 197n22
interracialism, 5, 48–49, 84, 99
intertextuality, 25–26, 28, 31, 40–41
In the Tradition (Baraka), 105, 127
In the Tradition (Blythe), 131
intuition, 29, 104, 129, 196n16
invention, 29–30, 38, 117, 201n7; of the concrete, 30; dimensions of, 119–25; inventory and, 104, 106, 110–11, 115, 133; isolated from past, 134; of subjectivity, 125. *See also* freedom
inventory, 77, 104, 106, 110–11, 115, 140–41; in "Black Dada Nihilismus," 119, 123; emergence as, 117; invention and, 104, 106, 110–11, 133
Invisible Man (Ellison), 97
Iton, Richard, 6, 68, 107, 124, 128, 132, 195n8, 196n10, 221n85
Iyer, Vijay, 161
Izenon, David, 42, 43

Jackson, Brian, 126, 131
Jackson, Milt, 113
Jacquet, Jean-Baptiste "Illinois," 78
Jain, Gitanjali, 58
James, Joy, 28, 131–32, 174, 230n96
Jameson, Fredric, 54, 109, 131
Jarman, Shaku Joseph, 2
Jazz, 18–20; "accompaniment," 74, 209n37; as "American classical music," 73, 111; "American pluralism" linked to, 135; as anticipatory, 61, 75, 91; bebop, 65, 72, 88; and black body as product, 44–45; "cool jazz," 77; exclusion in discourses of, 18–19, 111–12; "feeling of," 88; fusion, 113; as "high" art, 184; as intellectual tradition, 78; journals, 109, 217n24; Mingus's relationship to, 65, 77; neo-classicist/neo-formalist, 26, 135; new idioms/languages in, 88; as performative archive, 77; racialization of, 79; representations and narratives as constitutive of, 18–19; "soul jazz," 12, 70, 149, 214n91; styles, 225n17; "uglier modes," of 11, 44; white hipster appropriation of, 12, 73; "young lions" championed by record labels, 135. *See also* free jazz; swing
"Jazz as Communication" (Hughes), 61
Jazz Composer's Guild, 42, 49, 204n46
Jazz Workshop, 49, 67, 72–73, 76, 213n82; in *Weary Blues*, 92–93, 98, 100
Jihad Records, 115
Jim Crow, 49, 95
Jim Crow's Last Stand (Hughes), 99, 214n92
Joans, Ted, 176
Jobim, Antonio Carlos, 50, 53
John Coltrane Quartet, 216n10
Johnson, Cedric, 222n111
Johnson, J. J., 84
Johnson, Osie, 92
Jones, Meta DuEwa, 74, 92, 147, 209n37
Jones, Philly Joe, 177
Jones, Richard M., 85
Jordan, June, 181
Jost, Ekkerhard, 87, 167, 226n17, 229n75
Jujus/Alchemy of the Blues (Fabio), 45

Karenga, Ron, 39, 203n38
Kay, Connie, 113
Kelley, Robin, 95, 195n4
Kennedy, Peter, 182
King, Rodney, 4
Kingan, Renee M., 190, 231n12, 232n13
kinship, 36, 56–59, 152
Kirk, Rahsaan Roland, 182
Knepper, Jimmy, 82, 83, 84, 92, 94
Kristeva, Julia, 145, 150–53, 156, 166, 229n78
Kutzinski, Vera, 64, 69

Labelle, Brandon, 166
labor, 20–21, 38, 190
language, spoken, musicality of, 182–83
leadership, black, 9, 129, 134–35, 205n66
Lee, Don L., 176
Lee, Jeanne, 6, 64, 143, 148, 170–79, 191; black maternity and kinship in work of, 152; and European collaborators, 172; as post-cultural nationalist, 172–73; Shepp, collaboration with, 171–72; *Works:* "Angel Chile," 174; "Blasé" (with Shepp), 176–79; *Conspiracy,* 174; "Djinji's Corner" (with Brown), 175–76, 177
left, 6, 11, 66, 68, 198n28, 230n104; ambivalent relationship to, 69, 76; depoliticization of race, 132, 217n25. *See also* communism

legitimacy, 11, 19, 66, 129, 222n111; as component of social reproduction, 152; of hegemonic order, 9; intelligibility and, 15, 25; self-legitimation of present, 3
legitimation, 15, 25–26, 31, 66, 94, 114, 135, 173, 193
Leonard, Keith, 74
Lewis, George E., 46, 54, 172, 204n46
Lewis, John, 113
liberation: Black Liberation struggles, 24, 67, 129, 137, 173, 178; narratives of, 6–7; poetics of, 109–15
Liberator, 115
Lincoln, Abbey, 45, 57
liner notes: to *Fire Music*, 42, 43, 47; for *Live at Birdland*, 110, 139; Mingus's, 79, 80, 211n54; poetry as, 163; re-mediation through, 4, 30; Taylor's, 163
listening: as act of witness, 192; anticipatory, 122, 124; autonomy of, 21, 84; as creative act, 81, 111; distant, 230n95; embodied, 99; future-perfect time of, 21; grammars of, 13, 87, 194; Harlem as site of, 84; "he(a)rded"/herding, 2–3, 9, 13, 18, 21–22, 100; historical context of, 3–4; intersubjective relationships, 53; inventive, 105; lived experience and, 81; as proto-political, 22, 193; recursive, 78; reference, 110–11; shared, 83–84; Shepp's, 39; as site of reproduction, 125; Third World or diasporic public sphere, 52; transcription as, 160–61; transition from public to private, 11, 34; as trope, 161
lived experience, 3, 16, 81, 136, 149, 151, 153, 187
"lived time," 73–74, 81, 102, 108
"live" performance, 6, 54, 105, 164
living rooms, 11, 34, 36
local, the, 80, 97, 99
Loftin, Elouise, 174
logocentrism, 15
Lorde, Audre, 101, 191
Lordi, Emily, 204n45
Los Angeles uprisings, 1990s, 4
Lott, Eric, 12
love, 59, 115, 119, 121–22, 177–78, 230n106
Lowney, John, 100
lyric poetry, 147–48, 150, 225n16; Baraka and, 116, 120, 225n16; Hughes and, 90, 96–98, 101

Mackey, Nathaniel, 2, 21, 28, 143, 169, 204n55, 225n10; "hearded," concept of, 2, 21; as host of *Tanganyika Strut*, 21; on "outside," 91; "post-expectant," concept of, 104
magazines, 30, 109

Mailer, Norman, 101
"Malcolm, Malcolm—Semper Malcolm" (Shepp), 42–45
Malcolm X, 40, 42–43, 46, 58, 120, 124
marginality, 14, 83, 91
Marsalis, Wynton, 30, 131, 135, 201n11
Marx, Karl, 20, 46–47
Marxism, 38; aesthetic theory of, 107; Third World, Baraka's, 104–6, 126
masculinity, 94, 101, 207n9
mass culture and media, 9, 35, 46, 57, 66, 139; Baraka and, 104, 112; Hughes and, 90; modernism separated from, 80
materialist accounts, 20–21, 42, 106, 112
materiality: extra-discursive, 154; Moten's reading of, 33; of music, 111, 160, 183, 188; of voice, 57, 183
maternity, 34, 57, 151–52, 171, 174; "mother" vs. "mama," 151, 177–78; "oceanic space" of mother's body, 81
Mathes, Carter, 115
Mayfield, Julian, 111
McCaffery, Steven, 225n10
McCall, Steve, 105, 127, 133
McCarthy, Joseph, 69–70
McKay, Claude, 35
McKittrick, Katherine, 55
meaning: contests over, 4, 18; means of disclosed, 41; as movement, 167; production of, 32; re-signification of, 31; and semantemes, 18; in sound of words, 19
media: black sound disarticulated from, 35; commodity form and, 7; "human interest" fetishized by, 193; as ideological and conceptual condensation points, 4; legitimating role of, 31, 134–35; racialized contexts of, 11; of sound reproduction, 58; technologies, 26. *See also* liner notes; paratexts
media concept, black, 14, 26–27, 29, 31, 53–54
mediation, 24, 31, 53–55, 58, 101, 193n16; defined, 26; Douglass's, 32–33; of enslaved people's music, 32–34; of history, 38, 54; between "inside" and "outside," 225n16; mass, 139; naturalization of, 44; poetry as, 20; remediation, 30, 53–54, 58; textual, 33, 40–41; tradition as, 54; voice as index of, 41
medium, 11, 23–27, 31, 90–91, 163; black sound as, in opposition to capitalist modernity, 38; detaching work of, 175; durability of, 13, 25, 105–6, 111, 194; mediation and, 53–54; as proxy term for changes in social relations and technologies, 26–27; as recurring set of contingent social

relations and practices, 19; sound as, 38; text as, 13–14; as transmitter of values, 19, 33, 35, 60; voice as, 8, 171, 183

Melhem, D. H., 189

metaphor, 4, 97, 152; improvisation and, 16; meaningfulness and, 31, 33; Mingus and, 63, 69, 87–88; musico-tactile, 63; in Taylor's work, 163, 167, 170

metavoice, 28–29, 170

"methodologic fissures," 156, 159, 227n40

metonymy, 4, 8–9; Douglass's use of, 34, 38–39; line between synecdoche and, 8, 28, 34, 52, 54; saxophone "scream," 24, 25, 57. *See also* synecdoche

middle class: Baraka's view of, 107–8, 117–19, 136, 186–87, 218n39; black, 47, 107–8, 173, 215n4, 231n9; global, 124; U.S. political argot of, 107

mimesis, 31–32, 94, 192

Mingus, Charles, 5, 116; as "Angry Man of Jazz," 65, 207n9; "black authenticity" and, 89–90; circular and centripetal metaphors in, 88; composition and, 63–64, 76–78; Debut Records, 65; Hughes, collaboration with, 61–102; jazz, ambivalence toward, 210n44; Jazz Workshop, 49, 67, 72–73, 76, 92–93, 98, 100; liner notes, 79, 80, 211n54; literary aspects of, 64–65; multimedia experiments of, 72, 86; pianoless quartet, 88–89; poetry as central to compositional approach of, 77–78; as progenitor of "avant-garde" jazz, 77; radicalism of, 65; and "rotary perception," 65, 73, 75, 87–88, 91, 118, 209n32; titles, 78; as transitional figure, 78–79; *Works: Beneath the Underdog*, 73, 87–89; *The Black Saint and the Sinner Lady*, 78, 210n48; *Blues and Roots*, 70, 98–99, 214n91; *The Charles Mingus Quintet Plus Max Roach*, 211n55; "The Chill of Death," 78; "The Clown," 79–80; "A Colloquial Dream," 81, 211n59; "Fables of Faubus," 79, 212n64; "A Foggy Day," 80; *Let My Children Hear Music*, 78; "Meditations (On a Pair of Wire Cutters)," 97; *A Modern Jazz Symposium of Music and Poetry*, 64, 81; *Pithecanthropus Erectus*, 76, 211n54; "Scenes in the City," 80–90, 93; *Tijuana Moods*, 81, 210n47. *See also* Hughes, Langston

minstrelsy, 12, 30, 34, 123, 137–40

"mixtery," 169–70

modernism, 210–11n53; of Hughes, 96–97; hybrid, 172; Lee and, 172; neutralization of, 187; New Negro generation, 112–13; political, 186

modernism/mass culture binaries, 9, 80

modernity: blackness as unassimilable to, 71; black sound in opposition to, 38; black soundwork as constitutive of, 8; capitalist, 20, 38, 71, 106, 213n76; colonial relations hidden or obscured in, 12; "communities in transition" and, 75; plurality inherent in, 213n76; and public amnesia, 96; and racial anxieties, 80; self-definition of, 52. *See also* capitalism

Modern Jazz Quartet (MJQ), 113

Monk, Thelonious, 74, 76, 77, 84

montage, 43, 61, 79–80, 86, 91, 93–98

Montage of a Dream Deferred (Hughes), 66–67, 72–73, 90

Monterose, J. R., 80

Moore, Don, 42

Moor Mother (Camae Ayewa), 1–2

Moran, Jason, 182–83

Moreland, Mantan, 137–40

Morrison, Toni, 23

Morton, Jelly Roll, 80

Moses, J. C., 42, 43

Moten, Fred, 13, 14, 31, 57, 149–50, 201n2; on *a*calculation, 162; on anxieties about European influence, 158; on "Black Dada Nihilismus," 121; on interinanimation, 137; on materiality, 33; and Mingus's circles, implications of, 88; on Taylor, 159, 164, 228n47; and undercommons, concept of, 67

"motor responses," 157–58

murder of black people, extralegal, 4–5

Murray, Albert, 135, 225n10

Murray, David, 105, 127, 133, 137, 181

Murray, Sunny, 115–16, 118, 161. *See also* "Black Art" (Baraka/Murray)

music: "declassing" of, 130; as fantasy object, 82, 86, 88; "internal" categories of, 2–4; limits of poetry's relationship to, 62; mass politics awakened by, 132; materiality of, 111, 160, 183, 188; "natural language" and, 168; as outside history, 86; as poetry, 143–48; "proper," 161; as result of thought, 37, 110; revolutionary, 111; symbolic economy of, 4; textuality of, 162–63; as writing, 13, 194, 232n38

musicking, 74, 107, 209n38

musicology, Western, 7

musique concrete, 79–80

mystery, 96, 169

mystification, 96

myth, 176

Narrative (Douglass), 32, 201n2

narrative, transcription as production of, 160–61

narratives: as constitutive of jazz, 18–19; liberationist, 6–7; of resistance, 3
nationalism: black, 51, 124, 127, 135, 140, 203n37; as cover for bourgeois or anti-black politics, 173; cultural, 41–42, 104–6, 126, 130, 135, 172–74, 216n22; Du Bois on, 34; global class shuffle and, 107; post-cultural, 172–73; romantic, 198n29
nation-state, 6, 12, 68, 193; Baraka's view, 108, 110, 112, 114, 118–19, 126; reproduction of in New Black Music, 47
Neal, Larry, 38, 39, 47, 105, 145, 203n37; "white thing," critique of, 153
neconservatism, 129
Négritude poets, 186, 232n13
Negro: An Anthology (Cunard), 35
neocolonialism, 49, 76, 108
neoliberalism, 49, 76, 126, 129, 193
New Black Aesthetic, 187, 203n37
New Black Music, 8, 11, 28, 30, 45, 49; Baraka and, 108–10, 117, 154; composition, considerations of, 76–77; and manipulation of existing forms, 39; proletarian innovators of, 47
New Black Poetry, 109
New Communist Movement, 104
New Deal, 48
New Music—New Poetry (Baraka, Murray, and McCall), 131–34, 136
New Negro generation, 35, 112–13
Newport Jazz Festival, 72
New York Art Quartet (NYAQ), 105, 119–25, 134, 137–41
Ngai, Sianne, 190
Nielsen, Aldon, 5, 43, 208n29, 213n82, 219n63; on "Black Dada Nihilismus," 120, 122; on Cortez, 189–90; on free jazz as radical activity, 159; on modes of Baraka's poetry, 108
Niemöller, Martin, 79
Nigeria, 192
"Night in Tunisia, A" (Gillespie), 84–85
Nix, Bern, 185
non-art, 9, 20, 162
"nonfunctional" approach to sound, 156–57
non-meaning, 18

Obama, Barack, 138, 181
"oceanic space," 81–82, 84, 92
Oliver, King, 78
"one," the, 154–55, 162, 166–67, 170
Ongiri, Amy Obugo, 38, 50, 128, 205n70
ongoingness. *See* continuity/ongoingness

ontology, 4, 8–9, 168; "para-ontological," 13, 199n37; social ecstasy, 149
optimism, 125, 176; cruel, 140, 216n18
orature/literature binary, 27
"organic ideologies," 129, 132
Organization of Woman Writers of Africa, 185
origin, 81, 86, 96, 201n2; ōriri- (to rise, to be born), 168, 170; of racial being, 40, 128–29; of sound, 25, 31–32
Other than Art's Sake (film, Kennedy), 182
"outness/outsideness," 29, 32–33, 36–38, 114; anarchic potential of, 154; Mackey on, 91; in Taylor's work, 148, 160, 162, 167, 169; as theoretical practice, 146–49

Pace, Harry, 112, 231n9
Palmore, Gayle, 175, 176
Pan-Africanism, 34, 108, 178
paratexts, 4, 46, 79, 160, 195n6, 210n52
Parker, Charlie, 43, 65, 77, 78, 84, 88, 90, 211n53
Parker, William, 137
Parks, Suzan-Lori, 86
Parlan, Horace, 83, 92, 93, 213n82
past: as abstract individual-collective will to narrative, 108; alternative collectivity formed through, 14, 107–8, 190; anarchic regard of, 141; composition and, 63–64; invention isolated from, 134; as inventory, 104, 106; mediation of by previous texts, 14, 104; "premodern," 128, 134; refusal to narrate, 58–59; ruins of futures past, 49; as source and resource, 53; unresolved problems from, 119–20
Patterson, Anita Haya, 96–97
Peacock, Gary, 116
"people," the, 10–11, 13, 39, 192; alternative possibilities within, 174–75; anti-institutional practice and, 127; autonomy of, 114; as consumers, 52; fugitive voice and, 28; as homogenous, 49, 129–30; Shepp's view of, 42, 49; vernacular as sign of, 62–63. *See also* "folk"
performance: black, in context of capitalism, 113–14; of poetry, 19
performance style, 8–9, 193
performativity, 28, 147
personhood: black, 152; capitalist and patriarchal, 16–17, 123–24
petit bourgeoisie, 48, 49
phantom objectivity, 8, 199n45
phenotext, 169, 229n78
phonographic poetry, 2, 4; anticolonial phonopoetics, 35; early poetry performance and,

19; emergence of, 12; poetry-jazz nexus and, 5; resurgence of, 181; self-assertion of blacks through, 12-13; of Shepp, 41; during times of upheaval, 4-5. *See also* collaborations between poets and musicians; poetry; recording/reproduction technologies; textuality

phonography, 13, 73; legitimated through ethnographic recording, 11, 32

Piper, Adrian, 182-83

play, 17; agonistic, 74; in free jazz, 143-47, 193; and *jouissance*, 147, 150-51; non-teleological, 2, 72, 74; in poetry, 145, 148; as practice of freedom, 74-75; reciprocal attunement as a form of, 144; and reenchantment, 3, 40, 146, 155, 162, 175; as subversive gift, 59, 74, 178; unruly, 108-9

poetic essence of music, 143

poetics: anticipatory, 75; of black communism, 67-69, 71, 72-76, 93, 102; communist, 68, 73, 93, 102; of liberation, 109-15; "micro-poetics," 78; social, 30, 63, 84, 91, 95, 101, 118; "speech-based," 225n16; vernacular as, 67

poetry: Art Ensemble of Chicago, 1-2; Black Arts, 51; circulation of on record, 199n34; contemporary assumptions about, 52; as counterculture, 12; limits of music's relationship to, 62; music as, 143-48; oratory, roots in, 19; orchestration of, 187; performance of, 19; physicality of, 117; play in, 145, 148; pre-capitalist function of, 40; as rhythm, 91; sonic interplay in, 27; sound poetry, 166-67, 171-72, 225n16; spaces of encounter, 148. *See also* phonographic poetry; sound

poetry-jazz nexus, 5, 72-73, 208n31

police order, 15-16

politics: 1960s, 46-47; black as abstraction in, 130; black intellectuals in, 222n111, 223n113; collective, 11; control, desire for, 49; as count of community "parts," 14-15, 16; and depoliticization, 26, 46, 60, 132, 217n25; domination resisted, 15; electoralist, 60; limitations of, 60; no-longer-available, 50; performance of, 28; the political distinguished from, 14-16, 221n85; and proto-political stances, 22, 128, 136, 191-93, 210n44; Rancière's account of, 14-15; as unruly, 26

popular, the, 24, 50, 54, 99; avant-garde and, 10-11, 197n26; black culture vs. black people as, 67-69; Black Panther Party's role in creating, 128, 205n70; "folk," relationship with, 66; social responsibility and, 46; subaltern, relationship with, 54, 66, 183-84, 193

popular culture, 10, 50, 66, 127-28, 174, 198n29, 205n70, 230n95; artifacts of, 104; Hall on, 183-84

Popular Front, 10-11, 65

Porter, Eric, 47, 50, 171-72, 175, 203n37, 210n44

postcolonial context, 7, 145, 149, 181, 193, 197n24

post-cultural nationalism, 172, 173

post-expectant politics, 104, 108

poststructuralism, 144-45

potentiality, 9, 148, 154, 178, 190, 229n75

poverty, 189; in "Scenes in the City," 81, 82-83, 89

"Pov Piti Mamzelle Zizi" (Creole song), 58-59

Powell, Bud, 65, 78, 84, 90

power-knowledge relations, 145, 196n14

present, 2-3, 7, 10; historical, 3, 79; in Hughes and Mingus, 67; lived experience of, 81; "now" as claim of, 3, 136; "origin" inscribed in, 81; as political, 3, 106, 216n18; tradition enabled in, 125

Priestley, Brian, 76, 211n54, 212n64, 214n91

private space, development of, 11, 34, 52

production: aesthetic, 3, 41, 75, 104-5, 107, 114, 128-29, 131; alternative modes of, 71; of marginal social life, 14; of racial difference, 107; of value, 14, 32, 41, 117-18. *See also* aesthetic production; recording/reproduction technologies

proletariat, 46-49

promotional genres, 78

property, 16-17; black communist critique of, 67-68; status of voice and, 32-33

propriety/refinement, 7, 16-17, 36, 68, 110, 123-24, 197n24; of "folk" materials, 87, 112, 158-59

proto-political stances, 22, 128, 136, 191-93, 210n44

pseudomorphisis, 62

psychoanalysis, 73, 145, 151-52, 154

public, black, 70

public/private binary, 27

quotidian, the, 7, 9-10, 37, 43, 66-68; anti-institutional practices of, 66-67, 72, 95, 127; jazz and, 91-92, 95; separation from art, 107

race: (re)definition of, 140-41; depoliticized by left, 132, 217n25; production of through sound, 8; psychoanalysis and, 154

"racecraft," 81, 211n62

"race records," 12, 36

racial formation, 48

racialization, 11-13, 17, 107, 112, 119, 195, 197n24; blackness as form of, 17; of jazz, 79; of jazz texts, 161; of sexuality, 101; of sound, 12; and white bourgeois as "representative," 32

INDEX / 263

racial logics, 10–11, 132, 197n24
Ragin, Hugh, 1, 137
Rambsy, Howard, II, 115
Rampersad, Arnold, 72, 208n31
Rancière, Jacques, 14–15
rap music, 30, 183–85, 201n11
reappropriation, 10–11, 34, 69, 133, 152
rebel, 28
recording industry, critiques of, 44–45
recording/reproduction technologies, 10–12, 26–27, 31–33, 198n29, 202n16, 210n53; emergence of, 27, 52; and "live" performance, 6, 54, 164; media of, 58; and minstrel sounds as commodity, 34; new performance styles require changes in, 4, 9, 11; and overdubbing, 78; and platform change, 26, 135; poetry performance and, 19; voice and production of value, 32–33. *See also* phonographic poetry; sound technologies
records, 34, 135; anticolonial phonopoetics in, 35; Baraka and, 36–37; and CD reissues, 26, 92; as commodity, 20–22, 31; dominant values communicated through, 12; ethnographic, 11; history borne and distorted by, 37; learning through, 35; of oratory, 19; overlapping historical media, 26; "race records," 12, 36; social hygiene project, of early, 21, 69, 185. *See also* sound objects
Reed, Adolph, 128–29, 205n66, 221n89, 223n113
reenchantment, 3, 40, 146, 155, 162, 175
"refinement," 112–13
reflection, 116–17
reflexive stance, 2–3, 8, 16, 21, 55, 74, 145–46, 155, 188
refusals, 2, 8, 27, 39, 49, 57–59, 64; communism as, 68–69; Harlem's specificity and, 75
reification, 119–20, 122, 124–25; class obscured by, 188–89; of maternal body (Kristeva), 151, 152–53
reinscription, 9, 13, 66, 84, 147, 151, 165, 184, 194
relation, as product of intellectual labor, 54
relative autonomy, 18, 118, 128, 199n45
remediation, 53–54, 58
repetition, 7, 93, 103, 139, 150, 152, 169–70; Cortez's use of, 185, 191–92; note-for-note, expected of solos, 64
representation, 67; as constitutive of jazz, 18–19; moving beyond, 25–26; structure of, 196n16
reproduction technologies. *See* recording/reproduction technologies
resignification/re-signification, 13, 28, 31, 39, 136–37, 194
resistance, 3, 15; as spectacle, 50, 127–28; transformation and, 104; to universality, 90

resonance, 2, 4, 11, 124, 137, 149, 193, 225n16; emotional, 56; formal and historical, 65, 68
revolution, 47; art and music as revolutionary, 38, 42, 104, 111, 136; black protest as spectacle of capitalism, 50, 127–28; consumer goods, revolutionary, 128; multiple time scales, 53; past, use of in present, 136; post-revolutionary age, 126–41; as process, 136. *See also* insurgent practices
revolutionary, the: continuity/ongoingness of, 104; desire to understand things otherwise, 122; Hughes and, 66; in Shepp's thought, 25, 39, 47, 54, 203n37. *See also* Baraka, Amiri
Revolutionary Communist League, 104
"The Revolution Will Not Be Televised" (Scott-Heron), 173–74
Rexroth, Kenneth, 72, 199n34, 208n31
rhythm, 166, 167, 194; poetry as, 91; reappropriated sign of, 133–34
rhythm and blues, 30, 38–39, 43–44, 45, 126, 135
Richmond, Dannie, 82, 84, 89, 94
riotous, the, 9–10, 16, 17, 20, 22
Roach, Max, 57, 65, 84, 211n55; *Freedom Now* suite, 109
Roberts, Matana, 5–6, 24–25, 30, 31, 53–60; artistic statements of, 206n82, 206n88; *Coin Coin* series, 53–60
Robinson, Cedric, 17
rock and roll, 12, 52
Rollins, Sonny, 109
rotary perception (Mingus), 65, 73, 75, 87–88, 91, 118
"'Round Midnight" (Monk), 84–85
Rudd, Roswell, 103, 120–21, 137, 139
Ruff, Tom "Curly," 92

samba, 50
Sanchez, Sonia, 126
Sanders, Pharoah, 116
Santoro, Gene, 72
Saul, Scott, 74
saxophone "scream," as metonym, 24, 57
"Scenes in the City" (Mingus/Hughes), 64, 80–90, 93; ambivalence in, 89; blues references in, 81–83; harmonic progression in, 86; instrumentation, 82; and listening, shared, 83–84; "oceanic space" in, 81–82, 84; pedagogical introduction to jazz in, 84–85; poverty in, 81, 82–83, 89; social organization critiqued in, 81; sonic impressionism in, 83–84; text of, 81–83
Schwarz, David, 86, 212n63

264 / INDEX

scores, 76–77, 105
Scott, David, 153
Scott-Heron, Gil, 126, 173–74; *Pieces of a Man*, 174; *Small Talk at 125th and Lenox*, 174
"scream," 4, 43, 124, 162; Brown's, 40; saxophone, 24, 25, 57; technical constraints and, 192
"Seek Light at Once" (Baraka), 137–41
self: alternatives to, 145–46; and burdened individuality of black, 110, 114; concrete, reinvention of, 30, 145, 150, 153–54, 178; grammar of, 155; "killing" of, 108, 147, 154–55
self-determination, 6, 67, 134, 146
self-narration, 27
semantemes, 18
semantic, 145, 150
semiotic, the, 178–79; and improvisation, 150, 168, 171; Kristeva's account of, 145, 150–53, 156, 166; ongoingness of, 163; Symbolic and, 150–52, 171
Semple, Jesse B. (character in Hughes), 70, 211n58
sensible, the, 14–15, 33
sensory experience, 7, 27, 122, 158, 167–68
sexual relation, 101, 167
Shaw, Clarence "Gene," 82, 84, 85
sheet music, 34
Shepherd, Jean, 79
Shepp, Archie, 6, 23–25, 30–31, 38, 149; as "angry black tenor man," 25, 49, 133; Baraka's collaboration with, 103; consensus view of, 48; fugitive voice and, 34, 39, 42; Lee's collaboration with, 171–72; phonopoems of, 42–43; references to historical conditions, 25; relationship to culture industries, 46, 49–50; revolutionary thought in works of, 25, 39, 54, 203n37; saxophone improvisation, 43; "success" of, 50–51; voice of, 41–53; Works: *Attica Blues*, 52; "Blasé," 176–79; *The Cry of My People*, 52; *Fire Music*, 42, 47; *Four for Trane*, 42; "Funeral," 42; "The Funeral," 42; "The Girl from Ipanema," 50, 53; *Live at the Pan-African Festival*, 52, 176, 177; *Live in New York*, 103; *For Losers*, 52; *The Magic of Ju-Ju*, 52; "Malcolm, Malcolm—Semper Malcolm," 42–45; "Poem for Malcolm," 204n47; *Rufus*, 42; "We Have Come Back," 177
"Sidewalk Blues" (Morton), 80
signification, 122; material processes of, 145; re-signification/re-signification, 13, 28, 31, 39, 194; sign-ification, 8, 13, 39, 150, 194
simultaneity, 6–7, 9, 13–15, 56, 168–69
Sin and Soul (Brown), 59
singularity, 8, 147, 154; "one" as, 154, 166–67; slavery as, 34, 39

sixties, the, 101, 130, 137, 163, 182
slavery, 38–39; afterlives of, 55–56, 58–59, 182; continuity of through African ancestry, 34–35; domestic institutions tied to, 56; enslaved people's music, mediation of, 32–34; freedom's social forms predicated on, 17; idea of as singular culture, 34, 39
slave song, 32–34
slogans, commodification of, 108
Small, Christopher, 10, 74, 209n38
Smethurst, James, 10–11, 65, 66, 197n26, 207n11
Smith, Wadada Leo, 77
social hygiene project, of early sound recording, 21, 69, 185
social organization: alternative forms of, 8, 9–13, 69; Black Arts era, 25; capitalist, 6; communist, 14; "communities in transition," 67; new configurations of, 13–18; in "Scenes in the City," 81, 89–90; of sound, 11; "traditional African" forms of, 128; unorganizable within, 9, 126. *See also* community; institution-building, alternative
social poetics, 30, 63, 84, 91, 95, 101, 118
social reproduction, 7, 21, 36–37, 94, 118; avant-garde music's apposition to, 37; embodiment and, 152; and kinship, 36, 56–59, 152; Taylor and, 159, 166–67
solidarity, 30, 71, 121, 129, 132, 135; women's, 175. *See also* community
Sollors, Werner, 117–18, 216n10
somatic (embodied sound), 145
"Someday My Prince Will Come" (Davis), 85
"Song" (Bennett), 35
songfulness, 19, 56, 162, 200n49
"songs of the people," 35–36
sonic structures, as compositions, 29–30
"Sorrow Songs, The," 34
"soul jazz," 12, 70, 149, 214n91
soul music, 38, 214n91
Souls of Black Folk, The (Du Bois), 34
sound: Baraka on, 37; as basis of thought, 37; as medium, 38; non-meaning, 18; nonverbal, 5, 45, 164–65; "origin" of, 25, 31–32; physicality of, 25–26, 111, 117, 120; race produced through, 8; racialization of, 12; as resounding, 2; source, relationship with, 9, 27, 30; as text, 40; textual dimensions of, 25; unavailability of an origin for, 25; as work, 193–94. *See also* black sound; soundwork
sound engineering, 147
"sound for sounding," 41, 45, 203n43
soundful, word as, 19

sound media, 6, 17, 46, 65, 105, 111, 160, 198n29, 210n53
sound objects, 4, 27, 160; becoming-autonomous of, 11; capitalist production, relation to, 27; collection of, 20–22. *See also* records
sound poetry, 166–67, 171–72, 225n16
sound technologies, 7–9, 14, 27, 198n29. *See also* recording/reproduction technologies
soundwork, 58–59, 166, 171–72, 179, 182, 190, 194; calls to prospective audience, 14; as liberatory, 12; as material practice, 8, 14, 27, 150, 193; meaningful change due to, 4; multidisciplinary, 171; as practice of black collective thinking, 14; reframing as task of, 59; as theoretical work, 8–9; as way of inhabiting collective present, 3. *See also* black sound
sovereignty, 6, 12, 16–17, 108, 193
space-time, 31, 67, 123, 146, 159, 174
speaking *I*, authorial *I*, 51
specificity, 8–9, 73–75, 114–15, 168
spectacle, 50, 127–28, 173
speculative practices, 3, 16, 28–30, 69
speech, as inadequate, 204n55
Spellman, A. B., 36, 157, 227n43
Spillers, Hortense, 49–50, 126, 129, 132, 145, 151, 196n16, 205n68; insurgent ground of gendered difference, 171; "one," the, 154–55, 162, 166–67
spirituals, 35–36, 50, 114
Spiritual Unity (Ayler), 116
Spivak, Gayatri Chakravorty, 5, 16, 20, 28, 66, 144, 201n2, 207n14
spontaneity: community-in-progress, 63; in composition, 63–65, 73, 77–80, 83–84, 90, 97–98, 224n6; constructionism, 165; as discrediting, 9, 165; Mingus's view of, 65, 73, 78; rhetoric of, 9, 77–80; uprisings, 9, 118, 182, 221n89, 222n111; Taylor and, 165
"Squash People" (Taylor), 164, 167, 168–70
standardization, 74, 154
state cultural apparatuses, 4, 24, 46, 50, 159; neutralization of jazz forms, 159, 185; surveillance, 55
Sterne, Jonathan, 11, 44, 198n29, 202n16, 230n95
Stewart, Mel, 80, 81, 82, 211n58
Student Non-Violent Coordinating Committee, 185
subaltern, 24, 50, 196n10, 207n14; black communism and, 71, 73; Hughes and, 91–92, 94; "popular," relationship with, 54, 66, 183–84, 193; rap music and, 183–84
subjection, 58, 144, 166–67, 182

subjectivity: invention of, 125; subjecthood and, 44. *See also* individualism; singularity
subject/object relation, 147, 150, 162, 167
subordinativities, 68
subversion, 183–84; play as subversive gift, 59, 74, 178
Such, David, 225–26n17
"Sunni" (Loftin/Lee), 174
Sunny's Time Now (Murray), 115–19
Sun Ra, 6
supersession, rhetoric of, 10, 152, 183
supersurrealism, 187–89
surface/depth models, 145, 153
surprise, 17, 29, 116, 157, 175
"Sweet V" (Rudd), 121
swing, 43–44, 148, 222n109, 229n75; Mingus's relationship to, 65, 70, 73, 83, 87–89, 93
syllepsis, 189–90
Symbolic, 150–52, 171, 187
symbolic, the, 3–4, 19, 26, 30–31; stylistic choices and, 24, 118
Symphony Sid (disc jockey), 88
syncopation, 94–95; "Negro," 67–69, 91, 95; as popular music of America, 67–68, 69, 92; predetermined symbolic relations of, 18; in Shepp's music, 43
synecdoche, 8, 28, 34, 43, 51, 54–55, 89, 158. *See also* metonymy

Tacuma, Jamaaladeen, 181, 185
Tanganyika Strut (radio show), 21
Taylor, Cecil, 6, 29, 52, 77, 116, 148–50, 155–70; atonality in, 156–57; on feeling, 144, 191; on finite statement, 150; "instant composing," 162; "methodologic fissures," 156, 159, 227n40; "motor responses," use of, 157–58; "nonfunctional" approach to sound, 156–57; ongoingness in, 155, 163; poetry and music's relationship in thought of, 143–44, 148, 155, 162–66, 179, 228n64; "solo" performances, 163–64; Unit Core albums, 161, 163; *Works: Chinampas,* 164; *Double Holy House,* 164, 167–70, 179; "Elell," 164, 166; *Garden,* 163–65; *Indent,* 163; "Sound of Subculture Becoming Major Breath/Naked Fire Gesture," 163; "Squash People," 164, 167, 168–70; *Unit Structures,* 163
Taylor, Sam "The Man," 92
Tchicai, John, 29, 42, 120–21, 137, 139, 220n70
technologies: black role in development and popularization of, 26
teleological schemas, 2, 6–7, 63, 74, 146, 183–84; of black politics, 133; modular approach vs., 161;

rhythmic uncertainty and, 118; ruins of past, 181; soundwork avoids, 8-9
temporality: Baraka's presence in changed media landscape, 134-41; in Baraka's work, 103-4, 106-8, 118, 121, 123, 134-35, 140; habitus of, 153; in Lee's work, 173; and listening, 3, 21; Middle Passage ruptures, 35; simultaneity, 6-7, 168-69; speculative, 28; in Taylor's work, 162
text: destruction of, 145; improvisation as, 174-75; internal arrangement of material, 29, 160; mediation of tradition by, 54; Neal's call for destruction of, 39-40, 118; oral performative dimensions of, 25; parallel, 62; paratexts, 4, 46, 79, 160, 195n6, 210n52; as process of dissemination, 40-41; time and, 158; as transmission of effects, 31; as will to systematicity, 23-24
textuality, 25-26, 40, 147, 175, 195, 201n2; of black sound, primacy of, 23-25; intertextuality, 13-14, 25-26, 28, 31, 40-41; of music, 162-63. *See also* phonographic poetry
There It Is (Cortez), 188-89, 192
"Third Stream" movement, 113
Third World, 52, 189
Third World Marxism, 104-6, 126
Thompson, Malachi, 137, 138
timbre, 190, 193, 194
time: collection, 20-22; ecstatic, 146; future-perfect, 21; improvisation and, 150; of listening, 21; lived experience of, 153; orchestration of, 161, 163; problematic of, 65; recursive "disctortions," 90, 101; text and, 158
Time, 68; as dominant narrative, 63, 67; escape from, 95; rhythmic feeling for life and, 87, 91
time centrality of body to, 168
titles, 4, 79, 99
tonality, 190; atonality, 156-57
tone, 190, 193
Tracy, Steve, 65
tradition: as affiliation, 57; anarchic regard of, 108-9; as a "developing resource," 131; enabled in present, 125; inventory of, 111; learned through records, 35; loss and reconstitution of, 107; mediation of by texts, 54; media concept's role in, 26-27; multiple streams of, 133; "return," 26; as text, 29
transcription, 160-61
translation: as erotics of surrender, 144; lyrical, 147-48; from music to poetry, 62; from one medium to another, 13, 194
tropes, 3, 18, 74, 94, 163; of community, 128-29; listening as, 161; subjection as, 166-67; syllepsis, 189-90

trouble, tradition of, 190, 191
"Trouble in Mind" (Jones), 85
Trouillot, Michel-Rolph, 213n76
Truth Is on Its Way, The (Giovanni), 45
"truth," sonic, 13
Tucker, Sherrie, 18-19, 200n46
"tune-writing," 76-77
Tynan, John, 216n10

uncertainty, 95, 104, 124, 162, 174; historical context and, 11, 28, 39, 87, 118; of status of blackness, 115
underclasses, 63
undercommons, 17, 67-72, 84-85, 125
underdog, 72
unfreedom, 12, 30, 55-56, 108, 153
unions, 131
United States: and American standardization, 74; black life possibilities in, 47; built on exclusion and enslavement of blackness, 39; and destabilizing intent of Third World policies, 189; "Negro syncopation" as pulse of, 67-68, 69; Nigeria, treatment of black people in, 192; racial formation in, 48; Shepps' ambivalence toward, 51
universality, 16, 107, 121; exclusion and, 68; oneness, 143-44, 146; reconception of, 141; vernacular as resistant to, 90
unorganizable, the, 9, 19, 126
unsettling, sense of, 53-54, 70, 144, 166; in "Scenes in the City," 86-87
uprisings, 4, 15-16, 127, 173; Attica Prison, 79; current era, 182; discrediting of, 15; "marching" and "dancing" as, 127; Scythian slave revolt, 15; "spontaneous," 9, 118, 182, 221n89, 222n111
use-time, 21
use-value, 20-21, 38, 41, 89; pseudo-use value, 33
"U.S./Nigeria Relations" (Cortez), 192-93

value: aesthetic, 39, 114, 140, 149; alternative forms of, 20, 117-18; medium as transmitter of, 19, 33, 35, 60; production of, 14, 32, 41, 117-18
Varèse, Edgar, 211n53
vaudeville performers, African American, 11, 12, 80
vernacular: community and, 63; Ellison's definition of, 10, 197n24; "folk" as contrast to, 91; Hughes and, 62-63, 65-66, 68-70, 75; Mingus and, 5, 63, 67, 70, 75; as poetics, 67; pre-discursive, 150-51; as sign of "the people," 62-63; Taylor and, 159; time and, 90; "trans-African" music and, 52

vernacular avant-garde, 6, 9–13, 184–85; Baraka and, 105, 110, 132; international networks, 105; Mingus and, 67, 69, 72, 80; reappropriation of "outmoded" forms, 10–11; Shepp and, 46–49. *See also* avant-garde
vibration societies, 182, 189
victory, 1–2
voice: as alterity, 29; autonomy of, 46; Baraka's view of, 23, 27–28, 45–46, 107; black women's, 27; communal, 43–44; cultural status of, 32–33, 44; embodied, 152, 168; fugitive, 28–30, 34, 39, 42, 49, 51, 54, 202n16; "grain" of, 41; literal and figurative, 4; materiality of, 57, 183; as medium, 8, 171, 183; metavoice, 28–29, 170; in New Black Music ideologies, 7–8; nonverbal/extrasemantic, 45; political, 43–44; as property, 32–33; recited poetry, importance to, 41; resignified, 28; self-excessive, 29, 167–68; Shepp's, 41–53; "signature," 204n45; as sign of consciousness, 44; as sign of dispossession, 29; as sign of interiority, 29, 44; "sound for sounding," 41, 45, 203n43; split function of, 27–28; vocalization and, 170–71; whisper, 42–44, 46
voicing: ecstatic, 166; fugitive, 23–30; reciprocal, 225n10

Walker, T-Bone, 95
Watts Repertory Theater Company, 185
"we," 2, 17, 102, 103, 117, 141, 150, 159, 167; vibration societies, 182, 189
"We Are on the Edge" (Art Ensemble of Chicago), 1–2
Weary Blues, The (Hughes/Mingus), 61, 64, 90–102; band members, 92; "Consider Me," 92, 93–97; "Dead in There," 97–98; "Double G Train," 98–99; freedom in, 91–92; "Motto," 97–98; music written for, 92–93; "The Stranger," 97–98; "Warning: Augmented," 97–98, 99
"Weary Blues, The" (Hughes), 61–63, 68
"Wednesday Night Prayer Meeting" (Hughes), 98–100, 214n91
Weheliye, Alexander, 8, 25, 27

We Insist! (Lincoln), 45
West African languages, 163, 170
"West End Blues" (Oliver, Armstrong), 78
Westendorf, Lynette, 157
Western tradition: anxieties about, 158; black culture as protection against, 113; economic reasoning prioritized, 38; "interiority" of, 7, 162; as resource, 113–14
Weston, Randy, 70, 211n56
White, Simone, 30
white avant-garde, 5, 116, 124–25
white hipsters, 12, 111–12
"white thing," 153
white youth culture, 12
Williams, Al, 92
Williams, Raymond, 48, 117
Wilmer, Valerie, 156
women: black women's voices, 27; centrality of in transmission of culture, 36; exclusion of from jazz, 18; in Hughes's poetry, 101, 214n97; "improvising," 200n46; middle class, gender and, 50–51, 53; in "Scenes in the City," 82, 85–86; and solidarity, 175; voices of, 27; work roles of, 94, 95. *See also* gender; *and specific artists*
"wordspeak," 57, 58
worker, figure of, 132
working class, 46–50, 107
Workman, Reggie, 103, 137
world-making projects, 6–7, 71, 148
"world" music, 11, 12
World War II, 99
Worrell, Lewis, 115, 116, 120–23, 137, 220n70
Wright, Frank, 45
Wynter, Sylvia, 25, 30, 145, 153–54, 224n7, 226n29

Young, Cynthia, 124
Young, Robert, 68
young lions, 135, 187
Your Prayer (Wright), 45

Zaentz, Celia Mingus, 65
Zip Coon minstrel figure, 137–38

www.ingramcontent.com/pod-product-compliance
Lightning Source LLC
Chambersburg PA
CBHW050212240426
43671CB00013B/2303